LONELY PLANET PUBLICATIONS

REGIS ST LOUIS

RIO DE JANEIRO

CITY GUIDE

INTRODUCING RIO DE JANEIRO

Pão de Açúcar (Sugarloaf Mountain; p80) – one of Rio's dazzling icons

Rio de Janeiro stretches between beach and mountain, with colonial neighborhoods, modernist style and that addictive sound that ties it all together: samba. Welcome to the *cidade maravilhosa* (marvelous city).

Once the adopted home of the Portuguese crown, Rio has long entranced visitors. Magnificent festivals like Carnaval and Reveillon (New Year's Eve) are renowned, but the city has plenty of other occasions for revelry – weekend samba parties in Lapa, celebrations at a Flamengo soccer match, and impromptu music jams at sidewalk cafes in Leblon, Centro or any other corner of town.

Music is the lifeblood of Rio, with a soundtrack that begins with samba and encompasses old-school bossa nova, hip-hop, funk, and Brazil's many regional styles. Catch the beat at open-air bars, old-fashioned dance halls or hypermodern nightclubs and lounges.

The setting is another reason why visitors fall hard for Rio. Rain forest still covers large swaths of the metropolitan area, while the city's dramatic mountains and white-sand beaches weave together one of the world's most striking urban landscapes. On sunny days, Cariocas (residents of Rio) head outdoors to cycle the shoreline, surf the waves, sail on Baía de Guanabara, hike the forests of Tijuca or rock-climb the face of Pão de Açúcar.

The Rio experience is about many things, from watching the sunset over Arpoador to catching an impromptu samba jam in a tiny backyard club. It's people-watching in Ipanema, seafood feasts on Lagoa, and coming face-to-face with that spirit of spontaneity and joy seemingly found around every corner of this dynamic tropical city.

RIO DE JANEIRO LIFE

Life happens out-of-doors in Rio de Janeiro. Drawn outside by sunshine (and driven out by cramped apartments), Cariocas find love, conflict and all the other varieties of human experience on the streets and beaches of town. Big festivals like Carnaval and Reveillon are almost entirely outdoor events, while an afternoon at the beach, followed by a night of open-air eating, drinking and merry-making, are the preferred ways to spend a day.

Not surprisingly, gossip travels fast in this community. At cafés and juice bars, Cariocas swap the latest rumors. There are usually plenty of scandals to whet the appetite. Political scandals often hog the headlines. Like many other countries, the media leans toward sensationalism, and splashy stories get much play. Violence in the favelas (shanty towns) is another recurrent theme.

Celebrities also tend to come crashing into the headlines. Hot topics here are who's cheating on whom, which Hollywood playboy was frolicking with you-know-who on Saõ beach and which Brazilian actress is doing nude magazine-spreads this week. This kind of attention to frivolity is one of the reasons why Paulistas (residents of São Paulo) sometimes stereotype Cariocas as superficial beach bums obsessed with their bodies. Cariocas for their part describe Paulistas as being workaholics with no zeal for life.

Residents of both cities have more in common than they're sometimes willing to admit. They usually rate crime, for instance, as the number one problem in both towns. Middle- and upper-class Cariocas, like Paulistas, live in highly secured buildings, and some even hire private body-guards. Like São Paulo, Rio has a huge gap between the haves and have-nots. At one end are the million-odd Cariocas living in favelas, often struggling just to feed themselves, and at the other end are the stratospherically rich living in luxury high-rises, with a maid, a driver and various other servants to attend to their needs. The dividing line is often little more than a highway.

Despite the chasm between rich and poor, there are many ways in which the city comes together. The beaches in Rio, for instance, have always been free and open to all, and today on Ipanema beach it's possible to see soccer-playing kids from the favelas, cell phone-toting models, pensioners, hippies, yuppies and assorted tourists – all in the span of a few volleyball courts.

Dancing in the streets at Carnaval *(p50)*

HIGHLIGHTS

IPANEMA & LEBLON

Ipanema and Leblon have it all: beautiful beaches, great restaurants and bars, and elegant boutiques that can quickly drain your wallet. Bossa nova was born here, and there's still plenty of soul in these peaceful, tree-lined streets.

❶ Ipanema beach
Stroll, surf, sunbathe or simply people-watch (p63)

❷ Zazá Bistrô Tropical
Join the beautiful crowd over fusion fare at this handsome restaurant (p133)

❸ Londra
Rio's A-list bar of the moment, with an interior designed by Philippe Starck (p154)

❹ Osklen
Get an eyeful of the latest fashions at this stylish boutique (p115)

❺ Ponta do Arpoador
This rocky outcropping is one of the best vantage points in Rio for watching the sunset (p63)

❻ Cafeína
A good place to take in the scene on this vibrant street (p137)

❼ Banda de Ipanema
Join the rabble-rousers at this colorful Carnaval parade (p52)

GÁVEA, JARDIM BOTÂNICO & LAGOA

Just inland from Rio's picturesque saltwater lagoon, these upscale neighborhoods have a great dining and drinking scene, plus botanical gardens and a planetarium. Lakeside attractions include outdoor restaurants along the shoreline and a running and cycling track.

4

5

❶ Jardim Botânico
The botanical garden is a verdant refuge from big-city bustle (p72)

❷ Baixo Gávea
Join the people parade at one of Rio's many bustling bars (p154)

❸ Helicopter tour
Depart from the lake's helipad for a magnificent view over Rio (p225)

❹ Palaphita Kitch
A splendid Polynesian-style bar that's ideal for a sundowner (p155)

❺ Lagoa Rodrigo de Freitas
A great spot for a morning jog (p73)

❻ 00 (Zero Zero)
Inside the planetarium, this nightspot has one of Rio's best dance floors (p169)

6

COPACABANA & LEME

Once a Brazilian icon, Copacabana is a diverse neighborhood with a marvelous beach and plenty of hidden gems among its high-rises, including tiny samba bars, edgy dance clubs and top-notch restaurants. Tiny Leme, with its quiet beaches and sleepy streets, feels more town than big-city suburb.

1 Copacabana beach
One of Rio's icons, this long, scalloped beach is truly magnificent (p75)

2 Fruit markets
Sample the tastes of Brazil at one of Rio's many enticing fruit markets (p137)

3 Posto dos pescadores
Fishermen still head out from the post at Copacabana's southern end (p74)

4 Copacabana Palace
Dine or overnight in elegance at this symbol of Rio's golden age (p193)

5 Galeria 1618
More laid back than Copacabana, Leme has many charming restaurants like this (p142)

6 Beachside path
On Sunday the path closes to traffic, and joggers and cyclists take over (p75)

7 Morro do Leme
A peaceful vantage point for checking out divers and fishermen (p77)

BOTAFOGO & URCA

Botafogo is a traditional neighborhood with some intriguing museums, a lively boteco (open-sided bar) scene and several bohemian nightclubs. Urca is famed for Pão de Açúcar (Sugarloaf) soaring over its tree-lined streets; it's also an idyllic neighborhood for wandering around.

❶ Pão de Açúcar
For an adrenaline rush, climb to the top of the famous peak (p80)

❷ Urca's seawall
One of Urca's many tranquil spots for enjoying the view (p81)

❸ Enseada de Botafogo
For sunset views, go to Botafogo's picturesque inlet (p79)

❹ Praia Vermelha
A jewelbox-sized beach with a marvelous panorama (p80)

1 Arte Sesc Cultural Center
Visit this small gallery, housed in one of Flamengo's delightful old mansions (p83)

2 Casa Rosa
Head to the Sunday backyard parties here for great music and a fun crowd (p165)

3 Parque do Flamengo
Spend time exploring one of the world's largest urban parks (p83)

4 Cristo Redentor
Gaze out over the city from the Savior's lofty perch (p85)

FLAMENGO, LARANJEIRAS & COSME VELHO

The major attraction here is Rio's most recognizable symbol, Cristo Redentor (Christ the Redeemer). In addition to the open-armed savior, you'll find the long Parque do Flamengo, set with sports fields and museums, and there's some great exploring among the shady streets.

CENTRO & CINELÂNDIA

Rio's bustling commercial center is a medley of office towers and historic colonial buildings, with baroque churches, a photogenic opera house, lively plazas and the city's best museum. Narrow pedestrian streets crisscross Centro, many of which fill with drinkers and diners when the workday is done.

❶ Igreja de Nossa Senhora de Candelária
Pray for good weather at this baroque church (p92)

❷ Museu de Arte Moderna
Superb exhibits inside Rio's green Parque do Flamengo (p89)

❸ Museu Histórico Nacional
History is everywhere in Centro, with key relics preserved in this former royal armory (p89)

❹ Centro Cultural Banco do Brasil
Home to some of Rio's best exhibitions (p89)

❺ Samba clubs
For a primer on the relentless samba scene, head to Centro (p166)

❻ Theatro Municipal
One of many striking buildings in downtown Rio, home to some great performances (p94)

❼ Travessa do Comércio
Join Cariocas (residents of Rio) for a happy-hour drink on this narrow colonial lane (p94)

SANTA TERESA & LAPA

Bohemian Rio thrives at these edgy arts centers. Old-fashioned dance halls pack the streets of Lapa, with the addictive sound of samba spilling out of doorways. High up on the hill, Santa Teresa has lovely mansions where artists, intellectuals and Rio's free spirits hold court.

❶ Bonde
The best way up to Santa Teresa is on this old-fashioned tram (p97)

❷ Bar do Mineiro
This neighborhood classic serves tasty home-cooked meals and strong caipirinhas (cane-liquor cocktails; p149)

❸ Democráticus
An old-time samba club with a heart of gold (p166)

❹ B&Bs
For the inside scoop on Santa Teresa, stay in the colonial house of a local (p200)

❺ Arcos da Lapa
The former viaduct is now the backdrop to Lapa's incredible music scene (p100)

❻ Antique stores
Along Rua do Lavradio, this is one of numerous shops on Rio's antique row (p118)

❼ Parque das Ruínas
There are great views from many spots in Santa Teresa, including the ruins of a former mansion (p99)

GREATER RIO

Rio's outer regions have some highly recommended sights, including rowdy Maracanã football stadium, a national park with protected rain forest, and dozens of serene beaches that get wilder as you get farther out of town. Other adventures include sailing on the bay and visiting the island of Paquetá.

1 Museu do Arte Contemporânea
Oscar Niemeyer's whimsical museum has stunning views (p106)

2 Sitio Burle Marx
A verdant wonderland, the house and gardens on this lush estate warrant the trip (p107)

3 Maracanã Football Stadium
Don't miss the big match at this shrine to the beautiful game (p104)

4 Rocinha
Support the community by buying handicrafts directly from the source (p48)

CONTENTS

Continued from previous page.

THE AUTHOR

Regis St Louis

Regis' longtime admiration for the *cidade maravilhosa* (marvelous city) has led to his deep involvement with the country. The city's vibrant music scene, its colorful *botecos* (neighborhood bars) and samba clubs, and the alluring energy of the Cariocas (residents of Rio) are just a few of the reasons why he's returned so often. Regis speaks both Portuguese and Spanish, and he has written many articles on Rio. He is also the coordinating author of Lonely Planet's *Brazil* guide, and covered both Rio and Brazil's southern states for Lonely Planet's *South America on a Shoestring.* He splits his time between New York City and the tropics.

REGIS' TOP RIO DAY

Since this is my ideal day, the sun is shining when I rise and it's still early as I step outside. I decide to go for a stroll along Ipanema beach, pausing for *agua de coco* (coconut water) along the way. Afterwards, I grab an *açaí*, the world's most delicious (nonalcoholic) beverage, at Bibi Sucos (p137), take a look at *O Globo* newspaper and contemplate the day ahead. Seeing there's an exhibition I'm eager to see at the Centro Cultural Banco do Brasil (p89) – which is free, no less – I decide to head to Centro. Along the way, I'll take a peak at nearby eating spots (p146) and see what tempts me. Unable to decide between two of my favorites, I opt for Arte Temperada (p146) followed by Brasserie Rosário (p147) for coffee and dessert. Over lunch, I'll take a look at my walking tour of Centro (p95) and see if I can find some new places to add. Happily fed, I take a stroll through the pedestrian streets, stopping at shops and taking in the street scene before ultimately making my way to the music vendors, including Feira de Muśica (p118), on Rua Pedro Lessa. I'll buy a few records then catch the *bonde* (tram) up to Santa Teresa. There I'll stop in on a few friends, grab an afternoon drink at Jasmin Mango (p149) and make plans for the evening. If I'm lucky, a friend will call and invite me to the opening of a new samba club in Lapa; otherwise, I'll consider my options and go either to Semente (p167) if today is a Monday, Democráticus (p166) if it's Thursday or Beco do Rato (p163) if it's Friday. Afterwards, I'll taxi back to Ipanema for a final cocktail at Londra (p154).

LONELY PLANET AUTHORS

Why is our travel information the best in the world? It's simple: our authors are independent, dedicated travellers. They don't research using just the internet or phone, and they don't take freebies, so you can rely on their advice being well-researched and impartial. They travel widely, to all the popular spots and off the beaten track. They personally visit thousands of hotels, restaurants, cafés, bars, galleries, palaces, museums and more – and they take pride in getting all the details right, and telling it how it is. Think you can do it? Find out how at lonelyplanet.com.

PHOTOGRAPHERS

John Maier Jr

John is a journalist, photographer and videographer who has been living in Rio de Janeiro since 1985. His work has been featured in leading publications and networks, including *National Georgraphic, Time, The New York Times,* HBO, the BBC and Discovery (and Lonely Planet, of course). His work has been honored with two Emmys and a Peabody.

Ricardo Gomes

Ricardo is a native of Rio and an accomplished photographer, videographer and editor. He has worked for top Brazilian and international publications such as *O Globo, The New York Times, Spiegel* and *Adrenalin Magazine.* He specializes in covering nature and extreme sports, but he also photographs and films institutional videos for companies and nongovernment organizations.

GETTING STARTED

Before dashing off to Brazil, find out whether you need a visa. Many nationalities require them, including citizens from the US, Canada and Australia. See p228 for more details.

If you plan to visit during the high season, it's wise to book accommodations at least two or three months in advance. For Carnaval or Reveillon (New Year's Eve), it's never too early to start planning, with some hotels filling up six months in advance.

Aside from accommodations, Rio is an easy-going place, and you can reserve most other things (tours, outdoor activities, tables at top restaurants) after your arrival.

Money is, of course, the other major consideration – and no small one given the surge of the Brazilian *real* in recent years. In general, prices for most things are slightly lower than those in North America and Western Europe, with ample options for both budget travelers and visitors on generous expense accounts.

WHEN TO GO

There is never really a bad time to visit Rio, but whether you want to party like a rock star or escape the masses may help deciding when to go. Rio's high season coincides with the Brazilian summer, running from December to March. This is when the country fills with both foreign visitors and vacationing Brazilian families. Hotel rooms are about 30% higher at this time and you'll face more crowds, though this is also the most festive time in Rio. The low season runs from May to September, and if you're looking to beat the crowds and don't mind cooler weather, this is a fine time to visit.

If you plan any side trips in Rio, be mindful of weekends. Búzios, Paraty, Ilha Grande and other nearby destinations get packed on summer weekends, and you'll have more luck scoring rooms (and deal with fewer crowds) going mid-week.

Rio lies just inside the tropics, with rainfall and humidity playing no small part in the city's seasons. Summer temperatures hover around 82°F (28°C), but can often reach 95°F (35°C) or higher. In the winter, blue skies and mild weather is the norm, with temperatures around 70°F (mid-20s). Rain falls on the city all year long, though the wettest months are October to February.

FESTIVALS

Rio's Carnaval is deservedly popular, but that's not the end of the celebrating. Reveillon is another citywide celebration, when Cariocas and visitors pack Copacabana beach. Other *festas* (parties) occur throughout the year. For the dates of Rio's many public holidays, see p222.

January & February

DIA DE SÃO SEBASTIÃO

On January 20, the patron saint of Rio is commemorated with a procession that carries the image of São Sebastião from Igreja (church) de São Sebastião dos Capuchinos in Tijuca to the Catedral Metropolitana (p100), where the image is blessed in a Mass celebrated by the Archbishop of Rio de Janeiro.

CARNAVAL

www.rio-carnival.net

In February or March, the city puts on its famous no-holds-barred party. For information on how to celebrate with Cariocas, see p50.

ADVANCE PLANNING

In addition to organizing your visa (if you need one) and booking accommodation, there are a few things you might look into before flying to Rio.

The best guides often book up well in advance, so get in touch early if there's something particular you want to do (such as scuba diving or rock-climbing up the face of Pão de Açúcar, p181). If you plan on tandem gliding, get in touch with a pilot (p183) and find out what day might be best for flying.

Find out if there are going to be any football games on while you're in town (cbfnews.uol.com.br in Portuguese lists game schedules), and browse through listings – on Riotur (www.riodejaneiro-turismo.com.br) and other sites – for events on while you're in town.

March & April

SEXTA-FEIRA DA PAIXÃO

In March or April (depending when Easter falls), Good Friday is celebrated throughout the city. The most important ceremony re-enacts the Stations of the Cross under the Arcos da Lapa (p100), with more than 100 actors.

DIA DA FUNDAÇÃO DA CIDADE

On March 1, the city commemorates its founding in 1565 by Estácio de Sá with a Mass in the church of its patron saint, Igreja de São Sebastião dos Capuchinos.

FESTIVAL INTERNACIONAL DE DOCUMENTÁRIOS

www.itsalltrue.com

Latin America's most important documentary film festival takes place in late March and early April when more than 100 films from both Brazil and abroad are screened at theaters in Rio and São Paulo.

DIA DO ÍNDIO

April 19 is recognized in Brazil as Indians' day, with a week of special events held at the Museu do Índio (p79). Exhibitions, dance and film presentations are staged daily.

DIA DE SÃO JORGE

Igreja de São Jorge, Rua da Alfândega 382, Centro

On April 23, the city pays its respects to St George, an important figure in the Afro-Brazilian community. St George is the alter-ego of the god Ogum in the Candomblé religion (originating in Africa). There's a Mass and procession, and food vendors around.

May & June

RIO DAS OSTRAS JAZZ E BLUES FESTIVAL

www.riodasostrasjazzeblues.com

Located 170km east of Rio, on the way to Búzios, Rio das Ostras boasts lovely beaches and mangrove forests. In early June, it's the setting for one of Brazil's best jazz and blues fests, with a good mix of Brazilian and international performers.

FESTAS JUNINAS

Spanning the month of June, the feast days of various saints mark some of the most important folkloric festivals in Brazil. In Rio, celebrations are held in various public squares, with lots of food stands, music, fireworks and the occasional bonfire or two. The big feast days are June 13 (Dia de Santo Antônio), June 24 (São João) and June 29 (São Pedro).

RIO MARATHON

www.maratonadorio.com.br

Set along the coast, with the ocean always at your side, this marathon course must be one of the most beautiful in the world. Rio hosts its annual 42km run in mid- to late-June, when the weather is mild and the skies are clear and blue. There are also 6km and 21km runs.

July & August

GAY PRIDE RIO

Although nowhere near as large as São Paulo's massive parade, the Rio gay pride event is growing in popularity, attracting 500,000 people on average. It usually takes place in late June or early July.

PORTAS ABERTAS

www.artedeportasabertas.com.br in Portuguese

Artists in Santa Teresa open their studios for a week in July during this lively annual festival. Expect music, a diverse crowd and inventive installations that make good use of the atmospheric bohemian hood.

FESTA DA SÃO PEDRO DO MAR

On July 3, the fishing fraternity pays homage to its patron saint in a maritime procession. Their decorated boats leave from the fishing community of Caju and sail to the statue of São Pedro in Urca.

FESTA LITERÁRIA INTERNACIONAL DE PARATI

www.flip.org.br

This important literary festival brings authors from around the world to Paraty for five days each July. The opening concert features big names in Brazilian music.

FESTA DE NS DA GLÓRIA DO OUTEIRO

On August 15, a solemn Mass is held at the historic church overlooking Glória and the bay. From the church (ablaze with decorated lights), a procession travels out into the streets of Glória to mark the Feast of the Assumption. This *festa* includes music and colorful stalls set up in the Praça NS da Glória. Festivities start at 8am and continue all day.

September & October

SAMBA-SCHOOL REHEARSALS

In September (though some begin as early as July or August), samba schools host open rehearsals once a week (usually on Friday or Saturday night). In spite of the name, these are less a dress rehearsal than just an excuse to dance (to samba, of course), celebrate and pass on the good vibe before the big show come Carnaval time. Anyone can come, and it's a mixed crowd of Cariocas and tourists, though it gets more and more crowded the closer it is to Carnaval. For more information on attending the open rehearsals, see p163.

DIA DE INDEPENDÊNCIA DO BRASIL

On September 7, Independence Day is celebrated with a large military parade down Av Presidente Vargas. It starts at 8am at Candelária and goes down just past Praça XI.

FESTIVAL DO RIO

www.festivaldorio.com.br

Rio's international film festival is one of the biggest in Latin America. More than 200 films from all over the world are shown at some 35 theaters in Rio. Often the festival holds open-air screenings at locations around town. It runs from the last week of September through the first week of October.

FESTA DA PENHA

One of the largest (and most popular) religious festivals in the city takes place every Sunday in October and on the first Sunday in November. The lively celebrations commence in the northern suburb of Penha at Igreja NS da Penha de França, Largo da Penha 19.

FESTIVAL PANORAMA DE DANÇA

www.panoramafestival.com

One of Brazil's biggest dance festivals takes place in late October through early November and, at various locations around the city, features the work of around 200 different contemporary dance groups. The one-week festival features plenty of experimental troupes – from both Brazil and abroad – as well as traditional performers who don't get much attention.

RIO JAZZ FESTIVAL

Although dates for this October jazz festival vary, it's an opportunity for Rio's beautiful people to come together for three nights of great music. Local, national and international acts present a wide variety of music, playing jazz and its many relatives – samba-jazz, bossa nova, samba and *Música Popular Brasileira* (MPB).

TIM FESTIVAL

Tim, the über-successful cell-phone service provider, throws a huge music festival in October (currently the third weekend, though dates can vary). Expect Brazil's top names in pop, jazz and MPB in an eclectic line up of performers at one of Rio's big venues (most recently at the Marina da Glória). Tickets often sell out well before the three-day event, so keep an eye on *Veja* magazine, which announces details in advance.

November & December

NOITES CARIOCAS

oinoitescariocas.oi.com.br in Portuguese

Atop one of Brazil's most beguiling viewpoints, the city of Rio forms the backdrop to one of its best music fests during this annual summertime event. Beginning in November and running through February, all-night rock and MPB concerts are held on weekend nights, attracting a well-dressed Zona Sul crowd. Concerts are currently held at Pier Mauá, just north of Centro.

LIGHTING OF THE LAGOA CHRISTMAS TREE

From the end of November to the first week of January, the Christmas tree glows brightly on the Lagoa de Rodrigo de Freitas (p73). To celebrate its lighting, the city often throws big concerts in Parque Brigadeiro Faria Lima, usually on the first Saturday in December. Big Brazilian names have performed in the past.

VERÃO DA URCA

www.morrodaurca.com.br in Portuguese

From December through Carnaval, Morro da Urca becomes the setting for a great party above Rio. Concerts take place on periodic Saturday nights – and some Friday nights – and feature top Brazilian bands and magnificent views.

FESTA DE IEMANJÁ

Dwarfed by secular New Year's Eve celebrations, this Candomblé (a religion originating from Africa) festival on December 31 celebrates the feast day of Iemanjá, the goddess of the sea. Celebrants dress in white and place their petitions on small boats, sending them out to sea. If their petitions return, their prayers will not be answered. Along with the petitions, celebrants send candles, perfumes and talcum powder to appease the blue-cloaked *orixá* (spirits or deities). Until recently, devotees gathered in Copacabana, Ipanema and Leblon, but owing to the popularity of Reveillon, and its chaotic spillover, they are seeking more tranquil spots – Barra da Tijuca and Recreio dos Bandeirantes – to make their offerings.

REVEILLON

Rio's biggest holiday after its spectacular and rowdy Carnaval takes place on the famed Copacabana beach, where some two million people pack the sands to welcome the new year. A spectacular fireworks display lights up the night sky as top bands perform in the area. The hardiest of revelers keep things going all night long, then watch the sunrise the next morning.

COSTS & MONEY

Rio is less expensive than many cities in Western Europe and North America, but Brazil's booming economy and strong *real* mean that it isn't the bargain it once was. Still, it is possible to enjoy the city without breaking the bank.

Ascetics could get by on about R$60 a day, staying in cheaper hostels, preparing their own meals and avoiding pricey nights out. Midrange travelers should budget around R$300 a day, which will cover decent lodging near the beach and a good assortment of restaurant and bar expenses. High-end travelers will spend R$500 or more a day, which will cover hotel rooms with beach views, Rio's best restaurants, and drinks at top music halls and dance clubs.

Accommodations will probably be your biggest expense. The cheapest rooms in town can go for as little as R$20 per night for a bed in a hostel outside the Zona Sul (hostels in Ipanema, however, typically charge R$45 a night). A clean, fairly decent double room in Copacabana goes for about R$200 and up. In Ipanema, good rooms start around R$300. If you have money to burn, Rio's top hotel rooms will set you back a cool R$1000 or more.

Restaurants cater to an equally broad range of budgets. At the low-end are inexpensive per-kilo restaurants and cheap set lunches, which can fill a person up for R$10. If you're not scraping by, you can enjoy a good selection of local places with mains averaging R$20, or enjoy a dinner for two for R$80. Dinner at Rio's most expensive places will cost R$200 or so, including a few drinks. Keep in mind that many restaurants list their menu prices for two. If you're not sharing, be sure to clarify before ordering (and you can usually order a half portion).

Getting around town is fairly inexpensive, with cheap bus and metro tickets (under R$2.50 one way), while taxi rides will run to a bit more (R$20 to zip up to Lapa from Ipanema). Renting a car is expensive (starting at R$100), with high petrol prices to match, and it's not worth recommending unless you plan to do a lot of exploring outside of the main towns.

Brazil is not the cheapest destination for solo travelers. The cost of a single room in a hotel is not much less than for a double.

Lastly, during the December-to-February holiday season, lodging costs generally increase by about 30% (and sometimes more in places like Búzios and other popular resorts). You'll pay a premium if you come during Carnaval or Reveillon, with accommodation prices doubling or even tripling – with the added requirement of four-night minimum stays.

HOW MUCH?

Liter of gas R$2.20

Liter of bottled water R$1.50

Glass of chope (draft beer) R$4

Souvenir T-shirt R$20-30

Caipirinha (cocktail) on the beach R$5

Metro ticket R$2.40

Pair of Havaianas R$15-25

Admission to samba club R$10-25

Dinner for two at Bar do Mineiro R$60

Cable-car ride to the top of Pão de Açúcar R$35

INTERNET RESOURCES

Agenda de Samba e Choro (www.samba-choro.com.br in Portuguese) This no-nonsense site lists top places to catch live samba and *choro* in town.

Brazzil (www.brazzil.com) In-depth articles touching on Brazilian politics, economy, literature, arts and culture.

Carioca Forever (www.cariocaforever.com) Articles written by English-speaking expats living in Brazil, with info on cultural events, life in Rio and language-learning tips.

Gringos (www.gringoes.com) Articles written by Anglophones living in Brazil.

Hip Guide to Brazil (www.brazilmax.com) Excellent guide to Brazilian culture and society; good, selective articles and links.

Insider's Guide to Rio (www.ipanema.com) One of the best internet introductions to Rio, this guide has up-to-date tips on hotels, restaurants, nightlife and shopping, with special sections on Carnaval and Rio for gays.

Lana Lapa (www.lanalapa.com.br in Portuguese) Up-to-date listings of live concerts and other events in Lapa, plus a rundown of restaurants and bars in the area.

Lonely Planet (www.lonelyplanet.com) For summaries on Brazil travel, the popular Thorn Tree forum, online accommodation booking and links to a variety of other web resources.

Maria-Brazil (www.maria-brazil.org) An expat's recommendations of favorite dining, drinking, shopping and sightseeing in Rio, plus extensive recipes and links to blogs by other expats.

Rio This Week (www.riothisweek.com) Flashy photos and listings of what's-on around town, plus restaurant recommendations and other tips. You can download a colorful PDF of the current guide on the site.

Riotur (www.riodejaneiro-turismo.com.br) Rio's tourist information agency, Riotur keeps a current website of what's-on around town, as well as comprehensive listings of museums, restaurants and other info.

BACKGROUND

HISTORY

THE PORTUGUESE ARRIVAL

In the 15th century the small country of Portugal, ever infatuated with the sea, began its large-scale explorations that would eventually take Portuguese explorers to the coast of Brazil in 1500. A little over a year later, Gonçalo Coelho sailed from Portugal and entered a huge bay in January 1502. It was his chief pilot, Amerigo Vespucci, however, who would give the name. Mistaking the bay for a river (or possibly making no mistake at all since the old Portuguese 'rio' is another word for bay), he dubbed it Rio de Janeiro (River of January).

Although the Portuguese were the first European *arrivistes,* the French would become the first non-natives to settle along the bay. Like the Portuguese, the French had been harvesting dyewood along the Brazilian coast, but unlike the Portuguese they hadn't attempted any permanent settlements in this region until Rio. Regardless, the Portuguese were far from being the first to set foot on the tropical shoreline, as the land had already been inhabited for at least 10,000 years.

OF NOBLE SAVAGES & SAVAGE NOBLES

Some believe that the Guanabara Indians, the Tupinambá (better known as the Tupi), inspired works such as Sir Thomas Moore's *Utopia* (1516) and would later inspire Rousseau's Enlightenment-era idea of the 'noble savage'. This all started from the letters credited to Amerigo Vespucci on his first voyage to Rio in 1502. The idea common at the time was that there existed on earth an Eden, and that it lay undiscovered. Vespucci claimed to have found that Eden, from his cursory observations of the Tupi. They were described as innocent savages, carefree and well-groomed, with the unusual custom of taking daily baths in the sea. The fact that native women were freely offered to the strange foreigners probably added to the enthusiasm with which they spoke about the region upon their return to Portugal.

In fact, the honeymoon didn't last long. The conquerors soon came to see the forest-dwelling Indians as raw manpower for the Portuguese empire, and enslaved them and set them to work on plantations. The Indians, too, turned out to be different than the Europeans imagined. The Tupinambá were warlike and ate their enemies – through ritualistic cannibalism they believed they would receive the power and strength of the consumed opponent. They also didn't take to the work as the Portuguese had expected, and were dying off in large numbers from introduced diseases. By the 17th century the Tupinambá had been completely eradicated. To fulfill their growing labor demands, the Portuguese eventually turned to Africa.

AFRICANS IN BRAZIL

The Portuguese began bringing blacks, stolen from Africa, into the new colony shortly after Brazil's founding. Most blacks were brought from Guinea, Angola and the Congo and would constitute some four million souls brought to Brazil over its three-and-a-half centuries of human

TIMELINE

8000 BC

Ancestors of Tupinambá settle along Baía de Guanabara; they are descendents of hunter gatherers who crossed the Bering Strait from East Asia sometime between 10,000 BC and 12,000 BC.

AD 1502

Portuguese explorer Gonçalo Coelho leads an expedition from Portugal, sailing into Baía de Guanabara after an eight-month voyage. His chief pilot Amerigo Vespucci (after whom 'America' is named) dubbed the lovely setting Rio de Janeiro.

1567

After successfully driving the French and their Indian allies off the land, the Portuguese set up the first settlement on Morro do Castelo. It's called São Sebastião do Rio de Janeiro (after Portuguese king São Sebastião).

trafficking. The port of Rio had the largest number of slaves entering the colony – as many as two million in all. At open-air slave markets these new immigrants were sold as local help or shipped to the interior, initially to work on the thriving sugar plantations, and later – when gold was discovered in Minas Gerais in 1704 – to work back-breaking jobs in the mines.

Although slavery was rotten anywhere in the New World, most historians agree that the Africans in Rio had it better than their rural brethren. Those that came to Rio worked in domestic roles as maids and butlers and out on the streets as dock workers, furniture movers, delivery boys, boatmen, cobblers, fishermen and carpenters. The worst job was transporting the barrels of human excrement produced in town and emptying them into the sea.

As Rio's population grew, so too did the number of slaves imported to meet the labor needs of the expanding coffee plantations in the Paraíba Valley. By the early 19th century African slaves made up two-thirds of Rio's population.

Lots of illicit liaisons occurred between master and slave, and children born into mixed backgrounds were largely accepted into the social sphere and raised as free citizens. This contributed considerably to creating Brazil's melting pot. While escape attempts were fewer in Rio than in the more brutal climate of the northeast, there were attempts. Those seeking freedom often set their sights on *quilombos* (communities of runaway slaves). Some were quite developed – as was the case with Palmares, which had a population of 20,000 and survived through much of the 17th century before it was wiped out by Federal troops.

Rio's nearest *quilombo* in the 19th century was in Leblon – then quite distant from the city. Unlike other *quilombos,* it was headed by a white, progressive businessman who was in favor of slave abolition. Luggage manufacturer Jose de Seixas Magalhães kept farmland in Leblon, which was staffed entirely by runaway slaves, whom he hid and protected in his Leblon mansion. This was during Brazil's incipient abolition movement, and the farm operated under the eyes of the government. Magalhães, however, enjoyed the special patronage of Princesa Isabel, daughter of Dom Pedro II and regent of the Empire while he traveled overseas. Abroad, the country was receiving pressure to outlaw slavery, and trafficking in human cargo was eventually outlawed in 1830. This move, however, did nothing to improve the lives of slaves already in Brazil, who would have to wait another two generations to gain their freedom. Despite the ban, shipment of human cargo continued well into the 1850s, with 500,000 slaves smuggled into Brazil between 1830 and 1850. The British (out of economic self-interest) finally suppressed Brazil's trafficking with naval squadrons.

Pressure from home and abroad reached boiling point toward the end of the 19th century until finally, in 1888, from the steps of Royal Palace overlooking Praça Quinze de Novembro, slavery was declared abolished. Brazil was the last country in the New World to end slavery.

RIO'S EARLY DAYS

In order to get the colony up and running, the Portuguese built a fortified town on Morro do Castelo in 1567 to maximize protection from European invasion by sea and Indian attack by land. They named their town São Sebastião do Rio de Janeiro, in honor of King Sebastião of Portugal. Cobbled together by the 500 founding Cariocas (residents of Rio), early Rio was a poorly planned town with irregular streets in the medieval Portuguese style. It remained a small settlement through the mid-17th century, surviving on the export of brazilwood and sugarcane. In Rio's first census (in 1600), the population comprised 3000 Indians, 750 Portuguese and 100 blacks.

1580

The Portuguese bring 2000 slaves to the new colony. Over the next 300 years, more than four million blacks stolen from Africa will be relocated to Brazil.

1763

With wealth flowing from the gold mines of Minas Gerais through Rio, the city grows wealthy and swells in population to 50,000; the Portuguese court transfers the capital of Brazil from Salvador to Rio.

1807

Napoleon invades Portugal and the Portuguese prince regent (later known as Dom João VI) and his entire court of 15,000 flees for Brazil. The royal coffers shower wealth upon Rio.

With its excellent harbor and good lands for sugarcane, Rio became Brazil's third most important settlement (after Salvador da Bahia and Recife-Olinda) in the 17th century.

The gold rush in Minas Gerais had a profound effect on Rio and caused major demographic shifts on three continents. The rare metal was first discovered by *bandeirantes* (explorers and hired slave-hunters) in the 1690s, and as word spread gold seekers arrived in droves. Over the next half-century an estimated 500,000 Portuguese arrived in Brazil and many thousands of African slaves were imported. Rio served as the natural port of entry for this flow of people and commerce to and from the Minas Gerais goldfields.

In the 18th century Rio morphed into a rough-and-tumble place attracting a swarthy brand of European immigrant. Most of the settlement was built near the water (where Praça Quinze de Novembro stands today), beside rows of warehouses, with noisy taverns sprinkled along the main streets. Rio was a rough city full of smugglers and thieves, tramps and assassins, and slaves on the run. Smuggling was rampant, with ships robbed and the sailors murdered, with bribes given over to the cops. Gold flowing through the city created the constant menace of pirates. Adding a note of temperance to the place were the religious orders that came in small bands and built Rio's first churches.

RIO UNDER THE KING

In 1807 Napoleon's army marched on Lisbon. Two days before the French invasion, 40 ships carrying the Portuguese prince regent (later known as Dom João VI) and his entire court of 15,000 set sail for Brazil under the protection of British warships. After the initial landing in Bahia (where their unkempt state was met with bemusement), the royal family moved down to Rio, where they settled.

This had momentous consequences for the city as the king, missing the high culture of Europe, lavished his attention on Rio, envisioning a splendid European-style city for his new hometown. European artisans flooded the city. The British, rewarded for helping the king safely reach Brazil, gained access to Brazil's ports, and many Anglo traders and merchants set up shop in the town center. Anti-Napoleon French also arrived, as did other Europeans, creating an international air unknown until then. When the German prince and noted naturalist Alexander Philip Maximilian arrived in Brazil in 1815 he commented on the many nationalities and mixtures of people he encountered.

Dom João VI fell in love with Rio. A great admirer of nature, he founded the botanical gardens and introduced sea bathing to the inhabitants of Rio. He had a special pier built at Caju, with a small tub at the end, in which he would immerse himself fully clothed as the waves rocked gently against it. (His wife Carlota Joaquina bathed in the nude.) This was long before Copacabana was opened to the rest of the city, remaining a virgin expanse of white sand framed by rainforest covered mountains, reachable only by an arduous journey.

With the court came an influx of money and talent that helped build some of the city's lasting monuments, such as the palace at the Quinta da Boa Vista. Within a year of his arrival, Dom João VI also created the School of Medicine, the Bank of Brazil, the Law Courts, the Naval Academy and the Royal Printing Works.

Dom João VI was expected to return to Portugal after Napoleon's Waterloo in 1815, but instead stayed in Brazil. The following year his mother, mad Queen Dona Maria I, died, and Dom João VI became king. He refused demands to return to Portugal to rule, and declared Rio

1822

Left in charge of Brazil after his father Dom João VI returns to Portugal, the prince regent Dom Pedro I declares independence from Portugal and crowns himself 'emperor' of Brazil.

1831

Brazil's first homegrown monarch, Dom Pedro I, proves incompetent and abdicates the throne. His son Pedro II takes power and ushers in a long period of growth and stability.

1865

Brazil, allied with Uruguay and Argentina, wages the 'War of the Triple Alliance' on Paraguay. Although Brazil wins, it proves South America's bloodiest conflict, killing hundreds of thousands (and wiping out half of Paraguay's population).

THE FRENCH CONNECTION

Cariocas and the French share much more than just a few romance-language cognates. In fact, Franco-Brazilian history goes back five centuries. Within two years of the Portuguese landing in Brazil, French sailors (pirates, mostly) began appearing in the bay. In contrast to the more aggressive methods of the Portuguese, the French developed a strong friendship with the Tupinambá, and by 1710 there were bilingual people on both sides. The French also brought back brazilwood, parrots and tobacco, but they were the first to bring back a living Tupi, and paraded him before Franco King Henri II at a decadent 'Brazilian Festival'.

France was also the first in the region to set up a colony in what they called Antarctic France. They settled an island in the bay and present-day Flamengo beach, and called their 'town' Henriville. The colony didn't last as the Portuguese battled for control over the region, eventually driving the French off the land in 1565.

The French returned a few times in the early 18th century to try to get a piece of Brazil but, ironically, it wasn't until Dom João's arrival from Portugal that French culture truly thrived in Brazil. The king, who adored French culture (but was still an archenemy of Napoleon), invited a French mission to Brazil – a talented assortment of architects, painters, sculptors and other artists. They made substantial contributions to the young country, creating, among other things, the Imperial Academy of Fine Arts, Brazil's first school for the education of architects. The academy was headed by the architect Grandjean de Montigny, who ushered in Rio's neoclassical architectural period (see p42).

Early in the 19th century, Rio captured the public imagination in Paris at an exhibition of Felix-Émile Taunay's colorful panoramas. Rio was billed as the new Arcadia, a city whose emphasis was on natural beauty. This fired the imagination of some Parisians, and hot on the heels of the artistic mission came other elements of high culture – French dressmakers, florists, perfumers and wine sellers – who set up shop on Rua do Ouvidor, which quickly became the French quarter of the city.

Some of Rio's most important buildings that rose over the next century were decidedly French in flavor. The opera house, for instance, was modeled on the Paris Opera House, and Rio's grand avenue (today Av Rio Branco) was laid down in an attempt to re-create the Champs Elysées in the tropics. In the 20th century French architects such as Le Corbusier were extremely influential on urban design.

On the political front, the French influence was again significant. In fact, the most commonly seen slogan in Brazil today – Order and Progress (visible on any Brazilian flag) – comes from French philosopher Auguste de Comte (1797–1857), whose elevation of reason and scientific knowledge over traditional religious beliefs was extremely influential on the young Brazilian republic.

Today, the tropical mystique continues to entrance Parisians. The 'Year of Brazil in France' was celebrated in 2005 with hundreds of exhibitions, parties and events – celebrating Brazilian music, film, art and dance – held throughout France. Paris nightclubs have also tapped into Rio's allure with places like Favela Chic serving up caipirinhas (cane liquor cocktails) as DJs spin hip-hop straight out of the *baile funk*, while samba parties by the Seine are becoming a regular summertime event. Meanwhile, French visitors continue to flock to the *cidade maravilhosa* (marvelous city). Only the US and Germany send more travelers to Rio.

Rio for its part continues to hold French culture in high esteem. Top culinary honors consistently go to French restaurants and French chefs (with Le Pré Catalan and Le Saint Honoré often battling for top billing). And French filmmaking, French art and French fashion are usually regarded in Rio as the pinnacles of achievement. The perfect day in Rio for a Zona Sul *garota* (young woman) would probably entail a quick shop at Louis Vuitton or the French boutique Clube Chocolate (p124), catching the latest French film at Casa França-Brasil (p93), followed by dinner at Olympe (p138).

1888

Slavery is abolished in Brazil, the last country in the New World to do so. The law is signed into effect by Princesa Isabel, admired by many blacks as their benefactress.

1889

A military coup, supported by Brazil's wealthy coffee farmers, overthrows Pedro II. The monarchy is abolished and the Brazilian Republic is born. Pedro II goes into exile in Paris and dies a few years later.

1897

Some 20,000 refugees and former soldiers settle on the barren hillside of Morro da Providência just outside of downtown Rio. This becomes the country's first favela.

the capital of the United Kingdom of Portugal, Brazil and the Algarves. Brazil became the only New World colony to ever have a European monarch ruling on its soil.

Five years later Dom João VI finally relented to political pressure and returned to Portugal, leaving his 23-year-old son Pedro in Brazil as prince regent. In Portugal the king was confronted with the newly formed Côrtes, a legislative assembly attempting to reign in the powers of the monarchy. The Côrtes had many directives, one of which was restoring Brazil to its previous status as subservient colony. Word was sent to Dom Pedro that his authority was greatly diminished. According to legend, when Pedro received the directive in 1822, he pulled out his sword and yelled *'Independência ou morte!'* ('Independence or death!'), putting himself at the country's head as Emperor Dom Pedro I.

Portugal was too weak to fight its favorite son, not to mention the British, who had the most to gain from Brazilian independence and would have come to the aid of the Brazilians. Without spilling blood, Brazil had attained its independence and Dom Pedro I became the head of the Brazilian 'empire' (despite Pedro's claims to the contrary, Brazil was a regular monarchy, not an empire since it had no overseas colonies).

Dom Pedro I ruled for only nine years. From all accounts, he was a bumbling incompetent who scandalized even the permissive Brazilians by siring numerous illegitimate children. He also strongly resisted any attempts to weaken his power by constitutional means. Following street demonstrations in Rio in 1831, he surprised everyone by abdicating, leaving the power in the hands of his five-year-old, Brazilian-born son.

Until Dom Pedro II reached adolescence, Brazil suffered through a turbulent period of unrest, which finally ended in 1840 when Dom Pedro II, at the age of 14, took the throne. Despite his youth he proved to be a stabilizing element for the country, and ushered in a long period of peace and relative prosperity. The period of industrialization began with the introduction of the steamship and the telegraph, and the king encouraged mass immigration from Europe. His shortcomings during his half-century of rule were a bloody war with Paraguay (1865–70) and his slowness at abolishing slavery. He was well-liked by his subjects, but they finally had enough of a monarchy and he was pushed from power in 1889.

THE BELLE ÉPOQUE

Rio experienced boom days in the latter half of the 19th century. The spreading wealth of coffee plantations in Rio state (and in São Paulo) revitalized Brazil's economy, just as the city was going through substantial growth and modernization. Regular passenger ships began sailing to London (1845) and Paris (1851), and the local ferry service to Niterói began in 1862. A telegraph system and gas streetlights were installed in 1854. By 1860 Rio had more than 250,000 inhabitants, making it the largest city in South America.

For the wealthy, the goal of creating a modern European capital grew ever closer, as the city embraced all things European – with particular influence from the customs, fashion and even cuisine of Paris. The poor, however, had a miserable lot. In the 1870s and 1880s, as the rich moved to new urban areas by the bay or in the hills, Rio's marginalized lived in tenement houses in the old center of town. There conditions were grim: streets were poorly lit and poorly ventilated, with a stench filling the narrow alleyways.

Rio's flood of immigrants added diversity to the city. On the streets, you could hear a symphony of languages – African, Portuguese, English, French – mixing with the sounds of the

1900

Rio's mayor Pereira Passos ushers in a period of urbanization, with the creation of grand boulevards, the opening up of Copacabana (via a tunnel to Botafogo), and improving public health and sanitation.

1915

Praça Onze becomes the center of Afro-Brazilian culture, with Bahian immigrants gathering for music, dance and Candomblé celebrations. Samba is soon born, with the first songs heard on the radio by 1917.

1923

The Copacabana Palace opens its doors. The hotel quickly becomes an icon of Rio's tropical glamour, with jet-setters from Hollywood and Europe flying down to the city during its pre-Depression boom days.

bonde (tram), of carts drawn by mules, as the cadence of various dances – maxixes, lundus, polkas and waltzes – interpreted by anonymous performers.

The city went through dramatic changes in the first decade of 1900, owing in large part to the work of mayor Pereira Passos. He continued the work of 'Europeanization' by widening Rio's streets and creating grand boulevards such as Av Central and Mem de Sá. The biggest of these boulevards required the destruction of 600 buildings to make way for Av Central (later renamed Rio Branco), which became the Champs Elysées of Rio, an elegant boulevard full of sidewalk cafés and promenading Cariocas.

Passos also connected Botafogo to Copacabana by building a tunnel, paving the way for the development of the southern beaches. Despite his grand vision for Rio, his vision for the poor was one of wide-scale removal from the city center – a short-sighted policy that would dog Rio (and Brazilian) government for the next 80 years. In truth, the *cortiços* (poor, collective lodgings) were breeding grounds for deadly outbreaks of small pox, yellow fever and typhus. Sighting the widespread health and sanitation problems, the city destroyed thousands of shacks. With no homes, the poor fled to the hills, later creating some of the earliest favelas (shanty towns). The city also exterminated rats and mosquitoes and created a modern sewage system.

By the time Passos' term ended in 1906, Rio was the Belle Époque capital par excellence of Latin America. Its only possible rival in beauty was Buenos Aires. One visitor who commented on Rio's transformation was former US President Teddy Roosevelt. In 1913, during a tour through town, he noted that since Brazil had become a republic in 1889, Rio de Janeiro had gone 'from a picturesque pest-hole into a singularly beautiful, healthy, clean and efficient modern great city.'

BOOM DAYS, REFORM & REPRESSION UNDER VARGAS

At the end of the 19th century, the city's population exploded because of European immigration and internal migration (mostly ex-slaves from the declining coffee and sugar regions). By 1900 Rio boasted more than 800,000 inhabitants, a quarter of them foreign-born (by contrast, São Paulo's population was only 300,000).

Following Passos' radical changes, the early 1920s to the late 1950s were one of Rio's golden ages. With the inauguration of some grand luxury resort hotels (the Glória in 1922 and the Copacabana Palace in 1923), Rio became a romantic, exotic destination for Hollywood celebrities and international high society, with Copacabana its headquarters. In some ways Rio's quasi-mythic status as a tropical arcadia spans its entire history, but in the 1940s and '50s its reputation as the urban Eden of Latin America was vouchsafed as the world was introduced to Carmen Miranda, a Rio icon.

This was also a time when radical changes were happening in the world of music (see p35), and when Rio was first beginning to celebrate its 'Brazilianness', or its mixed heritage and multicolored population. Sociologist Gilberto Freyre's influential book *Masters and Slaves* (1933) turned things upside down as Brazilians, long conditioned to think of their mixed-race past with shame, began to think differently about their heritage – as an asset that set them apart from other nations of the world.

The 1930s was the era of President Vargas, who formed the Estado Novo (New State) in November 1937, making him the first Brazilian president to wield absolute power. Inspired by the fascist governments of Salazar in Portugal and Mussolini in Italy, Vargas banned political

1928

Deixa Falar becomes the first *escola de samba* (samba school; called a 'school' because it's located next to a primary school), followed by Mangueira later that year. In 1932, Rio holds its first Carnaval parade.

1930

Getúlio Vargas comes into power. Inspired by European fascists, President Vargas presides over an authoritarian state, playing a major role in Brazilian politics until his suicide in 1951.

1960

President Juscelino Kubitschek moves the capital of Brazil from Rio to the newly constructed Brasília, which leads to a decline in Rio's political and sociocultural prominence.

parties, imprisoned political opponents and censored artists and the press.

Despite all this, many liked Vargas. The 'father' of Brazil's workers, he created Brazil's minimum wage in 1938. Each year he introduced new labor laws to coincide with Workers' Day on May 1, to sweeten the teeth of Brazil's factory workers. His vision for Brazil was not to increase the country's output, but to improve the level of education among all Brazilians.

THE MILITARY DICTATORSHIP

The world's fascination with Rio was severely curtailed during the rise of the military dictatorship of the 1960s. The era of repression began with press censorship, silencing of political opponents (sometimes by torture and violence) and an exodus of political defectors abroad (including musicians, writers and artists). There were numerous protests during that period (notably in 1968 when some 100,000 marched upon the Palácio Tiradentes). And even Rio's politicians opposed the military regime, which responded by withholding vital federal funding for certain social programs.

Despite the repression, the '60s and '70s witnessed profound changes in the city, with the opening of tunnels and the building of viaducts, parks and landfills. (Perversely, this time of autocratic rule was also marked by a booming economy.) In the realm of public transportation, modernization was on the way. In the 1970s builders connected Rio with Niterói with the construction of the bay-spanning bridge, while beneath the city, the first metro cars began to run. This outmoded *bonde* has nearly disappeared: Rio's last streetcar line runs from Centro to Santa Teresa, and still conjures up those nostalgic prewar days.

Meanwhile, the Zona Sul saw skyscrapers rising over the beaches of Copacabana and Leblon, with the wealthy moving further away from neglected downtown Rio. The moving of Brazil's capital to Brasília in 1960 seemed to spell the end for Centro, which became a ghost town

top picks

HISTORICAL SITES

- **Paço Imperial** (p92) The former imperial palace was home to the royal family when they arrived from Portugal.
- **Praça Quinze de Novembro** (p92) Named after the date Brazil declared itself a republic (November 15, 1822), this plaza has witnessed a lot of historical action, including the crowning of two emperors and the abolition of slavery.
- **Travessa do Comércio** (p94) This narrow alley is a window into colonial Rio, with 18th-century buildings converted into bars and restaurants.
- **Museu Histórico Nacional** (p89) Set in the 18th-century royal arsenal, this museum houses Rio's best assortment of historical artifacts.
- **Jardim Botânico** (p72) Prince Regent Dom João VI insured the city would have no shortage of green spaces, and ordered this verdant garden planted in 1808.
- **Museu da República** (p86) Formerly known as the Palácio do Catete, this mansion was Brazil's presidential home from 1896 to 1954. Getúlio Vargas was the last president to live here, and committed suicide in one of the upstairs rooms.
- **Praça Floriano** (p94) Centro's picturesque main square has long been the meeting ground for popular demonstrations, including student uprisings against the military dictatorship in the 1960s and victory celebrations following World Cup finals.
- **Garota de Ipanema** (p135) Famed spot where Tom Jobim and Vinícius de Moraes penned the 'Girl from Ipanema', whose international success was a major moment in the history of bossa nova.

1964

President Goulart is overthrown by a military coup. Troops arrive in Rio and seize power. So begins the era of dictatorship, with generals running the show for the next 20 years.

1968

The government passes the repressive Institutional Act 5, which purges opposition legislators, judges and mayors from public office; most political parties are banned. Over 100,000 take to the streets in Rio, protesting against the dictatorship.

1985

Following a cautious period of *abertura* (opening), Brazil holds an indirect presidential election. Civilian rule returns to Brazil under José Sarney, though he proves unable to handle the rampant inflation and huge debt left by his predecessors.

RIO'S MALANDROS *Carmen Michael*

In the suffocating heat of a summer afternoon sometime in the 1930s, João Francisco dos Santos walked into the shabby, corrupt Lapa police station with vengeance on his mind. Wearing a silk shirt stretched across his taut frame and a gold ring engraved with St George, the formidable *capoeirista* (Brazilian martial arts practitioner) attacked five policemen who had previously assaulted his transvestite friends... At least, that's the story they tell in the more notorious drinking dens of Lapa. Born to slaves in the impoverished northeast of Brazil, swapped at age eight for a horse, and later emerging as a flamboyant transvestite cabaret performer, João Francisco dos Santos (or Madam Satã as he was later called) became the first of a new breed of social misfits known in Rio as *malandros* (con men).

In the tumultuous era of the 1930s, Lapa emerged as a seedy bohemian enclave of gambling houses, cabaret and brothels. In this setting, *malandros* consorted with a cast of exotic dancers, transvestites, penniless musicians and angst-ridden poets. Their exploits were told by the likes of Noel Rosa, Nelson Gonçalves and other musicians who sang of Meia Noite, Camisa Preta, Miguel Zinho and other legendary *malandros*. Originally portrayed as complicated Robin Hood types, the *malandro* today is more likely to be described as a sly con artist.

'First samba, then make love and then sleep,' wrote Chico Buarque, summing up the *malandro* philosophy in one of his many odes to 'the idle lifestyle'. For the poor and discriminated, *malandros* also became a symbol of rebellion. Carefully dodging the title of thief or gigolo, *malandros* used charm, persuasion and manipulation to fund their flamboyant lifestyle, and they often played the part in eye-catching white patent shoes, and silk shirts and scarves.

Rio's con artists have been largely relegated to the pages of history, though there are some who say a new breed of *malandro* has emerged, playfully targeting those who possess money and naïveté in equal quantities. When Brazilians talk about *malandros* today, mostly they mean that unnaturally good-looking *capoeirista*, *sambista* (samba dancer) or surfer who offers to 'show you around' and who will spend your money so fast it will make your head spin. And then, as all good *malandros* should do, he will disappear into the night to the local *botequim* (bar), ensuring his exploits are well known in the barfly history books. As they say in Rio: as long as *otários* (the gullible) exist, there will always be *malandros*.

after hours and retained none of the energy of its past. By the 1970s, its plazas and parks were dangerous places, surrounded by aging office towers.

The center of old Rio remained a bleak place until around 1985, when Brazil held its first direct presidential election in 20 years. With the slow return to civilian rule, Cariocas turned their attention to sadly abandoned parts of the city, like downtown. Over the next decade citizens, particularly local shop owners, launched a downtown revitalization campaign, sometimes collecting money by going door-to-door.

By 1995 it was clear that the drive was a success. Whole blocks in downtown received much-needed facelifts. Handsomely restored buildings attracted new investment, with new shops and cultural centers opening their doors alongside book publishers and art galleries. And nightlife returned to Lapa.

A CITY DIVIDED

Unfortunately, the latter half of the 20th century was also an era of explosive growth in the favelas, as immigrants poured in from poverty-stricken areas of the northeast and the interior, swelling the number of urban poor in the city. The *cidade maravilhosa* began to lose its gloss as crime and violence increased, and in the 1990s it became known as the *cidade partida* (divided

1994

The Favela-Bairro project is unveiled. Over the next decade, US$180 million in funding will be spent providing neglected communities with access to decent sanitation, health clinics and public transportation.

2002

After four unsuccessful attempts, Lula is elected president. The former union leader serves a moderate first-term, despite upper-class fears of radical agendas. Meanwhile, Brazil wins its fifth World Cup.

2007

Rio hosts the Pan American Games, spending an estimated US$2 billion. Brazilian athletes rank third overall in total medal rankings (behind the US and Cuba). Increased police presence helps insure relative calm in the city.

city), a term that reflected the widening chasm between the affluent neighborhoods of the Zona Sul and the shanty towns spreading across the region's hillsides.

As Rio entered the new millennium, crime remained one of the most pervasive problems afflicting the city. Violence continued to take thousands of lives – particularly in the favelas – with no signs of letting up. As a result of a worsening situation, Brazilian officials have finally begun to pay more than lip service to the problem. President Lula, who astutely sees the link between poverty and crime, announced in 2007 that Rio's favelas would receive US$1.7 billion to invest in running water, sanitation, roads and housing. He even paid a visit to the Cantagalo favela, a first for a Brazilian president. He later told a reporter that such investment – providing adequate services for the people – was the only way to combat drug lords.

Yet Rio police have clearly shown a different approach. As the popular film *Tropa Elite* (Elite Squad, 2007), made poignantly clear, violence isn't exclusively the work of drug gangs. The film, researched by former police officers and some drug traffickers, depicts killing and torture perpetrated by the police. Techniques of 'shoot first, ask questions later' have been all too common an approach by law enforcement – which is why over 1000 citizens are killed by police each year in Rio.

Yet it hasn't been entirely grim news for the city. Rio's most recent international success was hosting the 2007 Pan American Games, which went off with few hitches (the city was particularly peaceful – owing to an added 20,000-strong police presence). The city poured an estimated US$2 billion into the games (critics say the money would have been better spent on services for the poor). Shortly after the games, Brazil made the winning bid to host the 2014 World Cup, bringing the tournament back home for the first time since 1950.

On other fronts, Rio is basking in the glow of its successful campaign to make Cristo Redentor one of the world's new seven wonders. It's also enjoying enormous economic opportunities on the back of a strong *real*, which continues to lure foreign investors to the country. The million-dollar question for the future is whether economic gains will extend down to Rio's worst-off citizens, and whether the government can truly get a handle on the twin evils of violence and poverty.

ARTS

Since its founding 500 years ago, Rio has made enormous contributions to the arts. Its world-class music scene continues to dominate center stage, but there's much more ablaze than just samba in the *cidade maravilhosa*. The city's museums, cinemas, theaters and concert halls continue to be a strong source of innovation – and inspiration – just like its venerated music clubs. Support for the arts is strong, with a good mix of the classic and daring vying for attention on the many stages throughout town.

Music is undoubtedly one of Rio's great legacies. The memorable talents from the 1930s may have disappeared, but a new crop of singers and musicians have taken their place. The revitalized neighborhood of Lapa is the center of samba, its old *gafieiras* (dance halls) drawing a diverse crowd who come to dance and hear the latest rising star. But samba can be heard all over town, at tiny storefront bars in Copacabana, spacious clubs in Centro and the verandas of Santa Teresa. Rio also has its great contributors of rock, *Música Popular Brasileira* (MPB), *choro*, jazz, hip-hop and even a few nostalgic bossa nova voices, which you can still hear in certain parts of town. Other distinctly Carioca innovations include *baile funk* (enormous dance parties in the favelas).

Like its music, Rio's fine arts scene is a dynamic one, with well-attended museums and galleries hosting some of Brazil's best exhibitions. At avant-garde galleries like the Centro de Arte He'lio Oitícica (p92), wall space is the domain of Rio's experimental artists. More venerable institutions showcase Brazil's most talented artists, with the Museu de Arte Moderna (MAM; p89) and Centro Cultural Banco do Brasil (p89) leading the way. There's also plenty of evocative street art, with certain boulevards – like the southern end of Rua Jardim Botânico – hosting a riotous medley of color in its imaginative graffiti. Other artists use Rio as their backdrop, as is the case when Santa Teresa hosts its annual Portas Abertas (p21).

Brazilian cinema continues to speed ahead. Each year, the film industry produces some excellent homegrown productions, and Cariocas also have a healthy appetite for foreign and independent films. There are dozens of theaters about town, and some notable film festivals, including the Festival do Rio (p22), which screens over 300 films from across the globe and attracts huge audiences.

Theater, dance and classical music also play an important role in the city's cultural life. Enormous stages like the modern Teatro Nelson Rodrigues (p175) host some of the city's biggest and best productions, while the historic venues of Theatro Municipal (p175) and Sala Cecília Meireles (p175) also host some excellent performances.

Those with good Portuguese can immerse themselves in the literary world, catching local poets at spoken-word events like those hosted at Leblon's Da Conde (p113) and other bookstores in town. Literary lights such as José Saramago and Paulo Coelho also give readings when in town.

Rio's calendar is packed with festivals, and new events pop up all the time. These are great places to see what's hot and new in the city. See p20 for special events happening during your stay. For a complete list of venues to catch music, theater, dance and more, see p162 and p174.

MUSIC

Rio boasts an enormous musical heritage. Rock, jazz, electronic music and uniquely Brazilian styles all showcase the talents of an astounding pool of musical talent. Foremost of all is the city's signature sound of samba – a deeply ingrained part of life that is heard everywhere on the streets.

Samba

The birth of Brazilian music essentially began with the birth of samba, first heard in the early 20th century in a Rio neighborhood near present-day Praça Onze. Here, immigrants from northeastern Brazil (mostly from Bahia) formed a tightly knit community in which traditional African customs thrived – music, dance and the Candomblé religion. Local homes provided the setting for impromptu performances and the exchange of ideas among Rio's first great instrumentalists. Such an atmosphere nurtured the likes of Pixinguinha, one of samba's founding fathers, as well as Donga, one of the composers of 'Pelo Telefone,' the first recorded samba song (in 1917) and an enormous success at the then-fledgling Carnaval.

Samba continued to evolve in the homes and *botequims* around Rio. The 1930s are known as the golden age of samba. By this point, samba's popularity had spread beyond the working-class neighborhoods of central Rio, and the music evolved at the same time into diverse, less percussive styles of samba. Sophisticated lyricists like Dorival Caymmi, Ary Barroso and Noel Rosa popularized *samba-canção* (melody-driven samba). (For insight into Noel Rosa's poetically charged and tragically brief life, check out the 2006 film *Noel: Poeta da Vila.*) Songs in this style featured sentimental lyrics and an emphasis on melody (rather than rhythm), foreshadowing the later advent of cool bossa nova. Carmen Miranda, one of the big radio stars of the 1930s, would become one of the first ambassadors of Brazilian music.

The 1930s were also the golden age of samba songwriting for the Carnaval. *Escolas de samba* (samba schools), which first emerged in 1928, soon became a vehicle for samba songwriting and by the 1930s, samba and Carnaval would be forever linked. Today's theme songs still borrow from that golden epoch.

Great *sambistas* (samba singers) continued to emerge in Brazil over the next few decades, although other emerging musical styles diluted their popularity. Artists like Cartola, Nelson Cavaquinho and Clementina de Jesus made substantial contributions to both samba and styles of music that followed from samba.

Traditional samba went through a rebirth a little over a decade ago with the opening of old-style *gafieiras* (dance halls) in Lapa (see p36). Today, Rio is once again awash with great *sambistas.* Classic *sambistas* like Alcione and Beth Carvalho still perform, while rising stars like Teresa Christina and Grupo Semente are intimately linked to Lapa's rebirth. Other talents to look out for on Rio's stages include Diogo Nogueira, the deep-voiced samba son of legendary singer João Nogueira, and Thais Villela, a rising star on the Lapa stage.

Another immensely popular artist still active in Rio is Maria Rita, the talented singer and songwriter whose voice is remarkably similar to that of her late mother, Elis Regina – one of Brazil's top singers. Although much of Rita's work often falls into the MPB camp, her 2007 album *Samba Meu* ranks as one of the best releases of the year, with a brilliant collection of sambas.

MOTHER OF SAMBA

In the early 20th century, one of Rio's most momentous events was transpiring inside the working-class neighborhood of Praça Onze near downtown. In 1915 this was considered 'Africa in miniature' for the influx of immigrants from Bahia, who had been flocking to the region since the end of slavery in 1888. In Praça Onze, Afro-Brazilian culture – music, dance and religion (Candomblé) – thrived in the homes of old Bahian matriarchs, called *tias* (aunts). At the center of this thriving community was Tia Ciata, something of a self-made woman who rented out costumes for the Carnaval balls, worked as a healer (she was even consulted by president Wenceslau Brás, who had a leg wound that Ciata allegedly healed), and hosted large parties on Candomblé saints' days – all while looking after her 15 children. Within time, Ciata's house became the meeting point for the city's journalists, bohemians, Bahian expats and musicians. Today's now-legendary names – Pixinguinha, Donga, Heitor dos Prazeres and others – met regularly to play music and experiment with new forms, never imagining that their result – samba – would become one of the world's great musical forms. Coincidentally, this was also around the time that African-Americans in New Orleans were playing the music that would later be called jazz.

After the earliest musical creations, the performers gathering at Tia Ciata's went on to make records, and samba's popularity spread like wildfire across the city. They came first through the working class and, after initial resistance, on into the houses of the wealthy. Samba continued to evolve throughout the next few decades as it was adopted for Carnaval, yet the songs developed in those early years would live on (many are still played), and laid the foundation for which so much of Brazilian music is based on today.

Bossa Nova

In the 1950s came bossa nova (literally, new wave), sparking a new era of Brazilian music. Bossa nova's founders – songwriter and composer Antonio Carlos (Tom) Jobim and guitarist João Gilberto, in association with the lyricist-poet Vinícius de Moraes – slowed down and altered the basic samba rhythm to create a more intimate, harmonic style. This new wave initiated a new style of playing instruments and of singing.

Bossa nova's seductive melodies were very much linked to Rio's Zona Sul, where most bossa musicians lived. Songs like Jobim's 'Corcovado' and Roberto Meneschal's 'Rio' evoked an almost nostalgic portrait of the city with their quiet lyricism. Bossa was also associated with the new class of university-educated Brazilians, and its lyrics reflected the optimistic mood of the middle class in the 1950s.

By the 1960s, bossa nova had become a huge international success. The genre's initial development was greatly influenced by American jazz and blues, and over time, the bossa nova style came to influence those music styles as well. Bossa nova classics were adopted, adapted and recorded by such musical luminaries as Frank Sinatra, Ella Fitzgerald and Stan Getz, among others.

In addition to the founding members, other great Brazilian bossa nova musicians include Marcos Valle, Luiz Bonfá and Baden Powell, whose talented 20-something son Marcel Powell carries on the musical tradition (catch him live around Rio). Bands from the 1960s like Sergio Mendes & Brasil '66 were also influenced by bossa nova, as were other artists who fled the repressive years of military-dictatorship rule to live and play abroad. More recent interpreters of the seductive bossa sound include the Bahian-born Rosa Passos and the Carioca Paula Morelenbaum.

For the full story, check out Ruy Castro's *Bossa Nova: The Story of the Brazilian Music that Seduced the World.*

Tropicália

One of Brazil's great artistic movements, emerging in the late 1960s, was *tropicália,* a direct response to the repressive military dictatorship that seized power in 1964 (and remained in power until 1984). Bahian singers Caetano Veloso and Gilberto Gil led the movement, making waves with songs of protest against the national regime. (Gil, ironically, is today's Minister of Culture – see p38.) In addition to penning defiant lyrics, *tropicalistas* introduced the public to electric instruments, fragmentary melodics and wildly divergent musical styles. In fact, the *tropicalistas'* hero was poet Oswald de Andrade, whose 1928 *Manifesto Antropofágico* (Cannibalistic Manifesto) supported the idea that anything under the sun could be devoured and re-created in one's music. Hence, the movement fused elements of American rock and roll, blues, jazz and British psychedelic styles into bossa nova and samba rhythms. Important figures linked to *tropicália* include

Gal Costa, Jorge Benjor, Maria Bethânia, Os Mutantes and Tom Zé. Although *tropicália* wasn't initially embraced by the public, who objected to the electric and rock elements (in fact, Veloso was booed off the stage on several occasions), by the 1970s its radical ideas had been absorbed and accepted, and lyrics of protest were ubiquitous in songwriting of the time.

The world is still coming to grips with the complex musical legacy of the *tropicalistas.* A 2006 exposition at London's Barbican Centre was dedicated to the movement, and included the music of AfroReggae, one of Rio's leading funk groups, whose songs have elements of *tropicália.* Os Mutantes also helped reignite interest in *tropicália* during their 2006 world reunion tour (which unfortunately did not include Rita Lee).

Those who want a deeper understanding of the movement and its aftermath should read Caetano Veloso's self-congratulatory book *Tropical Truth.*

Música Popular Brasileira (MPB)

Música Popular Brasileira (MPB) is a catchphrase to describe all popular Brazilian music after bossa nova. It includes *tropicália, pagode* (relaxed and rhythmic form of samba), and Brazilian pop and rock. All Brazilian music has roots in samba; even in Brazilian rock, heavy metal, disco or pop, the samba sound is often present.

MPB first emerged in the 1970s along with talented musicians like Edu Lobo, Milton Nascimento, Elis Regina, Djavan and dozens of others, many of whom wrote protest songs not unlike the *tropicalistas.* Chico Buarque is one of the first big names from this epoch, and is easily one of Brazil's greatest songwriters. His music career began in 1968 and spanned a time during which many of his songs were banned by the military dictatorship – in fact his music became a symbol of protest during that era. Today the enormously successful Carioca artist continues to write new albums, though lately he has turned his hand to novel writing.

Jorge Benjor is another singer whose career, which began in the 1960s, has survived up to the present day. Highly addictive rhythms are omnipresent in Benjor's songs, as he incorporates African beats and elements of funk, samba and blues in his eclectic repertoire. The celebratory album *África Brasil,* along with his debut album *Samba Esquema Novo,* are among his best.

Carlinhos Brown is another popular artist (and workaholic) who continues to make immeasurable contributions to Brazilian music, particularly in the realm of Afro-Brazilian rhythms.

THE DANCE HALLS OF OLD *Carmen Michael*

If you're interested in Brazilian music and dance, shine up your dancing shoes and head for some of Rio's old-school-style dance halls, known as *gafieiras*. Originally established in the 1920s as dance halls for Rio's urban working class, *gafieiras* nowadays attract an eclectic combination of musicians, dancers, *malandros* (con men) and, of course, the radical chic from Zona Sul. Modern and sleek they are not. Typically held in the ballrooms of old colonial buildings in Lapa, the locations are magnificently old-world. Bow-tied waiters serve ice-cold *cerveja* (beer) under low, yellow lights and, while the setup initially looks formal, give it a few rounds and it will dissolve into a typically raucous Brazilian evening.

Before *gafieiras* were established, Rio's different communities were polarized by their places of social interaction, whether it was opera and tango for the Europeans or street *choro* (romantic, intimate samba) for the Africans. Responding to a social need and in tandem with the politics of the time, *gafieiras* quickly became places where musicians and audiences of black and white backgrounds alike could mix and create new sounds. Through the *gafieiras,* the street-improvised *choro* formations became big-band songs and a new Brazilian sound was born. The best and oldest dance halls are Democráticus (p166), attracting a young yet fashionably bohemian crowd on Wednesday, and Estudantina (p167) on Praça Tiradentes, which operates from Friday to Sunday.

The standard of dancing is outstanding in Brazil, so expect to see couples who would be considered professional in Europe or the US dancing unnoticed across the polished floors. While just about anything goes in Rio, it's an opportunity for the Cariocas to dress up a little, so you will see quite a few dresses and smart shoes. Don't be intimidated by the other dancers. Unlike in Buenos Aires, where the tango is for experts only, Brazilians are pretty relaxed about newcomers dancing. For those traveling solo, *gafieiras* are fantastic places to meet some intriguing locals and learn a few steps. Dance around the edge of the dance floor with the rest of the dancers to get a closer look at how the dance works – if you are a woman, you won't wait long before someone asks you to dance. Alternatively you can take a lesson and perhaps meet some fellow beginners to dance with. Estudantina has an in-house dance instructor with whom you can arrange lessons; otherwise, head for one of the nearby dance schools such as Fundição Progresso (p185).

THE IPOD 25: SOUNDS FROM BRAZIL

One of the world's great music cultures, Brazil has an astounding array of talented musicians. A list of our favorite songs could easily fill this chapter, but we've limited our highly subjective pick to 25 songs from 25 different artists.

- 'Aquarela do Brasil' – Ary Barroso
- 'Viagem' – Baden Powell
- 'Soy Loco Por Ti, America' – Caetano Veloso
- 'Alvorada' – Cartola
- 'Construção' – Chico Buarque
- 'Flor de Lis' – Djavan
- 'O Mar' – Dorival Caymmi
- 'Aguas de Março' – Elis Regina (written by Tom Jobim)
- 'Amor Perfeito' – Elza Soares
- 'Namorinho de Portão' – Gal Costa
- 'Domingo no Parque' – Gilberto Gil
- 'Desafinado' – João Gilberto
- 'Ponta de Lança Africana' – Jorge Benjor
- 'Asa Branca' – Luiz Gonzaga
- 'Alibi' – Maria Bethânia
- 'Recado' – Maria Rita
- 'Chuva no Brejo' – Marisa Monte
- 'Travessia' – Milton Nascimento
- 'Último Desejo' – Noel Rosa
- 'Panis et Circenses' – Os Mutantes
- 'Acenda O Farol' – Tim Maia
- 'Garota de Ipanema' – Tom Jobim
- 'Velha Infância' – Tribalistas
- 'Não me deixe só' – Vanessa da Mata
- 'Felicidade' – Vinícius de Moraes

Born in Bahia, Brown has influences that range from *merengue* (fast-paced dancehall music originating in the Domincan Republic) to Candomblé music to straight-up James Brown-style funk (the US artist from whom Carlinhos took his stage name). In addition to creating the popular percussion ensemble Timbalada, he has a number of excellent albums of his own (notably *Alfagamabetizado*).

Rock, Pop & Hip Hop

MPB tends to bleed into other genres, particularly into rock and pop. One artist who moves comfortably between genres is Bebel Gilberto (the sweet-voiced daughter of João Gilberto), who blends bossa nova with modern beats. Another heiress of Brazilian traditions is the Rio-born Marisa Monte, popular at home and abroad for her fine singing and songwriting. Mixing samba, *forró* (traditional, fast-paced music from the northeast), pop and rock, Marisa has been part of a number of successful collaborations in the music world, most recently with Arnaldo Antunes and Carlinhos Brown to create the hit album *Tribalistas* (2003). Two other notable young singers who hail from a bossa line include Fernanda Porto and Cibelle.

Brazilian hip-hop emerged from the favelas of Rio sometime in the 1980s, and has been slowly attracting followers ever since. Big names like Racionais MCs first emerged out of São Paulo, but Rio has its share of more recent success stories. One of the best on the scene is Marcelo D2 (formerly of Planet Hemp) impressing audiences with albums like *A Procura da Batida Perfeita* (2005) and *Meu Samba É Assim* (2006). Seu Jorge, who starred in the film *Cidade de Deus*, has also earned accolades for the release of *Cru* (2005), an inventive hip-hop album with politically charged beats.

Rock has its promoters, though it enjoys far less airtime than samba. Rio gets its share of mega-rockers on the world tour (the Rolling Stones played before an estimated 1.5 million on Copacabana beach in 2006). It also has a few homegrown talents. The group Legião Urbana from Brasília remains a national favorite even after the death of its lead singer in 2007. Skank, O Rappa, Paralamas Sucesso and the Rio-based Barão Vermelho are other essential names.

In other genres, indie-rock favorites Los Hermanos are among the best bands competing for airtime. Check out their excellent album *Ventura*. Another of our indie favorites is *Monokini Mondo Topless* (2004), an album that blends pop with electro grooves – think vaguely Stereolab in the tropics.

There's no doubt that more great artists will emerge by the time you read this. Your best bet: after arriving, head straight to a record store in Rio (try Modern Sound, p119) and find out who's the hottest pop star of the moment. It's unlikely the store clerk will answer Beyoncé, or any non-Brazilian artist for that matter. For a more detailed history of Brazilian music, check out the book *The Brazilian Sound* by Chris McGowan and Ricardo Pessanha.

BRAZIL'S FAVORITE POLITICO *Tom Phillips*

An active participant in both the World Economic Forum and the World Social Forum, Gilberto Gil is not exactly your cookie-cutter bureaucrat. Perhaps only in Brazil would you expect to find a pop star in government. Forget Silvio Berlusconi's crooning, or Tony Blair's attempts at Christian rock – Gilberto Gil has been one of Brazil's best-loved musicians since the 1960s.

Gil was always an *engajado* (activist) – during the 1960s he spent two years exiled in London after offending the dictatorship with his surreal, provocative lyrics. It's just that these days he's engaged in a different way, occupying an office in Brazil's Planalto, where he is the Minister of Culture in President Lula's cabinet.

A household name for decades, Gil hails from the northeastern state of Bahia. Born in 1942, he was raised in a middle-class family near Salvador. His career as a troubadour began in 1965, when he moved south to São Paulo with another Bahian musician, Caetano Veloso. Between them they were responsible for *tropicália,* an influential though short-lived cultural movement that blended traditional Brazilian music with the electric guitars and psychedelia of the Beatles. Years later Veloso even recorded a Tupiniquim (an indigenous group in the northeast) tribute to the Liverpudlian rockers – called *Sugar Cane Fields Forever*.

Over the decades Gil has notched up hit after hit – morphing from quick-footed *sambista* (samba dancer) to Stevie Wonderesque balladeer to dreadlocked reggae icon.

Since the release of *Louvaçao* in 1967, Gil has recorded dozens of albums, including *Kaya N'Gan Daya*, a tribute to his idol Bob Marley. He's shared the stage with many performers over the years, even playing with the former UN general Secretary Kofi Annan (on bongos) in New York.

In between world tours, book launches and his ministerial duties, the slender 60-something-year-old even finds time for the beach. Keep your eyes peeled – it's not uncommon to find Gil sunning himself at Ipanema's Posto 9.

Here is some essential listening:

- *Gilberto Gil (Frevo Rasgado, 1968)* – Gilberto Gil
- *Acoustic* (1994) – Gilberto Gil
- *Quanta* (1997) – Gilberto Gil
- *Refazenda* (1996) – Gilberto Gil
- *Tropicália 2* (1994) – Gilberto Gil and Caetano Veloso
- *Tropicália, ou Panis et Circencis* (1968) – Gilberto Gil, Caetano Veloso, Gal Costa and Os Mutantes

CINEMA

Brazil has a prolific film industry, though much of what it makes doesn't venture beyond the country's borders. One of the most-talked about films in recent years is *Tropa de Elite* (Elite Squad, 2007), which depicts police brutality in the favelas; it also makes a very clear link between middle-class college kids who buy drugs and the deaths of young children in the favelas who are recruited by drug lords to help meet the demand for coke and other substances. It was made by José Padilha, the acclaimed director of the disturbing documentary *Bus 174,* which depicts a high-profile bus hijacking that took place in Rio de Janeiro in 2000. (Do yourself a favor and watch it *after* your trip, rather than before it.)

The beautifully set *Casa da Areia* (House of Sand, 2006), directed by Andrucha Waddington, follows three generations of women as they struggle on the dramatic but desolate landscape in Maranhão. It stars real-life mother and daughter Fernanda Montenegro and Fernando Torres, with Seu Jorge in a supporting role.

Slightly more uplifting is *Dois Filhos do Francisco* (The Two Sons of Francisco, 2005), based on the true story of two brothers – Zeze and Luciano di Camargo – who overcame their humble origins to become successful country musicians. Despite some unfortunate melodrama, the film has plenty of merit, including a curious soundtrack created under the direction of Caetano Veloso. It is also the highest grossing film at the box office in the last 20 years.

Although made by two Americans, *Favela Rising* (2005) is so quintessentially 'Rio' that it deserves mention. A fine counterpoint to *Cidade de Deus* (more on that later), this documentary shows a different side of the favela through the eyes of Anderson Sá, founder of the very talented *Grupo Cultural Afro Reggae* (Afro-Reggae Group) and a massive symbol of hope for many poor children growing up in the favela. In the film, Sá, who turned his life around after involvement in gangs, starts a music school for youths and makes an enormous contribution to a number of lives as the Afro-Reggae movement spreads to other favelas.

Another worthwhile documentary is *Vinícius* (2005), a paean to the great poet and songwriter Vinícius de Moraes, directed by his ex-son-in-law Miguel Faria Jr. The film features archival footage of old interviews as well as performances of Vinícius' music as played by some of Brazil's best artists.

The documentary *Rio de Jano* (2003) shows an outsider perspective via interviews with the French cartoonist Jano. Jean le Guay (aka Jano) carefully avoids the stereotypes but captures the Carioca sense of humor while drawing a mixed gang at work (in blue-collar jobs), at the beach, dancing at a funk party and basking on the beach. Director Anna Azevedo did a marvelous job bringing Jano's vision to life.

For a trip back to the 1930s Lapa, check out Karim Aïnouz's compelling *Madame Satã* (2002). Rio's gritty red-light district of that time (which hasn't changed much in the last 75 years) is the setting for the true story of Madame Satã (aka João Francisco dos Santos), the troubled but good-hearted *malandro* (con artist), transvestite, singer and *capoeira* master, who became a symbol of Lapa's mid-century bohemianism.

One of Brazil's top directors, Fernando Meirelles earned his credibility with *Cidade de Deus* (City of God), the 2002 film based on a true story by Paolo Lins. The film, which shows brutality and hope co-existing in a Rio favela, earned four Oscar nominations, including one for best director. More importantly, it brought much attention to the plight of the urban poor in Brazil. After his success with *Cidade de Deus,* Meirelles went Hollywood with *The Constant Gardener* (2004), an intriguing conspiracy film shot in Africa.

Eu, Tu, Eles (Me, You, Them), Andrucha Waddington's social comedy about a northeasterner with three husbands, was also well received when it was released in 2000. It has beautiful cinematography and a score by Gilberto Gil (see opposite) that contributed to the recent wave of popularity of that funky northeastern music, *forró*.

Walter Salles is one of Brazil's best-known directors, whose Oscar award-winning *Central do Brasil* (Central Station, 1998) should be in every serious Brazilophile's film library. The central character is an elderly woman who works in the main train station in Rio writing letters for illiterates with families far away. A chance encounter with a young homeless boy leads her to accompany him into the real, unglamorized Brazil on a search for his father. Salles' latest foray into film is his big-budget biopic *Diarios de Motocicleta* (The Motorcycle Diaries, 2004), detailing the historic journey of Che Guevara and Alberto Granada across South America.

As with many filmmakers, some of Salles' best works came much earlier. In fact, his first feature film *Terra Estrangeiro* (Foreign Land, 1995) holds an important place in the renaissance of Brazilian cinema. The film won seven international prizes and was shown at over two dozen film festivals. It was named best film of the year in Brazil in 1996, where it screened for over six months. Salles is also a great documentary filmmaker; *Socorro Nobre* (Life Somewhere Else, 1995) and *Krajcberg, O Poeta dos Vestigios* (Krajcberg, the Poet of the Remains, 1987) have won awards at international festivals.

Bruno Barreto's *O Que É Isso Companheiro* (released as *Four Days in September* in the US, 1998) is based on the 1969 kidnapping of the US ambassador to Brazil by leftist guerrillas. It was nominated for an Oscar in 1998.

Another milestone in Brazilian cinema is the visceral film *Pixote* (1981), directed by the acclaimed Hector Babenco. This film shows life through the eyes of a street kid in Rio, who gets swept along on a journey from innocent waif to murderer by the currents of the underworld. The film is a damning indictment of Brazilian society, made all the more poignant when the actor who played Pixote was killed by police during a bungled robbery six years after the making of the film.

Another important film is *Bye Bye Brasil* (1980) by Carlos Diegues. The first major film produced after the end of the dictatorship, it chronicles the adventures of a theater troupe as it tours the entire country, charting the profound changes in Brazilian society in the second half of the 20th century. Diegues went on to direct *Orfeu* (1999), a lackluster remake of the Camus classic.

Prior to the military dictatorship (1964–85), which stymied much creative expression in the country, Brazil was in the grip of Cinema Novo. This 1960s movement focused on Brazil's bleak social problems, and was influenced by Italian neorealism. One of the great films made during this epoch is *O Pagador de Promessas* (The Payer of Vows, 1962), a poetic story about a man who keeps his promise to carry a cross after the healing of his donkey. It won the Palme d'Or at the Cannes Film Festival. Another great pioneer of Cinema Novo is the director Glauber

Rocha. In *Deus e o Diabo na Terra do Sol* (Black God, White Devil, 1963), Rocha touches on many of the elements in northeastern Brazil of struggle, fanaticism and poverty. It's one of the great films of the period.

Another important film of the 20th century is Marcel Camus' *Orfeu Negro* (Black Orpheus, 1959), which opened the world's ears to bossa nova by way of the Jobim and Bonfá soundtrack. Music aside, the film did a clever job recasting Ovid's original Orpheus-Eurydice myth in the setting of Rio's Carnaval (a fertile ground for mythmaking). Making an arguably larger impact on Brazilian cinema is the Nelson Pereira dos Santos film *Rio 40 Graus* (1955). This classic of Cinema Novo follows a number of characters and plots that intertwine at an electric pace. Because of its unglamorized portrait of the poor, it was banned on release and wasn't shown in theaters until a year later.

Brazilian cinema began in Rio; appropriately, the city itself starred in the first film made in the country – a slow pan of Baía de Guanabara, made in 1898.

LITERATURE

Carioca author Paulo Coelho, whose books have sold more than 100 million copies, is one of the world's most widely read novelists. While critics tend to knock his simplistic New Age spiritual fables, books such as *The Pilgrimage* (1987), *The Alchemist* (1988), and more recently *The Witch of Portobello* (2006) have struck a nerve with his global fan base, bringing him rock-star fame.

A writer of 'actual' rock-star fame is talented singer and songwriter Chico Buarque. The author of two rather mediocre novels, Buarque seemed to jump the fence successfully in his third effort, *Budapest* (2003), an engaging and meditative novel of love and language set in Budapest and Rio.

A far-different worldview is presented in works from the detective genre, with popular novels finally available in English. Often called the Raymond Chandler of Brazil, Luis Alfredo Garcia-Roza writes hard-boiled page-turners, often set in his Copacabana neighborhood. To explore the noir side of Rio check out his novels *Southwesterly Wind* (2004) and *Window in Copacabana* (2005). Patrícia Melo is another Brazilian crime novelist (and playwright), who's received praise from both readers and academics for her smart, psychologically complex thrillers. Among her best works are *The Killer* (1998) and *Inferno* (2002).

More widely respected in literary circles is the great Brazilian writer Jorge Amado, who died in 2001. Born near Ilhéus in 1912, and a longtime resident of Salvador, Amado wrote colorful romances of Bahia's people and places, with touches of magical realism. His early work was strongly influenced by communism. His later books were lighter in subject, but more picturesque and intimate in style. The most acclaimed are *Gabriela, Clove and Cinnamon* (1958), set in Ilhéus, and *Dona Flor and Her Two Husbands* (1966), set in Salvador. The latter relates the tale of a young woman who must decide between two lovers – the first being the man she marries after her first husband drops dead at Carnaval, the second being her deceased husband who returns to her as a (still amorous) ghost. Amado's other works include *Tent of Miracles* (1969), which explores race relations in Brazil, and provides an excellent introduction to Candomblé (Amado himself was a practitioner). *The Violent Land* (1943) is an early Amado classic – something of a dark frontier story. *Shepherds of the Night* (1964), three short stories about a group of Bahian characters, provides another excellent and witty portrait of Bahia.

In the 19th century, José de Alencar became one of Brazil's most famous writers. Many of his works are set in Rio, including *Cinco Minutos* and *Senhora,* both published in 1875. Another author from that era, Joaquim Manoel de Macedo was a great chronicler of the customs of his time. In addition to such romances as *A Moreninha,* he wrote *Um Passeio Pela Cidade do Rio de Janeiro* (1863) and *Memórias da Rua do Ouvidor* (1878).

Joaquim Maria Machado de Assis, another Carioca, is widely regarded as Brazil's greatest writer. The son of a freed slave, Assis worked as a typesetter and journalist in late-19th-century Rio. A tremendous stylist with a great command of humor and irony, Assis had a sharp understanding of human relations, which he used to great effect in his brilliantly cynical works. He used Rio as the background for most of the works he produced in the late 19th century, such as *The Posthumous Memoirs of Bras Cubas* (1881) and *Quincas Borba* (1891).

Mario de Andrade led the country's artistic renaissance in the 1920s, and became one of the leading figures in the modernist movement in Brazil. In works such as *Macunaíma* (1928) he pioneered the use of vernacular language in national literature. He stressed the importance of

Brazilian writers drawing from their own rich heritage. His work showed elements of surrealism and was later seen as a precursor to magical realism.

VISUAL ARTS

Although currently little known outside of Brazil, Rio's artists are slowly carving a name for themselves in the contemporary art world. At the forefront of the art movement are avant-gardists like Ducha, who utilizes the city's unique topography to create some of his boldest works. His best-known work is his 2001 *Projeto Cristo Redentor,* in which he turned the Christ statue blood-red by covering the white spotlights surrounding it with red gelatin film. This of course required breaking the law, which earned him a fair bit of notoriety.

Another Rio-based artist doing daring work is Jarbas Lopes. His politically and socially incisive work often takes aim at the corruption inherent in many spheres of Brazilian government. Lopes' *O Debate* (The Debate) series was created by manipulating posters, found on the street, of political candidates. Taking the posters of two opposing candidates, he'd weave them together, then place them back on the street, offering his views on the lack of choice in the elections.

Although he's not from Rio, the photographer Sebastião Salgado is Brazil's best-known contemporary artist outside the country. Noted for his masterful use of light, the black-and-white photographer has earned international acclaim for his stunningly beautiful and highly evocative photos of migrant workers and others on the fringes of society.

Going back a few years, the Carioca artist Hélio Oiticica (1937–80) was one of the most significant figures of the avant-garde of the '60s and '70s. He's best known for interactive works, like his controversial *Cosmococa,* an installation that invited viewers to lie on sand covered with plastic sheeting, while watching a projection in which lines of cocaine were arranged across a photo of Marilyn Monroe. Despite his short life, his impact on Brazilian art was profound. Today, there's even a cultural center, Centro de Arte Hélio Oiticica, named after him.

Rio-born artist Cildo Meireles (b 1948) has also made a sizable contribution to the contemporary art movement. Creating at the height of the military dictatorship, Meireles focused on the social environment, using silk screens and installations to question the legitimacy of the regime. In the US he garnered much attention for his designing and printing of fake banknotes that featured an image of Uncle Sam on one side and Fort Knox on the other, which he reintroduced into circulation.

Anna Bella Geiger (b 1933) is another important artist active since the 1960s. Following the warm reception of her early photographic work, she expanded her range, becoming one of Brazil's pioneers in video art. Her most recent work was her 2004 exhibition at Paço Imperial, entitled *Obras em Arquipélago,* a sublime composition uniting the language and design of cartography with the geography of the human body.

Getting his start a few decades earlier was the experimental artist Abraham Palatnik, one of the first Brazilians to explore the use of technology in art. He delighted critics with his masterful mixing of light and movement, which he fused in 'cinechromatic machines' – projections of colored light forms onto clear surfaces, innovative work for the 1950s. His last solo exhibition was held in Rio in 1986.

Throughout Brazil's recent history, the influence of European and other foreign art on Brazilian work is significant. In the 19th and 20th centuries, Brazilian artists followed international trends such as neoclassicism, romanticism, impressionism and modernism. The best-known Brazilian painter internationally is Cândido Portinari (1903–62). Early in his career he made the decision to paint only Brazil and its people. Strongly influenced by the Mexican muralists, such as Diego Rivera, he fused native, expressionist influences with a sophisticated, socially conscious style.

Rio's earliest painters were quite taken with the landscape – a tradition that continues today. The 19th-century French artists Jean-Baptiste Debret and Nicolas Taunay, who came via the French artistic mission, set the tone for the development of art over the next 100 years (some critics say they stifled Brazilian art by keeping it rooted in old-fashioned traditions). Regardless, Debret's and Taunay's works in watercolor are some of the first visual records of life in the colony. The neoclassical strand was continued in later works like Victor Meirelles' *A Primeira Missa* (the First Mass, 1861), which depicts the first Mass celebrated in the new colony, with Pedro Álvarez Cabral (Portuguese discoverer of Brazil) and his men in attendance.

THEATER & DANCE

One of the big names in Brazilian theater today is the avant-garde director Gerald Thomas. Raised in Rio, Thomas now lives in New York, but continues to have some of his biggest successes on Rio's stages. His work, which he calls Dry Opera, features the almost cinematic use of blackouts and atmospheric lighting, along with pre-recorded music and marionette-like acting. For some, it amounts to a complete reinvention of theater. The political comedy *Um Circo de Rins e Fígados* (A Circus of Kidneys and Livers) remains one of his long-running successes (already seen by over 80,000 people in both Brazil and Argentina). His drama isn't strictly limited to his plays: in 2003, following his production of *Tristan und Isolde,* several belligerent audience members shouted at the director, and he mooned them from onstage. This led to criminal proceedings, though his name was eventually cleared.

Equal parts dance, theater and performance art, Intrépida Trupa has been showcasing its avant-garde pieces since 1986. Expertly choreographed acrobatics, impressive special effects and dramatic tension have earned comparisons to Cirque du Soleil. Its popular show Metegol returns periodically to Rio, usually staged at Fundição Progresso (p100), where the troupe also gives classes in acrobatics (p185).

Rio's lively theater scene began long before the term 'indecent exposure' was in circulation. In fact, the first theater troupes were founded just after Brazil's independence in 1822, and playwrights soon developed a national style. The poet and writer Gonçalves Dias (1823–64) was among the first Brazilians to write plays. Only a handful of Dias' work survives, and the romantic figure (who later died in a shipwreck) is better known for his poetry. His lyric 'Canção do Exílio' (Song of Exile) is his dedication to Brazil's natural beauty.

During the early days of the republic, other great theater works were produced. Well-known writers, such as José de Alencar, Machado de Assis and Artur Azevedo, wrote plays in addition to literary works, expanding the national repertoire of Brazil's proliferating theaters.

In the 1940s, Nelson Rodrigues (1912–80), who's often characterized as the Eugene O'Neill of Brazil, was instrumental in transforming theater. His socially conscious plays revealed the moral hypocrisy of upper-class Brazilian families. The 1950s saw a flourishing of the theater arts as playwrights like Gianfranco Guarnieri, Jorge Andrade and Ariano Suassuna created more experimental works, creating a dynamic theater scene in Rio and São Paolo.

ARCHITECTURE

The capital of Brazil for many years, Rio has been the architectural setting for the beautiful, the functional and the avant-garde. Today one can see a sweeping range of styles that span the 17th to 20th centuries in archetypal buildings that often jockey for attention alongside one another.

Vestiges of the colonial period live on in downtown Rio. Some of the most impressive works are the 17th-century churches built by the Jesuits. The best examples from this, the baroque period, are the Convento de Santo Antônio (p92) and the Mosteiro de São Bento (p93). The incredibly ornate interiors, which appear almost to drip with liquid gold, show little of the restraint that would later typify Brazilian architecture.

The artist mission (a group of artists and architects chosen to bring new life to the city) that arrived from France in the early 19th century introduced a whole new design aesthetic to the budding Brazilian empire. Neoclassicism became the official style and was formally taught in the newly founded Imperial Academy. The works built during this period were grandiose and monumental, dominated by classical features such as elongated columns and wide domes. Among the many fine examples of this period are the Instituto Nacional de Belas Artes, the Theatro Municipal (p94) and the Casa França-Brasil (p93) – considered the most important from this period. There are a few curious features of the Casa: its alignment to the cardinal points, the large cross-shaped space inside, and its monumental dome.

The end of the 19th century saw the continuation of this trend of returning to earlier forms and featured works like the Real Gabinete Português de Leitura (p94). Completed in 1887, the Royal Reading Room shows inspiration from the much earlier manueline period (early 1500s), with a Gothic facade and the highlighting of its metallic structure.

During the 20th century, Rio became the setting for a wide array of architectural styles – including neoclassical, eclectic, art deco and modernist works. During the same period, Rio

BOHEMIAN RIO: A WIDE-EYED LOOK AT THE CIDADE MARAVILHOSA

Rio has turned heads for centuries, inspiring a string of admirers dating back to the city's earliest colonial days. Some visitors come for a week and decide they're not going home. That's what happened to Australian Carmen Michael when she left her job in London in 2003 for a short holiday in Brazil, and has been there ever since. In that time, Carmen has settled in Santa Teresa and delved deeply into Rio, which she describes in her book *Chasing Bohemia* (2007). When Lonely Planet got in touch with Carmen, she described a pivotal night in her decision to live in Rio: 'There was a moment running down the empty streets of Centro on the first night of Carnaval with 100,000 wild-eyed hedonists. I thought, yeah! Maybe this is the place for me! It was the stuff of fantasy – a street rebellion in sequins and feathers to the sound of a hundred drums.'

What are the things you most love about the city? To quote Vinícius de Moraes, I would say its 'adorable disorganization'. There is something deeply exciting about an anarchic culture when you are coming from a controlled and conservative society such as Australia. The apparent freedom of everyday life – staying up until sunrise on weekdays, not turning up to work, limited obligations within relationships – is fairly intoxicating for an Anglo Saxon girl who grew up between a farm in Western Australia and Canberra.

Why did you choose to live in Santa Teresa? Every city has its time. Paris had the '20s, New York had the '70s and I feel that Santa Teresa is in her moment. There is a higher intensity of life there than other places. I guess this extraordinary level of personal and creative liberty, combined with an explosive social situation, makes for heady times. It has a colorful, carefree mix of artists, travelers and intellectuals, all clinging onto a spectacular hill between the favelas and the bohemian red-light district. It is all very avant-garde!

Do you feel Rio has changed much since you settled there in 2003? In some ways the violent reputation of Rio de Janeiro has protected her from the mass tourism market. I think that a small amount of tourism adds an interesting cultural layer to any place, and Rio is a city sufficiently chaotic that it blends the presence of locals and foreigners quite well. I guess one way that Rio has changed is that Santa Teresa has become increasingly more popular with the 'seachangers' from Europe buying houses and turning them into B&Bs. This has, in part, gentrified the area, but it has also brought about desperately needed investment for a historically important area. Most of the foreigners leave in exasperation at the cultural differences after about four years anyway!

Samba seems to be an integral part of your Rio experience. Any bands or performers you're particularly fond of? For some live unsigned action, I would be looking out for Fabio da Lapa and Galo Canto for samba, Zo Paulo for *choro*, Thais Villolla for a powerful vocal performance, and MC Catra and MC Frank for *carioca* funk. If you want to buy an album – Tom Jobim, Cartola, Caetano Veloso, Nelson Cavaquinho, Elis Regina and Chico Buarque.

An interview with Carmen Michael, Australian expat now living in Rio

also restored some of its colonial gems (others fell to the wrecking ball), becoming one of Latin America's most beautiful cities.

This, of course, did not happen by chance. In the early 20th century, as capital of Brazil, Rio de Janeiro was viewed as a symbol of the glory of the modern republic and the president lavished beautiful neoclassical buildings upon the urban streetscape.

The early 1900s was also the period when one of Rio's most ambitious mayors, Pereira Passos, was in office. These twin factors had an enormous influence in shaping the face of Brazil's best-known city.

Mayor Passos (1902–06) envisioned Rio as the Paris of South America, and ordered his engineers to lay down grand boulevards and create manicured parks, as some of Rio's most elegant buildings rose overhead. One of the most beautiful buildings constructed during this period was the Palaçio Monroe (1906), a re-creation of a work built for the 1904 St Louis World's Fair. The elegant neoclassical Monroe Palace sat on the Praça Floriano and housed the Câmara dos Deputados (House of Representatives). Unfortunately, like many other of Rio's beautiful buildings, it was destroyed in 1976 in the gross 'reurbanization' craze that swept through the city.

The fruits of this early period were displayed at the International Exposition held in Rio in 1922. This was not only the showcase for neocolonial architecture and urban design; it also introduced Brazil's most modern city to the rest of the world. Another big event of the 1920s was the completion of the Copacabana Palace (p193), the first luxury hotel in South America. Its construction would lead to the rapid development of the beach regions.

top picks

ARCHITECTURAL ICONS

- **Copacabana Palace** (p193) The neoclassical gem that came to represent a glitzy new era.
- **Arcos da Lapa** (p100) Often used as a symbol of Lapa's bohemian rebirth.
- **Maracanã football stadium** (p104) Brazil's temple to football and its largest stadium.
- **Cristo Redentor** (p85) Recently voted one of the new seven modern wonders of the world, Christ the Redeemer still looms large over Rio's landscape.
- **Theatro Municipal** (p94) The flower of the Belle Époque and also the costliest opera house constructed outside of Europe.

Rio's 1930s buildings show the currents of modern European architecture, which greatly impacted upon the city's design. Rio's modernism was born along with the rise of President Vargas, who wanted to leave his mark on federal Rio through the construction of public ministries, official chambers and the residences of government power. The Ministry of Health & Education, the apotheosis of the modernist movement in Brazil, is one of the city's most significant public buildings, as it's one of the few works designed by French architect Le Corbusier, in conjunction with several young Brazilian architects. (Another Le Corbusier-influenced design is the Aeroporto Santos Dumont, completed in 1937.)

The 1930s was also the era of the art-deco movement, which was characterized by highly worked artistic details and an abundance of ornamentation. Good specimens include the central train station and the statue of Cristo Redentor (p85) on Corcovado.

Oscar Niemeyer, one of the young Brazilians who assisted on Le Corbusier's project, would turn out to be a monumental name in architectural history. Working in the firm of Lúcio Costa at the time of his initial collaboration with Le Corbusier, Niemeyer – along with Costa – championed the European avant-garde style in Brazil, making a permanent impact on the next 50 years of Brazilian design. Costa and Niemeyer collaborated on many works, designing some of the most important buildings in Brazil.

In Rio, Niemeyer and Costa broke with the neoclassical style and developed the functional style, with its extensive use of steel and glass, and lack of ornamentation. The Museu de Arte Moderna (inaugurated in 1958, p89) and the Catedral Metropolitana (begun in 1964, p100) are good examples of this style. One of the most fascinating modern buildings close to Rio is the Niemeyer-designed Museu do Arte Contemporânea (MAC; p106) in Niterói. Its fluid form and delicate curves are reminiscent of a flower in bloom (though many simply call it spaceship like). It showcases its natural setting and offers stunning views of Rio.

Niemeyer, whose work has often been described as harmonious, graceful and elegant, has continued to design innovative buildings for over half a century. He collaborated with Le Corbusier and other architects on the design of the UN headquarters in New York, completed in 1953. Now over 100, Niemeyer shows no sign of slowing down, and he still maintains an office in Copacabana. (Niemeyer, incidentally, was forced into exile in 1964 for his association with the Communist party, and he still maintains ties today.)

More recent building projects in Rio include the completion of the Hotel Fasano (p188), Philippe Starck's first project in Brazil. It opened in 2007 and is a stylish blend of wood, glass and steel, with mid-century elegance (harking back to Rio's golden days in the 1950s and '60s). It also has whimsical Starck touches, like amoeba-shaped mirrors and a huge 5m-long block of wood that serves as the front check-in desk. One project currently under construction is the enormous futuristic concert hall Cidade de Música (Music City) in Barra da Tijuca. It's designed by the Pritzker prize-winning architect Christian de Portzamparc and is due to open in 2009.

ENVIRONMENT & PLANNING

THE LAND

Rio – with its spectacular scenery – is more than blessed by nature. Its location between the mountains and the sea, bathed by the sun, has entranced visitors for many centuries. Darwin called it 'more magnificent than anything any European has ever seen in his country of origin.'

It all started millions of years ago, when the movement of the earth pushed rock crystal and granite, already disturbed by faults and fractures, into the sea. Low-lying areas were flooded and the high granite peaks became islands.

The plains and swamps on which the city is built were slowly created through centuries of erosion from the peaks and the gradual accumulation of river and ocean sediment.

The mountains, their granite peaks worn by intense erosion and their slopes covered with Atlantic rainforest, form three ranges: the Rural da Pedra Branca massif, the Rural Marapicu-Gericinó massif and the Tijuca-Carioca massif.

The Tijuca-Carioca massif can be seen from almost everywhere in Rio and is responsible for the coastline, which alternates between bare granite escarpments and Atlantic beaches. Its most famous peaks are Pão de Açúcar (Sugarloaf, p80), Morro do Leme, Ponta do Arpoador, Morro Dona Marta, Corcovado and Dois Irmãos at the end of Praia de Leblon.

The sea has also played its part. The stretch of coast between Dois Irmãos and Arpoador was once a large spit, and Lagoa Rodrigo de Freitas (p73) was a bay. Between Arpoador and Morro do Leme, the sea created the beautiful curved beach of Copacabana. Praia Vermelha, the smallest of Rio's Atlantic beaches, is the only one with yellow sand instead of white. Inside Baía de Guanabara, river sediment and reclamation projects formed the present bay rim.

GREEN RIO

Rio still has a long way to go toward protecting its natural beauty, and there are serious environmental problems affecting the city.

Although nowhere near as bad as burgeoning São Paulo to the south, the air quality in Rio is poor, a result of both the heavy volume of traffic throughout the metropolitan area and industrial emissions in neighboring regions. The mountains that surround the city enclose the air pollution, aggravating the problem. (One effect of this air pollution is high rates of asthma among children.)

Despite initial efforts to clean up the Baía de Guanabara following the Earth Summit (the UN Conference on Environment and Development) in 1992, an oil spill in 2000 brought further ecological damage to the bay, and no concerted efforts have been made to clean it up since then. In 2006, residents near the Praia de Ramos blamed the proliferation of dead fish washing up on the beach and oil slicks on environmentally damaging practices at Tom Jobim International Airport. It is foolish to swim at bay beaches. Ocean beaches are also polluted, although less so than the bay. Ipanema is cleaner than Copacabana, and the further you get from the city, the cleaner the waters will be. Refuse from storm drains and the open sewers still prevalent in the city add to the pollution after heavy rains (some 30% of households still lack access to sewer connections).

Another disturbing problem in the city is the continued destruction of Mata Atlântica (Atlantic rainforest) that remains on some of the hillsides around the city, as favelas continue to spread. Until recently, very few citizens took much interest in environmental cleanups. New projects, however, are beginning to reflect a growing concern over the degradation of Rio's natural beauty. Beach cleanup groups, spearheaded by nongovernmental organizations (NGOs) such as Aqualung, have begun appearing on the shores of Rio, and other groups have even set their sights on cleaning up the polluted Baía de Guanabara.

Although Rio is nothing like it was when tropical rainforest covered its landscape, there is still a variety of wildlife in the city.

top picks

GREEN SPACES

- **Floresta (Forest) da Tijuca** (p105) Rio's crown jewel of green spaces, with rainforests teeming with plant and animal life.
- **Sítio Burle Marx** (p107) Out of the way, but worth the trip, with thousands of plant species on an old, lushly landscaped estate.
- **Parque do Flamengo** (p83) Best on Sunday when through-streets close to traffic and joggers, cyclists and rollerbladers claim the myriad pathways through the seaside park.
- **Jardim Botânico** (p72) Stately royal gardens best suited to leisurely strolls.
- **Parque do Catete** (p87) Small but elegant, complete with swan-filled pond and garden-side bistro.

In Campo de Santana, *agoutis* (hamster-like native rodents), peacocks, white-faced tree ducks, geese, egrets and curassows abound.

The park near Leme (p77) has many plants and birds native to the Atlantic rainforest, such as saddle and bishop tanagers, thrushes and the East Brazilian house wren, which has a distinctive trill. The nearby Parque Nacional da Tijuca (p105) contains many more rainforest species.

The Jardim Botânico (p72) has a huge variety of native and imported plant species, including the Vítoria Régia water lilies from the Amazon and impressive rows of royal palms, whose seeds originally came from France. It has over 8000 plant species, including 600 varieties of orchid. Watch for the brightly plumed hummingbirds, known in Brazil as *beija-flores* (literally, flower-kissers).

Micos (capuchin monkeys) and other wildlife can be seen in surprising places in the city, including Pista Cláudio Coutinho (p80) in Urca and Parque Lage (p72) on the south side of Corcovado.

URBAN PLANNING & DEVELOPMENT

One of the world's 25 most populous cities, Rio suffers from the same urban sprawl affecting most other cities. Today Rio occupies around 1200 sq km, with 4800 people packed into each square kilometer.

Favelas contribute much to this urban density. The number of people living in them grows at an annual rate three times that of overall population growth. Some believe there are now over 500 favelas, with an estimated one million Cariocas living in them.

In earlier decades, federal officials paid very little attention to the problems of the urban poor. Things first began to change in 1994 with the city's launch of Favela-Bairro, a program aimed at bringing city infrastructure to some of the favelas. Although the project was imperfect, it was a good first step. Brazil's strong economy has allowed politicos to continue investing in favelas. In 2007, President Lula pledged around US$1.7 billion to improve conditions in Rio's favelas, by putting money into transportation, sanitation and education.

One of the big civic successes in recent years was the Pan American Games, which Rio hosted in 2007. Although the city scrambled to complete projects on time, the games ran smoothly. Brazil spent around US$2 billion on the event, bringing an estimated 80,000 visitors (and athletes from 42 countries) into the city. The city proved itself able to handle a huge logistical event, and Brazil earned the right to host the next World Cup in 2014. Shortly after the Pan Am games, Rio announced its bid to host the Olympic Games in 2016.

In other contexts, 'urban planning' amounts to very little planning at all. The city continues to expand north and west, taxing the environment with unbridled growth.

GOVERNMENT & POLITICS

Rio de Janeiro is the capital of the eponymous state (Brazil has 26 states), which manages its affairs in the Palaçio Tiradentes (p94) under the guidance of the state assembly. The head of Rio state is the governor, who is elected in four-year terms. On a city level, Rio is headed by a mayor, also elected for four-year terms, and a *câmara municipal* (municipal council), which meets at Praça Floriano (p94).

Political parties proliferate in Brazil, and at present there are over two dozen parties, the majority having formed in the last 10 years.

Sérgio Cabral, elected in 2006, is the current governor of Rio state. In Brazil, where it's business-as-usual in many public offices, the 40-something governor of Rio brings a bold new vision to the state. One of his role models is former New York City mayor Rudolph Giuliani, whose 'zero tolerance' crime policies are often credited with cleaning up New York City. Cabral has promised to root out corruption in the police force and bring reform to a justice system of short sentences, rampant inefficiencies and often bribed officials. He plans to build more prisons, alleviating the overcrowding that stigmatizes the Brazilian penal system.

Cabral seems determined. He has already moved some of the most dangerous criminals from local prisons to a new facility in another state, where their influence and means of communicating with gang leaders will be compromised. In his first four months in office, he fired more than 100 police officers and indicated the purges would continue. He suggested that perhaps as many as 10,000 would be fired if necessary, in order to stamp out corruption.

HAIL, CÉSAR

Although Rio has had its share of controversial figures, César Maia is certainly one of the more eccentric mayors the city has known in recent years. He's also the longest incumbent mayor in Rio's history, having completed his third term in 2008. Maia has undertaken some ambitious projects for Rio. He is best known for championing the Favela-Bairro project, having gained millions for favela development since unveiling the plan back in 1994. This has earned him much praise in certain favelas (though some favela dwellers feel left out of the equation). He has invested heavily in education (building 60 new schools in his tenure) and has decried the hypocrisy of the rich, who benefit from cheap labor found in the favelas, but want the poor to disappear from sight. This is not surprising for a man who went into exile in the 1960s for being a member of the Communist Party.

Yet despite his seemingly soft-hearted concern for the poor, Maia has said other things that reveal there's more to his politics than liberal rhetoric. In regards to the growing homeless population, he has suggested spraying toxic chemicals on the roads to discourage people from sleeping on the sidewalks. He has also said that police should be given more authority to shoot to kill – and that 'elimination' of drug lords is the best way to curtail drug trafficking.

The more one learns about Maia, the more his contradictions emerge. He was born not far from Maracanã to middle-class parents, and became active in politics when he joined the Communist Party in college. After his exile in Chile, he returned to Brazil and enlisted in the left-of-center Democratic Labor Party (PDT), but ended up jumping the fence to the conservative Liberal Front Party (PFL) when the Labor Party refused to endorse him in 2000.

Cesar Maia's legacy still remains uncertain. While Favela-Bairro has many advocates, it has its equal share of detractors who say funds are being mismanaged. His bid to bring the Olympics to Rio in 2016 follows on two past failed bids, although the city did secure and successfully host the Pan American Games in 2007. What remains on the horizon for César is still anybody's guess, though the cantankerous 60-something-year-old mayor has no plans to disappear from the spotlight.

Cabral also plans to bring new roads and city services into favelas, hoping to break the stranglehold gangs have on communities there. He has jumpstarted a family-planning program in poor neighborhoods, making condoms and the contraceptive pill more widely available.

Critics of Cabral's 'tough-on-crime' approach say it's the same message that's been tried and has failed in the past. Whether Cabral can bring meaningful change to Rio will undoubtedly play out on the city streets in the coming years.

Corruption is one of the greater challenges Cabral – and any ambitious politician – must grapple with in Brazil. Government scandals are commonplace, which has led to much disillusionment on the part of many Brazilians, who are resigned to the idea of dishonest political leadership.

MEDIA

Like many other cities in the world, Rio's news outlets are concentrated in the hands of the few. The Organizações (O) Globo empire, which was founded by patriarch Roberto Marinho in Rio in the 1920s, today has the world's fourth-largest TV network (behind NBC, CBS and ABC in the US). O Globo also includes Brazil's major radio network (Radio Globo), the country's second-biggest publishing house (Editora Globo) and of course the leading Rio newspaper *(O Globo)*. Today *O Globo* receives half of the total amount spent annually in Brazil on advertising.

Major dailies in Rio include the sometimes sensationalist *O Dia* as well as the nationwide *Jornal do Brasil,* a more moderate publication (not unlike *O Globo* in its political slant).

The variety of magazines on newsstands is astounding. Aside from Portuguese translations of popular magazines like *Cosmopolitan,* there are hundreds of glossies, covering everything from science, history and literature to sailing, dogs and astrology. Brazil's most popular magazines are *Veja,* a glossy mag full of journalism lite (not unlike *Time* magazine); *Época,* which has a similar format; and the more sophisticated *Isto É,* with more in-depth articles on politics and economic issues.

Although internet usage is growing, there are still few conduits of alternative news sources in Brazil. Globo Online tends to dominate this field as well. For further details of newspapers and magazines available in Rio, see p224.

THE NATIONAL ADDICTION

Although football is certainly near the top of the list of Brazil's national obsessions, *novelas* (soap operas) are more watched than anything else on TV. Aired nightly between 6pm and 9pm, these one-hour soaps feature some of Brazil's top actors and certainly Brazilian TV's racier subject matter – unlike American soaps, *novelas* aren't afraid to show some nudity and bloodshed. The plots tend to deal with historical themes, in settings ranging from 17th-century Salvador to a 19th-century coffee plantation or an estate in 1930s Minas Gerais. Period costume is just part of the fun. Also unlike American variants, Brazilian soaps run for a finite period – usually six to nine months – with wild finales often featuring over-the-top gun battles or improbable marriages. Incidentally, directors aren't averse to killing off a few characters along the way; this only adds to the excitement – particularly when audiences give unfavorable reviews of the death, and the screenwriter is compelled to resurrect the deceased character.

Despite the widespread popularity of *novelas,* there are a few critics. The most common gripe is the role to which blacks are relegated in the soaps. The maid, butler and chauffeur are invariably black, while the majority of leading characters have the fairest of skin. Defenders say this is merely a reflection of reality, particularly when filming period pieces. Regardless, things may be beginning to change as a few *novelas* are introducing meatier roles for their once-typecast actors.

FASHION

Rio's fashion has a lot to do with the belief in the body beautiful: Cariocas have them, and they're not afraid to show them off.

Top European labels must now jockey for attention beside rising homegrown luminaries. The city's biggest fashion event is the annual Fashion Rio, a week during which some three dozen or so Brazilian designers – the majority based in Rio – launch their upcoming spring and summer collections. What began as a small event in 2002 has grown to become a major media circus, with top models such as Gisele Bündchen showcasing the work of Lenny, Salinas, Walter Rodrigues, Blue Man, Complexo B and others slowly emerging onto the world stage.

In addition to the many boutiques in Ipanema and Leblon, a good opportunity to peruse the talents of upcoming designers is at the Babilônia Feira Hype market (see p118), held throughout the year.

Although the French invented the bikini in 1946, it's Brazilian designers – and the models promoting them – that breathe new life into it every season. *Fio dental* ('dental floss' bikinis) emerged in the '80s, and are still an icon on beaches here. Exposed *bundas* (bottoms), at least for the women, are generally the style. Whether you're six or 60, fat or skinny, the rule on the beach is to wear as little as possible, while still covering up the essentials (topless bathing is

FASHION CONSCIENCE

Coopa Roca (www.coopa-roca.org.br) is one favela organization that is garnering attention in some surprising places – top London fashion shows included. This craftwork and sewing collective began in Rocinha in the early 1980s under the guidance of sociologist Maria Teresa Leal. The idea began during Leal's repeat trips to the favela with her housekeeper, a Rocinha resident. During her stays, Leal encountered many women who were talented seamstresses but who had no opportunity to earn money for their skills. Wanting to give something to the community, Leal set up Coopa Roca, and the organization was off and running. Initially a small group of women joined the co-op, each working from home to produce quilts, pillows and craft items made of recycled fabrics and other materials.

The work grew more complex over the years, with more women joining the ranks, and soon the co-op began creating truly eye-catching pieces, using delicate techniques such as *fuxico* (embroidering with pieces of fabric).

The fashion world came calling in the early 1990s, with commissions from Brazilian designers Osklen and Carlos Miele, as well as the ubiquitous department store C&A. More recently, Coopa Roca has begun creating colorful crochet bags for British designer Paul Smith, and window displays for Ann Taylor, as well as assorted pieces for vanguard designers in France and Holland.

Today the co-op employs more than 150 women, most of whom would have little opportunity to earn money otherwise. All of the women continue to work from home and share the production and administrative responsibilities. Despite their growing success, the headquarters of Coopa Roca remains in the favela, where it will continue to be a source of inspiration for both those within the community and abroad.

not allowed in Rio, by the way) – this applies to men, to some extent. Maybe 15% of men wear Bermudas, while the vast majority stick to *sungas* (hip-hugging briefs).

Off the beach, women show up the men quite a bit. For most men, a night out means putting on a clean T-shirt and jeans. They are, according to one disgruntled Carioca woman, seriously fashion challenged. This is perhaps a bit unfair, as men are beginning to catch on; a growing number of boutiques in Ipanema, Leblon and the *shoppings* (shopping malls) are dedicated to pushing men in the right direction.

Regardless of gender or socioeconomic background, Havaianas are the quintessential item you'll find in every Carioca's wardrobe. The nifty rubber sandals are also one of Brazil's leading exports, with well over two billion pairs created since the inception of the company in 1962. Aside from sandals, a tan is the most common fashion accessory, and it's rare to find a Carioca who doesn't have at least some color to their skin, if not an outright deep, dark glow.

CARNAVAL

If you haven't heard by now, Rio throws one of the world's best parties, with music and dancing filling the streets for days on end. Officially, Carnaval is just five days of revelry – from Friday to Tuesday before Ash Wednesday – but Cariocas (residents of Rio) begin partying months in advance. The culmination of the big fest is the brilliantly colorful parade through the Sambódromo, with giant mechanized floats, pounding drummers and whirling dancers – but there's lots of action in Rio's many neighborhoods for those seeking more than just the stadium experience.

Out-of-towners add to the mayhem, joining Cariocas in the street parties and costumed balls erupting throughout town. There are free live concerts throughout the city (in Largo do Machado, Arcos da Lapa and Praça General Osório among other places), while those seeking a bit of decadence can head to the various balls about town. Whatever you do, prepare yourself for sleepless nights, an ample dose of caipirinhas (cane-liquor cocktails) and samba, and mingling with the joyful crowds spilling out of the city.

Joining the *bandas* (street parties, also called *blocos*) is one of the best ways to have the Carioca experience. These *bandas* consist of a procession of drummers and vocalists followed by anyone who wants to dance through the streets. Some *bandas* require costumes (drag, Amazonian attire etc), while others simply expect people to show up and add to the good cheer.

Although the city is blazing with energy during Carnaval, don't expect the party to come to you. To get more information on events during Carnaval, check *Veja* magazine's *Veja Rio* insert (sold on Sunday at newsstands) or visit Riotur (Map pp90–1; www.riodejaneiro-turismo.com.br; ☎ 2271 7000; 9th fl, Praça Pio X; 9am-6pm Mon-Fri), the tourist organization in charge of Carnaval. Also see p52 to get some ideas on how to celebrate the return of King Momo, the lord of the Carnaval. For those unacquainted with Momo, he's the modern embodiment of Momos, the Greek god of trickery, and when the chosen Momo is announced, Cariocas expect a portly, jolly ruler who can dance a mean samba. The revelry officially begins when the mayor hands King Momo the keys to the city on the Friday before Carnaval. The afternoon event usually takes place in front of the Palácio da Cidade (Map pp78–9; Rua São Clemente 360) in Botafogo.

Visit www.rio-carnival.net for a complete rundown on the latest Carnaval info.

HISTORY

Although the exact origins of Carnaval are shrouded in mystery, some believe the fest originated as a pagan celebration of spring's arrival sometime during the Middle Ages. The Portuguese brought the celebration to Brazil in the 1500s but it took on a decidedly local flavor by the adopting of Indian costumes and African rhythms. (The origin of the word itself probably derives from the Latin 'carne vale' –'farewell, meat' – whereby the Catholic population would give up meat and other fleshly temptations during the 40 days of Lent.)

The first festivals in Rio de Janeiro were called *entrudo,* with locals dancing through the streets in colorful costumes and throwing mud, flour and various suspect liquids at one another. In the 19th century, Carnaval meant attending a lavish masked ball or participating in the orderly and rather vapid European-style parade. Rio's poor citizens, bored by the finery but eager to celebrate, began holding their own parades, dancing through the streets to African-based rhythms. Then in the 1920s, the new sound of samba emerged in Rio. It was the music full of African flavors, brought to the city by former slaves and their poor descendents. It was a sound that would forever more be associated with Carnaval.

CARNAVAL DATES

The following are the Carnaval dates in coming years:

- 2009 February 20-24
- 2010 February 12-16
- 2011 March 4-8

CARNAVAL PARTY PLANNER *Marcos Silviano do Prado*

Cariocas start partying long before the big Sambódromo parades take place, but the city is at its wildest from Friday to Tuesday before Ash Wednesday. To make the most of your time, check out the long-standing *festas* (parties) listed below. You can dance through the streets in a *banda*, party like a rock star at one of many dance clubs scattered throughout town or find your groove at one of the samba-school rehearsals listed on p163. Those looking for free, open-air, neighborhood-wide celebrations shouldn't miss Rio Folia, in front of Acros da Lapa (Lapa Arches, p100) in Lapa. For up-to-date listings of what's on, visit www.ipanema.com or www.rio-carnival.net.

Saturday – two weeks before Carnaval

- Banda de Ipanema (p52) at 4pm
- Rehearsals at samba schools (p55)

Weekend before Carnaval

- Banda Simpatia é Quase Amor (p52), Saturday at 4pm
- Rehearsals at samba schools

Carnaval Friday

- Carnaval King Momo is crowned by the mayor at 1pm
- Shows start at Terreirão do Samba (Samba Land; p54) and Rio Folia from 8pm
- Children's samba schools parade at the Sambódromo (p53) from 9pm
- Cinelândia Ball from 9pm
- Red and Black Ball at the Scala (Leblon & Gávea; Av Afrânio de Melo Franco 296, Leblon) from 11pm
- Gay ball at Le Boy (p170)
- Dance party at Cine Ideal (☎ 2252 7766; www.idealparty.com.br in Portuguese; Rua da Carioca 62, Centro)

Carnaval Saturday

- Cordão do Bola Preta (p52) from 9.30am
- Banda de Ipanema at 4pm
- Deluxe costume competition at Glória (p198) from 7pm
- Parade of Group A samba schools at the Sambódromo from 7pm
- Street band competition (Av Rio Branco, Centro, admission free) from 8pm
- Shows start at Terreirão do Samba and Rio Folia from 8pm
- Copacabana Palace Luxury Ball (p52) from 11pm. Costume or black tie mandatory.
- Carnaval balls at Scala, Help (☎ 2522 1296; Av Atlântica 3432, Copacabana) and other venues from 11pm
- Gay balls at Le Boy and The Week (p170)
- X-Demente Party at Fundição Progresso (p100)
- Parties at 00 (p169) and other dance clubs

Carnaval Sunday

- Shows at Terreirão do Samba and Rio Folia from 8pm
- Samba parade at the Sambódromo from 9pm
- Carnaval balls at Scala and Help from 11pm
- Gay balls at Le Boy and Elite (☎ 2232 3217; Rua Frei Caneca 4, Lapa)
- Rave party at theme park Terra Encantada (p109)
- Parties at 00, Bunker (p169) and other dance clubs

Carnaval Monday

- Shows at Terreirão do Samba and Rio Folia from 8pm
- Samba parade at the Sambódromo from 9pm
- Carnaval balls at Scala, Help and others from 11pm
- Gay balls at Le Boy and Elite
- Parties at 00 and other dance clubs

Carnaval Tuesday

- Banda de Ipanema at 4pm
- Shows at Terreirão do Samba and Rio Folia from 8pm
- Parade of Group B samba schools at the Sambódromo from 9pm
- Scala Gay Costume Ball from 11pm
- Carnaval balls from 11pm at Help and other venues
- Gay balls at Le Boy and The Week
- X-Demente Party at Marina da Glória (Map p87)
- Parties at 00 and other dance clubs

Weekend after Carnaval

- Parade of champions, Sambódromo, Saturday 9pm
- Monobloco, Posto 6, Copacabana Beach, Sunday from 9am

Since those days, Carnaval has grown in leaps and bounds, with elaborate parades spreading from Rio de Janeiro to other parts of Brazil. It has also become a huge commercial enterprise, with the city spending in excess of R$100 million (US$56 million) to throw the party each year.

BANDAS: CARNAVAL ON THE STREETS

Attending a *banda* is one of the best ways to celebrate Carnaval and to join in; all you have to do is show up. Note that some *bandas* require that you to march in one of the *banda's* colors. Often you can buy shirts on the spot (around R$15) or you can just show up in the right colors. Dozens of *bandas* party through the streets before Carnaval. For complete listings, check Riotur (Map pp90–1; www.riodejaneiro-turismo.com.br; ☎ 2271 7000; 9th fl, Praça Pio X; 🕑 9am-6pm Mon-Fri) or www.carnavalvirtual.com.

Banda de Ipanema (Praça General Osório, Ipanema; 🕑 4pm 2nd Sat before Carnaval & Carnaval Sat) This long-standing *banda* attracts a wild crowd, complete with drag queens and others in costume. Don't miss it.

Banda de Sá Ferreira (cnr Av Atlântica & Rua Sá Ferreira, Copacabana; 🕑 4pm Carnaval Sat & Sun) This popular Copacabana *banda* marches along the ocean from Posto 1 to Posto 6.

Banda Simpatia é Quase Amor (Praça General Osório, Ipanema; 🕑 3pm 2nd Sat before Carnaval & Carnaval Sun) A big *bloco* with 15,000 participants and a 50-piece percussion band.

Barbas (cnr Ruas Assis Bueno & Arnoldo Quintela, Botafogo; 🕑 4pm Carnaval Sat) One of the oldest *bandas* of the Zona Sul parades through the streets with a 60-piece percussion band. A water truck follows along to spray the crowd of some 2500, all decked out in red and white.

Bloco das Carmelitas (cnr Rua Dias de Barros & Ladeira de Santa Teresa, Santa Teresa; 🕑 6pm Carnaval Fri & 5pm Carnaval Tue) Crazy mixed crowd (some dressed as Carmelite nuns) parades through Santa Teresa's streets.

Bloco de Bip Bip (Rua Almirante Gonçalves 50, Copacabana; 🕑 12.01am Carnaval Sat & 11.59pm Carnaval Tue) Has perhaps the best music of any *banda*, owing to the top-notch musicians who sometimes play in the procession. Meets in front of the old samba haunt Bip Bip (p163) at both the first and last minute of Carnaval.

Bloco de Segunda (Cobal Humaitá, Rua Voluntários de Pátria 446, Botafogo; 🕑 6pm Carnaval Mon) Excellent percussion band joins 2000 or so revelers.

Cordão do Bola Preta (cnr Rua Evaristo da Veiga & Rua 13 de Maio, Centro; 🕑 10am Carnaval Sat) The oldest *banda* still in action features lots of straight men dressed as women, and a chaotic march that often leads the group to stop at bars along the way. Costumes are always welcome, especially those with black-and-white spots.

Dois Pra Lá, Dois Pra Cá (Carlinho de Jesus Dance School, Rua da Passagem 145, Botafogo; 🕑 2pm Carnaval Sat) This fairly long march begins at the dance school and ends at the Copacabana Palace. Bring along your swimsuit for a dip in the ocean afterward.

Monobloco (Posto 6, Copacabana beach; 🕑 9am 1st Sun after Carnaval) Rise and shine! This huge *bloco* attracts upwards of 30,000 revelers who, nursing hangovers (or perhaps still inebriated) gather on the beach for a final bit of revelry before the city bids Carnaval farewell.

SIGHTS & ACTIVITIES

There are many ways to take part in Rio's Carnaval, whether joining an informal *banda*, attending a masked ball, or catching the parade up close at the Sambódromo. If you'd rather not be a spectator on the big night, you can don a costume and dance with a samba school – a highly rated experience by those who've done it (see boxed text, opposite).

CARNAVAL BALLS

Carnaval balls are giant, sometimes costumed, parties with live music and dancing, and an ambience that runs the gamut between staid and formal to wild and a bit tawdry. The most famous ball is held at the Copacabana Palace (p193). It's a formal affair, so you'll need a tux; there you'll have the opportunity to celebrate with Rio's glitterati as well as international stars. Tickets cost upwards of R$1000. Popular but less pricey balls are held at the Glória Hotel (p198) and Río Scenarium (p167).

Other balls are held at Scala (Map p66; ☎ 2239 4448; Leblon & Gávea; Av Afrânio de Melo Franco 296, Leblon) and Help (Map pp76–7; ☎ 2522 1296; Av Atlântica 3432, Copacabana). The most extravagant gay balls are found at Le Boy (Map pp76–7; ☎ 2513 4993; www.leboy.com.br in Portuguese; Rua Raul Pompéia 102, Copacabana).

Tickets go on sale about two weeks beforehand, and the balls are held nightly during Carnaval and the preceding week. The *Veja Rio* insert in *Veja* magazine has details.

SAMBA-SCHOOL PARADES

The highlight of any Carnaval experience is attending (or participating in) a parade at the Sambódromo. There before a crowd of some 30,000 (with millions more watching on TV), each of 14 samba schools has its 80 minutes to dance and sing through the open Oscar Niemeyer-designed stadium. The pageantry is not simply eye candy for the masses. Schools are competing for top honors in the parade, with winners announced (and a winner's parade held) on the Saturday following Carnaval.

Here's what to expect: each school enters the Sambódromo with amped energy levels, and dancers take things up a notch as they dance through the stadium. Announcers introduce the school, the group's theme colors and the number of *alas* (literally, wings – subgroups within a school, each playing a different role). Far away the lone voice of the *puxador* (interpreter) starts the samba. Thousands more voices join him, and then the drummers kick in, 200 to 400 per school. The pounding drums drive the parade. Next come the main wings of the school, the big allegorical floats, the children's wing, the drummers, the celebrities and the bell-shaped *baianas* (women dressed as Bahian aunts) twirling in elegant hoopskirts. The *baianas* honor the history of the parade itself, which was brought to Rio from Salvador da Bahia in 1877.

Costumes are fabulously lavish, with 1.5m feathered headdresses; long, flowing capes that sparkle with sequins; and rhinestone-studded G-strings.

The whole procession is also an elaborate competition. A handpicked set of judges chooses the best school on the basis of many components, including percussion, the *samba do enredo* (theme song), harmony between percussion, song and dance, choreography, costumes, story line, floats and decorations. The dance championship is hotly contested, with the winner becoming not just the pride of Rio but all of Brazil.

The Sambódromo parades start with the *mirins* (young samba-school members) on the night of Carnaval Friday, and continue on through Saturday night when the Group A samba schools strut their stuff. Sunday and Monday are the big nights, when the Grupo Especial – the 12 best samba schools in Rio – parade: six of them on Sunday night and into the morning, and six more on Monday night. The following Saturday, the six top schools strut their stuff again in the Parade of Champions. Each event starts at 9pm and runs until 4am.

Most visitors stay for three or four schools, and come to see their favorite in action (every self-respecting Carioca has a school they support, just as they have their favorite football team). If you're really gungho, wear your school's colors and learn the theme song so you can sing along when it marches through the Sambódromo.

Tickets

Getting tickets at legitimate prices can be tough. Many tickets are sold well in advance of the event. Check with Riotur about where you can get them, as the official outlet can vary from year to year. People line up for hours, and travel agents and scalpers snap up the best seats. Riotur reserves seats in bleacher sections for tourists for R$500, but you should be able to pick up regular tickets for much less from a travel agent. Try to get seats in the center, as this is the liveliest section and has the best views.

JOINING A SAMBA SCHOOL

There's nothing to stop you from taking part in a Carnaval parade. Most samba schools are happy to have foreigners join one of the wings. To get the ball rolling, you'll need to contact your chosen school far in advance; they'll tell you the rehearsal times and when you need to be in the city (usually a week or so before Carnaval). You'll also need to memorize the theme song, make it to the rehearsals and master that winning smile. For a list of samba schools and contact information see p163. The biggest investment, aside from making it to Rio, is buying a *fantasia* (costume), which will cost anywhere from R$500 to R$1500. You can read more about joining a school on the Rio Carnaval website, www.rio-carnival.net.

Those seeking an insider's perspective on what it's like to join a samba school should read Alma Guillermoprieto's excellent book, *Samba*.

By Carnaval weekend, most tickets will have sold out, but there are lots of scalpers. If you buy a ticket from a scalper (no need to worry about looking for them – they'll find you!), make sure you get both the plastic ticket with the magnetic strip and the ticket showing the seat number. The tickets for different days are color coded, so double-check the date as well.

If you haven't purchased a ticket but still want to go, during Carnaval you can show up at the Sambódromo at around midnight, three or four hours into the show. This is when you can get grandstand tickets for about R$30 from scalpers outside the gate. Make sure you check which sector your ticket is for. Most ticket sellers will try to pawn off their worst seats.

And if you can't make it during Carnaval proper, there's always the cheaper Parade of Champions the following Saturday.

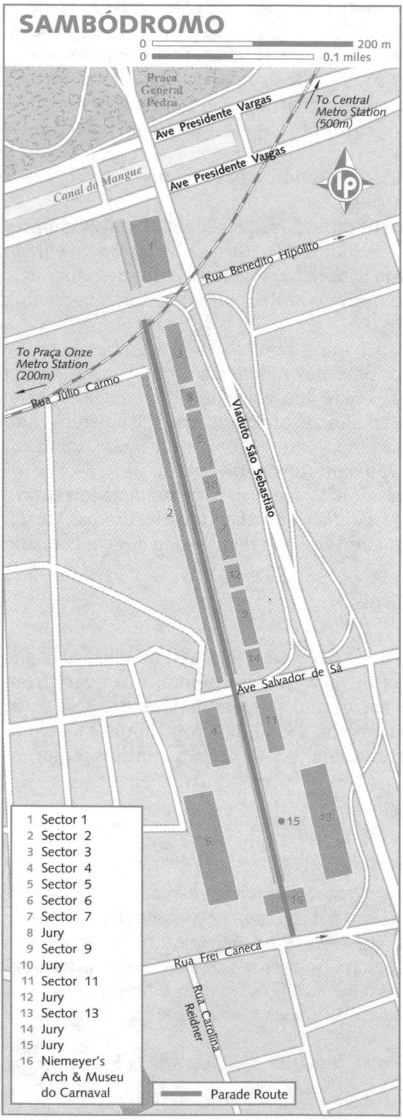

Getting to the Sambódromo

Don't take a bus to or from the Sambódromo (Map p54; Rua Marquês do Sapuçai, near Praça Onze metro station). It's much safer to take a taxi or the metro, which runs round the clock during Carnaval from Saturday morning until Tuesday evening. This is also a great opportunity to check out the paraders commuting in costume.

Make sure you indicate to your taxi driver which side of the stadium you're on. If you take the metro, the stop at which you get off depends on the location of your seats. For sectors 2, 4 and 6, exit at Praça Onze. Once outside the station, turn to the right, take another right and then walk straight ahead (on Rua Júlio Carmo) to Sector 2. For sectors 4 and 6, turn right at Rua Carmo Neto and proceed to Av Salvador de Sá. You'll soon see the Sambódromo and hear the roar of the crowd. Look for signs showing the entrance to the sectors. If you are going to sectors on the other side (1, 3, 5, 7, 9, 11 and 13) exit at the metro stop Central. You'll then walk about 700m along Av Presidente Vargas until you see the Sambódromo.

SAMBA CITY & SAMBA LAND

One of the biggest new developments in Rio's Carnaval world is Cidade do Samba (Samba City; ☎ 2213 2503; cidadedosambarj.globo.com; Rua Rivadávia Correa 60, Gamboa; 🕑 10am-5pm Tue-Sat), which opened in 2006. Constructed near the port, the 'city' is actually made up of 14 large buildings in which the top schools assemble the Carnaval floats.

Visitors can take tour through the area (R$10) or attend a twice-monthly live show (R$150), which features costumed dancers, live music and audience participation. It's touristy and pricey, but some visitors enjoy the Carnaval-style show nonetheless. For show times, call Cidade do Samba or check with Riotur.

SAMBA GLOSSARY FOR PARADE-GOERS

Alas – literally the 'wings.' These are groups of samba-school members responsible for a specific part of the central *samba do enredo* (theme song). Special *alas* include the *baianas* (women dressed as Bahian 'aunts' in full skirts and turbans). The *abre ala* of each school is the opening wing or float.

Bateria – the drum section is the driving beat behind the school's samba and is the 'soul' of the school.

Carnavalesco – the artistic director of each school, responsible for the overall layout and design of the school's theme.

Carros alegóricos – the dazzling floats, usually decorated with near-naked women. The floats are pushed along by the school's maintenance crew.

Desfile – the parade. The most important samba schools *desfilar* (parade) on the Sunday and Monday night of Carnaval. Each school's *desfile* is judged on its samba, drum section, master of ceremonies and flag bearer, floats, leading commission, costumes, dance coordination and overall harmony.

Destaques – the richest and most elaborate costumes. The heaviest ones usually get a spot on one of the floats.

Diretores de harmonia – the school organizers, who usually wear white or the school colors; they run around yelling and 'pumping up' the wings, making sure there aren't any gaps in the parade.

Enredo – the central theme of each school. The *samba do enredo* is the samba that goes with it. Radio stations and dance halls prime Cariocas with classic enredos on the weeks leading up to Carnaval.

Passistas – the best samba dancers of a school. They roam the parade in groups or alone, stopping to show off some fancy footwork along the way. The women are usually dressed in short, revealing skirts, and the men usually hold tambourines.

Puxador – the interpreter of the theme song. He (a *puxador* is invariably male) works as a guiding voice, leading the school's singers at rehearsals and in the parade.

An even more important staging ground is the Terreirão do Samba (Samba Land), an open-air courtyard next to the Sambódromo's sector 1, where bands play to large crowds throughout Carnaval (beginning the weekend before).

SAMBA-SCHOOL REHEARSALS

Around August or September, rehearsals start at the *escolas de samba* (samba schools or clubs). Some schools begin as early as July. Rehearsals usually take place in the favelas (shanty towns) and are open to visitors. They're fun to watch, but go with a Carioca for safety. Mangueira and Salgueiro are among the easiest schools to get to. See p163 for a complete listing of samba schools.

NEIGHBORHOODS

top picks

- **Ipanema Beach** (p63)
  Join the beautiful crowd for sunning, soccer and people-watching on Rio's loveliest stretch of shoreline.
- **Cristo Redentor** (p85)
  Take the cog train to eagle's-nest heights for an enchanting view beneath the open-armed redeemer.
- **Bonde to Santa Teresa** (p97)
  Hop aboard the old-fashioned streetcar as it clatters over the Lapa arches and through the cobblestone streets of bohemian Rio.
- **Copacabana Beach** (p75)
  Rise early for a sunrise stroll along the fabled beachfront.
- **Pão de Açúcar** (p80)
  Watch the sunset, caipirinha in hand, from atop magnificent heights.
- **Parque Nacional da Tijuca** (p105)
  Hike through rain forest amid Rio's lush, wildlife-filled backyard.

What's your recommendation? www.lonelyplanet.com/rio-de-janeiro

NEIGHBORHOODS

The *cidade maravilhosa* (marvelous city) is justly famed for its beaches and nightlife, but the city has lots more going on beyond its steamy seashore and samba-filled nights. Rio, after all, was once the mighty 'capital of the Brazilian empire' (as one Portuguese king crowned it), and its European settlement dates back more than five centuries. History lives on in its colonial quarters, cobbled lanes and 19th-century mansions, with many relics from the past waiting to be discovered.

'Wanderers and adventurers have a wealth of options when tackling the city'

Wanderers and adventurers have a wealth of options when tackling the city. Our recommendation is to head up to the heights of Pão de Açúcar (Sugarloaf) or Cristo Redentor (Christ the Redeemer) for an overview of the city. There you'll see the city's wild urban diversity, with beaches, mountains, skyscrapers and favelas (shanty towns) all woven into the landscape. The city itself can be divided into two zones: the Zona Norte, which consists of industrial, working-class neighborhoods in the northern part of the city and the Zona Sul, with its middle- and upper-class neighborhoods and well-known beaches in the city's southern half. Centro, Rio's business district, forms the boundary between the two.

After getting an overview, it's time to dive in. We've organized our neighborhoods chapter from south to north, and have included a number of walking tours for exploring the city streets.

The Zona Sul has the city's star attractions. At the far southern tip, the upscale neighborhoods of Ipanema and Leblon share the same stretch of south-facing shoreline. Rio's beautiful people flock to these beaches, while the tree-lined streets just inland hide some of the best eating, drinking and shopping in the city.

The northern border of Ipanema and Leblon is the Lagoa Rodrigo de Freitas, a saltwater lagoon fronted by the high-rent districts of Gávea, Jardim Botânico and Lagoa. Here you'll find open-air dining and drinking at lakeside restaurants, as well as the verdant botanical gardens to the west.

East of Ipanema begins the scalloped beach of Copacabana. Once a destination for international jetsetters, Copacabana is the city's somewhat ragged tourist magnet, with dozens of oceanfront hotels and sidewalk restaurants. The population density is high here with old-timers, favela kids and tourists all mixing on the streets, and you'll find an equal mix of high and low culture.

Botafogo lies just north of Copacabana, and is a desirable neighborhood with an active *boteco* culture and some intriguing museums in the area's old mansions. Next door, Urca retains a peaceful vibe that seems a world away from the Zona Sul's busier neighborhoods, and is famed for the iconic mountain Pão de Açúcar overshadowing its leafy streets.

Continuing north, are more residential neighborhoods, including low-key Flamengo, leafy Laranjeiras and further west Cosme Velho, where Cristo Redentor opens his arms atop Corcovado. Following the curve of the bay north is the Parque do Flamengo, a tree-lined park home to biking trails, football pitches and several monuments and museums. Inland from there, Catete and Glória hide much history in their battered streets, including the former presidential home.

One metro stop up, Centro is Rio's business hub; it's also one of Rio's oldest areas, with baroque churches, former palaces and excellent museums. On the southeastern edge of Centro is Lapa, Rio's nightlife nexus with dozens of samba-filled bars and clubs. Uphill from Lapa is Santa Teresa, a picturesque neighborhood of winding streets and old mansions that have been restored by the many artists who have settled there.

Greater Rio includes Zona Norte destinations like Maracanã soccer stadium, the Feira Nordestina (Northeastern Fair) and the Quinta da Boa Vista, former residence of the imperial family. It also includes the Baía de Guanabara, with the picturesque island of Paquetá. Across the bay is Niterói, home to one of Oscar Niemeyer's architectural creations. Another place to explore is the region west of Leblon, where you'll find lush rain forest and the beach of Barra da Tijuca. Other beaches dot the coast heading west, and get wilder and less populated the further out you go.

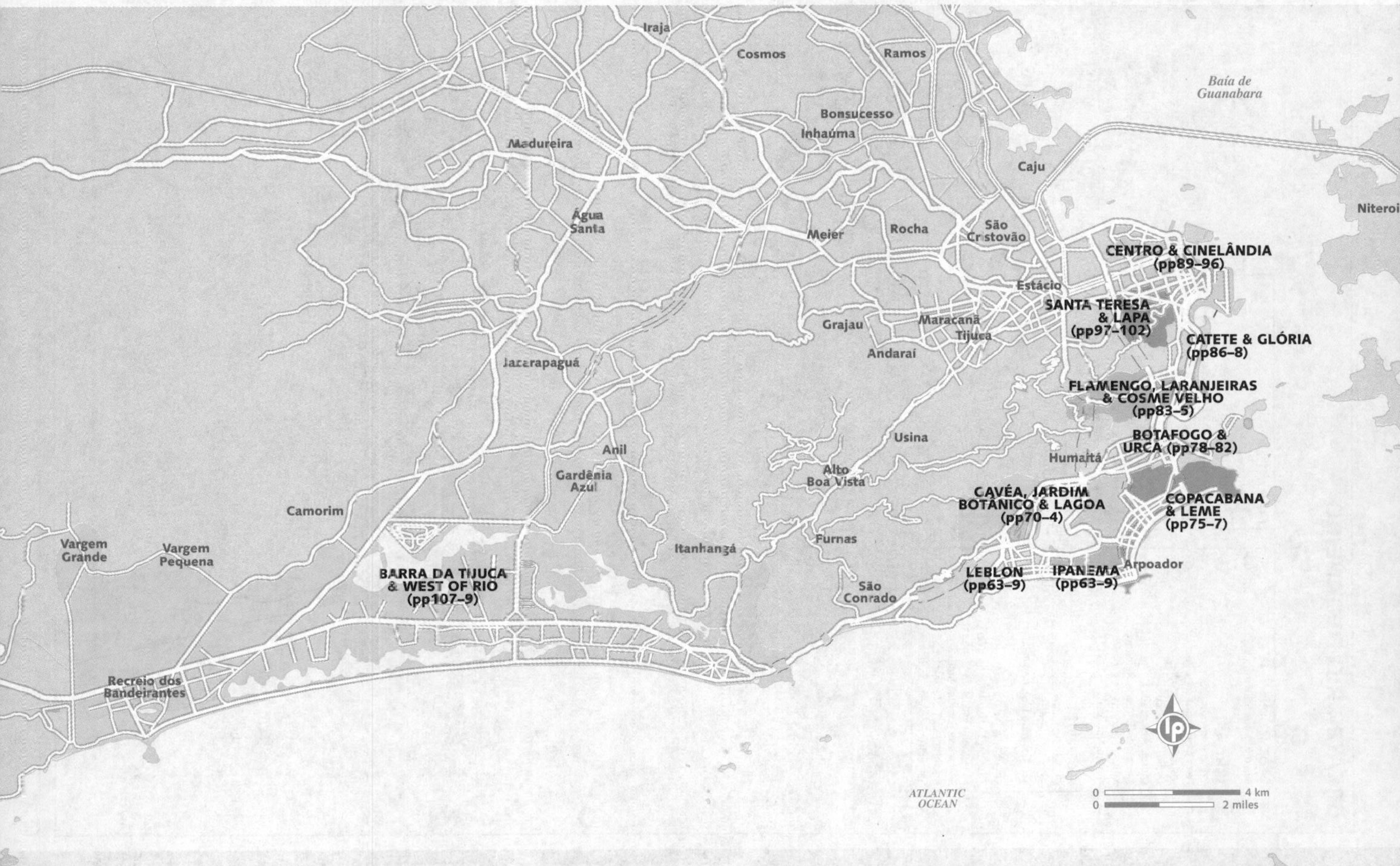

Iraja
Cosmos
Ramos
Baía de Guanabara
Bonsucesso
Inhaúma
Madureira
Caju
Niteroi
Água Santa
Meier
Rocha
São Cristovão
CENTRO & CINELÂNDIA (pp89–96)
Estácio
SANTA TERESA & LAPA (pp97–102)
Grajau
Maracanã
Tijuca
CATETE & GLÓRIA (pp86–8)
Jacarapaguá
Andaraí
FLAMENGO, LARANJEIRAS & COSME VELHO (pp83–5)
Usina
BOTAFOGO & URCA (pp78–82)
Anil
Humaitá
Alto Boa Vista
Gardênia Azul
CAVÉA, JARDIM BOTÂNICO & LAGOA (pp70–4)
COPACABANA & LEME (pp75–7)
Camorim
Vargem Grande
Vargem Pequena
Furnas
Itanhangá
Arpoador
BARRA DA TIJUCA & WEST OF RIO (pp107–9)
LEBLON (pp63–9)
IPANEMA (pp63–9)
São Conrado
Recreio dos Bandeirantes
ATLANTIC OCEAN
0
4 km
0
2 miles

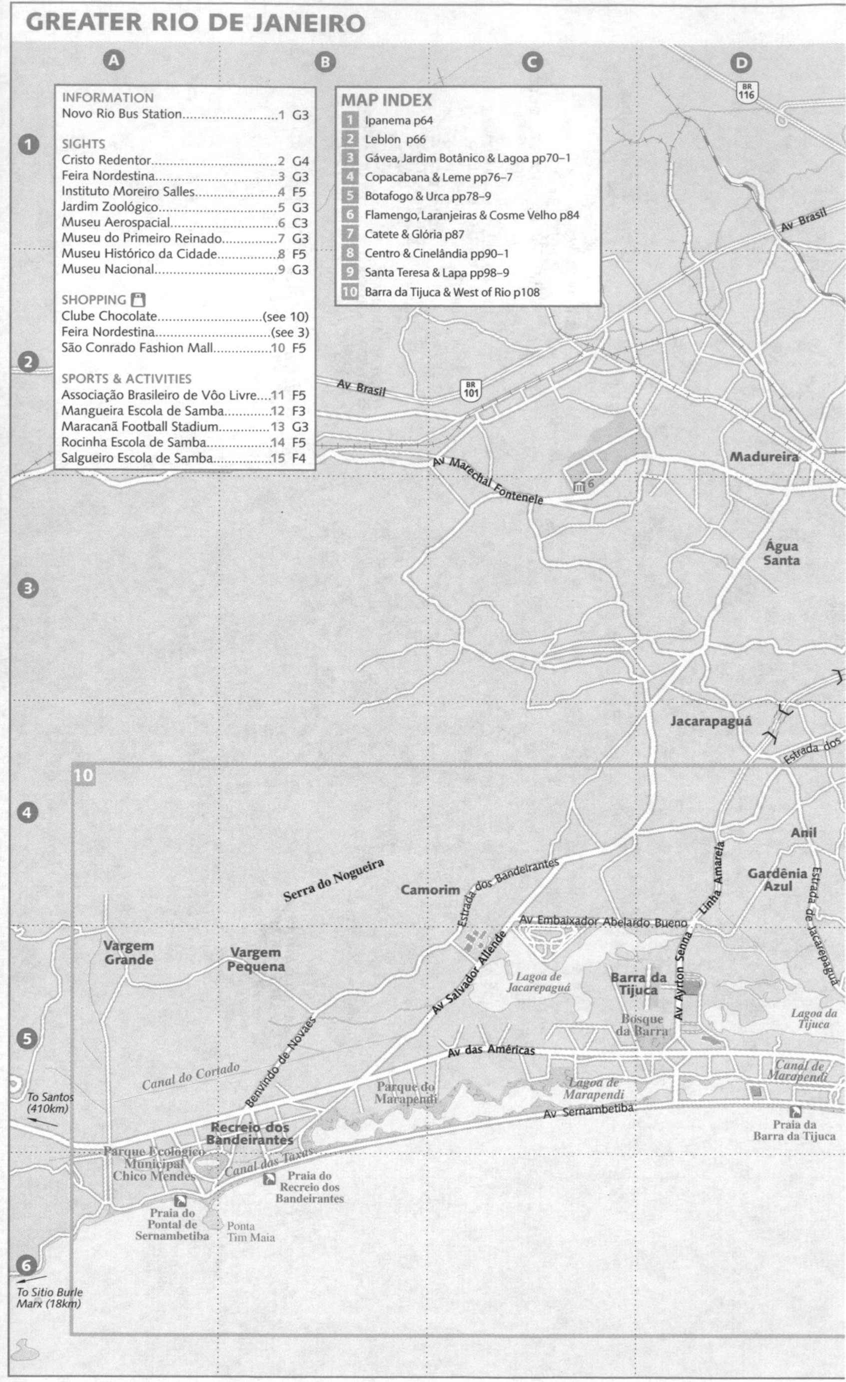

NEIGHBORHOODS GREATER RIO DE JANEIRO

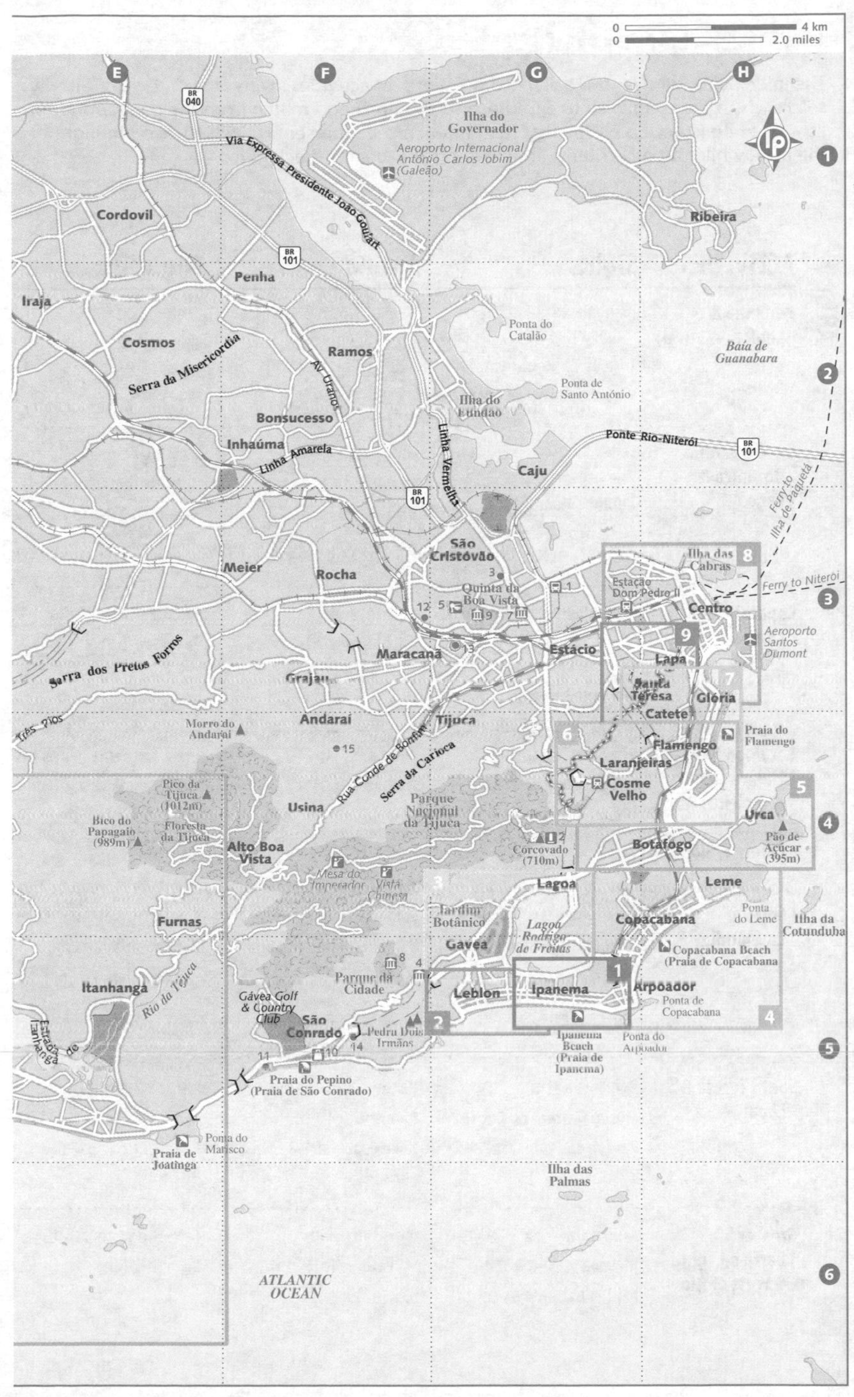

0 4 km
0 2.0 miles
E
F
G
H
BR 040
Ilha do Governador
Aeroporto Internacional Antônio Carlos Jobim (Galeão)
Via Expressa Presidente João Goulart
Cordovil
Ribeira
BR 101
Penha
Iraja
Cosmos
Serra da Misericordia
Ramos
Av Uranos
Ponta do Catalão
Baía de Guanabara
Ponta de Santo António
Ilha do Fundão
Bonsucesso
Inhaúma
Linha Amarela
Linha Vermelha
Ponte Rio-Niterói
Caju
Ferry to Ilha de Paquetá
São Cristóvão
Quinta da Boa Vista
Meier
Rocha
Ilha das Cabras
Estação Dom Pedro II
Ferry to Niterói
Centro
Aeroporto Santos Dumont
Maracanã
Estácio
Lapa
Serra dos Pretos Forros
Grajaú
Santa Teresa
Glória
Catete
Andaraí
Tijuca
Morro do Andaraí
Praia do Flamengo
Flamengo
Laranjeiras
Cosme Velho
Rua Conde de Bonfim
Serra da Carioca
Pico da Tijuca (1012m)
Floresta da Tijuca
Bico do Papagaio (989m)
Usina
Parque Nacional da Tijuca
Urca
Pão de Açúcar (395m)
Alto Boa Vista
Corcovado (710m)
Botafogo
Mesa do Imperador
Vista Chinesa
Lagoa
Leme
Jardim Botânico
Lagoa Rodrigo de Freitas
Copacabana
Ponta do Leme
Ilha da Cotunduba
Furnas
Gávea
Copacabana Beach (Praia de Copacabana)
Parque da Cidade
Itanhanga
Rio da Tijuca
Leblon
Ipanema
Arpoador
Ponta de Copacabana
Gávea Golf & Country Club
São Conrado
Pedra Dois Irmãos
Ipanema Beach (Praia de Ipanema)
Ponta do Arpoador
Praia do Pepino (Praia de São Conrado)
Praia de Joatinga
Ponta do Marisco
Ilha das Palmas
ATLANTIC OCEAN

ITINERARY BUILDER

The table below allows you to plan a day's worth of activities in any area of the city. Simply select which area you wish to explore, and then mix and match from the corresponding listings to build your day. The first item in each cell represents a well-known highlight of the area, while the other items are more off-the-beaten-track gems.

AREA / ACTIVITIES	Sights	Eating	Nightlife
Ipanema & Leblon	**Ipanema & Leblon Beach** (opposite) **Toca do Vinícius** (p65) **Mirante do Leblon** (opposite)	**Zazá Bistrô Tropical** (p133) **Gula Gula** (p133) **Bazzar** (p134)	**Melt** (p169) **Devassa** (p153) **Baronneti** (p169)
Gávea, Jardim Botânico & Lagoa	**Lagoa Rodrigo de Freitas** (p73) **Jardim Botânico** (p72) **Instituto Moreira Salles** (p71)	**Olympe** (p138) **Lulu** (p138) **Braz** (p138)	**00 (Zero Zero**; p169) **Braseiro da Gávea** (p154) **Palaphita Kitch** (p155)
Copacabana & Leme	**Copacabana & Leme Beach** (p75) **Forte de Copacabana** (p77) **Morro do Leme** (p77)	**Amir** (p141) **Miss Tanaka** (p140) **La Trattoria** (p141)	**Bip Bip** (p163) **Fosfobox** (p169) **Espelunca Chic** (p156)
Botafogo & Urca; Flamengo, Laranjeiras & Cosme Velho; Catete & Glória	**Pão de Açúcar** (p80) **Cristo Redentor** (p85) **Museu da República** (p86)	**Yorubá** (p143) **Intihuasi** (p144) **Casa da Suíça** (p145)	**Praia Vermelha** (p164) **Clube Guanabara** (p166) **Casa Rosa** (p165)
Centro & Cinelândia	**Paço Imperial** (p92) **Museu Histórico Nacional** (p89) **Centro Cultural Banco do Brasil** (p89)	**Confeitaria Colombo** (p147) **Brasserie Rosário** (p147) **Da Silva** (p146)	**Trapiche Gamboa** (p168) **Boteco Casual** (p158) **Cais do Oriente** (p164)
Santa Teresa & Lapa	**Bonde** (p97) **Museu Chácara do Céu** (p97) **Parque das Ruínas** (p99)	**Bar do Mineiro** (p149) **Aprazível** (p148) **Nova Capela** (p148)	**Rio Scenarium** (p167) **Carioca da Gema** (p165) **Democráticus** (p166)
Greater Rio, Barra da Tijuca & West of Rio	**Feira Nordestina** (p103) **Ilha de Paquetá** (p104) **Parque Nacional da Tijuca** (p105)	**Barreado** (p150) **Tia Palmira** (p150) **Bira** (p149)	**Feira Nordestina** (p103) **Nuth** (p170)

IPANEMA & LEBLON

Eating p130; Shopping p112; Sleeping p188

The favored address for Rio's young, beautiful and wealthy Cariocas (residents of Rio), these twin neighborhoods boast a magnificent beach and tree-lined streets full of enticing open-air cafés, restaurants and bars. It's also the city's high-end shopping district, with dozens of colorful boutiques and multistory *galerias* (shopping centers) selling pretty things that can quickly deplete a budget. While traditional sights are few, you can fill many days just exploring the leafy streets. Ipanema is also Rio's gay district, which revolves around the café and bar scene on the streets just west of Praça General Osório.

Ipanema acquired international fame in the early '60s as the home of the bossa nova character 'Girl from Ipanema.' It became the hangout of artists, intellectuals and wealthy liberals, who frequented the sidewalk cafés and bars. After the 1964 military coup and the resulting crackdown on liberals, many of these bohemians were forced into exile. During the '70s, Leblon became the nightlife center of Rio. The restaurants and bars of Baixo Leblon, on Av Ataúlfo de Paiva between Ruas Aristides Espínola and General Artigas, were the meeting point for a new generation of artists and musicians. While Lapa is where the live music is at, Leblon still has its allure. Some of the city's best old-fashioned bars are sprinkled about this neighborhood, with many dating from the 1950s.

IPANEMA & LEBLON BEACH Map p66

Av Delfim Moreira & Av Vieira Souto

Although the beaches of Ipanema and Leblon are one long beach, the *postos* (posts) along them subdivide the beach into areas as diverse as the city itself. Posto 9, right off Rua Vinícius de Moraes, is Garota de Ipanema, which is where Rio's most lithe and tanned bodies tend to migrate. The area is also known as the Cemetério dos Elefantes because of the handful of old leftists, hippies and artists who sometimes hang out there. In front of Rua Farme de Amoedo the beach is known as Bolsa de Valores or Crystal Palace (this is the gay section), while posto 8 further up is mostly the domain of favela kids. Arpoador, between Ipanema and Copacabana, is Rio's most popular surf spot. Leblon attracts a broad mix of single Cariocas, as well as families from the neighborhood. Posto 10 is for sport lovers, with ongoing volleyball, soccer and *frescobal* (played with wooden racquets and a rubber ball) games. There's also Baixo Bebê, between posts 11 and 12, where affluent parents with children migrate.

Whatever spot you choose, you'll enjoy cleaner sands and sea than those in Copacabana. Keep in mind that if you go on Saturday or Sunday, the sands get crowded. Go early to stake out a spot.

Incidentally, the word *ipanema* is Indian for 'bad, dangerous waters' – not so far off given the strong undertow and often oversized waves crashing on the shore. Be careful, and swim only where the locals do.

TRANSPORTATION: IPANEMA & LEBLON

Bus Botafogo (571); Corcovado train station (583); Urca (511); São Conrado (177); Centro (132); Novo Rio bus station (473); Copacabana (571)

Metrô-Ônibus (metro buses) connect Siqueira Campos station with Ipanema and Leblon (see p218 for more information)

PONTA DO ARPOADOR Map p64

Far eastern end of Av Vieira Souto

This rocky point juts out into the water and serves as one of Rio's best places for watching the sunset. Throughout the day, you'll spot fishermen casting off the rock, couples stealing a few kisses and photographers snapping that iconic stretch of Ipanema beach stretching off toward the towering peaks of Dois Irmãos. You'll also see large flocks of surfers jockeying for position offshore. Around the western edge of the rock is the tiny Praia do Diabo (Devil's Beach), a fine place to take in the views – but swim with caution. A very rustic gym is built into the rocks (think barbells with concrete weights and many chin-up bars).

MIRANTE DO LEBLON Map p66

Av Niemeyer

A few fishermen casting out to sea mingle with couples admiring the view at this overlook at the western end of Leblon

IPANEMA

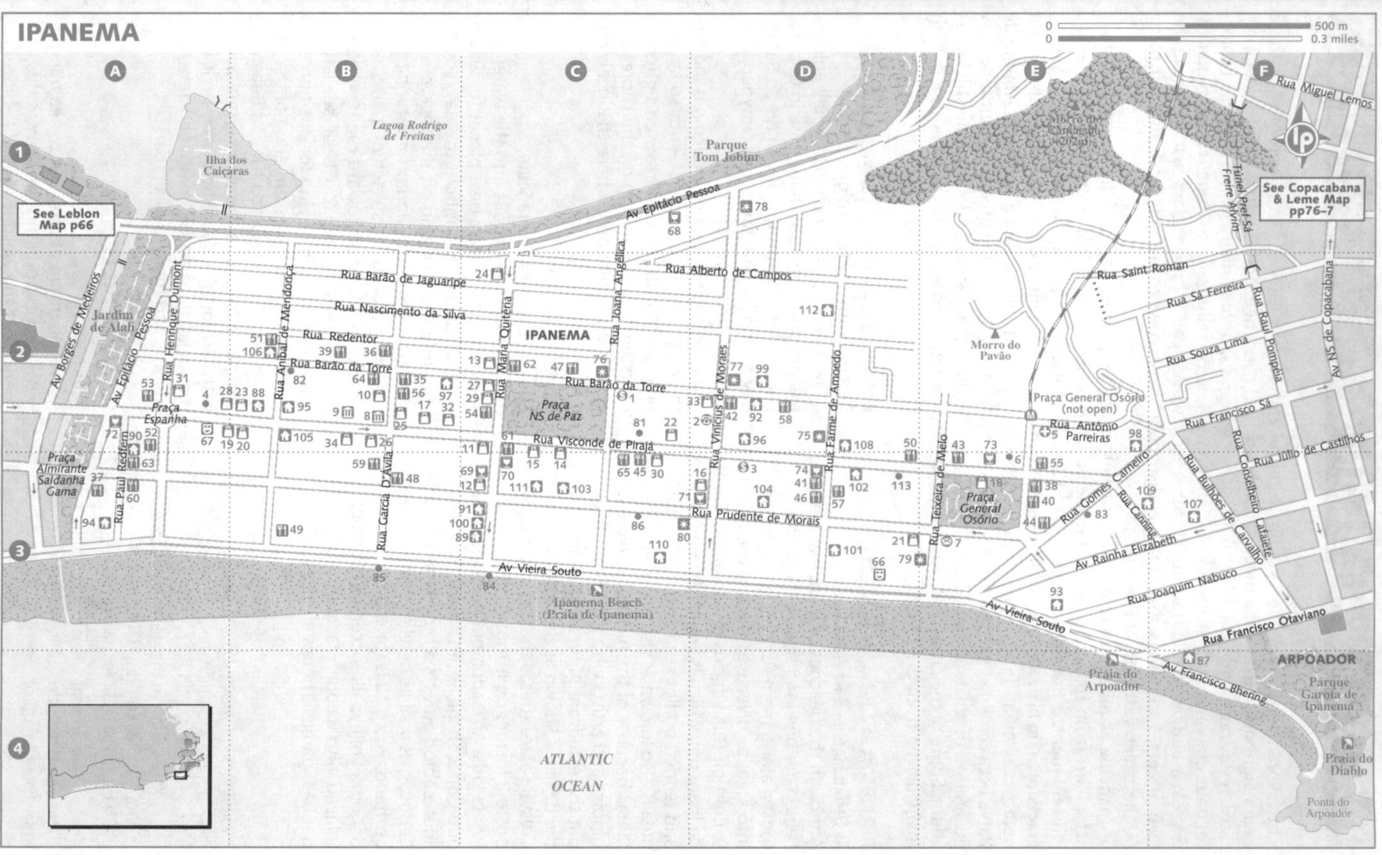
500 m
0.3 miles
Lagoa Rodrigo de Freitas
Ilha dos Caiçaras
Parque Tom Jobim
See Leblon Map p66
See Copacabana & Leme Map pp76-7
Av Epitácio Pessoa
Av Borges de Medeiros
Jardim de Alah
Praça Espanha
Praça Almirante Saldanha Gama
Rua Paul Redfern
Rua Henrique Dumont
Rua Aníbal de Mendonça
Rua Garcia D'Ávila
Rua Maria Quitéria
Rua Joana Angélica
Rua Vinícius de Moraes
Rua Farme de Amoedo
Rua Teixeira de Melo
Rua Barão de Jaguaripe
Rua Nascimento da Silva
Rua Redentor
Rua Barão da Torre
Rua Visconde de Pirajá
Rua Prudente de Morais
Rua Alberto de Campos
IPANEMA
Praça NS de Paz
Praça General Osório
Morro do Pavão
Praça General Osório (not open)
Rua Antônio Parreiras
Rua Gomes Carneiro
Rua Canning
Av Rainha Elizabeth
Rua Joaquim Nabuco
Rua Francisco Otaviano
Rua Bulhões de Carvalho
Rua Conselheiro Lafaiete
Rua Júlio de Castilhos
Rua Francisco Sá
Rua Souza Lima
Rua Sá Ferreira
Rua Saint Roman
Rua Raul Pompéia
Av NS de Copacabana
Rua Miguel Lemos
Túnel Pref Sá Freire Alvim
Av Vieira Souto
Ipanema Beach (Praia de Ipanema)
Praia do Arpoador
Av Francisco Bhering
ARPOADOR
Parque Garota de Ipanema
Praia do Diablo
Ponta do Arpoador
ATLANTIC OCEAN

IPANEMA

INFORMATION
Banco do Brasil 1 C2
Central Fone 2 D2
Citibank 3 D3
Drogaria Pacheco 4 A2
Hospital Ipanema 5 E2
Le Bon Voyage 6 E3
Letras e Expressões (Ipanema) (see 22)
Post Office 7 E3

SIGHTS
Museu Amsterdam Sauer 8 B2
Museu H Stern 9 B2

SHOPPING
Amsterdam Sauer (see 8)
Antonio Bernardo 10 B2
Brasil & Cia (see 100)
Contemporâneo 11 C2
Emporio Brasil (see 19)
Espaço Brazilian Soul 12 C3
Forum 13 C2
Forum de Ipanema 14 C2
Galeria Ipanema Secreta 15 C2
Garota de Ipanema 16 D3
Gilson Martins 17 B2
H Stern (see 9)
Hippie Fair 18 E3
Interstudio 19 A2
Ipanema 2000 20 B2
Ipanema.com 21 D3
Letras e Expressões (Ipanema) 22 C2
Livraria da Travessa 23 B2
Luko (see 20)
Maria Oiticica 24 C2
Mixed 25 B2
Musicale 26 B2
Osklen 27 C2
Oz 28 A2
Redley 29 C2
Renovar 30 C3
Sociedade Anônimo (see 14)
Sollas 31 A2
Teargas 32 B2
Toca do Vinícius 33 D2
Urucum Art & Design (see 67)
Vale das Bonecas (see 14)
Wöllner Outdoor 34 B2

EATING
Al Mare (see 93)
Alessandro E Federico 35 B2
Alessandro E Federico 36 B2
Artigiano 37 A3
Azul Marinho (see 87)
Banana Jack 38 E3
Bazzar 39 B2
Brasileirinho 40 E3
Caesar Park (see 89)
Cafeína 41 D3
Capricciosa 42 D2
Carretão 43 E3
Casa da Feijoada 44 E3
Chaika 45 C3
Colher de Pau 46 D3
Da Silva 47 C2
Delírio Tropical 48 B3
Doce Delícia 49 B3
Fontes (see 67)
Frontera 50 D3
Garota de Ipanema (see 71)
Gero 51 B2
Gula Gula 52 A2
Kilograma 53 A2
Koni Store 54 C2
Mel & Pimenta 55 E3
Mil Frutas 56 B2
Mio 57 D3
New Natural 58 D2
Nik Sushi 59 B3
Osteria Dell'Angolo 60 A3
Polis Sucos 61 C2
Sorvete Brasil 62 C2
Ten Kai 63 A3
Via Sete 64 B2
Zazá Bistrô Tropical 65 C3

THE ARTS
Casa da Cultura Laura Alvim 66 D3
Estação Ipanema 67 A2
Teatro Laura Alvim (see 66)

DRINKING
Bar Lagoa 68 C1
Empório 69 C3
Espelunca Chic 70 C3
Garota de Ipanema 71 D3
Londra (see 93)
Lord Jim 72 A2
Shenanigan's 73 E3
Tô Nem Aí 74 D3

NIGHTLIFE
Bar Bofetada 75 D2
Baronneti 76 C2
Casa da Lua 77 D2
Dama de Ferro 78 D1
Galeria Café 79 E3
Vinícius Piano Bar 80 C3

SPORTS & ACTIVITIES
Blyss Yôga 81 C2
Body Tech (Ipanema) 82 B2
Body Tech (Ipanema) 83 E3
Escolinha de Surf Paulo Dolabella 84 C3
Escolinha de Vôlei 85 B3
Spa Maria Bonita 86 C3

SLEEPING
Arpoador Inn 87 F4
Aurélio Rio Guide 88 B2
Caesar Park 89 C3
Che Lagarto Ipanema 90 A3
Everest Rio 91 C3
Hostel Harmonia 92 D2
Hotel Fasano 93 E3
Hotel Praia Ipanema 94 A3
Hotel San Marco 95 B2
Hotel Vermont 96 D2
Ipanema Beach House 97 B2
Ipanema Flat Hotel Residência 98 E2
Ipanema Hotel Residência 99 D2
Ipanema Inn 100 C3
Ipanema Plaza 101 D3
Ipanema Sweet 102 D3
Ipanema Tower 103 C3
Lighthouse Hostel (see 92)
Mango Tree 104 D3
Mar Ipanema 105 B2
Margarida's Pousada 106 B2
Parthenon Queen Elizabeth 107 F3
Rio Apartments 108 D2
Rio Hostel - Copacabana 109 E3
Sol Ipanema 110 C3
Terrasse Hostel (see 46)
Visconti 111 C3
Wave Hostel (see 92)
Yaya Hotel 112 D2

TRANSPORT
Special Bike 113 D3

beach. The luxury Sheraton Hotel looms to the west, with the not so luxurious favela of Vidigal nearby.

TOCA DO VINÍCIUS Map p64

2247 5227; www.tocadovinicius.com.br; Rua Vinícius de Moraes 129; 9am-9pm Mon-Fri, 10am-5pm Sun

A quintessential stop off for bossa nova fans, Toca do Vinícius is a music store (p116) named in honor of the famous Brazilian musician, Vinícius de Moraes. The 1st floor has a good selection of bossa, while upstairs a tiny museum displays original manuscripts and photos of the great songwriter and poet. Live bossa nova concerts are held in the small space several nights a week.

MUSEU AMSTERDAM SAUER Map p64

2512 1132; www.amsterdamsauer.com; Rua Garcia D'Ávila 105; admission free; 9am-7pm Mon-Fri, 9am-4pm Sat

Next door to Museu H Stern, the Amsterdam Sauer Museum houses an impressive

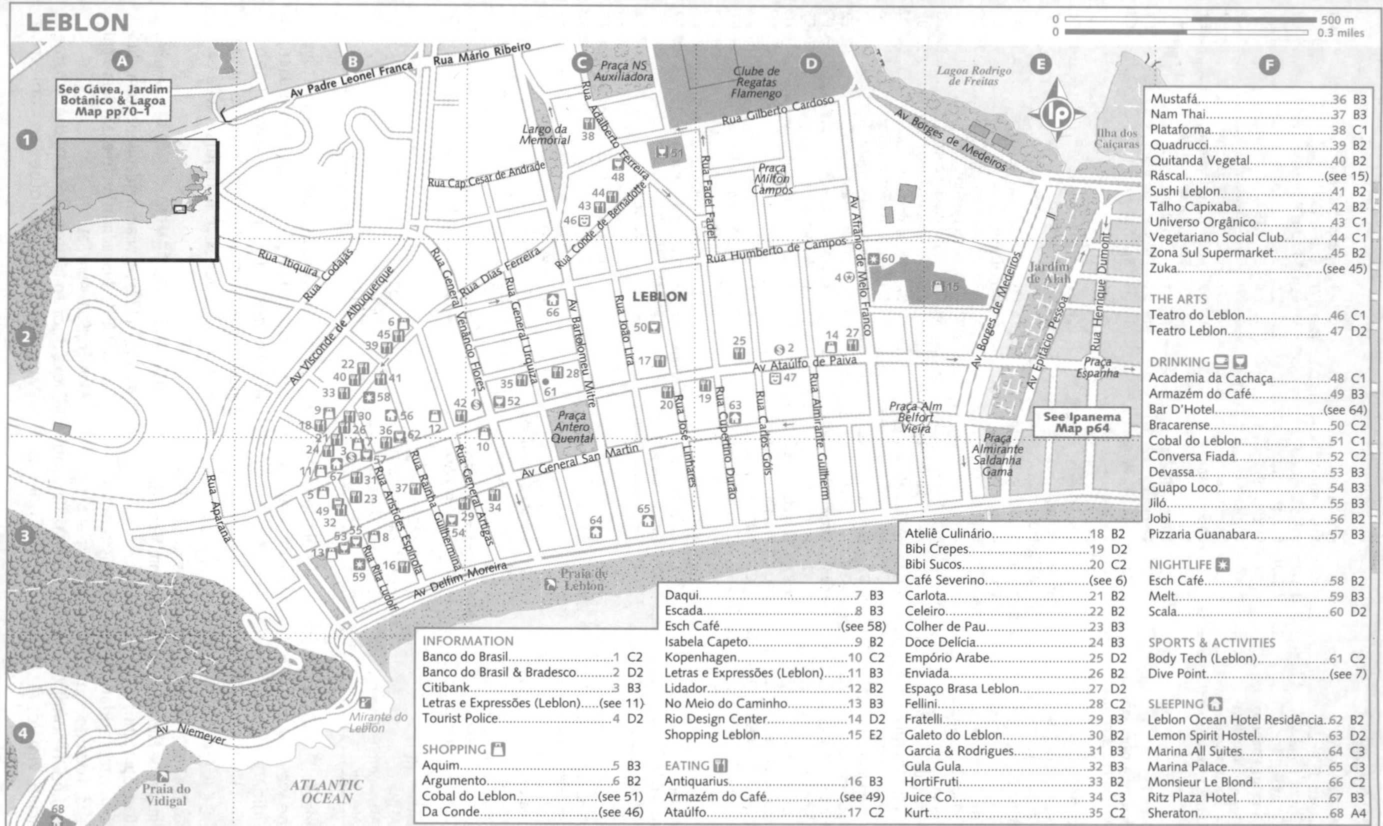
LEBLON
0 500 m
0 0.3 miles
See Gávea, Jardim Botânico & Lagoa Map pp70–1
See Ipanema Map p64
INFORMATION
Banco do Brasil 1 C2
Banco do Brasil & Bradesco 2 D2
Citibank 3 B3
Letras e Expressões (Leblon) (see 11)
Tourist Police 4 D2
SHOPPING
Aquim 5 B3
Argumento 6 B2
Cobal do Leblon (see 51)
Da Conde (see 46)
Daqui 7 B3
Escada 8 B3
Esch Café (see 58)
Isabela Capeto 9 B2
Kopenhagen 10 C2
Letras e Expressões (Leblon) 11 B3
Lidador 12 B2
No Meio do Caminho 13 B3
Rio Design Center 14 D2
Shopping Leblon 15 E2
EATING
Antiquarius 16 B3
Armazém do Café (see 49)
Ataúlfo 17 C2
Ateliê Culinário 18 B2
Bibi Crepes 19 D2
Bibi Sucos 20 C2
Café Severino (see 6)
Carlota 21 B2
Celeiro 22 B2
Colher de Pau 23 B3
Doce Delícia 24 B3
Empório Arabe 25 D2
Enviada 26 B2
Espaço Brasa Leblon 27 D2
Fellini 28 C2
Fratelli 29 B3
Galeto do Leblon 30 B2
Garcia & Rodrigues 31 B3
Gula Gula 32 B3
HortiFruti 33 B2
Juice Co. 34 C3
Kurt 35 C2
Mustafá 36 B3
Nam Thai 37 B3
Plataforma 38 C1
Quadrucci 39 B2
Quitanda Vegetal 40 B2
Ráscal (see 15)
Sushi Leblon 41 B2
Talho Capixaba 42 B2
Universo Orgânico 43 C1
Vegetariano Social Club 44 C1
Zona Sul Supermarket 45 B2
Zuka (see 45)
THE ARTS
Teatro do Leblon 46 C1
Teatro Leblon 47 D2
DRINKING
Academia da Cachaça 48 C1
Armazém do Café 49 B3
Bar D'Hotel (see 64)
Bracarense 50 C2
Cobal do Leblon 51 C1
Conversa Fiada 52 C2
Devassa 53 B3
Guapo Loco 54 B3
Jiló 55 B3
Jobi 56 B2
Pizzaria Guanabara 57 B3
NIGHTLIFE
Esch Café 58 B2
Melt 59 B3
Scala 60 D2
SPORTS & ACTIVITIES
Body Tech (Leblon) 61 C2
Dive Point (see 7)
SLEEPING
Leblon Ocean Hotel Residência 62 B2
Lemon Spirit Hostel 63 D2
Marina All Suites 64 C3
Marina Palace 65 C3
Monsieur Le Blond 66 C2
Ritz Plaza Hotel 67 B3
Sheraton 68 A4
LEBLON
Av Padre Leonel Franca
Rua Mário Ribeiro
Praça NS Auxiliadora
Clube de Regatas Flamengo
Lagoa Rodrigo de Freitas
Ilha dos Caiçaras
Rua Gilberto Cardoso
Av Borges de Medeiros
Largo da Memórial
Rua Adalberto Ferreira
Rua Fadel Fadel
Praça Milton Campos
Rua Cap Cesar de Andrade
Rua Conde de Bernadotte
Av Afrânio de Melo Franco
Rua Humberto de Campos
Jardim de Alah
Rua Henrique Dumont
Av Epitácio Pessoa
Rua Itiquira
Rua Codajás
Rua Dias Ferreira
Av Visconde de Albuquerque
Rua General Venâncio Flores
Rua General Urquiza
Av Bartolomeu Mitre
Rua João Lira
Av Ataúlfo de Paiva
Praça Espanha
Praça Alm Belfort Vieira
Praça Antero Quental
Rua José Linhares
Rua Cupertino Durão
Rua Carlos Góis
Rua Almirante Guilherm
Praça Almirante Saldanha Gama
Av General San Martin
Rua Aristides Espínola
Rua Rainha Guilhermina
Rua General Artigas
Rua Aparana
Rua Rita Ludolf
Av Delfim Moreira
Praia de Leblon
Mirante do Leblon
Av Niemeyer
Praia do Vidigal
ATLANTIC OCEAN

collection of precious stones – over 3000 items in all. Visitors can also take a peek at the two life-sized replicas of mines.

MUSEU H STERN Map p64

☎ 2274 8897; www.hstern.com.br; Rua Visconde de Pirajá 490; admission free; 9am-6pm Mon-Fri, 9am-2pm Sat

The headquarters of the famous jeweler H Stern incorporates a museum displaying a permanent exhibition of fine jewelry, some rare mineral specimens and a large collection of tourmalines. There is a 12-minute tour, which displays the process of turning the rough stones into flawlessly cut jewels as the gems pass through the hands of craftsmen, cutters, goldsmiths and setters. With a coupon, you can get a free cab from anywhere in the Zona Sul to the shop. Call them at ☎ 2274 6171 and they'll pick you up from your hotel.

PARQUE GAROTA DE IPANEMA Map p64

Off Rua Francisco Otaviano, near Rua Bulhões Carvalho; 7am-7pm

This small park next to the Arpoador rock features a tiny playground, a concrete area popular with skaters and a lookout with a view of Ipanema beach. On weekends in summer, there are occasional concerts here.

SHOPPING IN IPANEMA

Walking Tour

Ipanema's many boutiques make for some excellent browsing when you need a break from the beach. In addition to high-end clothing stores, you'll find a good assortment of wine, music, books and even handicrafts. Off the avenue, pretty streets with cafés, ice-cream stands and open-air restaurants provide a nice break from bargain hunting.

1 Rua Farme de Amoedo Before hitting the streets, boost up your energy levels with coffee and a pastry at Cafeína (p137), a pleasant open-air spot one block west of Praça General Osório. From there, walk over to Rua Vinícius de Moraes, named after the famed Carioca composer.

2 Toca do Vinícius One of the best little music stores in Rio, Toca do Vinícius (p116) lies along this street, and stocks all the great bossa nova hits of the legend for whom it's named. You'll also find samba, MPB *(Música Popular Brasileira)* and a good mix of Brazilian and international labels. Just across the road is Lidador, a handy wine shop.

3 Praça NS de Paz – west side On the west side of the plaza, you'll find a few noteworthy clothing shops, including Forum (p114), Redley (p115) and Osklen (p115). These shops stock men's and women's swimwear, T-shirts and outerwear in eye-catching styles.

WALK FACTS

Start Rua Farme de Amoedo
End Praça Espanha
Distance 2km
Duration 2½ hours

4 Hidden boutiques Down on busy Rua Visconde de Pirajá, you'll find dozens of shops, but some – like Forum de Ipanema (p114) and Galeria Ipanema Secreta (p114) – are hidden from view. Take a wander through these multistory centers for a peak at lots of colorful fashion stores.

5 Handicrafts One block south, you'll find Brasil & Cia (p116), one of the best handicrafts shops in the Zona Sul. Here you can check out the colorful works of artists from Minas Gerais, Bahia and other states.

6 Music and handbags Nearby are two unique Rio flagship stores. Contemporâneo (p114) has racks of men's and women's fashions in a stylish setting above the street. Gilson Martins (p112) receives much press for its iconic vinyl bags bearing images either of the Brazilian flag or of Corcovado.

7 Rua Garcia D'Ávila Probably Ipanema's toniest street, Rua Garcia D'Ávila is the address of three high-end jewelers, a Louis Vuitton store and several cafés and restaurants. Our picks: Antonio Bernardo (p116), maker of exquisite, custom-made jewelry, followed by a trip to Mil Frutas (p136), the highly satisfying ice- cream and snack shop.

8 Livraria da Travessa Although the bookseller has a number of shops in Rio, this Livraria da Travessa (p113) is one of our favorites, if only for the cozy café on the second floor. You can browse coffee-table books, listen to CDs in the music section and finish off with coffee and dessert.

PUB CRAWL IN LEBLON

Walking Tour

The neighborhood *boteco* is something of a Leblon institution, with ice-cold beer, excellent-but-terrible-for-you appetizers, and a festive, mixed crowd who aren't averse to solving the problems of the world or just having a laugh with friends over a few pints. We recommend doing the pub tour on a weekend afternoon – particularly on game days, when things are at their liveliest. Obviously, if you're planning a late-night drinking event, it's wise to take a taxi between bars.

1 Academia da Cachaça There's nothing like a shot of cachaça to take the edge off before a big evening out. In addition to tasty cocktails (try the passion-fruit caipirinha), the festive Academia da Cachaça (p152) serves up traditional Brazilian dishes. If you can't find a table, there are a handful of other bars next door.

2 Cobal do Leblon Just across the way, is the flower and vegetable market Cobal do Leblon (p153), which transforms into a festive open-air drinking spot most nights. While it's nothing fancy – think plastic tables and chairs – this place is popular, particularly with the 20-something crowd.

3 Bracarense Once your thirst is slaked (but not too slaked – the night is young), head south to Bracarense, the first of Leblon's classic botecos. Bracarense (p153) has been around since 1951 and has long been known for its tasty appetizers particularly the *bolinhos de bacalhau* (codfish balls).

4 Jobi Further west lies another classic old-timer, Jobi (p153). To call this tiny 50-something-year-old bar a neighborhood favorite is an understatement. The tiny bar has won *Veja* magazine's 'best boteco' award for five years running. Good appetizers, droll waiters and the ever-flowing ice-cold *chope* are a few reasons for success.

5 Pizzaria Guanabara A mainstay of the Leblon drinking scene, Pizzaria Guanabara (p154) attracts a youngish beer-drinking crowd and becomes a major destination in the wee hours (it stays open until 7am), when the post-party crowd comes for food. Keep in mind that the pizza is not particularly good, but tastes great when hunger strikes at 3am.

6 Esch Café Much better food lies around the corner on restaurant-packed Rua Dias Ferreira. This is also the street where you'll find the Esch Café (p114) a fairly staid wood-toned bar with a good selection of Cuban cigars and live jazz and bossa nova throughout the week.

7 Devassa A few blocks south, you'll find lively Devassa (p153), which is deservedly famous for its creamy rich draft beer. Now a franchise around Rio, the Leblon branch was the first. The open-sided ground floor has a happy chatty crowd, while bands sometimes bring the dance crowd upstairs.

8 Melt Speaking of dancing, Melt (p169) is just up the street, and if you're in a dancing mood

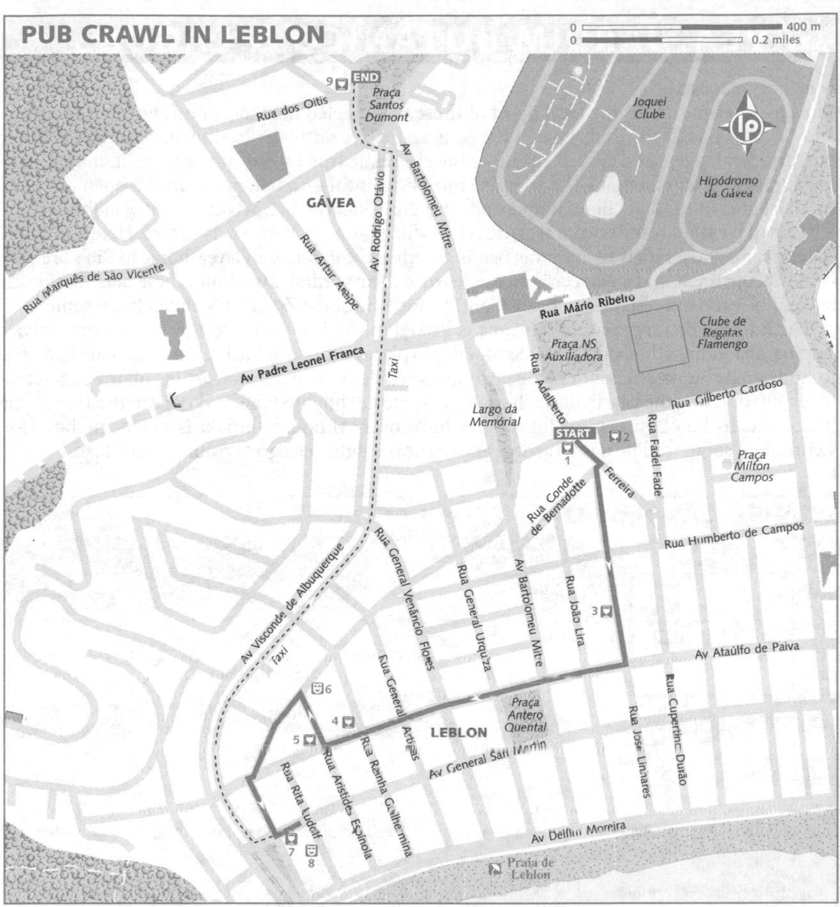

(and it's late enough) this is a good place to pop by. There is a lounge on the first floor, with DJs or bands performing on the second floor.

9 Baixo Gávea If you're not ready to call it a night but ready for a change of venue, catch a taxi up to the Praça Santos Dumont. Most nights of the week, the bars, such as Braseiro da Gávea (p154), facing the square pack with revelers, making for one of Rio's best informal drinking scenes.

WALK FACTS

Start Rua Conde de Bernadotte
End Praça Santos Dumont
Distance 2km
Duration Four-12 hours

GÁVEA, JARDIM BOTÂNICO & LAGOA

Eating p137; Shopping p117

Rio's picturesque lake is the focal point of these well-heeled neighborhoods north of Ipanema and Leblon. The Lagoa Rodrigo de Freitas, is actually a saltwater lagoon and is much utilized by Cariocas. Joggers and cyclists zip along the shoreline trail by day, while at night, the lakeside restaurants fill with couples and friends enjoying a meal and live music in the open air. Two small islands in the lake, Ilha Piraquê and Ilha dos Caiçaras, are private country clubs.

West of the lake are the botanical gardens for which the neighborhood is named. Here you'll find stately palms and a variety of flowering plants. South of the gardens is Gávea, home to Rio's premier horse-racing track, and a planetarium. Aside from their natural attractions, these neighborhoods have some excellent restaurants, lively nightlife and one of the Zona Sul's best cultural centers.

Much of the development of this area is linked to the lake. Prior to the Portuguese arrival, Tupinambá Indians dubbed the lake Sacopenapã (place of the soco birds), but it was later changed to Rodrigo de Freitas, in honor of the Portuguese settler who made his fortune off the sugarcane fields surrounding the lake in the 16th century. Factories blighted the landscape in the 1900s, and it took much of the 20th century for the area to recover. Although the lake is still too polluted for swimming, some wildlife has returned, and visitors might see egrets fishing in the lake.

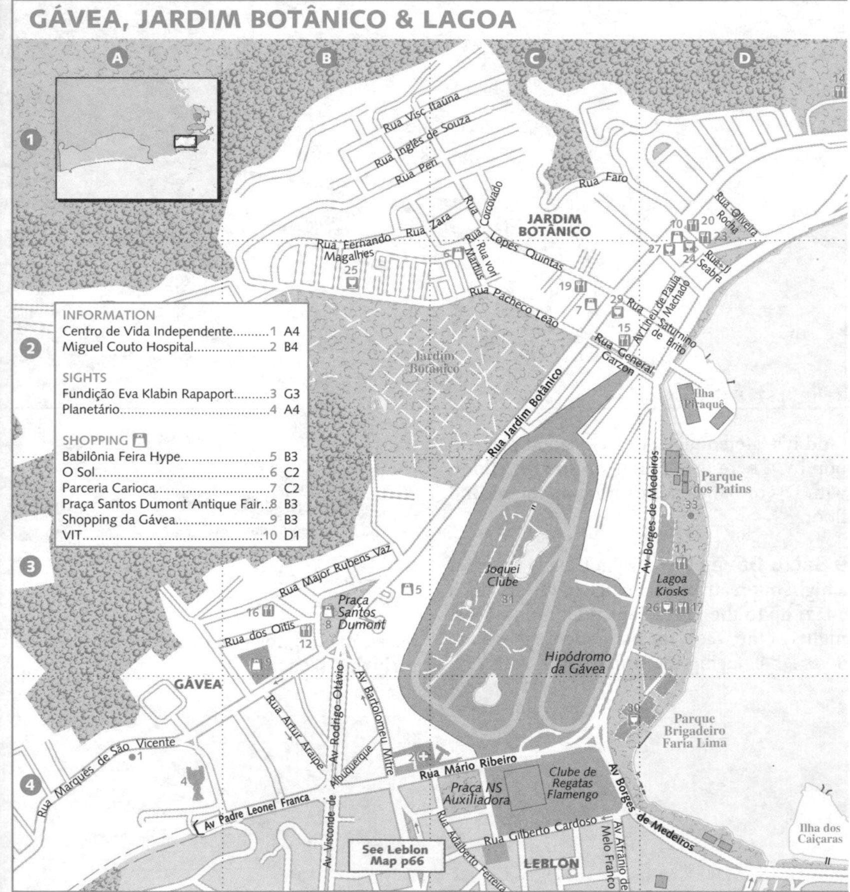

GÁVEA

INSTITUTO MOREIRA SALLES

Map pp60–1

☎ 3284 7400; www.ims.com.br in Portuguese; Rua Marquês de Sao Vicente 476; admission free; 🕑 1-8pm Tue-Sun

This beautiful cultural center is next to the Parque da Cidade and contains an archive of more than 80,000 photographs, many portraying old streets of Rio as well as the urban development of other Brazilian cities over the last two centuries. It also hosts impressive exhibitions, often showcasing the works of some of Brazil's best photographers and artists. Check its website for details of what's on when you're in town.

The gardens, complete with artificial lake and flowing river, were designed by Brazilian landscape architect Burle Marx. There's also a craft shop and a quaint café that serves lunch or afternoon tea.

MUSEU HISTÓRICO DA CIDADE

Map pp60–1

☎ 2512 2353; www.rio.rj.gov.br/culturas in Portuguese; Estrada de Santa Marinha 505; admission R$4; 🕑 10am-4pm Tue-Fri, 10am-3pm Sat & Sun

The 19th-century mansion located on the lovely grounds of the Parque da Cidade now houses the City History Museum. In addition to its permanent collection, which portrays Rio from its founding in 1565 to the mid-20th century, the museum has exhibitions of furniture, porcelain, photographs and paintings by well-known artists. The park itself is free, open from 7am to 6pm.

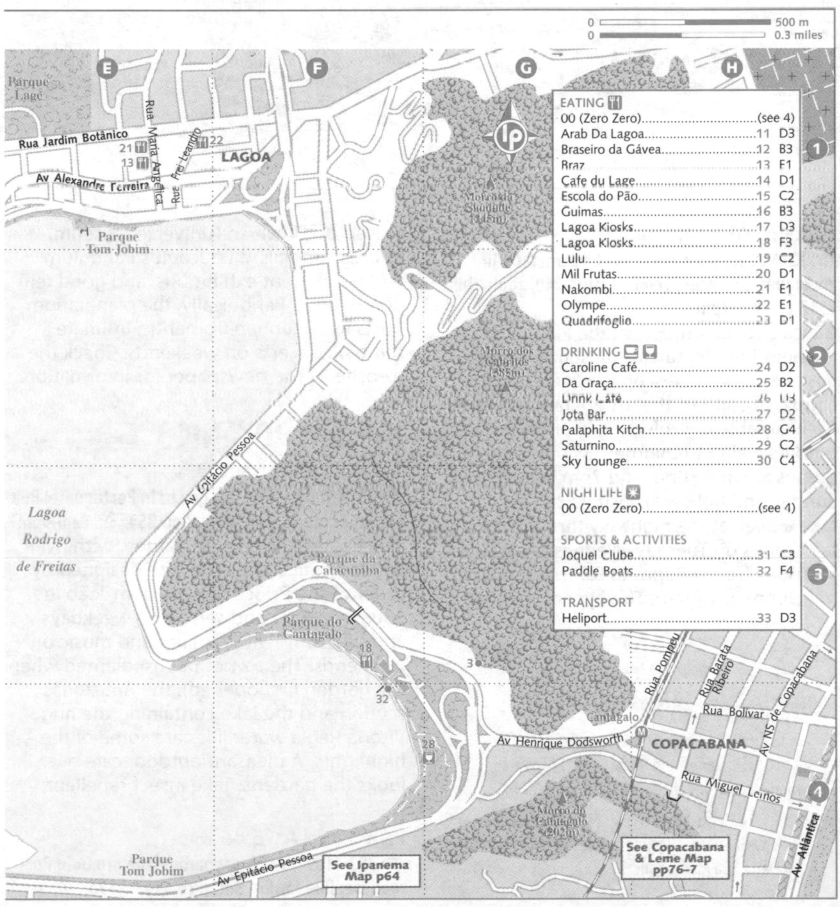

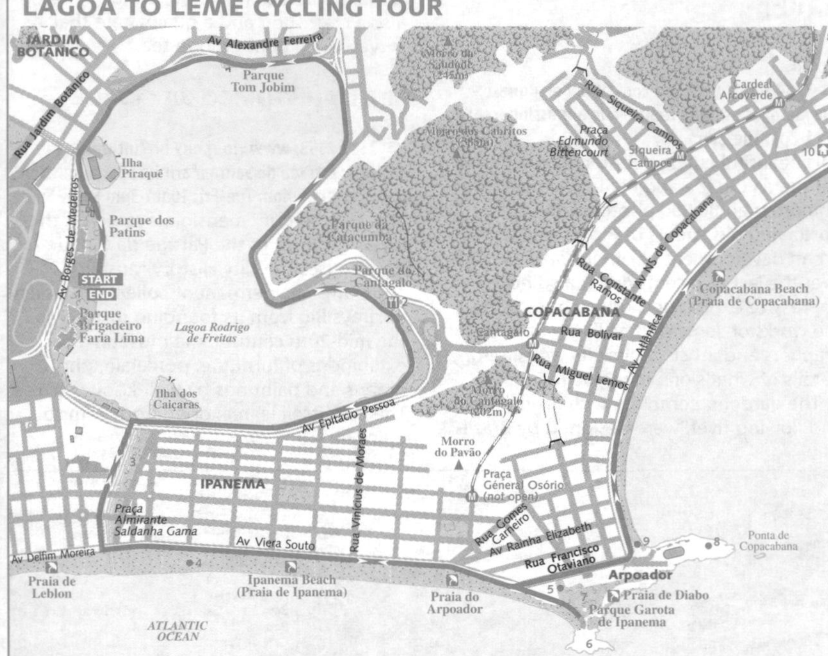

PLANETÁRIO Map pp70–1

☎ 2274 0046; www.rio.rj.gov.br/planetario in Portuguese; Av Padre Leonel Franca 240; adult/child R$12/6; 🕒 3-7pm

Gávea's stellar attraction, the Planetário (Planetarium) features a museum, a *praça dos telescópios* (telescopes' square) and a couple of state-of-the-art operating domes, each capable of projecting over 6000 stars onto its walls (40-minute sessions in the domes are at 5.30pm and 7pm Saturday, Sunday and holidays). Visitors can also take a peak at the night sky through the telescopes on Tuesday, Wednesday and Thursday from 7.30pm to 8.30pm (6.30pm to 7.30pm in winter). The hyper-modern Museu do Universo (Universe Museum) houses sundials, a Foucault's Pendulum and permanent exhibitions, and good temporary ones. Periodically, the planetarium hosts live *chorinho* (romantic, intimate samba) concerts on weekends. Check the website or the newspaper for information.

TRANSPORTATION: GÁVEA, JARDIM BOTÂNICO & LAGOA

Bus Jardim Botânico and Gávea: Centro (170); Botafogo, Flamengo and Glória (176, 178); Leblon, Ipanema and Copacabana (571, 572, 574)

Metro-Bus Metro-buses connect Siqueira Campos station with Gávea, stopping at Rua Padre Leonel França and Rua Marquês de São Vicente

JARDIM BOTÂNICO

JARDIM BOTÂNICO Map pp70–1

☎ 3874 1808; www.jbrj.gov.br in Portuguese; Rua Jardim Botânico 920; admission R$4; 🕒 8am-5pm

This exotic 137-hectare garden, with over 5500 varieties of plants, was designed by order of the Prince Regent Dom João in 1808. It's quiet and serene on weekdays and blossoms with families and music on weekends. The row of palms (planted when the garden first opened), the Amazonas section and the lake containing the huge Vitória Régia water lilies are some of the highlights. A pleasant outdoor café overlooks the gardens. Take insect repellent.

PARQUE LAGE Map pp70–1

☎ 2538 1091; www.eavparquelage.org.br in Portuguese; Rua Jardim Botânico 414; 🕒 7am-6pm

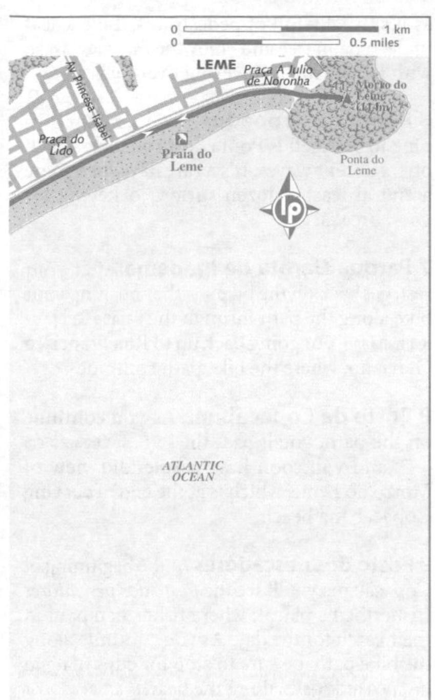

This beautiful park, at the base of Parque Nacional da Tijuca, is about 1km from Jardim Botânico. It has English-style gardens, little lakes and a mansion that now houses the Instituto Nacional de Belas Artes, which often hosts art exhibitions and occasional performances. The park is a tranquil place and particularly popular on weekends when the Café du Lage (p140) whips up a delightful brunch. Native Atlantic rain forest surrounds Parque Lage. This is the starting point for challenging hikes up Corcovado (best to go with a guide).

LAGOA

LAGOA RODRIGO DE FREITAS

Map pp70–1

One of the city's most picturesque spots, Lagoa has 7.2km of cycling/walking path around the lake. Bikes are available for hire (p215) near Parque Brigadeiro Faria Lima. And there's also a helipad (p225) on the shoreline for those who want a bird's-eye of the *cidade maravilhosa.* It may sound cheesy, but hiring a paddle boat is another way to enjoy the lake, especially when the Christmas tree is lit up across the water.

RIDE FACTS

Start **Parque Brigadeiro Faria Lima**
End **Parque Brigadeiro Faria Lima**
Distance **25km**
Duration **Three hours**

Boat rental is available on the lake's east side in Parque do Cantagalo, December through early January. For those who prefer caipirinhas to plastic swan boats, the kiosks in Parque dos Patins offer lakeside dining al fresco, often accompanied by live *forró* (traditional music from the northeast).

FUNDAÇAO EVA KLABIN RAPAPORT

Map pp70–1

☎ 3202 8550; Av Epitácio Pessoa 2480; guided visits by appointment 2.30 & 4pm Wed-Sun

An old mansion full of antiques, the former residence of Eva Klabin Rapaport houses the works of art she collected for 60 years. Reflecting Eva's diverse interests, the collection has 1100 pieces from ancient Egypt, Greece and China. Paintings, sculptures, silver, furniture and carpets are also on display.

PARQUE DA CATACUMBA Map pp70–1

Av Epitácio Pessoa; 8am-7pm

Inaugurated in 1979, Catacumba is the site of Brazil's first outdoor sculptural garden. The site of a former favela (which was demolished to create the park), Catacumba sits atop Morro dos Cabritos, which rises from the Lagoa Rodrigo de Freitas. It's a choice place to escape the heat while strolling through some fascinating works by artists such as Roberto Moriconi and Bruno Giorgi. Superb views await those willing to climb to the top of the hill (385m). During summer, Catacumba hosts free Sunday afternoon concerts featuring top performers in its outdoor amphitheater. Check the weekend listings in *O Globo* for details.

LAGOA TO LEME

Cycling Tour

It's hard to think of a better setting for a bike ride than the Zona Sul's lovely coastline and its nearby lakeside jewel, Lagoa Rodrigo de Freitas (left). The mountains rising out of the sea and the white-sand beaches facing them are a big part of the allure of the *cidade maravilhosa* and you'll be rewarded with a number of panoramic views along this journey. Beaches, bay, Corcovado, Pão de Açúcar and many of Rio's other lush peaks are the backdrop for your ride.

Bring some money for snacks and *agua de coco* (coconut water) – both prevalent along the beach – and a meal at the end of your ride. You'll work up an appetite out in the sun.

Most of this journey follows a bike path separate from the traffic on the street. Sunday is the best day to do this ride, as the road bordering the bike path is closed then – giving you more room to connect to your inner Armstrong.

1 Parque Brigadeiro Faria Lima Begin in this park on the edge of Lagoa. Conveniently, there's a bike-rental place right there. You can also rent bikes at a number of other places in town (p215).

2 Lagoa kiosks Once you're on the bike path, follow it north as it loops around the lake. Continue south, pedaling past some of the Lagoa kiosks, popular spots for al fresco dining in the evening.

3 Jardim de Alah In another 400m, you'll pass the Ilha dos Caiçaras on your right. Go just past it and take Av Borges de Medeiros south, following along the canal and the Jardim de Alah opposite. In a few blocks you'll reach the beach.

4 Posto 10 From Leblon, start pedaling east on the bike/jog path along Av Vieira Souto. As you ride along, you'll catch an eyeful of *frescobal*, soccer and volleyball games, with plenty of good people watching.

5 Praça do Arpoador When you reach Arpoador, pull off the bike path for your first *agua de coco* from a kiosk near the Praça do Arpoador. You'll need to walk your bike here, as it's usually full of pedestrians. Take a seat under a palm tree and enjoy the fine view west, with Dois Irmãos towering over Leblon.

6 Ponta do Arpoador The rock outcropping to your left is Ponta do Arpoador, which offers decent waves. It's a rare day when there aren't at least a dozen surfers jockeying for good breaks.

7 Parque Garota de Ipanema After your rest, get back on the bike – either pushing your bike along the path through the Parque Garota de Ipanema (p67), or going back up to Rua Francisco Otaviano, where the bike path continues.

8 Forte de Copacabana As you continue on the path, you'll pass the Forte de Copacabana (p77) and will soon have a splendid view of Morro do Leme, which is at the end of curving Copacabana beach.

9 Posto dos pescadores At the beginning of Copacabana you'll see the *posto dos pescadores* (fishermen's place), where fishermen haul in their catch for the day. As you continue along the bike path, be sure to stop for cups of *agua de coco* at kiosks along the beach.

10 Copacabana Palace Although you'll probably be watching the beach, the mountains and the sea, keep an eye out for the whitewashed Copacabana Palace (p193), Copa's first hotel (1923) back when the beach was still a remote getaway from Centro.

11 Morro do Leme In Leme the path ends at the Morro do Leme, where you'll probably see kids fishing off the rocks. Take a break before starting the return journey, which follows the same route back. If you haven't eaten by the time you return to Lagoa, grab a meal at one of the lakeside restaurants.

COPACABANA & LEME

Eating p140; Shopping p117; Sleeping p193

Synonymous with Rio's golden age, Copacabana was once an icon of Brazil, with ritzy beachfront hotels once frequented by international celebrities. One look around the place today, and you'll note that a lot has changed since the 1940s. Today's Copa is a chaotic mix of discount stores and noisy traffic-filled avenues, with a throbbing red-light district and an edgy feeling of crime lurking around every third street corner. While paradise it clearly is not, the beach is still undeniably beautiful. Framed by mountains and deep blue sea, the magnificent curve of shoreline stretches more than 4km from end to end.

Packing the beach are sun-worshippers of every age and background – from favela kids to aging socialites, with tourists and families from the Zona Norte thrown into the mix. Despite its obvious shortcomings, Copacabana is still a fascinating place, with many rare finds hidden beneath its weather-beaten facade. Old-school *botecos*, eclectic restaurants and nightclubs, myriad shops and of course the handsome beach still cast a spell on many visitors.

As in Ipanema, part of the beachside street (Av Atlântica in this case) closes on Sunday and holidays (until 6pm), giving freer reign to the joggers, cyclists and rollerbladers normally jostling for space on the sidewalks.

The name Copacabana comes from a small Bolivian village on Lake Titicaca. Historians believe a statue of the Virgin Mary (Our Lady of Copacabana) was brought to Rio and consecrated inside a small chapel near Arpoador. Copacabana remained a small fishing village until Túnel Velho opened in 1891, connecting it with the rest of the city.

The construction of the neoclassical Copacabana Palace Hotel in 1923 heralded a new era for Copacabana – and Rio – as South America's most elegant destination. Copacabana remained Rio's untarnished gem until the 1970s, when the area began to fall into decline.

COPACABANA & LEME BEACH

Map pp76–7

Av Atlântica

A magnificent confluence of land and sea, the long, scalloped beach of Copacabana and Leme runs for 4km, with a flurry of activity always stretching along its length: over-amped soccer players singing their team's anthem, Cariocas and tourists lining up for caipirinhas at kiosks, favela kids showing off their soccer skills, beach vendors shouting out their wares among the beached and tanned bodies.

As in Ipanema, each group stakes out their stretch of sand. Leme is a mix of older residents and favela kids, while the area between the Copacabana Palace Hotel and Rua Fernando Mendes is the gay and transvestite section, known as the Stock or Stock Market – easily recognized by the rainbow flag. Young soccer and *futevôlei* (soccer volleyball) players hold court near Rua Santa Clara. Posts five and six are a mix of favela kids and Carioca retirees, while the beach next to the Forte de Copacabana is the fishermen's community beach. In the morning, you can buy the fresh catch of the day.

The beach is lit at night and police are in the area, but it's still not wise to walk there after dark – stay on the hotel side of

TRANSPORTATION: COPACABANA & LEME

Bus Ipanema (570), Leblon (574), Gávea (432), Centro (123)

Metro Siqueira Campos and Cardeal Arcoverde

top picks

FOR CHILDREN

- Slipping and sliding along waterfalls at the gigantic Rio Water Planet (p109).
- Stargazing at the Planetário (p72).
- Meeting some of Brazil's native creatures at the Jardim Zoológico (p104).
- Admiring the city skyline at sunset during a cruise (p224) along the bay.
- Renting bikes (p215) for a cycle around Lagoa, followed by lunch at one of the lakeside kiosks.
- Playing in the sand in the family friendly beach area (between posts 11 and 12) in Leblon (p63).
- Checking out the submarine and nautical equipment at the Museu Naval (p94).

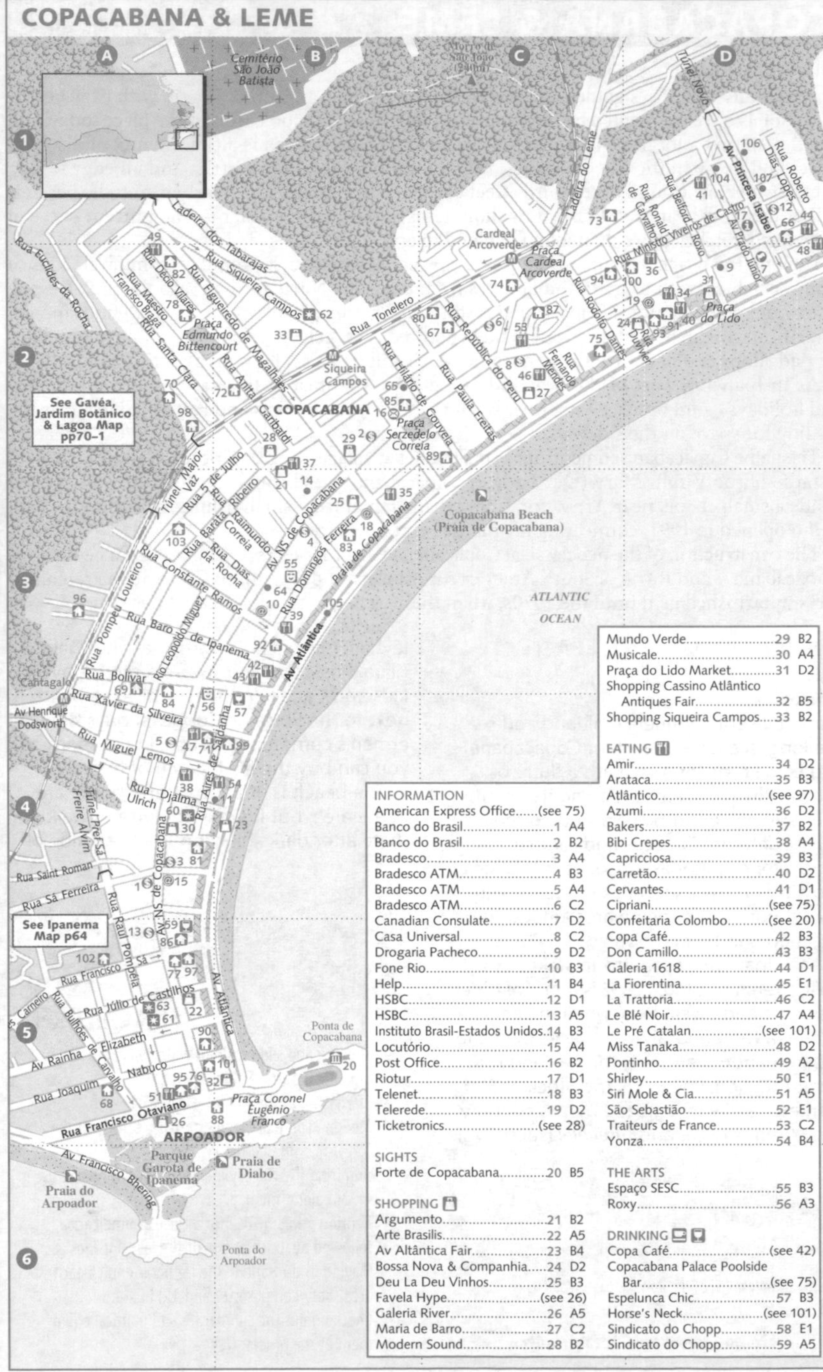
COPACABANA & LEME
Cemitério São João Batista
Morro de São João (240m)
Túnel Novo
Av Princesa Isabel
Rua Roberto Dias Lopes
Ladeira do Leme
Rua Ronald de Carvalho
Rua Belford Roxo
Rua Ministro Viveiros de Castro
Av Prado Júnior
Cardeal Arcoverde
Praça Cardeal Arcoverde
Rua Rodolfo Dantas
Rua Duvivier
Praça do Lido
Rua Tonelero
Rua República do Peru
Rua Fernando Mendes
Rua Paula Freitas
Rua Hilário de Gouveia
Praça Serzedelo Correia
Ladeira dos Tabajaras
Rua Siqueira Campos
Rua Figueiredo de Magalhães
Rua Euclides da Rocha
Praça Edmundo Bittencourt
Rua Santa Clara
Rua Anita Garibaldi
Siqueira Campos
COPACABANA
See Gavéa, Jardim Botânico & Lagoa Map pp70–1
Túnel Major Vaz
Rua 5 de Julho
Rua Ribeiro
Rua Barata Ribeiro
Rua Raimundo Correia
Rua Dias da Rocha
Av NS de Copacabana
Rua Domingos Ferreira
Praia de Copacabana
Copacabana Beach (Praia de Copacabana)
ATLANTIC OCEAN
Rua Constante Ramos
Rua Pompeu Loureiro
Rua Leopoldo Miguez
Rua Baro de Ipanema
Av Atlântica
Cantagalo
Rua Bolívar
Rua Xavier da Silveira
Av Henrique Dodsworth
Rua Miguel Lemos
Rua Djalma Ulrich
Rua Aires de Saldanha
Túnel Pref Sá Freire Alvim
Rua Saint Roman
Rua Sá Ferreira
Rua Raul Pompéia
See Ipanema Map p64
Rua Francisco Sá
Rua Júlio de Castilhos
Rua Bulhões de Carvalho
Av Rainha Elizabeth
Rua Nabuco
Rua Joaquim
Rua Francisco Otaviano
Praça Coronel Eugênio Franco
Ponta de Copacabana
ARPOADOR
Parque Garota de Ipanema
Praia de Diabo
Av Francisco Bhering
Praia do Arpoador
Ponta do Arpoador
INFORMATION
American Express Office......(see 75)
Banco do Brasil......1 A4
Banco do Brasil......2 B2
Bradesco......3 A4
Bradesco ATM......4 B3
Bradesco ATM......5 A4
Bradesco ATM......6 C2
Canadian Consulate......7 D2
Casa Universal......8 C2
Drogaria Pacheco......9 D2
Fone Rio......10 B3
Help......11 B4
HSBC......12 D1
HSBC......13 A5
Instituto Brasil-Estados Unidos..14 B3
Locutório......15 A4
Post Office......16 B2
Riotur......17 D1
Telenet......18 B3
Teleredo......19 D2
Ticketronics......(see 28)
SIGHTS
Forte de Copacabana......20 B5
SHOPPING
Argumento......21 B2
Arte Brasilis......22 A5
Av Altântica Fair......23 B4
Bossa Nova & Companhia......24 D2
Deu La Deu Vinhos......25 B3
Favela Hype......(see 26)
Galeria River......26 A5
Maria de Barro......27 C2
Modern Sound......28 B2
Mundo Verde......29 B2
Musicale......30 A4
Praça do Lido Market......31 D2
Shopping Cassino Atlântico Antiques Fair......32 B5
Shopping Siqueira Campos......33 B2
EATING
Amir......34 D2
Arataca......35 B3
Atlântico......(see 97)
Azumi......36 D2
Bakers......37 B2
Bibi Crepes......38 A4
Capricciosa......39 B3
Carretão......40 D2
Cervantes......41 D1
Cipriani......(see 75)
Confeitaria Colombo......(see 20)
Copa Café......42 B3
Don Camillo......43 B3
Galeria 1618......44 D1
La Fiorentina......45 E1
La Trattoria......46 C2
Le Blé Noir......47 A4
Le Pré Catalan......(see 101)
Miss Tanaka......48 D2
Pontinho......49 A2
Shirley......50 E1
Siri Mole & Cia......51 A5
São Sebastião......52 E1
Traiteurs de France......53 C2
Yonza......54 B4
THE ARTS
Espaço SESC......55 B3
Roxy......56 A3
DRINKING
Copa Café......(see 42)
Copacabana Palace Poolside Bar......(see 75)
Espelunca Chic......57 B3
Horse's Neck......(see 101)
Sindicato do Chopp......58 E1
Sindicato do Chopp......59 A5

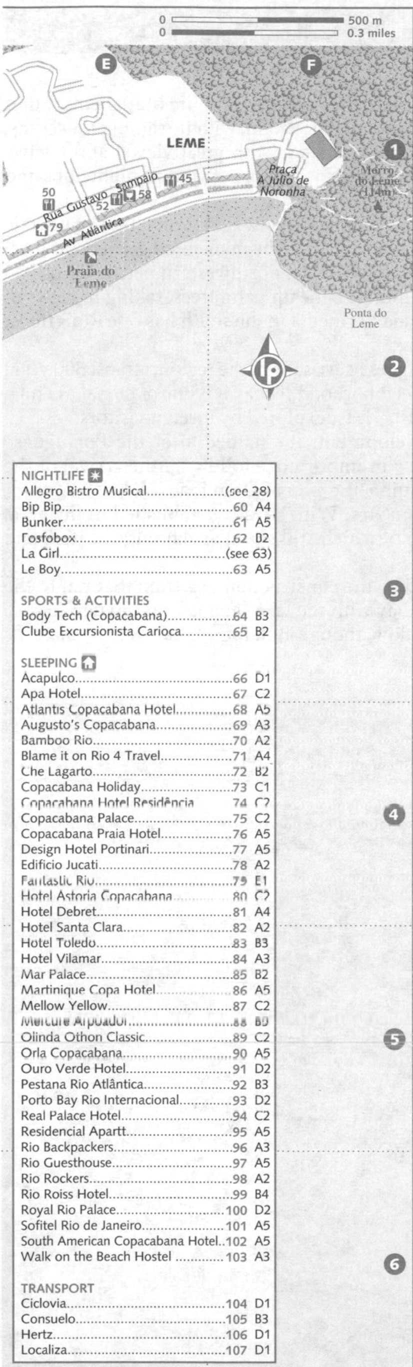

Av Atlântica if you take a stroll. Av NS de Copacabana (NS stands for *Nossa Senhora*, meaning Our Lady) is also dangerous – watch out at weekends, when the shops are closed and there are few locals around.

FORTE DE COPACABANA Map pp76–7

2521 1032; Av Atlântica & Rua Francisco Otaviano; admission R$4; 10am-4pm Tue-Sun

Built in 1914 on the promontory of the old Our Lady of Copacabana chapel, the fort of Copacabana was one of Rio's premier defenses against attack. You can still see its original features, including walls up to 12m thick, defended by Krupp cannons. Inside is a museum with several floors of exhibits tracing the early days of the Portuguese colony to the mid-19th-century, the exhibits aren't the most tastefully done, but the view alone is worth a visit. Be sure to stop in the beautifully sited Confeitaria Colombo (p142).

MORRO DO LEME Map pp76–7

2275 7696; 8am-4pm Sat & Sun, tour reservations required

East of Av Princesa Isabel, Morro do Leme contains an environmental protection area. The 11 hectares of Atlantic rain forest are home to numerous species of birds, such as the saddle and bishop tanagers, thrushes and the East Brazilian house wren. An hour-long tour is available by booking ahead. Tours meet at the Praça Almirante Júlio de Noronha.

BOTAFOGO & URCA

Eating p143; Shopping p120; Sleeping p197

The traditional, middle-class neighborhood of Botafogo may lack the allure of Ipanema, but it doesn't lack much else. There's a lot going on in this neighborhood, with intriguing museums, several movie theaters, quaint bookshops, a shopping center (with great views) and festive, open-air bars set along tranquil back streets. There are also a couple of vibrant nightclubs and a boulevard dotted with old mansions.

Neighboring Urca is even more idyllic, with shaded, quiet streets. Here, you'll find an eclectic mix of architecture, with art-deco and modernist houses backed by manicured gardens, as local residents stroll past them. Along the seawall, which forms the northwestern perimeter of Pão de Açúcar, fishermen cast for dinner as couples lounge beneath palm trees, taking in views of Baía de Guanabara and Cristo Redentor. Tiny Praia Vermelha in the south has one Rio's finest beach views. A pleasant walking trail begins there.

Although it was the site of one of the first Portuguese garrisons in the region, almost 300 years elapsed before Urca developed into a residential neighborhood. Today it is one of the safest and – in spite of the Pão de Açúcar cable car in its midst – least explored by foreign visitors.

Botafogo, on the other hand, saw early development. It's named after the Portuguese settler João Pereira de Souza Botafogo, and grew in importance following the arrival of the Portuguese court in the late 1800s. Carlota Joaquina, the wife of Dom João VI, had a country villa, and she used to bathe in the Baía de Guanabara. With royalty established in the area, arriving aristocrats built many mansions, some of which still stand as schools, theaters and cultural centers.

In the 19th century, development was spurred by the construction of a tram that ran to the botanical garden (Jardim Botânico), linking the bay with the lake (Lagoa Rodrigo de Freitas). This artery still plays a vital role in Rio's traffic flow, though Botafogo's main streets are now extremely congested.

BOTAFOGO & URCA

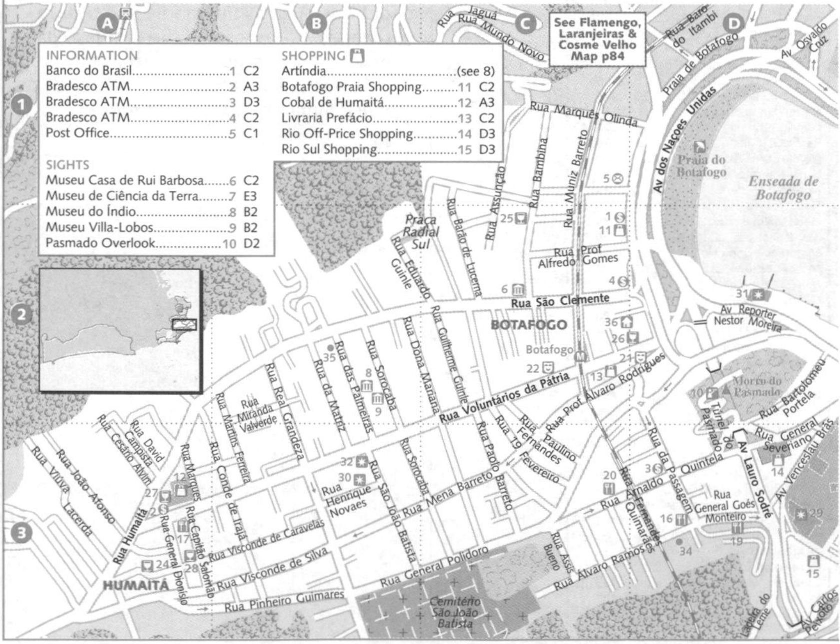

INFORMATION
Banco do Brasil 1 C2
Bradesco ATM 2 A3
Bradesco ATM 3 D3
Bradesco ATM 4 C2
Post Office 5 C1
SIGHTS
Museu Casa de Rui Barbosa 6 C2
Museu de Ciência da Terra 7 E3
Museu do Índio 8 B2
Museu Villa-Lobos 9 B2
Pasmado Overlook 10 D2
SHOPPING
Artíndia (see 8)
Botafogo Praia Shopping 11 C2
Cobal de Humaitá 12 A3
Livraria Prefácio 13 C2
Rio Off-Price Shopping 14 D3
Rio Sul Shopping 15 D3
See Flamengo, Laranjeiras & Cosme Velho Map p84
BOTAFOGO
HUMAITÁ
Enseada de Botafogo
Praia do Botafogo
Morro do Pasmado
Cemitério São João Batista
Praça Radial Sul
Rua São Clemente
Rua Voluntários da Pátria
Av dos Nações Unidas
Praia de Botafogo
Rua Marquês Olinda
Rua Humaitá
Rua Real Grandeza
Rua General Polidoro
Av Lauro Sodré

BOTAFOGO

MUSEU CASA DE RUI BARBOSA

Map pp78–9

☎ 3289 4600; www.casaruibarbosa.gov.br in Portuguese; Rua São Clemente 134; admission R$2; 🕑 9am-5.30pm Tue-Fri, 2-6pm Sat & Sun

The former mansion (completely restored in 2003) of famous Brazilian journalist and diplomat Rui Barbosa is now a museum housing his library and personal belongings, along with an impressive archive of manuscripts and first editions of other Brazilian authors, such as Machado de Assis and José de Alençar. Barbosa played a major role in shaping the country's socioeconomic development in the early 20th century.

MUSEU DO ÍNDIO Map pp78–9

☎ 2286 8899; www.museudoindio.org.br; Rua das Palmeiras 55; admission R$3; 🕑 9am-5.30pm Tue-Fri, 1-5pm Sat & Sun

Featuring multimedia exhibitions on Brazil's northern tribes, the small Museu do Índio provides an excellent introduction to the economic, religious and social life of Brazil's indigenous people. Next to native food and medicinal plants, the four life-size dwellings in the courtyard were actually built by four different tribes. As a branch of Funai (the National Indian Foundation), the museum contains an excellent archive of more than 14,000 objects, 50,000 photographs and 200 sound recordings. Its indigenous ethnography library containing 16,000 volumes by local and foreign authors is open to the public during the week.

PRAIA DO BOTAFOGO Map pp78–9

Av dos Naçoes Unidas

Although the waters of the bay are too polluted for swimming, the beach overlooking the Enseada de Botafogo (Botafogo Inlet) makes a photogenic setting for a stroll. Hopeful soccer stars play pick-up games along the shore against the backdrop of sailboats bobbing on the water and Pão de Açúcar off in the background.

PASMADO OVERLOOK Map pp78–9

Rua Bartolomeu Portela

Sweeping views of Enseada de Botafogo, Pão de Açúcar and Corcovado await visitors who make the journey up Pasmado. It's best reached in early morning or late

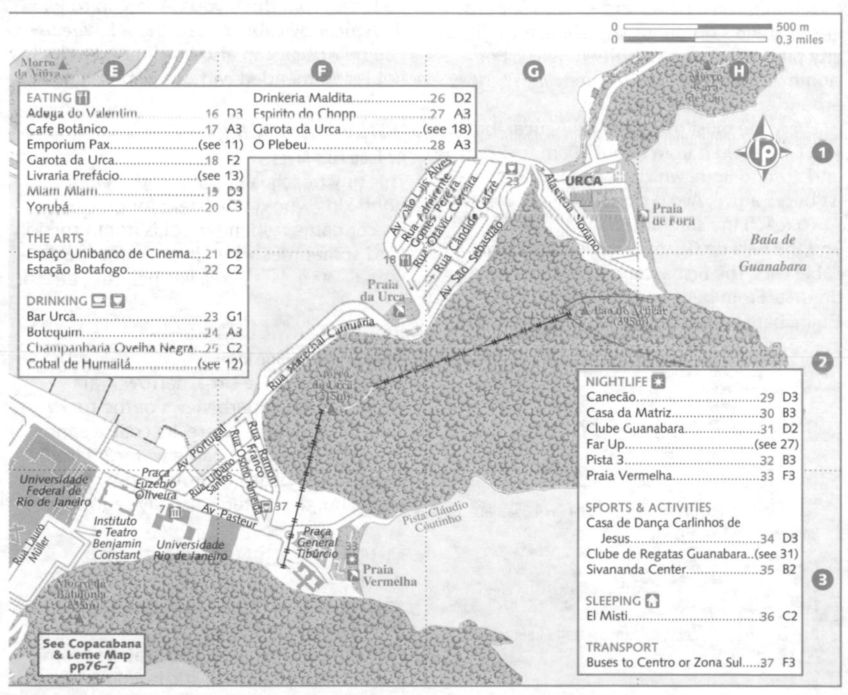

afternoon, when the light is at its best for capturing the postcard panorama. Visitors will also be able to see details of a favela from above. The overlook is best reached by taxi via Rua General Severiano.

MUSEU VILLA-LOBOS Map pp78–9

☎ 2266 3845; Rua Sorocaba 200; admission free; 🕑 10am-5.30pm Mon-Fri

Housed in a century-old building, the modest museum is dedicated to the memory of Brazil's greatest classical composer – and founder of the Brazilian Academy of Music – Heitor Villa-Lobos. In addition to scores, musical instruments – including the piano on which he composed – and personal items, the museum contains an extensive sound archive. Classical concerts are sometimes held in the adjoining courtyard.

URCA

PÃO DE AÇÚCAR Map pp78–9

☎ 2546 8400; Praça General Tibúrcio; adult/child R$35/17; 🕑 8am-10pm

One of Rio's dazzling icons, Pão de Açúcar (Sugarloaf) offers a vision of Rio at its most disarming. Following a steep ascent up the mountain, you'll be rewarded with superb views of Rio's gorgeous shoreline, and the city planted among the green peaks. For prime views of the *cidade maravilhosa,* go around sunset on a clear day.

Everyone must go to Pão de Açúcar, but if you can, avoid it from about 10am to 11am and 2pm to 3pm, which is when most tourist buses arrive. Avoid cloudy days as well.

To reach the summit, 395m above Rio and the Baía de Guanabara, you take two cable cars. The first ascends 215m to Morro da Urca. From here, you can see Baía de Guanabara and along the winding coastline.

TRANSPORTATION: BOTAFOGO & URCA

Botafogo

Bus Ipanema, Leblon and Copacabana (574), Jardim Botânico and Gávea (158)

Metro Botafogo

Urca

Bus Centro (107), Leblon, Ipanema and Copacabana (511 & 512)

On the ocean side of the mountain is Praia Vermelha, in a small, calm bay. Morro da Urca has a restaurant, souvenir shops, a playground, outdoor theater and a helipad (p225).

The second cable car goes up to Pão de Açúcar. At the top, the city unfolds beneath you, with Corcovado mountain and Cristo Redentor off to the west, and the long curve of Copacabana beach to the south. If the breathtaking heights unsteady you, a drink stand is on hand to serve caipirinhas or cups of Skol (beer). The two-stage cable cars depart every 30 minutes.

Those who'd rather take the long way to the summit should sign up with one of the granite-hugging climbing tours (p181) offered by various outfits in Rio.

PISTA CLÁUDIO COUTINHO Map pp78–9

🕑 6am-sunset

Everyone loves this paved 2km trail winding along the southern contour of Morro do Urca. It's a lush treed area, with the waves crashing on the rocks below. Look out for families of capuchin monkeys with their gray fur, striped tails and tiny faces. About 300m along the path, there's a small unmarked trail leading off the path to Morro da Urca. From there you can go up to Pão de Açúcar by cable car, saving a few *reais*. Pão de Açúcar can also be climbed – but it's not recommended without climbing gear.

PRAIA DA URCA Map pp78–9

Av João Luis Alves

This tiny beach is popular with neighborhood kids who gather here for pick-up soccer games when school is not in session (and sometimes when it is). A small restaurant, Garota da Urca (p143), lies near the beach.

PRAIA VERMELHA Map pp78–9

Praça General Tibúrcio

Beneath Morro da Urca, narrow Praia Vermelha has superb views of the rocky coastline from the shore. Its coarse sand gives the beach the name *vermelha* (red). Because the beach is protected by the headland, the water is usually calm.

MUSEU DE CIÊNCIA DA TERRA Map pp78–9

☎ 2295 7596; Av Pasteur 404; admission free; 🕑 10am-4pm Tue-Sun

With curved staircases and statues looming out front, this majestic building went through a number of incarnations before it finally ended up housing the Earth Science Museum. The museum mostly appeals to children, who still marvel at some of the life-sized dinosaurs on display. The four-room exhibit gives a quick overview of the natural history of Brazil since the big bang. Other rooms showcase the museum's extensive collection of minerals, rocks and meteorites – 5000 pieces in all.

URCA, THE VILLAGE BY THE SEA

Walking Tour

One of Rio's most charming neighborhoods is also one of its least explored. The peaceful streets are lined with trees, beautiful houses and lush gardens. Out by the bay, fishermen cast their lines just beyond the rocky shoreline as couples lounge on the seawall, Corcovado framing the scene.

1 Cassino da Urca Our walk begins where Rua Marechal Cantuária meets Av São Sebastião. On your left, you'll see Cassino da Urca, or at least what remains of the once popular gambling and nightspot, where Carmen Miranda and Josephine Baker both performed.

2 Carmen Miranda's former residence Veer to the right along Av São Sebastião, following the road uphill. You'll pass Carmen Miranda's former residence at number 131 and soon reach the wall that separates the military fort from the neighborhood.

3 Bar Urca When you get to the end of the street, take the steps down to Av João Luis Alves. Stop for a cold drink at Bar Urca (p156), while admiring the splendid views across the bay.

4 Rua Otávio Correira Explore the backstreets of Urca by heading down Rua Otávio

> **WALK FACTS**
>
> Start Rua Marechal Cantuária
> End Praia Vermelha
> Distance 4km
> Duration Three hours
> Fuel stop Garota da Urca (p143)

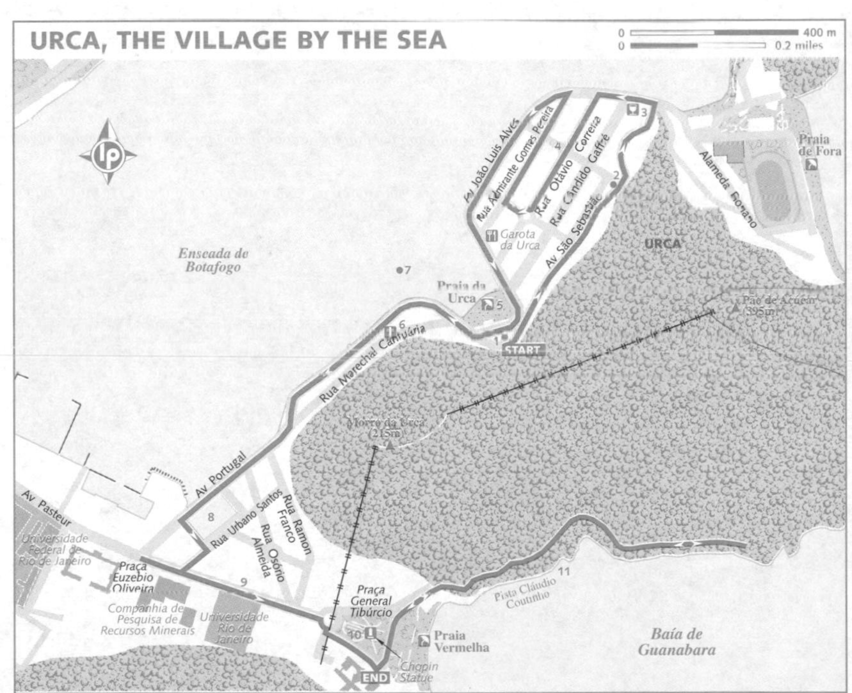

Correira and looping back along Rua Admirante Gomes Pereira to get a glimpse of the charming houses in the neighborhood.

5 Praia da Urca Cut back to Av João Luis Alves and follow it to Praia da Urca (p80). You have the option of walking across the sand or taking the road around.

6 Igreja de Nossa Senhora do Brasil Stick to the bay side as the road forks. Look for the small Igreja de Nossa Senhora do Brasil. Peek inside the small church (the chapel is on the ground floor; the church is upstairs), noting the small Brazilian flag on the Madonna's cloak on your way out.

7 São Pedro no Mar statue Facing the church is the floating statue of São Pedro no Mar. On June 29, St Peter's feast day, the fishermen make a procession across the bay, past the statue, scattering flowers across the water.

8 Quadrado da Urca Keep going along the avenue, now called Av Portugal, and you'll reach a bridge. To your left is the Quadrado da Urca, which is a harbor for a small collection of fishing boats. After crossing the bridge, turn left onto Rua Elmano Cardim and right onto Rua Urbano Santos, which runs into Av Pasteur.

9 Av Pasteur Follow this avenue southeast, passing Urca's most majestic buildings, including the Companhia de Pesquisa de Recursos Minerais (guarded by a lion) and the neoclassical Universidade Federal do Rio de Janeiro.

10 Praça General Tibúrcio Just beyond the cable-car station to Pão de Açúcar, is the nicely laid-out Praça General Tibúrcio. Keep walking toward the sea and you'll reach the statue of Chopin, donated to the city by Rio's Polish community.

11 Pista Cláudio Coutinho The last part of the tour follows the paved Pista Cláudio Coutinho (p80) out and back. Keep an eye out for capuchin monkeys and parrots, and enjoy the verdant setting, the waves crashing against the rocks below and the panoramic views out to sea.

FLAMENGO, LARANJEIRAS & COSME VELHO

Eating p143; Shopping p121; Sleeping p197

Running east from the bay out to Corcovado, these three residential neighborhoods have much history hidden in their old streets. Some even believe Flamengo was the site of Rio's first Portuguese-built house. The neighborhood was certainly Rio's finest residential district in the 19th century, though it lost its luster when the tunnel to Copacabana was completed, and the upper classes migrated south. Today this region contains both remnants from the colonial past and some highly successful urban development projects from more recent times.

The Parque do Flamengo dominates the region. Also known as the *aterro* (landfill), this beach-fronting green space is one of the world's largest urban parks, with a nationally recognized art museum, biking and running trails, sports fields and thousands of trees and flowering plants. Inland from the park, the shaded streets of Flamengo are sprinkled with a few cafés, historic botecos and gossip-filled juice bars.

West of Flamengo, Laranjeiras is a tightly interwoven community with a small-town feel to the district. Charming plazas like the Praça São Salvador are a great spot for just taking in the neighborhood.

Cosme Velho lies beyond Laranjeiras and is a major destination for visitors heading up to the statue of Cristo Redentor by the old-fashioned cog train. Nearby is the colorful Largo do Boticário, a frozen-in-time plaza from 19th-century Rio. Cosme Velho and Laranjeiras both have a few nightlife options, including several jazz cafés and nightclubs.

FLAMENGO

PARQUE DO FLAMENGO Map p84

Officially called Parque Brigadeiro Eduardo Gomes, Parque do Flamengo was the result of a landfill project that leveled the São Antônio hill in 1965, and now spreads all the way from downtown Rio through Glória, Catete and Flamengo, and on around to Botafogo. The 1.2 million sq meters of land reclaimed from the sea now stages every manner of Carioca outdoor activity. Cyclists and rollerbladers glide along the myriad paths, while the many soccer fields and sports courts are framed against the sea. On Sundays and holidays, the avenues through the park are closed (from 7am to 6pm).

Designed by famous Brazilian landscaper Burle Marx (who also landscaped Brasília), the park features some 170,000 trees of 300 different species. In addition there are three museums in the park: the Museu de Arte Moderna (p89), the Monumento Nacional aos Mortos da II Guerra Mundial (p95) and the Museu Carmen Miranda (right).

ARTE SESC CULTURAL CENTER Map p84

☎ 3138 1343; www.sescrio.org.br in Portuguese; Rua Marquês de Abrantes 99; admission free; noon-6pm Tue & Wed, noon-8pm Thu-Sat, 11am-5pm Sun

This small cultural center is housed in an early-20th-century mansion built by Czech entrepreneur Frederico Figner. His record company is better known than he is – Odeon records being one of the top labels in the country. The small gallery features good exhibits, often highlighting Rio's development in the early 20th century. Downstairs is the excellent Senac Bistrô (p144).

MUSEU CARMEN MIRANDA Map p84

☎ 2299 5586; facing Av Rui Barbosa 560; admission free; 10am-5pm Tue-Fri, 1-5pm Sat & Sun

Carmen Miranda was once the highest-paid entertainer in the USA. She's the only Brazilian to leave her prints in Hollywood's

TRANSPORTATION: FLAMENGO, LARANJEIRAS & COSME VELHO

Flamengo

Bus Leblon, Ipanema and Copacabana (571 and 572)

Metro Flamengo, Largo do Machado

Laranjeiras

Bus Copacabana (426), Ipanema (456), Leblon (435)

Cosme Velho

Bus From Copacabana, Ipanema or Leblon (570); to Copacabana, Ipanema or Leblon (569); from Centro, Glória or Flamengo (180); to Centro, Glória or Flamengo (422)

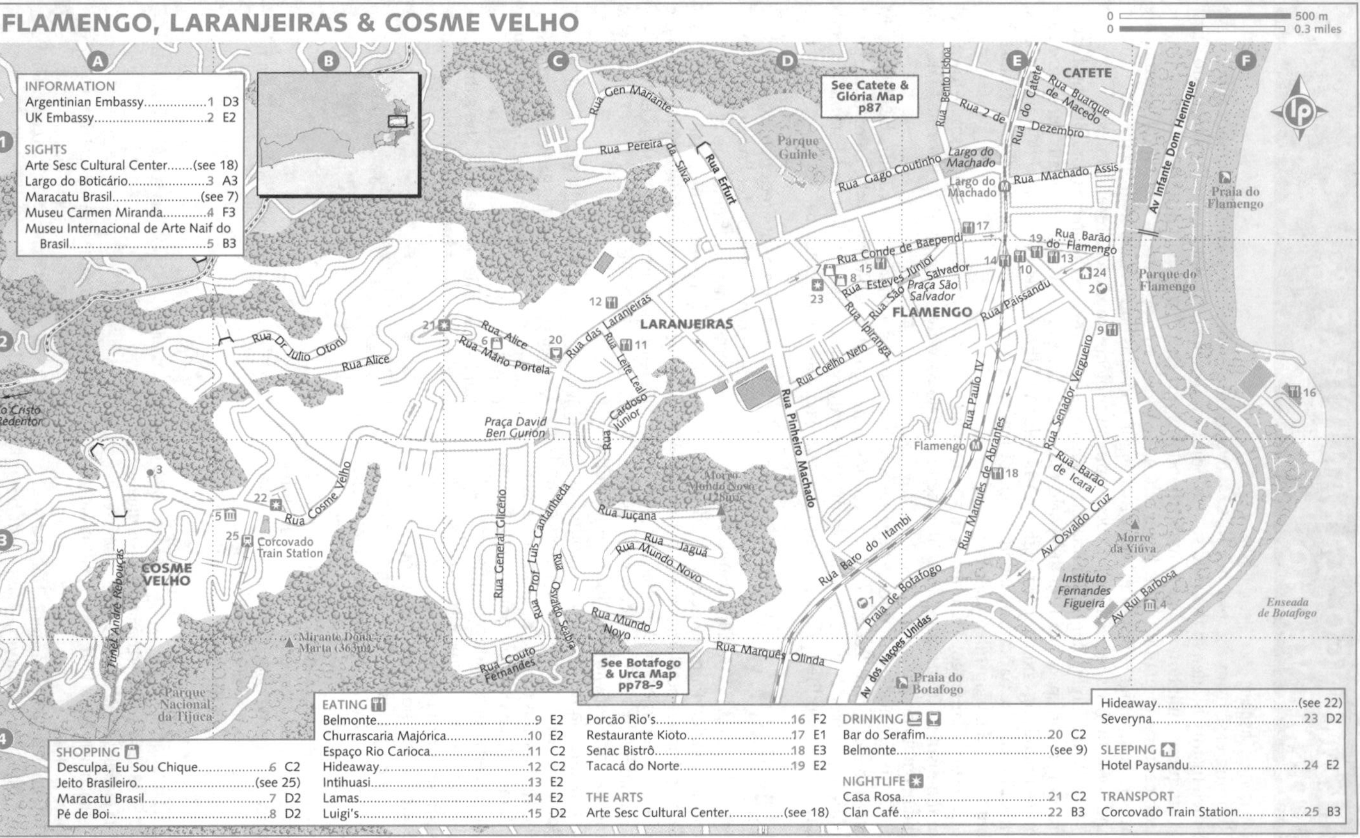
FLAMENGO, LARANJEIRAS & COSME VELHO
0 500 m
0 0.3 miles
INFORMATION
Argentinian Embassy.....1 D3
UK Embassy.....2 E2
SIGHTS
Arte Sesc Cultural Center.....(see 18)
Largo do Boticário.....3 A3
Maracatu Brasil.....(see 7)
Museu Carmen Miranda.....4 F3
Museu Internacional de Arte Naif do Brasil.....5 B3
SHOPPING
Desculpa, Eu Sou Chique.....6 C2
Jeito Brasileiro.....(see 25)
Maracatu Brasil.....7 D2
Pé de Boi.....8 D2
EATING
Belmonte.....9 E2
Churrascaria Majórica.....10 E2
Espaço Rio Carioca.....11 C2
Hideaway.....12 C2
Intihuasi.....13 E2
Lamas.....14 E2
Luigi's.....15 D2
Porcão Rio's.....16 F2
Restaurante Kioto.....17 E1
Senac Bistrô.....18 E3
Tacacá do Norte.....19 E2
THE ARTS
Arte Sesc Cultural Center.....(see 18)
DRINKING
Bar do Serafim.....20 C2
Belmonte.....(see 9)
NIGHTLIFE
Casa Rosa.....21 C2
Clan Café.....22 B3
Hideaway.....(see 22)
Severyna.....23 D2
SLEEPING
Hotel Paysandu.....24 E2
TRANSPORT
Corcovado Train Station.....25 B3
See Catete & Glória Map p87
See Botafogo & Urca Map pp78-9
CATETE
LARANJEIRAS
FLAMENGO
COSME VELHO
To Cristo Redentor
Parque Guinle
Parque do Flamengo
Praia do Flamengo
Praia do Botafogo
Enseada de Botafogo
Morro da Viúva
Instituto Fernandes Figueira
Mirante Dona Marta (363m)
Parque Nacional da Tijuca
Praça David Ben Gurion
Praça São Salvador
Largo do Machado
Flamengo
Corcovado Train Station
Av Infante Dom Henrique
Rua Pinheiro Machado
Rua das Laranjeiras
Rua Cosme Velho
Rua Alice
Rua Dr Julio Otoni
Rua Mário Portela
Túnel André Rebouças
Rua Marquês de Abrantes
Rua Senador Vergueiro
Rua do Catete
Rua Machado Assis
Rua Gago Coutinho
Rua Pereira da Silva
Rua Gen Mariante
Rua Erfurt
Rua Conde de Baependi
Rua Paissandu
Rua Paulo IV
Rua Coelho Neto
Rua Ipiranga
Rua Esteves Júnior
Rua São Salvador
Rua Barão do Flamengo
Rua Barão de Icaraí
Av Osvaldo Cruz
Av Rui Barbosa
Praia de Botafogo
Av dos Nações Unidas
Rua Baro do Itambi
Rua Marquês Olinda
Rua Mundo Novo
Rua Jaguá
Rua Juçana
Rua Osvaldo Seabra
Rua Prof Luís Cantanheda
Rua General Glicério
Rua Couto Fernandes
Rua Cardoso Júnior
Rua Leite Leal
Rua Bento Lisboa
Rua 2 de Dezembro
Rua Buarque de Macedo

RIO'S FAVORITE SAVIOR

Named one of the world's seven new wonders in 2007, Cristo Redentor is Brazil's largest monument and certainly its most widely recognized. The Redeemer, who turned 75 in 2006, is not a gift from the French – as popular urban legend has it. In fact, Cristo was designed by the Carioca architect-engineer Heitor Silva Costa (1873–1947), who also designed the Cathedral of Petrópolis. Many organizations helped make the statue a reality including several individuals who went door-to-door asking for contributions. The idea of the statue originated in 1921 when a group called Círculo Carioca held a competition for a religious monument to commemorate Brazil's upcoming 100 years of independence. Heitor's winning project, which took 10 years to build, was considered particularly ambitious at the time – naysayers doubted whether it could be accomplished at all. Heitor's original idea depicted Christ as a vertical form with a long cross held against his side, but the committee wanted something recognizable from a great distance, so the cross-like outstretched arms were chosen instead. Today it's one of Brazil's most visited sites, welcoming more than 600,000 people a year.

Walk of Fame. Although she's largely forgotten there, the talented Brazilian singer still has her fans in Rio and has become a cult icon among the gay community. For those interested in getting to know one of Brazil's stars of the '40s, the small museum dedicated to her is an excellent starting point. It has photographs and music of that era and the starlet's iconographic costumes and jewelry.

LARANJEIRAS

MARACATU BRASIL Map p84

☎ 2557 4754; www.maracatubrasil.com.br; 2nd fl, Rua Ipiranga 49; ⏰ 10am-6pm Mon-Sat

One of Rio's best places to study percussion, Maracatu Brasil is very active in music events throughout the city. Instructors here offer courses in a number of different drumming styles: *zabumba, pandeiro,* symphonic percussion and others. If you plan to stick around a while, you can arrange private lessons (R$250 for four one-hour classes) or sign up for group classes (R$80 to R$120 a month). On the 1st floor of the lime-green building, Maracatu sells instruments (p121).

COSME VELHO

CRISTO REDENTOR Map pp60–1

☎ 2558 1329; www.corcovado.org.br; Rua Cosme Velho 513 (cog station); cog train & admission R$36; ⏰ 8.30am-6.30pm

One of Rio's most identifiable landmarks, the magnificent 38m-high Cristo Redentor (Christ the Redeemer) looms large atop Corcovado. From here, the statue – all 1145 tons of him – has stunning views over Rio (which explains the contented expression on his face). Corcovado, which means 'hunchback,' rises straight up from the city to a height of 710m, and at night, the brightly lit statue is visible from nearly every part of the city.

When you reach the top, you'll notice the Redeemer's gaze directed at Pão de Açúcar (p80), with his left arm pointing toward the Zona Norte, and Maracanã football stadium crowding the foreground. You can also see the international airport on Ilha do Governador just beyond and the Serra dos Órgãos mountain range in the far distance. Beneath Christ's right arm is the Lagoa Rodrigo de Freitas, Hipódromo de Gávea, Jardim Botânico, and over to Ipanema and Leblon.

Corcovado lies within the Parque Nacional da Tijuca. You can get here by car or by taxi, but the best way is to go up in the cog train (departures every 30 minutes). For the best view, sit on the right-hand side going up. You can also drive to the top. Taxi drivers typically charge around R$10 per person (plus R$5 per person entrance fee) for return trips with waiting time.

Be sure to choose a clear day to visit.

LARGO DO BOTICÁRIO Map p84

Rua Cosme Velho 822

The brightly painted houses on this picturesque square date from the early 19th century. Largo do Boticário was named in honor of the Portuguese gentleman – Joaquim Luiz da Silva Souto – who once ran a *boticário* (apothecary), utilized by the royal family. The sound of a brook coming from the nearby forest adds to the square's charm. Occasional art and cultural events are hosted here.

CATETE & GLÓRIA

Eating p145; Sleeping p197

The aging buildings of bustling Catete and Glória have certainly seen better days. Like Flamengo, these twin districts flourished in the mid-19th century. In those days, their location at the outskirts of the city made them highly desirable places to live. Many noblemen and merchants built stately homes in this district, including the Barão de Novo Friburgo, who built the stately Palácio do Catete. By the end of the century, though, the wealthy began moving further out as the inner city expanded – a trend that continues today.

The Palácio do Catete, which once served as the republic's seat of power, remains the jewel of the neighborhood, and its attached gardens are a peaceful refuge from the often chaotic streets outside.

A few blocks north lies another historic beauty, the Igreja de Nossa Senhora da Glória do Outeiro. Atop a small hill overlooking the bay, the baroque church dates from the 18th century and was a favorite of Dom Pedro II and the royal family.

Aside from these vestiges of the past, most of the area is now a working-class area of greasy lunch counters, discount clothing and hardware shops and unkempt juice bars. Some of the once magnificent mansions now house second-rate hotels in serious need of renovation. With many budget options among these crumbling façades, Glória and Catete attract shoestring travelers who don't mind the workaday bustle.

CATETE

MUSEU DA REPÚBLICA Map p87

☎ 3235 2650; www.museudarepublica.org.br; Rua do Catete 153; admission R$6, free on Wed & Sun; 🕑 noon-5pm Tue-Fri, 2-6pm Sat & Sun

The Museu da República, located in the Palácio do Catete, has been wonderfully restored. Built between 1858 and 1866 and easily distinguished by the bronze condors on the eaves, the palace was home to the president of Brazil from 1896 until 1954, when President Getúlio Vargas committed suicide here.

He had made powerful enemies in the armed forces and the political right wing, and was attacked in the press as a communist for his attempts to raise the minimum wage and increase taxes on the middle and upper classes. Tensions reached a critical level when one of Vargas' bodyguards fired shots at a journalist. Although the journalist was unharmed, an air force officer guarding him was killed, giving the armed forces the pretext they needed to demand the resignation of Vargas. In response, Vargas committed suicide, and his emotional suicide note read, 'I choose this means to be with you [the Brazilian people] always…I gave you my life; now I offer my death.' The bedroom in which the suicide occurred is eerily preserved on the 3rd floor.

The museum has a good collection of art and artifacts from the Republican period, and also houses a good lunch restaurant, art-house cinema and bookstore.

TRANSPORTATION: CATETE & GLÓRIA

Bus Ipanema, Leblon and Copacabana (571)

Metro Largo do Machado, Catete, Glória

CENTRO CULTURAL OI FUTURO Map p87

☎ 3131 3060; www.oifuturo.org.br; Rua Dois de Dezembro 63; admission free; 🕑 11am-8pm Tue-Sun

One of Rio's most visually exciting new additions is this modern arts center on the edge of Flamengo. With 2000 sq meters of exhibition space spread across six floors, the center features temporary multimedia installations that run the gamut between architecture and urban design to photojournalism to pop art, to eye-catching video art. There's also a permanent exhibition on the history of telecommunications in Brazil. The top floor houses an auditorium where visitors can attend concerts and plays, or catch a documentary.

PARQUE GUINLE & THE PALÁCIO DAS LARANJEIRAS Map p87

☎ 2299 5689; Rua Paulo Cesar de Andrade 407; 🕑 palace guided visits by appointment 2pm & 3pm, Tue & Thu

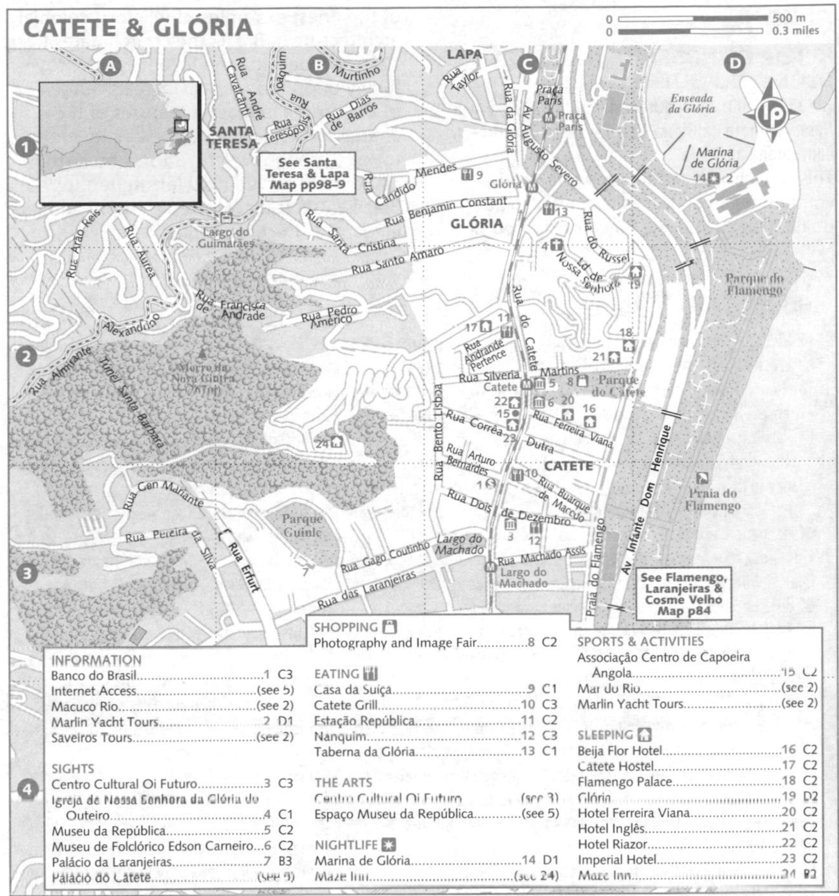

Designed by French landscaper Gochet, the park has a European air, and has a small lake, lanes and lawns. Overlooking the park is the resplendent Palácio da Laranjeiras, built between 1909 and 1914 by architect Silva Telles. Today it is the official residence in Rio of the state governor, and contains the same artwork, furniture and ornamental objects from when the palace was built. You can tour parts of the palace by guided appointments.

MUSEU DE FOLCLÓRICO EDSON CARNEIRO Map p87

☎ 2285 0441; Rua do Catete 179; admission free; 🕑 11am-6pm Tue-Fri, 3-6pm Sat & Sun

Created in 1968, the museum is an excellent introduction to Brazilian folk art, particularly from the northeast. Its permanent collection comprises 1400 pieces, and includes Candomblé costumes, ceramic figurines and religious costumes used in festivals. The museum also features a folklore library and a small shop, selling handicrafts, books and folk music. The museum is located next door to the Palácio do Catete.

PARQUE DO CATETE Map p87

☎ 2205 0090; Rua do Catete 181; admission free; 🕑 11am-6pm Tue-Fri, 3-6pm Sat & Sun

The small landscaped park on the grounds of the Palácio do Catete provides a quiet refuge from the city. Its pond and shade-covered walks are popular with neighborhood strollers and children. Special performances in the park include concerts and plays.

GLÓRIA

IGREJA DE NOSSA SENHORA DA GLÓRIA DO OUTEIRO Map p87

☎ 2557 4600; www.outeirodagloria.org.br; Praça Nossa Senhora da Glória 135; ⏲ 8am-5pm Tue-Fri, 8am-noon Sat & Sun

This tiny church atop Ladeira da Glória commands lovely views out over Parque do Flamengo and the bay. Considered one of the finest examples of religious colonial architecture in Brazil, the church dates from 1739 and became the favorite of the royal family upon their arrival in 1808. Some of the more fascinating features of the church are its octagonal design, its single tower (through which visitors enter), the elaborately carved altar (attributed to the Brazilian sculptor Mestre Valentim) and its elegant, 18th-century tiles.

HOPE IN RIO'S FAVELAS

Residents of Rio de Janeiro's favelas (shanty towns) face enormous obstacles. Many families live in communities lacking basic essentials (sewers, medical clinics, roads). Children attend some of the city's worst schools (many indeed drop out). The long bus commute to work can often take hours on traffic-snarled roads for a salary that may not even meet living expenses. There's also the social stigma of living in the slums, some of which are run by local drug lords.

Yet, it isn't all gloom for Rio's estimated one million favela residents. In the last two decades, locally managed organizations have begun appearing in favelas across the city. While small in scale, these non-profits offer residents the chance to learn new skills, gain a sense of pride, and give something often in short supply: hope.

For many poor favela children, the Grupo Cultural Afro Reggae (GCAR) is a lifeline. In 1997 in the Vigário Geral favela, GCAR opened a cultural center offering workshops in music, theatre, dance, hip-hop and capoeira. The center provided kids with a chance to get off the street, tap into their Afro-Brazilian heritage and gain self-esteem in setting and fulfilling goals. Owing to the center's wide popularity, the ideas have spread. GCAR and its favela affiliates now offer more than 60 different programs for poor residents around Rio.

Rocinha, Brazil's largest favela, creates similar opportunities for local residents at its Casa da Cultura. Founded in 2003 by Gilberto Gil, Minister of Culture, singer and neighbor, the center draws on the favela's rich artistic tradition, and offers classes in music, theater and painting. The favela next door, Vidigal, perched on a hillside overlooking Ipanema beach, is the base of the group Nos do Morro (Us from the Favela). This theater group won fame after some of its young actors appeared in the award-winning film *Cidade de Deus* (City of God). Ten of its members performed in *The Two Gentlemen of Verona* for the Royal Shakespeare Company in August 2006.

As many have discovered, the favela has a deep well of talent, but few opportunities. Opportunity is exactly what sociologist Maria Teresa Leal had in mind when she founded a sewing collective in Rocinha in the 1980s. The idea began during Leal's repeat trips to the favela where she encountered many talented seamstresses who had no chance to earn money for their skills. So began Coopa Roca (www.coopa-roca.org.br), a small group of women, each working from home to produce quilts, pillows and craft items made of recycled fabrics and other materials. Today the co-op employs some 150 women, and has even caught the eye of the fashion world, with commissions from Brazilian designers Osklen and Carlos Miele, as well as British designer Paul Smith.

For their part, favelas have made numerous contributions to the city. Rio's biggest party, Carnaval, was born in the favelas, and they continue to be pivotal to the fest. That favelas throw the best parties has long been known to many Cariocas. Today, Baile Funks are the biggest party craze to lure both rich and poor to the gritty neighborhoods on the hillsides. There, DJs spin a blend of Rio's bass-heavy funk music to packed dance floors.

Travellers interested in seeing beneath the stereotypes can visit a favela on a tour (p225), volunteer (p229) or even stay overnight in a favela such as Maze Inn (p198) or Pousada Favelinha (p200).

CENTRO & CINELÂNDIA

Eating p146; Shopping p121

Rio's business and financial hub is a wild architectural medley of old and new, with striking baroque churches and narrow colonial streets juxtaposed with looming office towers and wide, traffic-filled boulevards. During the week, it's all fuss and hurry as Rio's lawyers, secretaries and clerks jostle among the crowded streets. But despite the pace, it's well worth joining the fray as Centro has some of the city's best museums and its most intriguing historical sights, with avant-garde art galleries, 18th-century cathedrals and sprawling royal collections in former imperial buildings.

Many pedestrian-only areas crisscross Centro, and for the urban wanderer, there's no better destination in Rio. The most famous sub-district is known as Saara, a giant street bazaar crammed with discount stores and sprinkled with Lebanese restaurants.

Speaking of eating, Centro's restaurants suit every taste and budget, from greasy diners to elegant French bistros, with excellent per-kilo spots, art-nouveau cafés and old-fashioned pubs. After lunch, Cariocas browse the bookstores, music shops, galleries and curio shops. By workday's end, the bars and streetside cafés buzz with life as Cariocas unwind over ice-cold draughts.

At the southern edge of the business district, Cinelândia's shops, bars, restaurants and movie theaters are popular day and night. The bars and restaurants get crowded at lunch and after work, when street musicians sometimes wander the area. There's a greater mix of Cariocas here than in any other section of the city.

CENTRO

MUSEU DE ARTE MODERNA Map pp90–1

☎ 2240 4944; www.mamrio.org.br in Portuguese; Av Infante Dom Henrique 85; admission R$5; 🕑 noon-6pm Tue-Fri, noon-7pm Sat & Sun

At the northern end of Parque do Flamengo, the Museu de Arte Moderna (MAM) is immediately recognizable by the striking postmodern edifice designed by Alfonso Eduardo Reidy. The landscaping of Burle Marx is no less impressive.

After a devastating fire in 1978 that consumed 90% of its collection, the Museu de Arte Moderna is finally back on its feet, and now houses 11,000 permanent works, including pieces by Brazilian artists Bruno Giorgi, Di Cavalcanti and Maria Martins. Curators often bring excellent photography and design exhibits to the museum, and the cinema hosts regular film festivals throughout the year.

CENTRO CULTURAL BANCO DO BRASIL Map pp90–1

☎ 3808 2000; Rua Primeiro de Março 66; admission free; 🕑 noon-8pm Tue-Sun

Reopened in 1989, the Centro Cultural Banco do Brasil (CCBB) is housed in a beautifully restored 1906 building. It's one of Brazil's best cultural centers, with more than 120,000 visitors per month. Facilities include a cinema, two theaters and a permanent display of the evolution of currency in Brazil. CCBB hosts excellent exhibitions that are among the city's best. A recent display of African art garnered international attention.

There is always something going on at the Centro Cultural Banco do Brasil, from exhibitions, lunchtime and evening concerts, to film screenings, so look at *O Globo's* entertainment listings before you go. Don't miss this place, even if you only pass through the lobby while you're on a walking tour.

MUSEU HISTÓRICO NACIONAL Map pp90–1

☎ 2550 9224; www.museuhistoriconacional.com.br; off Av General Justo near Praça Marechal Âncora; admission R$6; 🕑 10am-5.30pm Tue-Fri, 2-6pm Sat & Sun

One of Rio de Janeiro's best museums, the large National History Museum contains over 250,000 historic relics relating to the history of Brazil – from its founding to its early days as a republic. Its extensive collection is housed on the old arsenal (built in 1764) and includes a full-sized model of a colonial pharmacy, enormous canvases depicting the bloody war with Paraguay, imperial carriages and tiny relics like the writing quill Princesa Isabel used to sign the document abolishing slavery in Brazil.

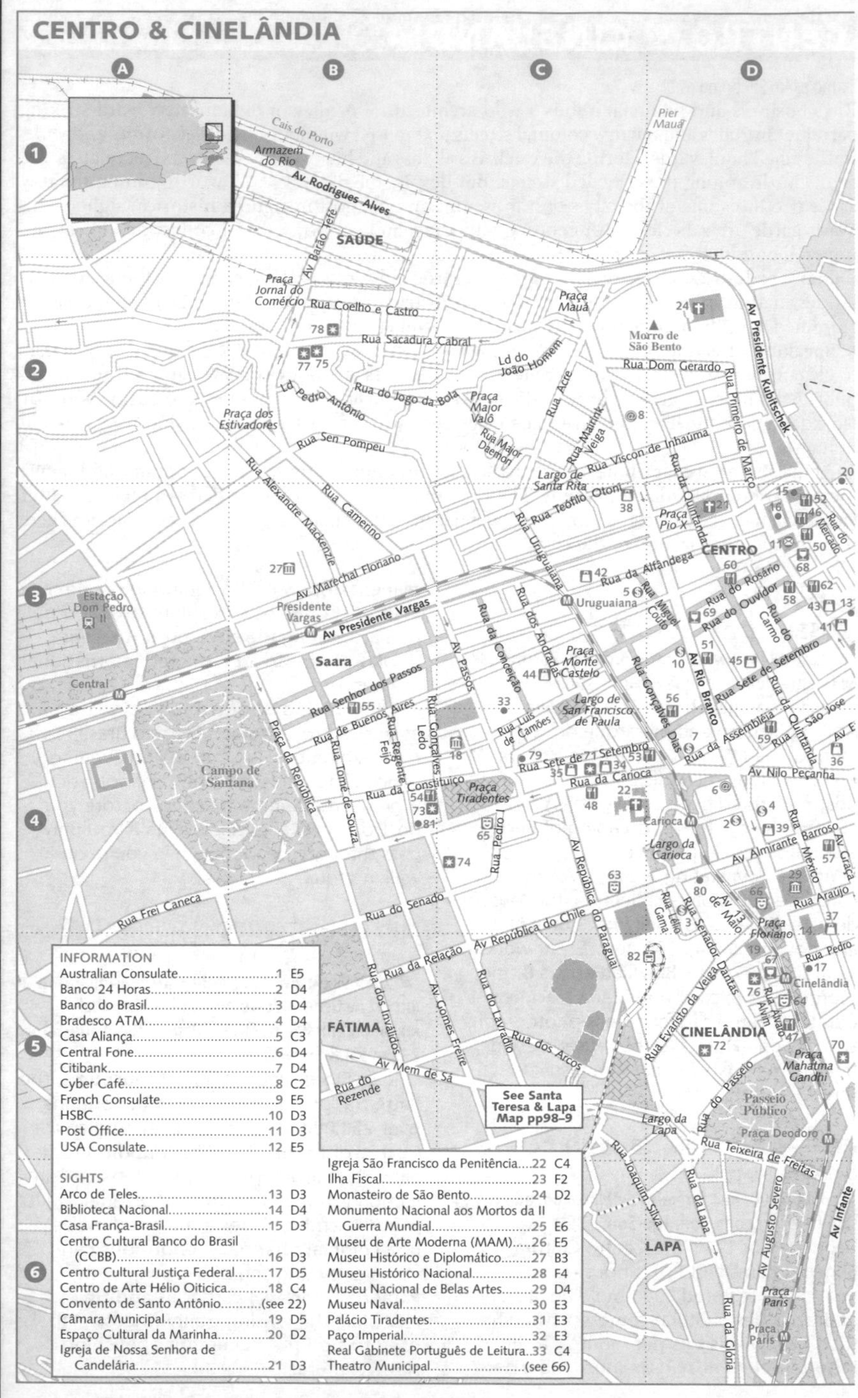
CENTRO & CINELÂNDIA
INFORMATION
Australian Consulate 1 E5
Banco 24 Horas 2 D4
Banco do Brasil 3 D4
Bradesco ATM 4 D4
Casa Aliança 5 C3
Central Fone 6 D4
Citibank 7 D4
Cyber Café 8 C2
French Consulate 9 E5
HSBC 10 D3
Post Office 11 D3
USA Consulate 12 E5
SIGHTS
Arco de Teles 13 D3
Biblioteca Nacional 14 D4
Casa França-Brasil 15 D3
Centro Cultural Banco do Brasil (CCBB) 16 D3
Centro Cultural Justiça Federal 17 D5
Centro de Arte Hélio Oiticica 18 C4
Convento de Santo Antônio (see 22)
Câmara Municipal 19 D5
Espaço Cultural da Marinha 20 D2
Igreja de Nossa Senhora de Candelária 21 D3
Igreja São Francisco da Penitência 22 C4
Ilha Fiscal 23 F2
Monasteiro de São Bento 24 D2
Monumento Nacional aos Mortos da II Guerra Mundial 25 E6
Museu de Arte Moderna (MAM) 26 E5
Museu Histórico e Diplomático 27 B3
Museu Histórico Nacional 28 F4
Museu Nacional de Belas Artes 29 D4
Museu Naval 30 E3
Palácio Tiradentes 31 E3
Paço Imperial 32 E3
Real Gabinete Português de Leitura 33 C4
Theatro Municipal (see 66)
See Santa Teresa & Lapa Map pp98–9
SAÚDE
CENTRO
Saara
FÁTIMA
CINELÂNDIA
LAPA
Cais do Porto
Armazem do Rio
Av Rodrigues Alves
Pier Mauá
Praça Mauá
Morro de São Bento
Av Presidente Kubitschek
Rua Dom Gerardo
Av Presidente Vargas
Av Marechal Floriano
Av Rio Branco
Campo de Santana
Estação Dom Pedro II
Central
Uruguaiana
Carioca
Cinelândia
Praça Tiradentes
Largo da Carioca
Passeio Público
Largo da Lapa
Praça Floriano
Praça Mahatma Gandhi
Praça Paris
Av República do Chile
Av Mem de Sá
Rua do Senado
Rua Frei Caneca
Av Almirante Barroso
Av Nilo Peçanha
Rua Sete de Setembro
Rua da Carioca
Rua do Ouvidor
Rua do Rosário
Rua da Alfândega
Rua da Quitanda
Rua Primeiro de Março
Rua Uruguaiana
Rua Teixeira de Freitas
Rua Joaquim Silva
Rua da Lapa
Av Augusto Severo
Rua da Glória
Av Infante

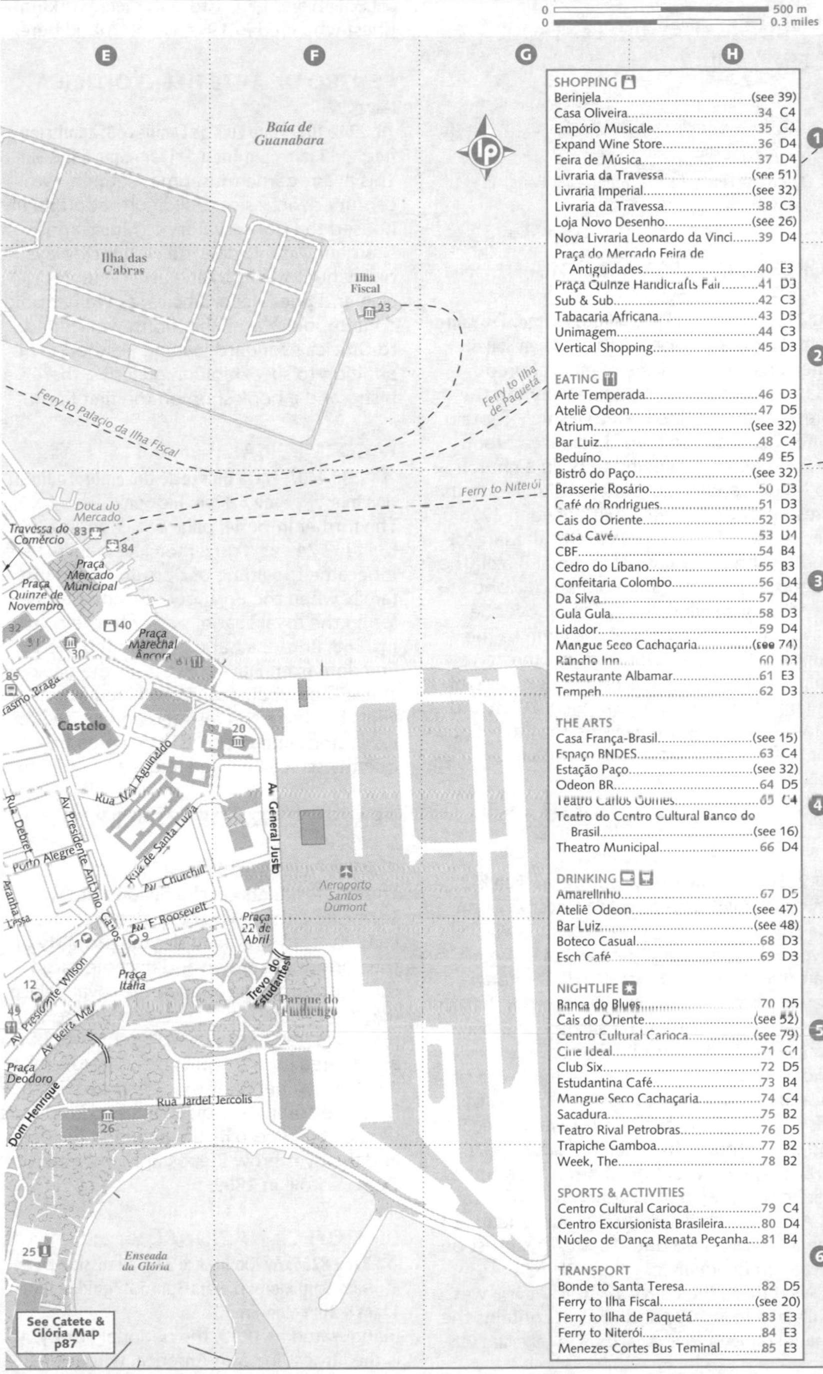
0 500 m
0 0.3 miles
E
F
G
H
Baía de Guanabara
Ilha das Cabras
Ilha Fiscal
Ferry to Palácio da Ilha Fiscal
Ferry to Ilha de Paquetá
Ferry to Niterói
Doca do Mercado
Travessa do Comércio
Praça Mercado Municipal
Praça Quinze de Novembro
Praça Marechal Âncora
Castelo
Rua Erasmo Braga
Rua Debret
Av Presidente Antônio Carlos
Rua de Santa Luzia
Porto Alegre
Av Churchill
Av F Roosevelt
Praça 22 de Abril
Av General Justo
Aeroporto Santos Dumont
Trevo dos Estudantes
Parque do Flamengo
Praça Itália
Av Presidente Wilson
Av Beira Mar
Praça Deodoro
Dom Henrique
Rua Jardel Jercolis
Enseada da Glória
See Catete & Glória Map p87
1
2
3
4
5
6
SHOPPING
Berinjela ...(see 39)
Casa Oliveira ...34 C4
Empório Musicale ...35 C4
Expand Wine Store ...36 D4
Feira de Música ...37 D4
Livraria da Travessa ...(see 51)
Livraria Imperial ...(see 32)
Livraria da Travessa ...38 C3
Loja Novo Desenho ...(see 26)
Nova Livraria Leonardo da Vinci ...39 D4
Praça do Mercado Feira de Antiguidades ...40 E3
Praça Quinze Handicrafts Fair ...41 D3
Sub & Sub ...42 C3
Tabacaria Africana ...43 D3
Unimagem ...44 C3
Vertical Shopping ...45 D3
EATING
Arte Temperada ...46 D3
Ateliê Odeon ...47 D5
Atrium ...(see 32)
Bar Luiz ...48 C4
Beduíno ...49 E5
Bistrô do Paço ...(see 32)
Brasserie Rosário ...50 D3
Café do Rodrigues ...51 D3
Cais do Oriente ...52 D3
Casa Cavé ...53 D4
CBF ...54 B4
Cedro do Líbano ...55 B3
Confeitaria Colombo ...56 D4
Da Silva ...57 D4
Gula Gula ...58 D3
Lidador ...59 D4
Mangue Seco Cachaçaria ...(see 74)
Rancho Inn ...60 D3
Restaurante Albamar ...61 E3
Tempeh ...62 D3
THE ARTS
Casa França-Brasil ...(see 15)
Espaço BNDES ...63 C4
Estação Paço ...(see 32)
Odeon BR ...64 D5
Teatro Carlos Gomes ...65 C4
Teatro do Centro Cultural Banco do Brasil ...(see 16)
Theatro Municipal ...66 D4
DRINKING
Amarelinho ...67 D5
Ateliê Odeon ...(see 47)
Bar Luiz ...(see 48)
Boteco Casual ...68 D3
Esch Café ...69 D3
NIGHTLIFE
Banca do Blues ...70 D5
Cais do Oriente ...(see 52)
Centro Cultural Carioca ...(see 79)
Cine Ideal ...71 C4
Club Six ...72 D5
Estudantina Café ...73 B4
Mangue Seco Cachaçaria ...74 C4
Sacadura ...75 B2
Teatro Rival Petrobras ...76 D5
Trapiche Gamboa ...77 B2
Week, The ...78 B2
SPORTS & ACTIVITIES
Centro Cultural Carioca ...79 C4
Centro Excursionista Brasileira ...80 D4
Núcleo de Dança Renata Peçanha ...81 B4
TRANSPORT
Bonde to Santa Teresa ...82 D5
Ferry to Ilha Fiscal ...(see 20)
Ferry to Ilha de Paquetá ...83 E3
Ferry to Niterói ...84 E3
Menezes Cortes Bus Teminal ...85 E3

TRANSPORTATION: CENTRO & CINELÂNDIA

Bus From the Zona Sul look for the following destinations printed in the window: 'Rio Branco,' 'Praça XV,' 'Praça Tiradentes,' and 'Castelo'

Metro Cinelândia, Carioca, Uruguaiana, Presidente Vargas

IGREJA DE NOSSA SENHORA DE CANDELÁRIA Map pp90–1

☎ 2233 2324; Praça Pio X; admission free; 🕐 8am-4pm Mon-Fri, 9am-noon Sat, 9am-1.30pm Sun

The construction of the original church (dating from the late 16th century) on the present site was credited to a ship's captain who was nearly shipwrecked at sea. Upon his safe return he vowed to build a church to NS de Candelária. A later design led to its present-day grandeur. Built between 1775 and 1894, NS de Candelária was the largest and wealthiest church of imperial Brazil. The interior is a combination of baroque and Renaissance styles. The ceiling above the nave reveals the origin of the church. The cupola, fabricated entirely from limestone shipped from Lisbon, is one of its most striking features. Mass is said at 9am, 10am and 11am on Sunday. But be sure to watch out for traffic as you cross to the church.

IGREJA SÃO FRANCISCO DA PENITÊNCIA & CONVENTO DE SANTO ANTÔNIO Map pp90–1

☎ 2262 0197; Largo da Carioca 5; admission R$2; 🕐 church 8am-6pm, convent 9am-noon & 1-4pm Tue-Fri

Overlooking the Largo da Carioca is the baroque Igreja São Francisco da Penitência, dating from 1726. Recently restored to its former glory, the church's sacristy, which dates from 1745, has blue Portuguese tiles and an elaborately carved altar made out of jacaranda wood. It also has a roof panel by José Oliveira Rosa depicting St Francis receiving the stigmata. The church's statue of Santo Antônio is an object of great devotion to many Cariocas in search of a husband or wife.

A garden on the church grounds leads to the catacombs, used until 1850. Visits must be arranged in advance.

Next door, the Convento de Santo Antônio was built between 1608 and 1615. It contains the chapel of Nossa Senhora das Dores da Imaculada Conceição. Fabiano de Cristo, a miracle-working priest who died in 1947, is entombed here.

CENTRO DE ARTE HÉLIO OITICICA

Map pp90–1

☎ 2242 1012; Rua Luis de Camões 68; admission free; 🕐 11am-6pm Tue-Fri, 11am-5pm Sat & Sun

This avant-garde museum is set in a 19th-century neoclassical building that originally housed the Conservatory of Music and Dramatic Arts. Today, the center displays permanent works by the artist, theoretician and poet Hélio Oiticica, as well as bold contemporary art exhibitions, well-tuned to Oiticica's forward-leaning aesthetics. In addition to six exhibition galleries, there's a bistro and a book shop on the first floor.

PAÇO IMPERIAL Map pp90–1

☎ 2533 4407; Praça Quinze de Novembro; admission free; 🕐 noon-6.30pm Tue-Sun

The former imperial palace was originally built in 1743 as a governor's residence. Later it became the home of Dom João and his family when the Portuguese throne transferred the royal seat of power to the colony. In 1888, Princesa Isabel proclaimed the Freedom from Slavery Act from the palace's steps. The building was neglected for many years but has been restored and is used for exhibitions and concerts; its cinema frequently screens foreign and art-house films.

PRAÇA QUINZE DE NOVEMBRO

Map pp90–1

Near Rua Primeiro de Março

The first residents on this historic site were Carmelite fathers who built a convent here in 1590. It later came under the property of the Portuguese crown and became Largo do Paço, which surrounded the royal palace (Paço Imperial). The square was later renamed Praça Quinze de Novembro after Brazil declared itself a republic on 15 November 1822. A number of historic events took place here: the coronation of Brazil's two Emperors (Pedro I and Pedro II), the abolition of slavery and the overthrow (deposition) of Emperor Dom Pedro II in 1889.

BIBLIOTECA NACIONAL Map pp90–1

☎ 2262 8255; Av Rio Branco 219; admission free; 🕐 9am-8pm Mon-Fri, 9am-3pm Sat, guided tours 11am & 3pm Mon-Fri

Inaugurated in 1910, the national library is the largest in Latin America, with more than 8 million volumes. It was designed by Francisco Marcelino de Souza Aguiar. On the ground floor, the periodical section is to the left, and general works are to the right. On the 2nd floor are many rare books and manuscripts, including two copies of the precious Mainz Psalter Bible, printed in 1492. Owing to their fragility, most of these rare books can be viewed only on microfilm.

CAMPO DE SANTANA Map pp90–1

Praça da República & Rua Frei Caneca

Campo de Santana is a pleasant park that, on 7 September 1822, was the scene of the proclamation of Brazil's independence from Portugal by Emperor Dom Pedro I of Portugal. The landscaped park with an artificial lake and swans is a fine place for a respite from the chaotic streets, and you're liable to see a few agoutis (a hamster-like rodent native to Brazil) running wild here.

CASA FRANÇA-BRASIL Map pp90–1

☎ 2253 5366; www.casafrancabrasil.rj.gov.br in Portuguese; Rua Visconde de Itaboraí 78; admission free; 🕒 10am-8pm Tue-Sun

In a neoclassical building dating from 1820, the Casa França-Brasil opened in 1990 for the purpose of advancing cultural relations between France and Brazil. The main hall features changing exhibitions often dealing with political and cultural facets of Carioca society. The building is considered the most important classical revival structure in Brazil, and once served as a customs house.

CENTRO CULTURAL CARIOCA Map pp90–1

☎ 2242 9642; www.centroculturalcarioca.com.br in Portuguese; Rua do Teatro 37; 🕒 noon-8pm Tue-Sun

This restored theater on Praça Tiradentes is once again a major contributor to the arts in downtown Rio. Its exposed brick walls and large wood-framed windows form the backdrop to superb musical groups – often samba – performing throughout the week (p166), and also has dance recitals, book releases and ongoing exhibitions. They also teach dance classes here (p185).

CENTRO CULTURAL JUSTIÇA FEDERAL Map pp90–1

☎ 2510 8846; Av Rio Branco 241; admission free; 🕒 noon-7pm Tue-Sun

The stately building overlooking the Praça Floriano served as the headquarters of the Supreme Court (Supremo Tribunal Federal) from 1909 to 1960. Following its recent restoration, it's become the Federal Justice Cultural Center, featuring exhibitions focused above all on photography and Brazilian art, though some fascinating exhibits from abroad sometimes make their way here. The store on the 1st floor has a tiny selection of books and handicrafts.

MOSTEIRO DE SÃO BENTO Map pp90–1

☎ 2206 8100; Rua Dom Gerardo 68; guided visits R$7; 🕒 8-11am & 2.30-6pm

This is one of the finest colonial churches in Brazil. Built between 1617 and 1641 on Morro de São Bento, the monastery has a fine view over the city. The simple facade hides a baroque interior richly decorated in gold. Among its historic treasures are wood carvings designed by Frei Domingos da Conceição (and made by Alexandre Machado) and paintings by José de Oliveira Rosa. On Sunday, the High Mass at 10am includes a choir of Benedictine monks singing Gregorian chants.

To reach the monastery from Rua Dom Gerardo, go to No 40 and take the elevator to the 5th floor.

MUSEU HISTÓRICO E DIPLOMÁTICO Map pp90–1

☎ 2253 2828; Av Marechal Floriano 196; 🕒 tours 2pm, 3pm, 4pm Mon, Wed & Fri

Housed in the neoclassical Palácio Itamaraty, the Museum of History and Diplomacy served as the private presidential home from 1889 until 1897. The museum has an impressive collection of art, antiques and maps. Visits are by guided 45-minute tours. Call ahead to ensure you get an English- or French-speaking guide. The museum is just a short walk west from Presidente Vargas metro station.

MUSEU NACIONAL DE BELAS ARTES Map pp90–1

☎ 2240 0068; Av Rio Branco 199; admission R$4; 🕒 10am-6pm Tue-Fri

Rio's fine arts museum houses more than 800 original paintings and sculptures ranging from the 17th to the 20th century. One of its most important galleries is the Galeria de Arte Brasileira, with 20th-century classics such as Cândido Portinari's *Café*. Other galleries display Brazilian folk art, African art and furniture, as well as contemporary exhibits. Guided tours are available in English (call ahead).

MUSEU NAVAL Map pp90–1

☎ 2533 7626; Rua Dom Manuel 15, Praça Quinze de Novembro; admission free; ⏰ noon-4pm Tue-Sun

Chronicling the history of the Brazilian navy from the 16th century to the present, the museum also has exhibitions of model warships, maps and navigational instruments.

Naval enthusiasts should also visit the nearby Espaço Cultural da Marinha (ECM; Map pp90–1; ☎ 2104 6992; admission free; ⏰ noon-5pm, Tue-Sun), on the waterfront near the eastern end of Av Presidente Vargas. It contains the *Riachuelo* submarine, which you can wander through, the *Bauru* (a WWII torpedo boat) and the royal family's large rowboat. The boat tour to Ilha Fiscal (p104) leaves from the docks here.

PALÁCIO TIRADENTES Map pp90–1

☎ 2588 1411; Rua Primeiro de Março; admission free; ⏰ 10am-5pm Mon-Sat, noon-5pm Sun

In the looming building overlooking the bay, the stately Tiradentes Palace today houses the seat of the legislative assembly. Visitors can wander through exhibits on the 1st and 2nd floors that relate – through photographs and documents – some of the historic events that took place in the nearby chambers between 1926 and the present. One of its darkest hours was when the National Assembly was shut down in 1937 under the Vargas dictatorship – it later served as his Department of Press and Propaganda. Most information is in Portuguese, though you can listen to a rundown of history in English at the interactive machine in the foyer. The statue in front, incidentally, is not a likeness of Russian mystic Rasputin, but rather that of martyr Tiradentes, who led the drive toward Brazilian independence in the 18th century.

PASSEIO PÚBLICO Map pp90–1

Rua do Passeio; admission free; ⏰ 9am-5pm

The oldest park in Rio, the Passeio Público was built in 1783 by Mestre Valentim, a famous Brazilian sculptor, who designed it after Lisbon's botanical gardens. In 1860 the park was remodeled by French landscaper Glaziou. The park features some large trees, a pond with islands and an interesting crocodile-shaped fountain. The entrance gate was built by Valentim. Before the Parque do Flamengo landfill, the sea came right up to the edge of the park.

REAL GABINETE PORTUGUÊS DE LEITURA Map pp90–1

☎ 2221 3138; Rua Luís de Camões 30; admission free; ⏰ 9am-6pm

Built in the Portuguese manueline style in 1837, the gorgeous Portuguese Reading Room houses over 350,000 works, many dating from the 16th, 17th and 18th centuries. It also has a small collection of paintings, sculptures and ancient coins.

THEATRO MUNICIPAL Map pp90–1

☎ 2299 1711; www.theatromunicipal.rj.gov.br; Rua Manuel de Carvalho; ⏰ guided tour 1-4pm Mon-Fri

Built in 1905 in the style of the Paris Opera, the magnificent Municipal Theater is the home of Rio's opera, orchestra and ballet. Its lavish interior contains many beautiful details – including the stage curtain painted by Italian artist Eliseu Visconti, which contains portraits of 75 major figures from the arts: Carlos Gomes, Wagner and Rembrandt among others. Guided tours are a good way to see the theater, call ☎ 2299 1667 to book one. If you get a chance, come to a performance here (see p175).

TRAVESSA DO COMÉRCIO Map pp90–1

Near Praça Quinze de Novembro

Beautiful two-story colonial townhouses line this narrow cobblestone street leading off Praça Quinze de Novembro. The archway, called Arco de Teles, leading into the area was once part of an old viaduct running between two buildings. Today, Travessa do Comércio contains half a dozen restaurants and drinking spots that open onto the streets. It's a favorite spot for Cariocas after work.

CINELÂNDIA

PRAÇA FLORIANO Map pp90–1

Av Rio Branco

The heart of modern Rio, the Praça Floriano comes to life at lunchtime and after work when the outdoor cafés are filled with beer drinkers, samba musicians and political debate. The square is also Rio's political marketplace. There are daily speechmaking, literature sales and street theater. Most city marches and rallies culminate here on the steps of the old Câmara Municipal (Town Hall) in the northwestern corner of the plaza.

MONUMENTO NACIONAL AOS MORTOS DA II GUERRA MUNDIAL

Map pp90–1

☎ 2240 1283; Av Infante Dom Henrique 75; admission free; 🕑 10am-4pm Tue-Sun

This delicate monument to the soldiers who perished in WWII contains a museum, a mausoleum and the Tomb of the Unknown Soldier. The museum exhibits uniforms, medals and documents from Brazil's Italian campaign. There's also a small lake and sculptures by Ceschiatti and Anísio Araújo de Medeiros.

HISTORIC CENTRO

Walking Tour

A mélange of historic buildings and young skyscrapers, the center of Rio is an excellent place to discover the essence of the city away from its beaches and mountains. Among the hustle and bustle of commerce, you'll find fascinating museums, atmospheric bars and theaters, open-air bazaars and the colonial-antique stores set near old samba clubs. This tour is best done during the week, as it gets rather deserted (and unsafe) on weekends.

1 Praça Floriano Start at the Praça Floriano (opposite), the heart of modern Rio. Praça Floriano comes to life at night when the outdoor cafés are filled with beer drinkers and political debate. The neoclassical Theatro Municipal (p175) overlooking the plaza is one of Rio's finest buildings.

2 Feira de Música On the east side of Av Rio Branco facing Praça Floriano is the Rua Pedro Lessa, where you can browse through the record and CD stalls at the open-air music market called the Feira de Música (p118).

3 Museu Nacional de Belas Artes Stroll up a few blocks along busy Av Rio Branco to

WALK FACTS

Start Praça Floriano (metro Cinelândia)
End Praça Pio X
Distance 4.4km
Duration Four hours

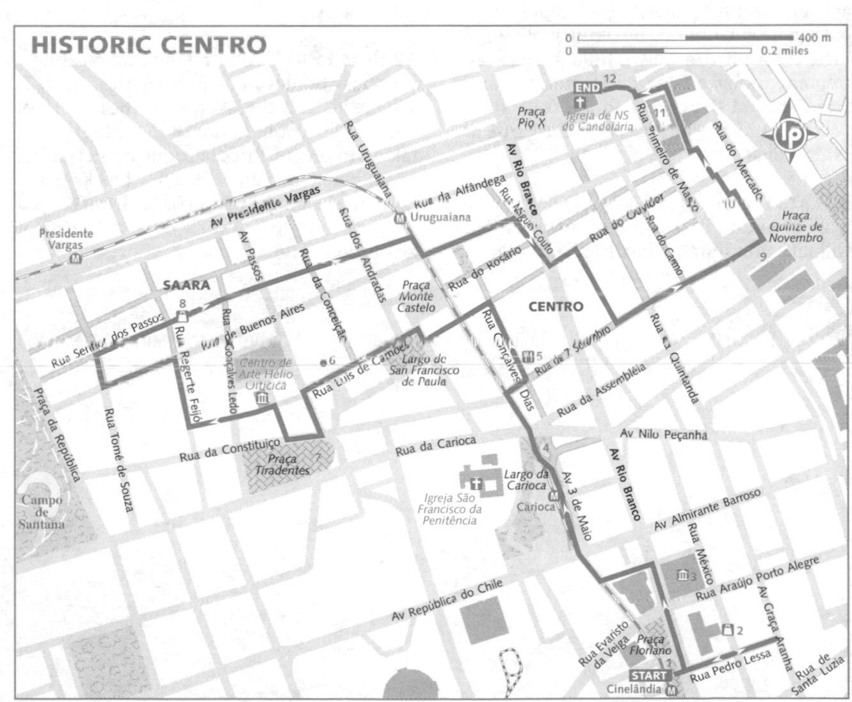

get a glimpse of the neoclassical Museu Nacional de Belas Artes (p93). It's worth venturing inside for a look at some of Rio's best-known 19th-century painters.

4 Largo da Carioca Cross over Av Rio Branco and turn right onto Av 13 de Maio. You'll soon pass through the Largo da Carioca, a bustling area with a small market. Up on the hill is the Igreja São Francisco da Penitência (p92), a 17th-century church which you can reach via elevator near the Carioca metro station.

5 Confeitaria Colombo After taking in the views, descend to the streets and continue along Av 13 de Maio. Turn right onto Rua Sete Setembro and left onto Gonçalves Dias to reach Confeitaria Colombo (p147) for a dose of caffeine and art nouveau.

6 Real Gabinete Português de Leitura From Rua Gonçalves Dias, turn left on Rua do Ouvidor, following it across the Largo de San Francisco de Paula. One block further is the Real Gabinete Português de Leitura (p94), a historic reading room that's well worth a look.

7 Praça Tiradentes Go one block west and one south to the Praça Tiradentes, an old square surrounded by century-old buildings. It's a bit run down, though some entrepreneurs have begun restoring the area. Head around the corner to the Centro de Arte Hélio Oiticica (p92), which hosts avant-garde art exhibitions.

8 Saara Walk over to Rua Regente Feijó and loop around to Rua Senhor dos Passos. This will take you into the heart of Saara (Portuguese for 'Sahara'), a narrow neighborhood bazaar packed with discount shops, pedestrians and a few Lebanese restaurants. Walk, shop and snack your way east to Rua Miguel Couto and turn right.

9 Paço Imperial Leaving Saara, turn left on Rua do Ouvidor, and jog down to Rua Sete de Setembro. Follow it until it ends at Rua Primeiro de Março. Across the road, the Paço Imperial (p92), was once the seat of imperial power in Brazil. This is a good spot to check out current exhibitions in the galleries or browse for music in the bookshop.

10 Travessa do Comércio As you leave the imperial building, cross Praça Quinze de Novembro and take the narrow lane beneath the arch. You'll walk along one of Centro's oldest lanes, through Travessa do Comércio (p94), with open-air restaurants and bars that fill with revelers around happy hour.

11 Centro Cultural Banco do Brasil If you still have energy, pop around the corner to the Centro Cultural Banco do Brasil (p89), a huge exhibition space (and cinema, theater and cafés), where you can often find Rio's best exhibitions.

12 Praça Pio X After taking care crossing a very busy boulevard, you reach the Igreja de NS de Candelária (p92), the last stop on the tour. Have a rest in the cool interior of the church while taking in one of Rio's baroque masterpieces. From here, you can walk a few blocks to the Uruguaiana metro station or back to Travessa do Comércio for a much-deserved drink at an outdoor café.

SANTA TERESA & LAPA

Eating p148; Shopping p123; Sleeping p198

Icons of bohemian Rio, Santa Teresa and Lapa are two rough-and-tumble neighborhoods that have contributed considerably to the city's artistic and musical heritage. On a hill overlooking the city, Santa Teresa has an impressive collection of 19th-century mansions set along winding lanes, with an old tram still rattling through the neighborhood. The Carmelite convent founded here in 1750 gave the district its name and became the first of many impressive buildings in the area. Santa Teresa was the uppermost residential neighborhood in the 19th century, when Rio's upper class lived here and rode the *bonde* (tram) to work in Centro. Many beautiful colonial homes stretch skyward, their manicured gardens hidden behind gabled fences. Like other areas near Centro, the neighborhood fell into neglect in the early 20th century as the wealthy moved further south. During the 1960s and '70s many artists and bohemians moved into Santa Teresa's mansions, initiating a revitalization process that still continues. Today, Santa Teresa is a buzzword about Rio for its vibrant arts scene. Throughout the year, impromptu festivals and street parties fill the air, ranging from *maracatu* drumming along Rua Joaquim Murtinho to live jazz at the Parque das Ruínas to the annual Portas Abertas event, where dozens of artists open their studios and cover the streets with living installations.

The neighborhood's ongoing restoration has led to an influx of restaurants, bars and cultural centers, and some have compared Santa Teresa to Paris' Montmartre. Yet this rugged neighborhood is unlikely to ever completely lose its edginess, if only for the omnipresent favelas spreading down the hillsides. Be cautious when walking around Santa Teresa.

The streets of Lapa lie down the hill from Santa Teresa and south of Cinelândia. Formerly a residential neighborhood of the wealthy, Lapa became a red-light district in the 1930s, its brothels and taverns the stomping ground for bohemians, intellectuals, politicians and malandros. Although Lapa is still a derelict area, it's also one of the music capitals of Brazil. At night, revelers from all over the city mingle among its samba clubs and music-filled bars. The music scene has brought some gentrification to the area, including new restaurants and hostels. Despite some signs of renewal, Lapa still has its share of crime. Take care when strolling around the neighborhood, which is actually safer on busy weekend nights than it is during the day.

Lapa's landmark aqueduct, Arcos da Lapa (Lapa Arches), is one of the neighborhood's most prominent features. Narrow tracks course over the 64m-high structure, carrying the famous *bonde* to and from Santa Teresa.

SANTA TERESA

BONDE Map pp98–9

☎ 2240 5709; station at Rua Lélio Gama 65; fare R$0.60; ⏲ departures every 30min

The *bonde* that travels up to Santa Teresa from Centro is the last of the historic streetcars that once crisscrossed the city. Its romantic clatter through the cobbled streets has made it the archetype for bohemian Santa Teresa. The two routes currently open have been in operation since the 19th century. Both travel high atop the narrow Arcos da Lapa (p100) and along curving Rua Joaquim Murtinho before reaching Largo do Guimarães (p100). From there, one line (Paula Matos) takes a northwestern route, terminating at Largo das Neves (p100). The longer route (Dois Irmãos) continues from Largo do Guimarães uphill and southward before terminating near the water reservoir at Dois Irmãos (Two Brothers – named after the twin stone pyramids used to collect water from the Carioca River).

Although a policeman often accompanies the tram, the favelas down the hillsides still make this a high-crime area. Go by all means, but don't bring any valuables. Local kids jumping on and off the tram lend a festive air to the journey. An unspoken tradition states that those who ride on the running board ride for free.

Tram tours (p226) depart every Saturday, highlighting historic points in the neighborhood.

MUSEU CHÁCARA DO CÉU Map pp98–9

☎ 2507 1932; Rua Murtinho Nobre 93; admission R$2; ⏲ noon-5pm Wed-Mon

The former mansion of art patron and industrialist Raymundo Ottoni de Castro Maya, the museum contains a small but diversified collection of modern art – formerly Ottoni's private collection, which he

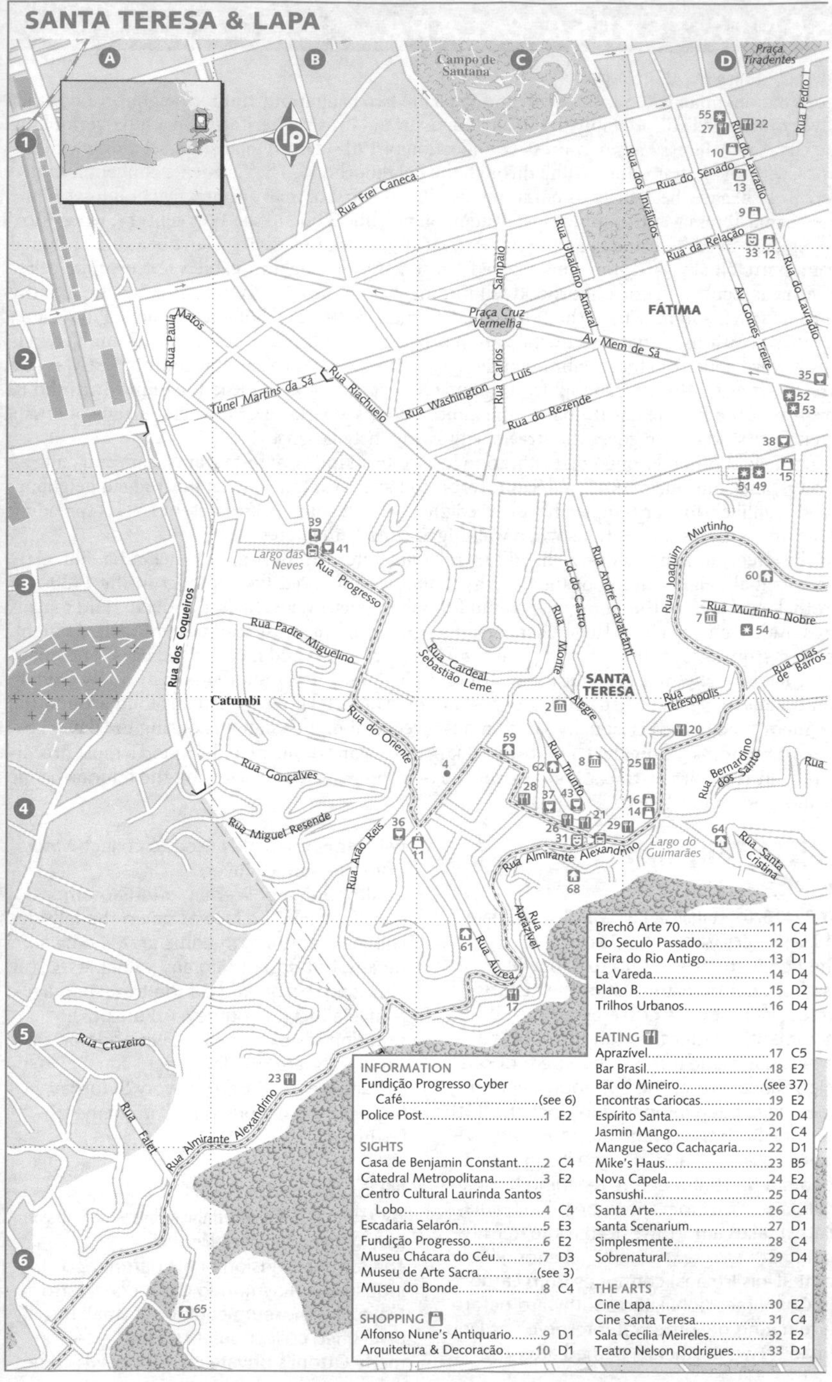
SANTA TERESA & LAPA
Campo de Santana
Praça Tiradentes
Rua Frei Caneca
Rua do Senado
Rua do Lavradio
Rua dos Inválidos
Rua da Relação
Rua Ubaldino Amaral
Rua Pedro I
Praça Cruz Vermelha
FÁTIMA
Av Mem de Sá
Av Gomes Freire
Rua Paula Matos
Túnel Martins da Sá
Rua Riachuelo
Rua Washington Luis
Rua Carlos Sampaio
Rua do Rezende
Largo das Neves
Rua Progresso
Rua dos Coqueiros
Rua Padre Miguelino
Rua Cardeal Sebastião Leme
Ld do Castro
Rua André Cavalcanti
Rua Monte Alegre
Rua Joaquim Murtinho
Rua Murtinho Nobre
Rua Dias de Barros
Rua Teresópolis
SANTA TERESA
Catumbi
Rua do Oriente
Rua Gonçalves
Rua Triunfo
Rua Bernardino dos Santo
Rua Miguel Resende
Rua Arão Reis
Rua Almirante Alexandrino
Largo do Guimarães
Rua Santa Cristina
Rua Aprazível
Rua Áurea
Rua Cruzeiro
Rua Falet
INFORMATION
Fundição Progresso Cyber Café (see 6)
Police Post 1 E2
SIGHTS
Casa de Benjamin Constant 2 C4
Catedral Metropolitana 3 E2
Centro Cultural Laurinda Santos Lobo 4 C4
Escadaria Selarón 5 E3
Fundição Progresso 6 E2
Museu Chácara do Céu 7 D3
Museu de Arte Sacra (see 3)
Museu do Bonde 8 C4
SHOPPING
Alfonso Nune's Antiquario 9 D1
Arquitetura & Decoracão 10 D1
Brechô Arte 70 11 C4
Do Seculo Passado 12 D1
Feira do Rio Antigo 13 D1
La Vareda 14 D4
Plano B 15 D2
Trilhos Urbanos 16 D4
EATING
Aprazível 17 C5
Bar Brasil 18 E2
Bar do Mineiro (see 37)
Encontras Cariocas 19 E2
Espírito Santa 20 D4
Jasmin Mango 21 C4
Mangue Seco Cachaçaria 22 D1
Mike's Haus 23 B5
Nova Capela 24 E2
Sansushi 25 D4
Santa Arte 26 C4
Santa Scenarium 27 D1
Simplesmente 28 C4
Sobrenatural 29 D4
THE ARTS
Cine Lapa 30 E2
Cine Santa Teresa 31 C4
Sala Cecília Meireles 32 E2
Teatro Nelson Rodrigues 33 D1

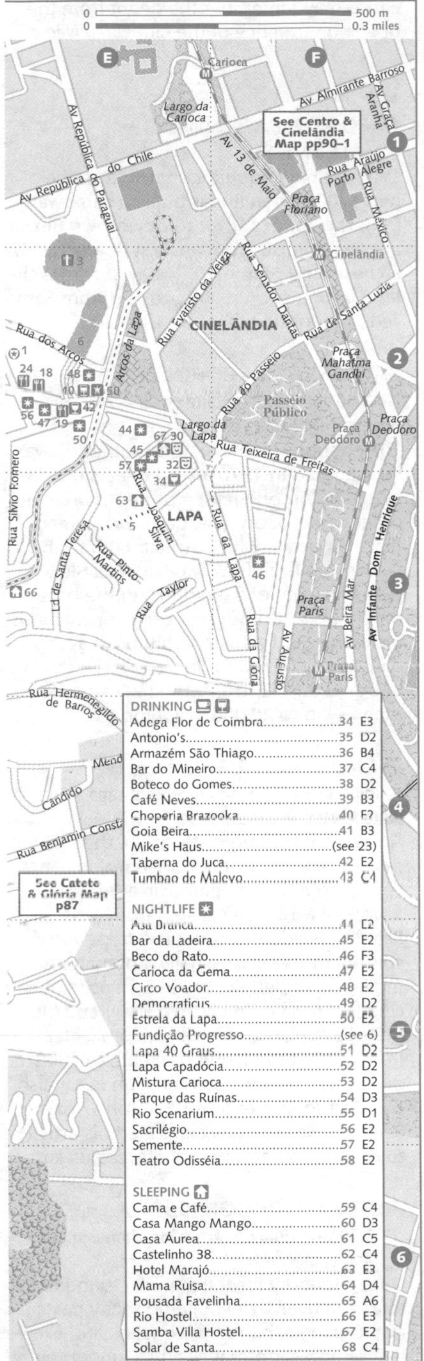

bequeathed to the nation. In addition to works by Portinari, Di Cavalcanti and Lygia Clark, the museum displays furniture and Brazilian maps dating from the 17th and 18th centuries. Unfortunately, some of the museum's most valuable pieces were stolen during a robbery in 2006. Beautiful gardens surround the museum, and a panoramic view of Centro and Baía de Guanabara awaits visitors.

PARQUE DAS RUÍNAS Map pp98–9

☎ 2252 1039; Rua Murtinho Nobre 169; admission free; ⏲ 10am-8pm Tue-Sun

Connected to the Museu Chácara do Céu by a walkway, this park contains the ruins of the mansion belonging to Brazilian heiress Laurinda Santos Lobo. Her house was a meeting point for Rio's artists and intellectuals for many years until her death in 1946. Today, the park stages open-air concerts periodically. Don't miss the excellent view from the top floor. There's a small outdoor café that makes a great spot to recharge.

CASA DE BENJAMIN CONSTANT Map pp98–9

☎ 2509 1248; Rua Monte Alegre 255; admission R$2, free Wed; ⏲ guided tours 1-5pm Wed-Sun

This country estate served as the residence for one of Brazil's most influential politicians in the founding of the young republic. Benjamin Constant (1837–91) was an engineer, military officer and professor before taking an active role in the Provisional Government. He is also remembered for founding a school for blind children. Painstakingly preserved, his house provides a window into his life and times. The lush gardens surrounding his estate provide a fine view over Centro and the western side of Santa Teresa.

CENTRO CULTURAL LAURINDA SANTOS LOBO Map pp98–9

☎ 2224 3331; Rua Monte Alegre 306; admission free; ⏲ 8am-5pm

The large mansion built in 1907 once served as a salon for artists from Brazil and abroad as socialite Laurinda Santos Lobo hosted her parties there. Villa-Lobos and Isadora Duncan among others attended. Today, the cultural center still plays an active role in the neighborhood by hosting exhibitions and open-air concerts throughout the year.

TRANSPORTATION: SANTA TERESA & LAPA

Santa Teresa

Bus Centro (206A, 206B and 214), all of which travel along Arcos da Lapa and Rua do Lavradio

Bonde Paula Matos, Dois Irmãos

Lapa

Bus Leblon bus (571) travels between Largo da Lapa and Leblon via Jóquei; 572 travels between the same points, going via Copacabana

Metro Cinelândia

LARGO DAS NEVES Map pp98–9

End of Rua Progresso

A slice of small-town life in the city, this small square is the gathering point of neighborhood children and families who lounge in the benches by day. At night, the bars surrounding the square come alive with revelers crowding the walks. At times, MPB bands perform to a young crowd here. Largo das Neves is the terminus of the Paula Matos *bonde* line.

LARGO DO GUIMARÃES Map pp98–9

Rua Almirante Alexandrino

The square named after Joaquim Fonseca Guimarães (a local resident whose house became Hotel Santa Teresa just up the road) now forms the center of bohemian Santa Teresa. A festive Carnaval street party originates here, and a number of restaurants, handicrafts and thrift shops lie within a short distance.

MUSEU DO BONDE Map pp98–9

☎ 2242 2354; Rua Carlos Brant 14; admission free; 9am-4.30pm

The tiny one-room Tram Museum at the depot close to Largo do Guimarães offers a history of Rio's tramways since 1865 – when the trams were pulled by donkeys. A few photographs, trip-recorders and conductor uniforms are just about the only objects documenting their legacy. Uplifting music plays overhead. The term *bonde*, incidentally, means just that – bond – indicating the way in which the first electric trams were financed – through public bonds. While you're at the museum, wander down to the old workshop that houses the trams. Cineastes may remember the depot from the opening sequence of the film *Orfeu Negro*.

LAPA

ARCOS DA LAPA Map pp98–9

Near Av Mem de Sá

The landmark aqueduct dates from the mid-1700s when it was built to carry water from the Carioca River to downtown Rio. In a style reminiscent of ancient Rome, the 42 arches stand 64m high. Today, it carries the famous *bonde* on its way to and from Santa Teresa atop the hill.

CATEDRAL METROPOLITANA Map pp98–9

☎ 2240 2669; Av República do Chile 245; admission free; 7am-5.30pm

The enormous cone-shaped cathedral was inaugurated in 1976 after 12 years of construction. Among its sculptures, murals and other works of art, the four vivid stained-glass windows, which stretch 60m to the ceiling, are breathtaking. The Museu de Arte Sacra (Museum of Sacred Art) in the basement contains a number of historical items, including the baptismal font used at the christening of royal princes and the throne of Dom Pedro II. The cathedral can accommodate up to 20,000 worshippers.

ESCADARIA SELARÓN Map pp98–9

Stairway btwn Rua Joaquim Silva in Lapa & Rua Pinto Martins in Santa Teresa

An ever-expanding installation, the staircase leading up to the Convento de Santa Teresa from Rua Joaquim Silva became a work of art when Chilean-born artist Selarón decided to cover the steps with colorful mosaics. Originally a homage to the Brazilian people, the 215 steps feature ceramic mosaics in green, yellow and blue. He uses mirrors as well as tiles collected from around the world to create the illustrious effects. A hand-painted sign in English and Portuguese explains Selarón's vision. Recently, Selarón has expanded his artistry to include mosaics near the Arcos da Lapa.

FUNDIÇÃO PROGRESSO Map pp98–9

☎ 2220 5070; Rua dos Arcos 24; admission free; 9am-6pm Mon-Fri

Once a foundry for the manufacturing of safes and ovens, the building today hosts avant-garde exhibitions, concerts and excellent samba performances throughout the year. It is one of the few buildings in the area that survived the neighborhood redistricting project in the 1950s to widen the avenue.

SANTA TERESA Walking Tour

Colorful colonial buildings, narrow brick-lined streets and sweeping views of downtown are a few of the reasons artists flocked here in the mid-'70s. Today the 'hood is still experiencing a cultural renaissance. You never know what you'll find here: old mansions hosting African drumming, bossa-jazz in a bombed-out building or impromptu music jams. No other neighborhood has quite the energy that Santa Teresa has. Do be careful when exploring this neighborhood, as muggings still occur. Travel in groups, and keep an eye out for pairs of young men on mopeds. We recommend not straying too far off the *bonde* line. The weekends are the liveliest time to visit, but if you plan to take the *bonde* then, travel to the *bonde* station by taxi as Centro is deserted (and dangerous) on Saturday and Sunday.

1 Largo das Neves Our saunter begins in the small square of Largo das Neves (opposite), also the end of the *bonde* line. The first part of our walk will follow the tracks, removing the possibility of getting lost among the winding streets.

2 Igreja de Nossa Senhora das Neves Above the Largo das Neves are the twin spires of Igreja de Nossa Senhora das Neves, one of many 19th-century churches in the area. On weekend nights, the Largo becomes the set piece for the music-filled cafés and bars that open onto it.

3 Armazém São Thiago Start following the tracks. You'll pass through a few curves before reaching an even sharper turn leading to Rua Monte Alegre. If you need a drink stop in the old-time Armazém São Thiago (p159), still called by its former name of Bar do Gomes by most.

4 Centro Cultural Laurinda Santos Lobo Keep following the tracks and you will pass Centro Cultural Laurinda Santos Lobo (p99), which often hosts exhibitions and the occasional concert.

5 Largo do Guimarães Continue following the tracks, passing a few restaurants, including the popular Bar do Mineiro (p149). Eventually, you'll reach the Largo do Guimarães (opposite), which is where you'll find the densest concentration of Santa Teresa shops and restaurants.

6 Museu do Bonde If you take a left on Rua Carlos Brandt, you can visit the tiny Museu do

WALK FACTS

Start Largo das Neves
End Rua Almirante Alexandrino
Distance 3.5km
Duration 2½ hours
Fuel stop Jasmin Mango (p149)

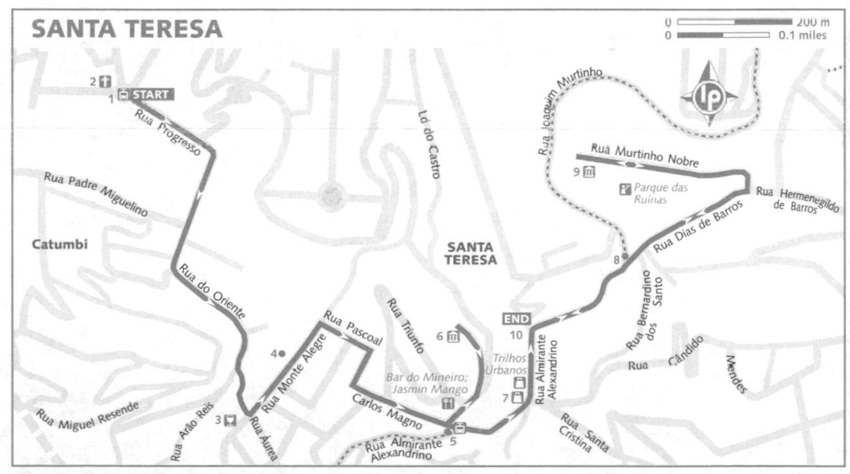

Bonde (p100) for a symphonic journey back to the *bonde*'s once-glorious day in the sun.

7 La Vareda After checking out the museum and the tram-storage building next door, walk back up to Largo do Guimarães and head up along Rua Almirante Alexandrino to La Vareda (p124) and Trilhos Urbanos (p124), both good spots to purchase Brazilian handicrafts.

8 Curvelo Keep walking downhill. Soon you'll reach Curvelo, a *bonde* shelter. Here, turn right (leaving the tracks behind, so get your bearings) onto Rua Dias de Barros. Follow this street until you reach a road branching off to the left (Rua Murtinho Nobre).

9 Museu Chácara do Céu Loop around and head up to the Museu Chácara do Céu (p97), with its small collection of modern art, and the Parque das Ruínas (p99) next door. Don't miss the excellent views up top.

10 Rua Almirante Alexandrino After exploring, stop in for a bit at one of the restaurants along the main strip of Rua Almirante Alexandrino before taking the *bonde* back down to Centro.

GREATER RIO

Shopping p124

Attractions here are fewer than those in the Zona Sul and Centro, but you'll still find some excellent reasons to venture out, including soccer rowdiness at Maracanã and island allure on the bay.

The neighborhood of São Cristóvão is home to the Quinta da Boa Vista, a large somewhat scruffy park containing the Museu Nacional and the zoo. It's also the site of the soccer stadium and the Feira Nordestina, one of Brazil's biggest weekend markets. In the 19th century the suburb was the home of the nobility, including the monarchs themselves. It has since become a heavily populated, working-class suburb.

Rio's lovely but heavily polluted bay lies east and north of Centro. This is a fine setting for a cruise to either Ilha de Paquetá or Niterói. The bay has a prominent place in Rio's history. In 1502 Portuguese explorers sailed into the bay and, mistaking it for the entrance to a large river, named it Rio de Janeiro (River of January). Even though they were mistaken in their geography, the name stuck and was later extended to the new settlement as a whole. Of course, the history doesn't begin with the Portuguese arrival. The indigenous Tamoio people lived along the shore long before their arrival, and the bay provided much of their sustenance. They were the ones who named the bay 'Guanabara,' which means 'arm of the sea.' In those days it was a tropical wilderness teeming with tapirs and jaguars. Today the wild animals (and much of the aquatic life as well) have disappeared from Baía de Guanabara. Much of its area has also disappeared. Owing to several landfill projects – which created Parque do Flamengo and Aeroporto Santos Dumont – the bay is also disappearing. The best way to experience the bay is by boat, taking a cruise (p224) or catching the ferry to either Niterói or Ilha de Paquetá.

São Cristóvão

FEIRA NORDESTINA Map pp60–1

☎ 3860 9976; Campo de São Cristóvão; admission R$1; Fri-Sun

This enormous fair (32,000 sq meters with 658 stalls) is not to be missed. The fair showcases the culture from the northeast, with *barracas* (food stalls) selling Bahian dishes as well as beer and *cachaça* (cane liquor), which flows in great abundance here. Bands play throughout the weekend – accordion, guitar and tambourine players performing *forró,* samba groups and comedy troupes, MPB and *rodas de capoeira* (*capoeira* circles). The vibrant scene starts around 8pm on Friday and continues nonstop through to Sunday evening. (Many club kids stop by here just before sunrise). In addition to food and drink, you can stock up on secondhand clothes, some well-priced hammocks and a wide (and wild) assortment of handicrafts.

TRANSPORTATION: GREATER RIO

Maracana

Bus From Copacabana, Ipanema & Leblon (463); to Copacabana, Ipanema & Leblon (432)

Metro Maracana

Quinta da Boa Vista

Bus Copacabana, Ipanema and Leblon (474)

Metro São Cristóvão (for Museu Nacional and Jardim Zoológic)

QUINTA DA BOA VISTA Map pp60–1

☎ 2234 1609; 9am-5pm

Quinta da Boa Vista was the residence of the Portuguese imperial family until the Republic was proclaimed. Today, it's a large and busy park with gardens and lakes. At weekends it's crowded with soccer games and families from the Zona Norte. The former imperial mansion houses the Museu Nacional (below) and Museu da Fauna. The Jardim Zoológico (p104), Rio's zoo, is 200m away.

MUSEU NACIONAL Map pp60–1

☎ 2568 8262; Quinta da Boa Vista; admission R$3; 10am-4pm Tue-Sun

This museum and its imperial entrance are still stately and imposing, and the view from the balcony to the royal palms is majestic. However, the weathered buildings and unkempt grounds have clearly declined since the fall of the monarchy.

There are many interesting exhibits: dinosaur fossils, saber-toothed tiger skeletons, beautiful pieces of pre-Columbian ceramics from the littoral and high plains of

Peru, a huge meteorite, hundreds of stuffed birds, mammals and fish, gruesome displays of tropical diseases, and exhibits on the peoples of Brazil.

JARDIM ZOOLÓGICO Map pp60–1

☎ 3878 4200; Quinta da Boa Vista; admission R$6; 9am-4.30pm Tue-Sun

Covering over 120,000 sq meters, the zoo at Quinta da Boa Vista has a wide variety of reptiles, mammals and birds – mostly indigenous to Brazil. Special attractions include the large walk-through aviary and the night house, which features nocturnal animals. The monkey house is also a crowd favorite.

MARACANÃ FOOTBALL STADIUM

Map pp60–1

☎ 2568 9962; gate 18, Rua Professor Eurico Rabelo; 9am-5pm Mon-Fri

Brazil's temple of soccer easily accommodates more than 100,000 people. On certain occasions, such as the World Cup match of 1950 or Pelé's last game, it has squeezed in close to 200,000 crazed fans – although it's now been modified to hold fewer.

If you like sports, if you want to understand Brazil, or if you just want an intense, quasi-psychedelic experience, then by all means go see a game of *futebol* – preferably a championship game or one between local rivals Flamengo, Vasco, Fluminense or Botafogo. See p180 for details.

There's a sports museum (open 9am to 5pm Monday to Friday) inside the stadium. It has photographs, posters, cups and the uniforms of Brazilian sporting greats, including Pelé's famous No 10 shirt. There's also a store where you can buy soccer shirts. Enter through gate 18 on Rua Professor Eurico Rabelo.

MUSEU DO PRIMEIRO REINADO

Map pp60–1

☎ 2299 2148; Av Dom Pedro II 293; admission free; 11am-5pm Tue-Fri

A 10-minute walk east of the Quinta da Boa Vista, this former mansion of the Marquesa de Santos depicts the history of the First Reign (the reign of bumbling Dom Pedro I before he was driven out of the country). The collection includes documents, furniture and paintings, but the main attraction is the building and its interior, with striking murals by Francisco Pedro do Amaral.

Baía De Guanabara & Niterói

ILHA DE PAQUETÁ

☎ ferry 2533 6661, hydrofoil 2533 7524

This tropical island in the Baía de Guanabara was once a very popular tourist spot and is now frequented mostly by families from the Zona Norte. There are no cars on the island. Transport is by foot, bicycle (with literally hundreds for rent) or horse-drawn cart. There's a certain dirty, decadent charm to the colonial buildings, unassuming beaches and businesses catering to local tourism. The place gets crowded at weekends.

Go to Paquetá for the boat ride through Rio's famous bay and to see Cariocas at play – especially during the Festa de São Roque, which is celebrated with fireworks, a procession and music on the weekend following 16 August.

Boats leave from near the Praça Quinze de Novembro (Map pp90–1) in Centro. The regular ferry takes 70 minutes and costs R$8 return on weekdays, R$15 return on weekends. The more comfortable hydrofoil takes only 25 minutes and costs R$16 return, but was out of commission at research time. Ferry service goes from 5.30am to 11pm, leaving every two to three hours.

ILHA FISCAL Map pp90–1

☎ 3870 6992; admission R$8; 1pm, 2.30pm & 4pm Thu-Sun except on the 2nd weekend of month

This eye-catching lime-green, neo-Gothic palace sitting in the Baía de Guanabara looks like something out of a child's fairy-tale book. It was designed by engineer Adolfo del Vecchio and completed in 1889. Originally used to supervise port operations, the palace is famous as the location of the last Imperial Ball on 9 November 1889. Today it's open for guided tours three times a day from Thursday to Sunday; tours leave from the dock near Praça Quinze (usually by boat, but sometimes by van).

NITERÓI

Niterói's principal attraction is the famous Museu do Arte Contemporânea (MAC). The cruise across the bay, however, is perhaps just as valid a reason for leaving Rio. Out on the water, you'll have impressive views of downtown, Pão de Açúcar (p80) and the other green mountains rising up out of the city; you'll also see planes (quite close)

FLORESTA (FOREST) DA TIJUCA – PARQUE NACIONAL DA TIJUCA

The Tijuca is all that's left of the Atlantic rain forest that once surrounded Rio de Janeiro. In just 15 minutes you can go from the concrete jungle of Copacabana to the 120-sq-km tropical jungle of the Parque Nacional da Tijuca (Map p105). A more rapid and dramatic contrast is hard to imagine. The forest is an exuberant green, with beautiful trees, creeks and waterfalls, mountainous terrain and high peaks. It has an excellent, well-marked trail system. Candomblistas leave offerings by the roadside, families have picnics and serious hikers climb the 1012m to the summit of Pico da Tijuca.

The heart of the forest is the Alto da Boa Vista area in the Floresta (Forest) da Tijuca, with many lovely natural and manmade features. Among the highlights of this beautiful park are several waterfalls (Cascatinha de Taunay, Cascata Gabriela and Cascata Diamantina), a 19th-century chapel (Capela Mayrink) and numerous caves (Gruta Luís Fernandes, Gruta Belmiro, Gruta Paulo e Virgínia). Also in the park is a lovely picnic spot (Bom Retiro) and two restaurants (Restaurante Os Equilos and Restaurante a Floresta, which is near the ruins of Major Archer's house – Ruínas do Archer).

The park is home to many different bird and animal species, including iguanas and monkeys, which you might encounter on one of the excellent day hikes you can make here (the trails are well-signed). Maps can be obtained at the small artisan shop just inside the park entrance, which is open from 7am to 9pm.

The entire park closes at sunset. It's best to go by car, but if you can't, catch a 221, 233 or 234 bus. Alternatively, take the metro to Saens Peña, then catch a bus going to Barra da Tijuca and get off at Alto da Boa Vista.

The best route by car is to take Rua Jardim Botânico two blocks past the Jardim Botânico (heading east from Gávea). Turn left on Rua Lopes Quintas and then follow the Tijuca or Corcovado signs for two quick left turns until you reach the back of the Jardim Botânico, where you turn right. Then follow the signs for a quick ascent into the forest and past the Vista Chinesa (Map pp60–1) – get out for a good view – and the Mesa do Imperador (Map pp60–1). As soon as you seem to come out of the forest, turn right onto the main road and you'll see the stone columns to the entrance of Alto da Boa Vista on your left after a couple of kilometers. You can also drive up to Alto da Boa Vista by heading out to São Conrado and turning right up the hill at the Parque Nacional da Tijuca signs.

Warning: there have been occasional reports of robbery within the park. Most Cariocas recommend going at weekends when there are more people around. Ask at Riotur (p228) about the present situation.

BEACHES EAST OF RIO

A number of beaches lie just east of Niterói. The ones closest to town are too polluted for swimming, but as you continue out, you'll reach some pristine beaches – Piratininga, Camboinhas, Itaipu and finally Itacoatiara, the most fabulous of the bunch. Framed by two looming hills on either side of the shore and backed by vegetation, the white sands of Itacoatiara seem like a world away from the urban beaches of Rio. *Barracas* (food stalls) sell scrumptious plates of fish, and there are also food stands overlooking the beach. The surf is strong here – evidenced by the many surfers jockeying for position – so swim with caution. To get there, you can take bus 38 or any bus labeled Itacoatiara from the ferry terminal (R$3, 50 minutes). If you're traveling in a group you can negotiate a return fare with a taxi driver.

landing and taking off at Aeroporto Santos Dumont. Try to be on the water at sunset when Centro glows with golden light. The ferry costs R$4.60 return and leaves from Praça Quinze de Novembro in Centro every 15 to 30 minutes; it's usually packed with commuters. The faster and more comfortable alternative is the jumbo catamaran, which runs every 20 minutes from 7.20am to 8pm and costs R$11 return. Once you reach the dock, there isn't much to see in the immediate area. It's a busy commercial area, full of pedestrians, and crisscrossing intersections. From here catch a bus to the MAC or to one of the beaches.

MUSEU DO ARTE CONTEMPORÂNEA

☎ 2620 2400; www.macniteroi.com.br in Portuguese; Mirante da Boa Viagem, Niterói; admission R$4; 🕑 10am-6pm Tue-Fri, 11am-7pm Sat & Sun

Designed by Brazil's most famous architect, Oscar Niemeyer, the MAC has a wild curvilinear design that blooms like a flower (or more prosaically, a flying saucer) against sweeping bay views. Unfortunately, the exhibits inside the museum are somewhat less inspiring. To get to the MAC from the Niterói ferry terminal, turn right as you leave and walk about 50m across to the bus terminal in the middle of the road; a 47B minibus will drop you at the museum door.

PONTE RIO–NITERÓI

The Ponte (bridge) Rio–Niterói (Ponte Pres Costa E Silva) offers spectacular views of Baía de Guanabara. It is 15.5km long, 60m high and 26.6m wide, with two three-lane roads. There's a tollbooth 3km from the Niterói city center.

BARRA DA TIJUCA & WEST OF RIO

Eating p149; Shopping p124; Sleeping p200

The Miami of Rio, Barra – as it's known locally – is a sprawling suburb with huge malls and entertainment complexes, long traffic corridors and very little pedestrian movement. The beach here is the real attraction, a wide and lovely 15km-long stretch of pristine shoreline. The commercial area feels quite different from other parts of Rio as Barra's development happened fairly recently. The middle classes first began moving here in the 1970s, when the situation in urban Rio seemed as if it had reached boiling point. Cariocas fled crime and the crowded city to live on a gorgeous stretch of sand. Today, Barra is still a safe neighborhood, but the influx of new residents has created crowded conditions once again.

While first-time visitors don't always make it to Barra da Tijuca, there are some extraordinary sights here, aside from the beach. The lush Sitio Burle Marx contains some of the loveliest gardens in Rio, while the Casa do Pontal houses a fascinating collection of folk art. Once you get beyond the development of Barra, the region gets less and less urban. Some of Rio's loveliest beaches lie out this way. There are also some great restaurants in idyllic settings that seem a far cry from busy downtown Rio.

SITIO BURLE MARX Map p108

☎ 2410 1412; Estrada da Barra de Guaratiba 2019, Guaratiba; admission R$5; 🕑 9.30am & 1pm, by advance appointment only

This huge 350,000-sq-meter estate was once the home of Brazil's most famous landscape architect, Roberto Burle Marx. The estate's lush vegetation includes thousands of plant species, some of which are rare varieties from different corners of the globe. A 17th-century Benedictine chapel also lies on the estate, along with Burle Marx's original farmhouse and studio, where you can see displays of paintings, furniture and sculptures by the talented designer.

CASA DO PONTAL Map p108

☎ 2490 4013; www.popular.art.br/museucasdopontal; Estrada do Pontal 3295, Recreio dos Bandeirantes; admission R$10; 🕑 9am-5.30pm Tue-Sun

Owned by French designer Jacques Van de Beuque, this impressive collection of over 5000 pieces is one of the best folk-art collections in Brazil. The assorted artifacts are grouped according to themes, including music, Carnaval, religion and folklore. The grounds of the museum are surrounded by lush vegetation, which alone makes it worth the trip out here.

BOSQUE DA BARRA Map p108

☎ 3325 6519, guided tours 2509 5099; Km 7, Av das Américas (intersection of Av Ayrton Senna), Barra da Tijuca; 🕑 7am-6pm

Covering 500,000 sq meters of salt-marsh vegetation, the park provides a refuge and breeding area for many small birds and animals. The woods have a jogging track and bicycle path.

MUSEU AEROSPACIAL Map pp60–1

☎ 2108 8954; www.musal.aer.mil.br in Portuguese; Av Marechal Fontenele 2000, Campo dos Afonsos; admission free; 🕑 9am-3pm Tue-Fri, 9.30am-4pm Sat & Sun

This museum maintains expositions on Santos Dumont (the Brazilian father of aviation), Air Marshal Eduardo Gomes, the history of Brazilian airmail and the role of Brazil's air force in WWII. There are lots of old planes, motors and flying instruments. Highlights are replicas of Santos Dumont's planes, the *14 Bis* and the *Demoiselle*. You can also arrange guided visits if you call at least three days in advance.

PARQUE DO MARAPENDI Map p108

Av Sernambetiba, Recreio dos Bandeirantes; 🕑 8am-5pm

At the end of Av Sernambetiba in Recreio dos Bandeirantes, this biological reserve sets aside 700,000 sq meters for study and has a small area for leisure, with workout stations and games areas.

TRANSPORTATION: BARRA DA TIJUCA

Bus Copacabana, Ipanema, Leblon, Flamengo, Centro (175)

BARRA DA TIJUCA & WEST OF RIO

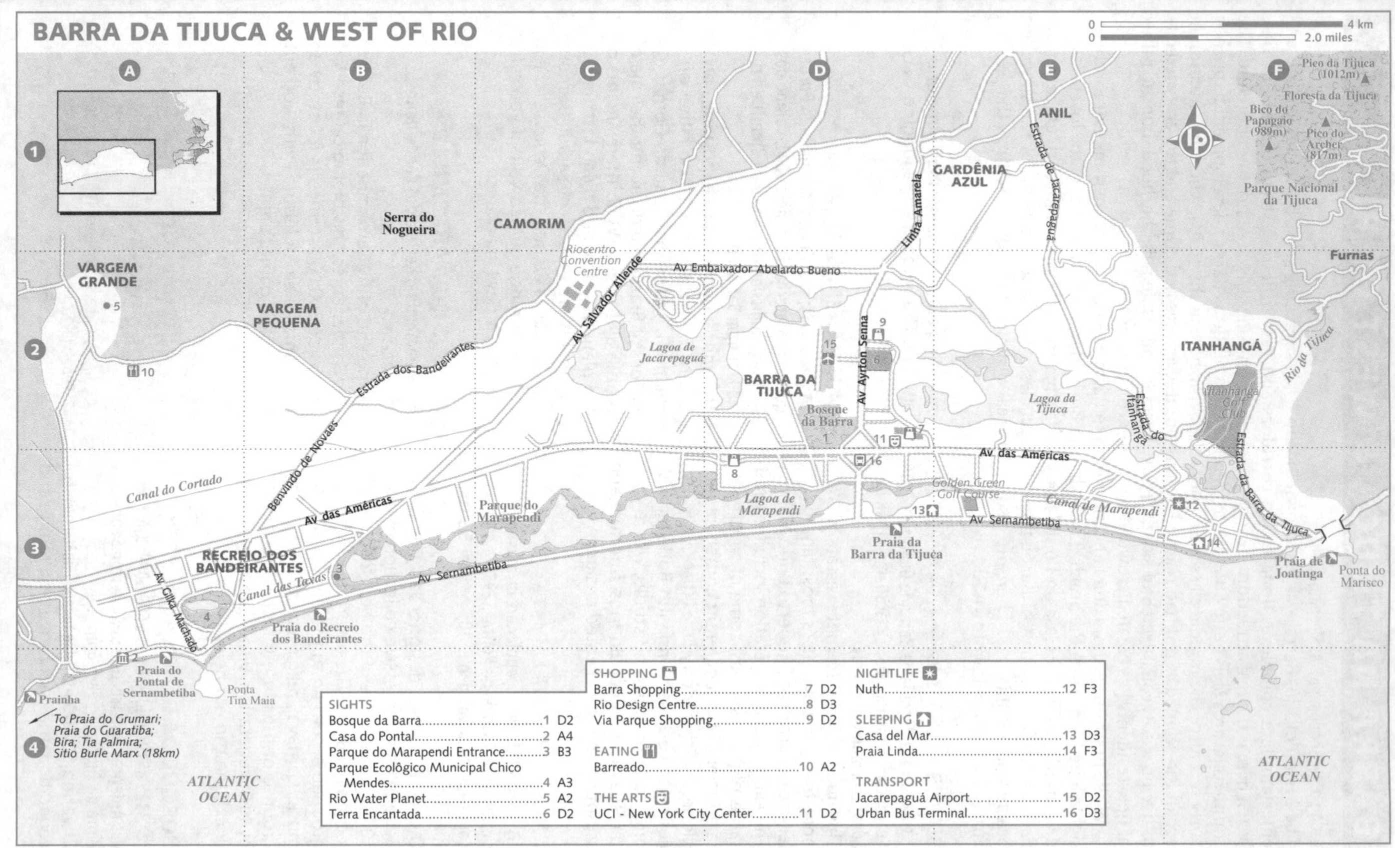

SIGHTS
Bosque da Barra....1 D2
Casa do Pontal....2 A4
Parque do Marapendi Entrance....3 B3
Parque Ecológico Municipal Chico Mendes....4 A3
Rio Water Planet....5 A2
Terra Encantada....6 D2

SHOPPING
Barra Shopping....7 D2
Rio Design Centre....8 D3
Via Parque Shopping....9 D2

EATING
Barreado....10 A2

THE ARTS
UCI - New York City Center....11 D2

NIGHTLIFE
Nuth....12 F3

SLEEPING
Casa del Mar....13 D3
Praia Linda....14 F3

TRANSPORT
Jacarepaguá Airport....15 D2
Urban Bus Terminal....16 D3

BEACHES WEST OF RIO

Although Copacabana and Ipanema are Rio's most famous stretches of sand, there are many stunning beaches in the area, some in spectacular natural settings.

The first major beach you'll reach heading west of Leblon is Praia do Pepino (Map pp60–1) in São Conrado. Pepino is a beautiful beach, and is less crowded than Ipanema. It's also where hang-glider riders like to lounge when they're not soaring overhead.

Although it gets crowded on weekends, Recreio dos Bandeirantes is almost deserted during the week. The large rock acts as a natural breakwater, creating a calm bay. The 2km-long stretch of sand is popular with families.

The secluded 700m-long Prainha lies just past Recreio. It's one of the best surfing beaches in Rio, so it's always full of surfers. Waves come highly recommended here.

The most isolated and unspoiled beach close to the city, Grumari is quiet during the week and packed on weekends with Cariocas looking to get away from city beaches. It is a gorgeous setting, surrounded by mountains and lush vegetation.

From Grumari, a narrow road climbs over a jungle-covered hillside toward Guaratiba. West of here is a good view of the Restinga de Marambaia (the vegetation-rich strip between the beach and the mainland), closed off to the public by a naval base. Cariocas enjoy eating lunch at several of the seafood restaurants in the area.

PARQUE ECOLÔGICO MUNICIPAL CHICO MENDES Map p108

☎ 2437 6400; Km 17, Av Jarbas de Carvalho 679, Recreio dos Bandeirantes; 8.30am-5.30pm

This 400,000-sq-meter park was created in 1989 and named after the Brazilian ecological activist who was murdered for his work. The park protects the remaining sand-spit vegetation from real estate speculators. The facilities include a visitors' center and ecological trails leading to a small lake. Animals protected in the park include butterflies, lizards, tortoises and the broad-nosed caiman.

PRAIA DA BARRA DA TIJUCA Map p108

Av Sernambetiba, Recreio dos Bandeirantes

The best thing about Barra is the beach. It's 12km long, with the lovely blue sea lapping at the shore. The first few kilometers of the eastern end of the beach are filled with bars and seafood restaurants.

The young and hip hang out in front of *barraca* No 1 – also known as the *barraca do Pepê,* after the famous Carioca hang-gliding champion who died during a competition in Japan in 1991.

The further out you go, the more deserted it gets, and the stalls turn into trailers. It's calm on weekdays and crazy on hot summer weekends.

RIO WATER PLANET Map p108

☎ 2428 9000; Estrada das Bandeirantes 24000, Recreio dos Bandeirantes; admission R$78; 10am-5pm Sat, Sun & holidays

Rio Water Planet claims to be the biggest aquatic park in Latin America. Waterfalls, artificial beaches (a bit surprising in this part of the world) and lazy rafting rivers are part of the attractions, as are Rio Kart Planet (an open-air kart track), Rio Show Planet (an area for shows) and Rio Circus Planet.

TERRA ENCANTADA Map p108

☎ 2421 9369; www.terra-encantada.com.br in Portuguese; Av Ayrton Senna 2800, Barra da Tijuca; adult/child R$36/18; 2-9pm Thu-Sat, noon-9pm Sun

The Enchanted Land is a large amusement park in Barra. It includes Cabhum (a 64m, 100km/h free fall), Ressaca (a toboggan ride that goes over a waterfall) and many other rides.

SHOPPING

top picks

- **Pé de Boi** (p121) Best handicrafts
- **Parceria Carioca** (p117) Best guilt-free buying
- **Desculpa, Eu Sou Chique** (p121) Best vintage shop
- **Forum** (p114) Best fashion boutique
- **Modern Sound** (p119) Best record shop
- **Nova Livraria Leonardo da Vinci** (p121) Best bookshop

What's your recommendation? www.lonelyplanet.com/rio-de-janeiro

SHOPPING

Shopping in Rio can mean many things, from browsing eye-catching boutiques in peaceful Leblon to strolling the teeming stalls at the Feira Nordestina on weekends. Not surprisingly, beach and casual wear are a big part of Rio's shopping scene, but less well known are the great variety of stores selling antiques, custom-made handicrafts, wine and spirits, handmade jewelry, records and CDs, coffee-table books and one-of-a-kind goods found only in Rio (like colorful Gilson Martins' handbags).

If you're looking for a hot new outfit for the night, start your shopping foray in Ipanema, and keep in mind that many stores are hidden inside multistory buildings. See p114 for a cheat sheet on some of these well-concealed boutiques. For a more colorful, chaotic experience, metro it up to Centro, where the narrow pedestrian lanes of Saara are packed with discount goods of all shapes and sizes. Copacabana has a bit of high-end and plenty of frenzy for those wanting the complete experience.

Something of an institution in Rio is the *shopping* (mall), which is a good place to hide away when bad weather arrives. In addition to hunting for sales, you can grab a bite (some malls, like Shopping Botafogo, have restaurants with panoramic views) or catch a film.

No matter where you are in Rio, you're probably not far from an open-air market. Delectable tropical fruits and vegetables dominate, but you'll also find markets selling used CDs and records, furniture, clothing and handicrafts.

All listings in this chapter are organized by shopping genre (accessories, music, wine etc) within each neighborhood.

OPENING HOURS

Most stores in Centro open from 9am to 6pm Monday to Friday. A few open on Saturday, usually from 10am to 1pm. In the Zona Sul, stores open from 10am to 6pm Monday to Friday, though some stay open until 8pm or 9pm. On Saturday, shopping hours are 10am to 2pm. Only a few of the big shopping malls open on Sunday – from about 3pm to 8pm.

CONSUMER TAXES

Most stores list their prices with the tax already included, so what you see on the price tag is the total price you'll pay for the goods.

IPANEMA & LEBLON

Ipanema and Leblon are the best hunting grounds for top fashion designs (both homegrown and foreign labels). You'll also find curio and novelty stores, galleries, bookshops, liquor stores and plenty of cafés in which to refuel along the way. There's a lot going on along the main thoroughfare (Rua Visconde de Pirajá in Ipanema and Av Ataulfo de Paiva in Leblon).

GILSON MARTINS Map p64 — Accessories

☎ 2227 6178; Rua Visconde de Pirajá 462, Ipanema; 🕓 10am-8pm Mon-Fri, 10am-4pm Sat

Designer Gilson Martins turns the silhouette of Corcovado into a fashion statement in his flagship store in Ipanema. In addition to glossy handbags, wallets and other accessories, the shop sports a gallery in the back with ongoing exhibitions.

DAQUI Map p66 — Accessories & Home Decor

☎ 2529 8576; Av Ataúlfo de Paiva 1174, Leblon; 🕓 9am-8pm Mon-Fri, 9am-4pm Sat

This tiny boutique is a fun place for a quick stop-off while strolling the neighborhood. Here you'll find handmade jewelry, purses, colorfully designed clothes and curiosities for the home, including tiny mirrors and seductively shaped pencils.

ESCADA Map p66 — Antiques

☎ 2274 9398; Av General San Martin 1219, Leblon; 🕓 5pm-10pm Mon-Sat

One step inside this rambling antique shop, and you'll just know there's some treasure hidden within. The only problem is that it may not fit in your suitcase. Chandeliers, papier-mâché sculptures, along with antique rings, rugs, little statues and countless other objects litter the interior of this store. Peer beneath the dust and you might find a gem.

top picks

RIO SOUVENIRS

- Music Rio is one of the world's best places to expand your CD or vinyl collection. Don't overlook local favorites like singers Maria Rita or Diogo Nogueira.
- Cachaça (cane liquor) Connoisseurs rate the smooth Germana as one of the best brands.
- Swimwear You may not be able to take the beach home, but you can at least flaunt your new tan in a tiny *sunga* (Speedo) or *fio dental* (string bikini).
- Maracatu drum If you don't think the massive northeastern instrument will fit on your coffee table, consider the smaller, gentler *cavaquinho* (small ukulele-like instrument). Maracatu Brasil (p121) and Casa Oliveira (p122) are the best places to look.
- Havaianas The many styles and colors mean there's one for every mood.
- Favela paintings You can find some fantastic art-naïf works for sale on Rocinha's main street, and help support the community.
- Soccer jersey Forget the well-known yellow label. Try and score a jersey for one of Rio's teams: Flamengo, Fluminense, Botafogo or Vasco da Gama.
- Folk art Tap into Brazil's rich handicraft traditions at stores such as Pé de Boi (p121) and Brasil & Cia (p116).

INTERSTUDIO
Map p64 Art & Home Decor

☎ 2511 1237; Rua Visconde de Pirajá 595, Ipanema; 🕑 10am-7pm Mon-Fri, 10am-4pm Sat

This small Ipanema shop sells some beautifully made art pieces. You'll find works in colored glass, wooden boxes, paintings and some intriguing papier-mâché objets d'art. Nearly everything here comes from Brazil (Minas and Recife in particular). Worldwide shipping is available for bigger pieces.

NO MEIO DO CAMINHO
Map p66 Art & Home Decor

☎ 2294 1330; Av General San Martin 1247, Leblon; 🕑 10am-7pm Mon-Fri, 10am-2pm Sat

Showcasing the work of talented Brazilian artisans, No Meio do Caminho has two floors full of pottery, vases, ceramics and woodwork. Decorative items here are more akin to art pieces – and are priced accordingly. It will ship anywhere.

URUCUM ART & DESIGN
Map p64 Art & Home Decor

☎ 2540 9990; Rua Visconde de Pirajá 605, Ipanema; 🕑 10am-8pm Mon-Fri, 10am-5pm Sat

This small, trim shop is in the same complex as the cinema Estação Ipanema (p176) Make your choice from the vases, block prints, playful sculptures, pottery and other artworks for sale.

ARGUMENTO
Map p66 Books & Music

☎ 2239 5294; Rua Dias Ferreira 417, Leblon; 🕑 9am-midnight Mon-Sat, 10am-midnight Sun

One of Leblon's fine neighborhood bookstores, Argumento stocks a small but decent selection of foreign-language books and magazines. The charming café in the back is a perfect place to disappear with a book – or a new friend. A new branch in Copacabana (Map pp76–7) opened recently.

DA CONDE
Map p66 Books & Music

☎ 2274 0359; store 125, Rua Conde de Bernadotte 26, Leblon; 🕑 11am-midnight Mon-Sat

Secreted inside a tiny shopping plaza, this little multilevel bookstore stocks a small selection of English-language titles. You'll also find CDs, DVDs and a café and lounge on the 2nd floor that hosts occasional book signings and other literary events.

LETRAS E EXPRESSÕES
Map p64 Books & Music

☎ 2521 6110; Rua Visconde de Pirajá 276, Ipanema; 🕑 8am-midnight

One of Ipanema's growing assortment of bookshops, Letras e Expressões carries a decent selection of foreign-language books from architectural tomes to fiction and travel books (Lonely Planet titles notwithstanding). It also has a variety of English-language magazines and an internet café (Café Ubaldo), which is nice for sipping cappuccino and sending envy-worthy missives back home. There is also a 24-hour location in Leblon (Map p66).

LIVRARIA DA TRAVESSA
Map p64 Books & Music

☎ 2249 4977; Rua Visconde de Pirajá 572, Ipanema; 🕑 9am-midnight Mon-Sat, 1pm-midnight Sun

One of a growing chain of bookstores around the city, Livraria da Travessa has a small selection of foreign-language books and periodicals. Upstairs it has a good music collection – most of which you can listen to by scanning the discs under the headphone stations. After browsing stop in at the cozy, second-floor café for tasty salads, quiches and desserts.

RENOVAR Map p64 Books & Music

☎ 2287 4080; Rua Visconde de Pirajá 273, Ipanema; 🕑 9am-8pm Mon-Sat

This bookshop has a charming old-world aesthetic and carries some 20,000 titles (a small portion of which are in English). The cozy café in the back is a choice meeting spot for Ipanema's literary minded.

AQUIM Map p66 Chocolates

☎ 2274 1001; Av Ataulfo de Paiva 1321, Leblon

This new neighborhood favorite sells beautifully designed chocolates out of its picture-book store. The artisanal truffles, chocolate cakes and mini tarts look too lovely to eat – though not doing so would be a serious mistake.

KOPENHAGEN Map p66 Chocolates

☎ 2511 1112; Av Ataúlfo de Paiva 1025, Leblon; 🕑 10am-7pm Mon-Fri, 10am-2pm Sat

Serving up tasty bonbons and other decadent chocolate treats, Kopenhagen has been satisfying children and chocoholics since 1928. There's a tiny café on hand if you can't resist the temptation to devour those cognac-filled truffles right there. There's another store in Copacabana (Map pp76–7).

ESCH CAFÉ Map p66 Cigars

☎ 2512 5651; Rua Dias Ferreira 78, Leblon; 🕑 noon until last customer

This restaurant-bar is also the 'house of the Havana,' which means if you have a taste for the Cubans, this is your place. The humidor is stocked with a decent selection, which you can enjoy there over a glass of port, or a few blocks away on the beach. They also have a branch in Centro (Rua do Rosário 108).

CONTEMPORÂNEO Map p64 Clothing

☎ 2287 6204; Rua Visconde de Pirajá 437, Ipanema; 🕑 9am-8pm Mon-Sat

A glowing boutique reminiscent of something you'd find in the center of Soho – better yet Nolita (the fashionistas' neighborhood of choice in New York). See the work of Brazil's best up-and-coming designers here. There's an excellent restaurant (serving contemporary fare of course) inside the store.

FORUM Map p64 Clothing

☎ 2521 7415; www.forum.com.br; Rua Barão da Torre 422, Ipanema; 🕑 10am-6pm Mon-Fri, 10am-2pm Sat

Much touted Brazilian designer Tufi Duek has set up his wildly designed flagship store on a peaceful, tree-lined street just up from the main avenue. Here you'll find elegant, beautifully made pieces from his men's and women's collections – which have secured his reputation among high-end retailers in São Paulo.

ISABELA CAPETO Map p66 Clothing

☎ 2540 5232; Rua Dias Ferreira 45B, Leblon; 🕑 10am-8pm Mon-Fri, 10am-3pm Sat

One of Brazil's rising young stars, Isabela Capeto creates beautifully handmade pieces with seductive lines and a masterful

HIDDEN BOUTIQUES

Lovely shops abound in Ipanema and Leblon, though they're not always obvious to the eye. Some of the best finds are secreted in *galerias* (small shopping plazas) like these:

Forum de Ipanema (Map p64; Rua Visconde de Pirajá 351, Ipanema; 🕑 10am-8pm Mon-Sat) Top stores here include Via Milano shoes; Yes, Brazil apparel; and Bum Bum and Salinas (both selling men's and women's swimwear).

Galeria Ipanema Secreta (Map p64; Rua Visconde de Pirajá 371, Ipanema; 🕑 10am-8pm Mon-Sat) Featuring a number of elegant designs, including the überhip T-shirt shop Ausländer.

Ipanema 2000 (Map p64; Rua Visconde de Pirajá 547, Ipanema; 🕑 10am-8pm Mon-Fri) Ipanema's fashion-conscious shoppers flock to this store gallery in search of something new for the after-office soiree – or the upcoming trip to Búzios.

Rio Design Center (Map p66; ☎ 3206 9100; Av Ataúlfo de Paiva 270, Leblon; 🕑 10am-10pm Mon-Fri, 10am-8pm Sat, 3-9pm Sun) Four floors of galleries and stores, most dedicated to home decor.

use of color. All of her pieces are embroidered and feature add-ons of vintage lace, sequins or fabric trims. A good place to see some of the dresses and skirts that have earned her accolades from *O Globo, Vogue* and others.

OSKLEN Map p64 Clothing

☎ 2227 2911; Rua Maria Quitéria 85, Ipanema; 🕙 10am-7pm Mon-Fri, 10am-2pm Sat
One of Brazil's hottest labels in recent years. The fashions here are light and playful with subdued colors. The company was started in 1988 by outdoor enthusiast Oskar Metsavaht, the first Brazilian to scale Mont Blanc.

OZ Map p64 Clothing

☎ 3204 0754; store 302, Rua Visconde de Pirajá 580, Ipanema; 🕙 10am-7pm Mon-Fri, 10am-2pm Sat
Complete with ruby-red heels and a yellow-brick road of sorts, Oz is a playful send-up of the old Dorothy story. T-shirts are the specialty here and, not surprisingly, come in whimsical designs that work for both the club and the beach.

REDLEY Map p64 Clothing

☎ 2287 4843; Rua Maria Quitéria 99, Ipanema
In the heart of Ipanema, this new multilevel fashion store is a fine place to browse for couture beach duds and streetwear. Unlike most other Ipanema boutiques, this one's aimed at the men, with an excellent assortment of T-shirts, shorts and swim suits.

ESPAÇO BRAZILIAN SOUL Map p64 Clothing & Accessories

☎ 2522 3641; Rua Prudente de Morais 1102, Ipanema
Set in a picturesque little villa, Espaço Brazilian Soul is a two-story boutique selling designer duds (Osklen among them) in the form of board shorts, T-shirts, flip-flops and button-downs. There's more men's apparel than women's, though the dresses are still worth a peak.

GAROTA DE IPANEMA Map p64 Clothing & Accessories

☎ 2521 3168; Rua Vinícius de Moraes 53, Ipanema
Next to the famous restaurant of the same name, this tiny boutique is an excellent place to browse for attractive, reasonably priced bikinis and beachwear. There are also eye-catching T-shirts (for men and women) as well as bags and other accessories.

IPANEMA.COM Map p64 Clothing & Accessories

☎ 2227 1288; Rua Prudente de Morais 237c, Ipanema; 🕙 10am-7pm Mon-Fri, 10am-4pm Sat
Featuring local and international designers, Ipanema.com focuses on men – though it also has women's wear. A good spot if you need a new look in a hurry for that special night out.

LUKO Map p64 Clothing & Accessories

☎ 2540 0589; store 111, Rua Visconde de Pirajá 547, Ipanema; 🕙 10am-7pm Mon-Fri, 10am-4pm Sat
This charming boutique has an eclectic collection of youthful women's couture. Slim, beaded necklaces and bracelets, silk scarves, form-fitting tops and skirts, and slinky lingerie are among the pieces you'll find here. Rumor has it that Luko is a great favorite among TV production companies looking for pieces for their actors.

MIXED Map p64 Clothing & Accessories

☎ 2259 9544; www.mixed.com.br in Portuguese; Rua Visconde de Pirajá 476, Ipanema; 🕙 10am-8pm Mon-Fri
One of Rio's premier boutiques, Mixed actually originated in São Paolo. Ipanemans, however, love it as their own. The shoes and platforms, blouses and pants sold here aim to capture the essence of Carioca (resident of Rio) sensuality. And they do it quite well.

TEARGAS Map p64 Clothing & Accessories

☎ 2512 9163; Rua Visconde de Pirajá 529, Ipanema; 🕙 10am-7pm Mon-Fri, 10am-3pm Sat
Daring men's and women's fashions are for sale at this innovative store and design studio in Ipanema. Stylized T-shirts (including one bearing the company logo, a gas mask), intricately embroidered button-downs, sleek jackets, pants and jeans are suitable not just for the mass demonstration, but for the posh after-party as well.

VALE DAS BONECAS Map p64 Clothing & Accessories

☎ 2523 1794; 2nd fl, Rua Visconde de Pirajá 351, Ipanema; 🕙 10am-8pm Mon-Fri, 10am-2.30pm Sat
Youthful street fashion is the focal point at this small Ipanema boutique. Local designers play with color and material here – not

always successfully. But if you're looking for something a little edgy, the Vale das Bonecas (Valley of the Dolls) is a fine destination.

WÖLLNER OUTDOOR
Map p64 Clothing & Accessories

☎ 2512 6531; Rua Visconde de Pirajá 511, Ipanema; 🕑 10am-9pm Mon-Fri

The great outdoors, and the shirt and shorts you'll need to enjoy it, seem to be the inspiration for Wöllner. Clothes and accessories are ruggedly styled, not unlike Abercrombie and American Eagle. Once you've browsed the selections, grab a *cafézinho* (small black coffee) and a chocolate tort at the café in the front.

SOCIEDADE ANÔNIMO
Map p64 Clothing & Kitsch

☎ 3201 2064; Rua Visconde de Pirajá 351, Ipanema

The 'Anonymous Society' is a playful store full of young women's fashions (good for both the beach and a night out) as well as colorful jewelry, kids clothes, silly postcards, bags of plastic dinosaurs, Buddhas in little cases and other assorted toys and accessories that may be just the thing for an inventive night on the town.

BRASIL & CIA Map p64 Handicrafts

☎ 2267 4603; Rua Maria Quitéria 27, Ipanema; 🕑 10am-7pm Mon-Sat, 10am-4pm Sun

This new handicrafts shop sells colorful works in papier-mâché, porcelain and glass, showcasing Brazil's rich artisan traditions. Figurines, wooden boxes, dolls and other crafts are made by artists from Pernambuco and Alagoas. Perfect for keepsakes of your travels.

EMPÓRIO BRASIL Map p64 Handicrafts

☎ 2239 3567; store 108, Rua Visconde de Pirajá 595, Ipanema; 🕑 9am-8pm Mon-Sat

Hidden in the back of a small shopping center, Empório Brasil has a small, attractive collection of regional handicrafts, as well as incense and beauty products showcasing the fruits of the Amazon. The store also offers massage and other treatments.

MUSEU AMSTERDAM SAUER
Map p64 Jewelry

☎ 2512 1132; www.amsterdamsauer.com; Rua Garcia D'Ávila 105, Ipanema; 🕑 9.30am-2.30pm Mon-Fri, 10am-2pm Sat

Well known for its impressive collection of precious stones, Amsterdam Sauer also sells finely crafted jewelry. Watches, pens, wallets and other accessories are available too. Visitors can also check out the museum (p65) while they are here.

ANTONIO BERNARDO Map p64 Jewelry

☎ 2512 7204; Rua Garcia D'Ávila 121, Ipanema; 🕑 10am-8pm Mon-Fri, 11am-4pm Sat

Designer-goldsmith Antonio Bernardo has garnered attention for his lovely bracelets, earrings and necklaces. His boutiques in Rio include one in Forum de Ipanema (p114).

MARIA OITICICA Map p64 Jewelry

☎ 2522 2447; Rua Barão de Jaguaripe 176

Using native materials found in the Amazon, Maria Oiticica has created some lovely handcrafted jewelry inspired by indigenous art. Seeds, plant fibers and tree bark are just some of the ingredients of bracelets, necklaces and earrings, and her work helps support struggling local communities with craft-making traditions.

H STERN Map p64 Jewelry & Accessories

☎ 2259 7442; hstern@hstern.com.br; Rua Garcia D'Ávila 113, Ipanema; 🕑 8.30am-6.30pm Mon-Fri, 8.30am-2pm Sat

The famous jeweler H Stern has an array of finely crafted jewelry, watches and other accessories for sale. At the company's headquarters you can also take a tour of the H Stern gem museum (p67).

MUSICALE Map p64 Music

☎ 2540 5237; Rua Visconde de Pirajá 483, Ipanema; 🕑 10am-7pm

This small music shop has narrow aisles, but you'll come across some real finds if you brave the elbow jousting at Musicale. Used and new CDs are organized somewhat by category, and you can listen to any used CD at one of the in-store decks. There's a small café on hand.

TOCA DO VINÍCIUS Map p64 Music

☎ 2247 5227; www.tocadovinicius.com.br; Rua Vinícius de Moraes 129, Ipanema; 🕑 9am-9pm Mon-Fri, 10am-9pm Sat & Sun

Bossa nova fans shouldn't miss this store. In addition to its ample CD selection of contemporary and old performers, Toca do Vinícius sells music scores and composition books. Upstairs a tiny museum displays memorabilia of the great songwriter and poet Vinícius de Moraes. Occasional concerts in the afternoon fill this neighborhood with smooth bossa sounds.

SOLLAS Map p64 Shoes
☎ 2511 5239; Av Henrique Dumont 68, Ipanema
Designer Carla Guglielmetti has gained a notable following for her eye-catching footwear at this glammy Ipanema boutique. Styles range from the understated to the bold, with stripes and animal prints featured on some of her flats and platforms. She also has handbags and leather sandals for men.

SHOPPING LEBLON Map p66 Shopping Center
☎ 3138 8000; Av Afrânio de Melo Franco 290, Leblon
The hottest, newest shopping destination in Rio is this glittering multistory shopping center packed with top-name Brazilian and foreign labels. There are plenty of tempting stores that will drain your vacation funds as well as good restaurants, a cinema and a lavish café, complete with a piano player and an expedition jet hovering over the tables.

LIDADOR Map p66 Wine & Spirits
☎ 2512 1788; Av Ataúlfo de Paiva 1079, Leblon; 🕑 10am-8pm Mon-Fri, 10am-5pm Sat
One of Leblon's best wine shops, Lidador stocks a decent variety of good Chilean and Argentinean wines as well as vintages from Europe and beyond. *Cachaças,* rums and even Brazilian wines are available if you're looking for something with a little more bite.

GÁVEA, JARDIM BOTÂNICO & LAGOA

Aside from a few scattered shops, there isn't much of a shopping scene in Jardim Botânico or Lagoa. Residents from the neighborhood typically head to Ipanema, Leblon or the huge Shopping da Gávea mall to satisfy their retail cravings. On weekends, however, several interesting markets make the journey here worthwhile: the Babilônia Feira Hype (p118) and the Praça Santos Dumont Antique Fair (p118).

VIT Map pp70–1 Antiques
☎ 2294 2410; Rua JJ Seabra 18, Jardim Botânico; 🕑 10am-6pm Mon-Fri, 10am-3pm Sat
In a small but flourishing block in Jardim Botânico, this rambling antiques shop is a fun place for browsing while checking out the neighborhood. You'll find old globes, furniture from the '30s to the '60s, stylized lamps, vases, crockery and other curios from the past.

PARCERIA CARIOCA
Map pp70–1 Clothing & Accessories
☎ 2259 1437; store 108, Rua Jardim Botânico 728, Jardim Botânico
This sweet little store sells clever T-shirts, colorful handbags and accessories, and an assortment of shoes, jewelry and decorative pieces, all of which combine elements of craftwork with contemporary fashion. As a bonus, Parceria Carioca works with NGOs and co-ops that provide jobs for artisans from poor communities. They also have stores in Forum Ipanema (Rua Visconde de Pirajá 351, Ipanema) and Shopping da Gávea.

O SOL Map pp70–1 Handicrafts
☎ 2294 5099; Rua Corcovado 213, Jardim Botânico; 🕑 9am-6pm Mon-Fri, 9am-1pm Sat
O Sol is run by Leste-Um, a nonprofit social-welfare organization. This delightful store displays the works of regional artists and sells Brazilian folk art in clay, wood and porcelain. It also sells baskets and woven rugs.

SHOPPING DA GÁVEA
Map pp70–1 Shopping Center
☎ 2274 9896; Rua Marquês de São Vicente 52, Gávea; 🕑 10am-10pm Mon-Sat, 3-9pm Sun
Shopping da Gávea touts itself as the preferred mall of artists and intellectuals, which may or may not matter to you when you're laying down serious cash for those sneakers. There are 200 stores, four performance theaters and numerous restaurants, including La Pasta Gialla, Brazil's bruschetta capital with 29 different types.

COPACABANA & LEME

Copacabana's shops, just like its local residents, are a diverse bunch, with everything from *cachaça* to soccer jerseys on hand, as well as shoe stores, surf shops and record stores thrown in the mix. Fashion hunters will find lower-tier labels than in Ipanema, along with lower prices to match. Between Copa and Ipanema is the Galeria River, a low-rise shopping mall lined with surf and swimwear shops.

MARKET LOVERS GUIDE TO RIO

Rio's many excellent markets are ideal places for exploring the subcultures lurking beneath the city's skin – whether brushing elbows with antique lovers, recent migrants from the northeast or the youthful flocks of fashionistas from the Zona Sul. Several markets, like the Feira Nordestina, the Babilônia Feira Hype and the once-monthly Feira do Rio Antigo, are as much about food and music as they are about shopping. A little bargaining is expected when making purchases, but keep in mind that sellers generally don't overinflate their prices and so aren't willing to haggle very much.

Av Atlântica Fair (Map pp76–7; Av Atlântica near Rua Djalma Ulrich, Copacabana; 7pm-midnight) Paintings, drawings, jewelry, clothing and a fair bit of tourist junk make up this Copacabana market. It's located on the median along Av Atlântica.

Babilônia Feira Hype (Map pp70–1; ☎ 2267 0066; www.babiloniahype.com.br; admission R$4; 2-10pm every other Sat & Sun) A festival atmosphere pervades this popular weekend fair. Young crowds mill through the clothing, sunglasses and jewelry stalls as live bands play nearby. There are also places to get your fortune read by *misticos* (psychics) or receive a henna tattoo. Food stalls (of the fried-sausages-and-beer variety) litter the fairgrounds. The event is held either in the Joquei Clube (Rua Jardim Botânico 971, Jardim Botânico) or in Barra (Av das Américas 1510). Call or check website for details.

Feira de Música (Map pp90–1; Rua Pedro Lessa, Centro; 9am-5pm Mon-Fri) On weekdays, next to the Biblioteca Nacional, record and CD stalls line the small lane. You'll find everything from American indie rock to vintage Brazilian funk, and most vendors will let you listen to any of their discs for sale – new or used.

Feira do Rio Antigo (Map pp90–1; ☎ 2224 6693; Rua do Lavradio, Centro; 10am-6pm 1st Sat of month) Although the Rio Antiques Fair happens just once a month, don't miss it if you're in town. The colonial buildings become a living installation as the whole street fills with antiques, and samba bands add to the ambience.

Feira Nordestina (Map pp60–1; ☎ 3860 9976; Campo de São Cristóvão, São Cristóvão; 10am-4pm Tue-Thu, nonstop 10am Fri to 10pm Sun) For details see p103.

Hippie Fair (Map p64; Praça General Osório, Ipanema; 9am-5pm Sun) The Zona Sul's most famous market, the Hippie Fair (aka Feira de Arte de Ipanema) has lots of artwork, jewelry, handicrafts and leather goods plus the occasional piece of furniture for sale. A stall in the southeast corner of the plaza sells tasty northeastern cuisine. Don't miss it.

Photography and Image Fair (Map p87; ☎ 2558 6350; Museu da República, Rua do Catete 153, Catete; 9am-5pm last Sun of month) Works from amateur and professional photographers are for sale at this once-monthly market in the verdant Parque do Catete. There's also a multimedia room, which hosts workshops, talks and slide projections.

Praça do Lido Market (Map pp76–7; Praça do Lido, Copacabana; 8am-6pm Sat & Sun) Copacabana's response to Ipanema's widely popular Hippie Fair, this weekend affair features handicrafts and souvenirs, soccer jerseys, a few jewelry stands and, from time to time, a man selling amazing slices of chocolate cake.

Praça do Mercado Feira de Antiguidades (Map pp90–1; Praça do Mercado; 9am-5pm Sat) This antique market next to the Niterói ferry terminal has a vast array of antique and not-so-antique finds – silverware, carpets, pocket watches, jewelry, typewriters, records and art-deco and art-nouveau items. You can find nearly anything out here, making it a browser's paradise.

Praça Santos Dumont Antique Fair (Map pp70–1; Praça Santos Dumont, Gávea; 9am-5pm Sun) Small but substantial, Gávea's antique fair features jewelry, records, watches, dinnerware, books and other odds and ends.

Praça Quinze Handicrafts Fair (Map pp90–1; Praça Quinze de Novembro, Centro; 8am-6pm Thu-Fri) This street fair near the Imperial Palace features craftsmen selling their works of leather, wood, porcelain, glass and silver. There are also stalls with regional Brazilian fare.

Shopping Cassino Atlântico Antiques Fair (Map pp76–7; Av Atlântico 4240, Copacabana; 11am-7pm Sat) Inside an air-conditioned shopping center, this antique fair consists of three floors of blown glass, sculpture, carpets, silverware and jewelry. Pieces are in much better condition here, which is clearly reflected in the prices. A tearoom and live music help bring on the mood.

FAVELA HYPE Map pp76–7 Clothing & Accessories

☎ 3201 0406; Rua Francisco Otaviano 67, Arpoador

Inside the Galeria River, this stylish boutique sells daring youthful fashions for men and women. Founded by the sisters Kananda and Krishna Soaras in Santa Teresa in 2001, Favela Hype incorporates a mix of retro and vintage design in the clothing, accessories and shoes, and the label deserves credit for its socially responsible employment practices.

ARTE BRASILIS Map pp76–7 Handicrafts

☎ 2513 1238; Av NS de Copacabana 1313, Copacabana; 9am-6pm Mon-Sat

One of Copacabana's few decent handicraft stores, Arte Brasilis sells colorful wall hangings, wooden carvings, place settings and other handmade objects from Minas Gerais and the northeast. There are better places to shop for souvenirs, but this one is convenient if you're based in Copacabana.

MARIA DE BARRO Map pp76–7 Handicrafts

☎ 2235 4339; Av Atlântica 1998, Copacabana; 10am-10pm Mon-Sat, 3-9pm Sun

This tiny shop sells a small selection of handcrafted pieces from the northeast of Brazil. Wooden geometric vases with animals such as capybaras carved in the side, tiny clay pots and sculptures in stone are among the simple, art-naïf pieces.

MUNDO VERDE Map pp76–7 Health Food

☎ 2257 3183; www.mundoverde.com.br in Portuguese; Av NS de Copacabana 630, Copacabana; 9am-6pm Mon-Fri, 9am-2pm Sat

Brazil's largest health-food retailer, Mundo Verde sells organic products, including *salgados* (bar-type snacks), and other snacks besides; jams made from Amazonian fruits; and other assorted goods. The sun-care products are usually cheaper here than in pharmacies – and much better for your skin.

BOSSA NOVA & COMPANHIA Map pp76–7 Music

☎ 2295 8096; Rua Duvivier 37A, Copacabana; 9am-7pm Mon-Sat

This new, well-lighted music shop is a nice addition to the neighborhood, with a fine assortment of bossa, *choro* and samba CDs and LPs as well as coffee-table books, sheet music and biographies of top Brazilian composers.

top picks

SHOPPING STRIPS

- Av Ataúlfo de Paiva, Leblon Boutiques selling haute couture sprinkled among cafés, bookshops and restaurants.
- Av Nossa Senhora (NS) de Copacabana, Copacabana Packed during the week, this strip is lined with shops selling everything from chocolates to soccer balls, with plenty of street vendors hawking their wares along the sidewalks.
- Rua do Lavradio, Lapa Rows of antique stores mixed with hypermodern furniture shops, along with a few cafés and bars – sometimes inside the stores.
- Rua Visconde de Pirajá, Ipanema Ipanema's vibrant shopping strip has boutiques, shopping centers and scores of dining and coffee-sipping options.
- Senhor dos Passos, Centro One of the main streets coursing through the Middle Eastern bazaar-like Saara, with clothing and curio shops packing the street.

MODERN SOUND Map pp76–7 Music

☎ 2548 5005; www.modernsound.com.br; Rua Barata Ribeiro 502, Copacabana; 9am-9pm Mon-Fri, 9am-8pm Sat

One of Brazil's largest music stores, Modern Sound makes a fine setting for browsing through the many shelves of samba, electronica, hip-hop, imports, classical and dozens of other well-represented categories. The café in the store features live concerts daily.

MUSICALE Map pp76–7 Music

☎ 2267 9607; Av NS de Copacabana 1103C, Copacabana; 10am-8pm Mon-Sat

Musicale has a small but decent selection of used and new CDs. In keeping with the neighborhood that surrounds the store, a diverse bunch shops here – club kids, old samba softies, expats trapped in the '80s – which is reflected in the range of albums for sale. Musicale also buys and trades CDs.

GALERIA RIVER Map pp76–7 Shopping Center

Rua Francisco Otaviano 67, Arpoador; 10am-6pm Mon-Sat

Surf shops, skateboard and rollerblade outlets, and shops selling beachwear and fashions for young nubile things fill this shopping gallery in Arpoador. Shorts, bikinis, swim trunks, party attire and gear for outdoor adventure are in abundance. The shops here – like Ocean Surf Shop – are a good place to inquire about board rentals, which cost about US$10 per day. Those interested in rock climbing and trekking should stop by the Casa do Montanhista, a trekking-apparel store for more information about courses.

SHOPPING SIQUEIRA CAMPOS

Map pp76–7 Shopping Center

☎ 2549 0650; Rua Siqueira Campos 143, Copacabana; 10am-8pm Mon-Sat

One of Rio's first malls, this quirky shopping mall packs an intriguing mix of stores along an upward-winding ramp. You'll find numerous antique shops, jewelry, no-nonsense art galleries, a pet shop and dozens of other surprising finds that you won't come across in Leblon. There's also a grocery store on the first floor.

DEU LA DEU VINHOS

Map pp76–7 Wine & Spirits

☎ 2235 7287; Rua Domingos Ferreira 66, Copacabana

Copacabana's best wine shop is hidden on a quiet street one block from the beach. In addition to a fair assortment of Chilean and Argentine vintages, you'll find a few decent Brazilian labels like Casa Vadulga and Miolo. A wide assortment of *cachaças* and other spirits round out the offerings.

top picks

RECORD STORES

- Feira de Música (p118) During the week browse through bins of records and CDs at this open-air market in Centro.
- Modern Sound (p119) One of Brazil's largest music stores stocks an impressive selection, with lots of staff recommendations, top Rio artists and imports. Live music shows are staged here daily.
- Plano B (p124) An underground favorite among local DJs, Plano B has new and used records and CDs, as well as a tattoo parlor in the back.
- Toca do Vinícius (p116) Bossa nova's smooth grooves live on in this shop dedicated to old and new artists of the genre. Upstairs, Vinícius' fans can get a glimpse of his life's work in the small museum dedicated to him.

BOTAFOGO & URCA

Shopping in Botafogo usually means heading to the high-rise mall overlooking the bay. There are, however, other good options, such as the Museu do Indio's small handicrafts shop (with all pieces made by Brazilian tribes) as well as a cozy bookshop near the cinemas with a back-room café. Urca, quiet old soul that she is, has nothing in the way of shopping.

LIVRARIA PREFÁCIO

Map pp78–9 Books & Music

☎ 2527 5699; Rua Voluntários da Pátria 39, Botafogo; 10am-10pm Mon-Fri, 2-10pm Sat & Sun

This charming bookshop stocks a small selection of foreign titles as well as music. And perusers need not go hungry or thirsty while they browse for titles: a slender bar in front delivers refreshing glasses of *chope* (draft beer), while seating upstairs and in the café (p143) in the back offers heartier fare. The bookshop hosts an occasional poetry reading or record-release party.

ARTÍNDIA

Map pp78–9 Handicrafts

☎ 2286 8899; Museu do Índio, Rua das Palmeiras 55, Botafogo; 9.30am-5.30pm Tue-Fri, 1-5pm Sat & Sun

Inside the grounds of the Museu do Índio, Artíndia sells a variety of indigenous handicrafts – masks, musical instruments, toys, pots, baskets and weapons. Regional artists, mostly from northern tribes, craft objects using native materials like straw, clay, wood and feathers.

BOTAFOGO PRAIA SHOPPING

Map pp78–9 Shopping Center

☎ 2559 9880; Praia de Botafogo 400, Botafogo; 10am-10pm Mon-Sat, 3-10pm Sun

Botafogo's large shopping center has dozens of stores, featuring Brazilian and international designers to suit every style – and clothe every part of the body. The 3rd floor's the best: for top designers check stores like Philippe Martins, Giselle Martins, Osklen and Equatore. The mall also has a cinema and several top-floor restaurants, such as Emporium Pax (p143), with great panoramic views.

RIO OFF-PRICE SHOPPING

Map pp78–9 Shopping Center

☎ 2542 5693; Rua General Severiano 97, Botafogo; 🕑 10am-10pm Mon-Sat, 3-9pm Sun

Near Rio Sul Shopping, Rio Off-Price Shopping is something of a factory outlet center. It has many of the same stores as other malls – domestic and international designers – but prices are about 20% lower. It also has two cinemas and meal options (mostly fast food).

RIO SUL SHOPPING

Map pp78–9 Shopping Center

☎ 2545 7200; www.riosul.com.br in Portuguese; Rua Lauro Müller 116, Botafogo; 🕑 10am-10pm Mon-Sat, 3-10pm Sun

The biggest shopping center you can reach without heading to Barra, Rio Sul has over 400 shops, featuring both the prominent and the obscure, cinemas, restaurants and, on weekends, overwhelming crowds.

FLAMENGO, LARANJEIRAS & COSME VELHO

While not a traditional shopping destination, this area offers some worthwhile exploring, particularly if you stop in the whimsical vintage shop on Rua Alice and the art gallery-handicrafts emporium known as Pé de Boi in Laranjeiras.

DESCULPA, EU SOU CHIQUE

Map p84 Clothing & Home Decor

☎ 2225 6059; Rua Alice 75, Laranjeiras

On bohemian Rua Alice, 'Sorry I'm Chic' is a delightful store selling a rambling assortment of vintage fashion, modish relics from the '60s and plenty of great finds from decades past. The upstairs area with a bar is also a theater space with periodic performances throughout the year.

JEITO BRASILEIRO Map p84 Handicrafts

☎ 2205 7636; Rua Ererê 11A, Cosme Velho; 🕑 9am-6pm Mon-Fri, 9am-4pm Sat, 9am-1pm Sun

Next to the Corcovado train terminal in Cosme Velho, Jeito Brasileiro has a wide selection of handicrafts from all over the country, including folk art made by members of the Camucim tribe.

PÉ DE BOI Map p84 Handicrafts

☎ 2285 4395; Rua Ipiranga 55, Laranjeiras; 🕑 9am-7pm Mon-Fri, 9am-1pm Sat

Although everything is for sale here, Pé de Boi feels more like an art gallery than a handicrafts shop, owing to the high quality of the wood and ceramic works, and the tapestries, sculptures and weavings. This is perhaps Rio's best place to see one-of-a-kind pieces by artists from Bahia, Amazônia, Minas Gerais and other parts of Brazil.

MARACATU BRASIL

Map p84 Percussion Instruments

☎ 2557 4754; www.maracatubrasil.com.br; Rua Ipiranga 49, Laranjeiras; 🕑 10am-6pm Mon-Sat

You can't miss the lime-green building that houses this small percussion store and workshop. Inside, you can buy an *afoxê* (a gourd shaker with beads strung around it), conga and bongo drums, tambourines and other Brazilian percussion instruments. Upstairs is a drum clinic, where you can study a number of styles with local musician-teachers; see p85 for more details.

CENTRO & CINELÂNDIA

For a break from the chrome and glass of the Zona Sul, check out the old-school shops of historic Centro. Bargains abound in the narrow pedestrian streets around Saara (p89), where shops peddle everything from clothes and cosmetics to toys, jerseys and all the fabric and sequins you'd ever need to make your own Carnaval costume. Nearby streets offer a little of everything, including discounted record shops, used bookshops and percussion stores often set behind century-old storefronts. Centro also boasts the city's largest antique market, Praça do Mercado Feira de Antiguidades (p118), open on Saturday.

NOVA LIVRARIA LEONARDO DA VINCI Map pp90–1 Books

☎ 2533 2237; Av Rio Branco 185, Centro; 🕑 9am-7pm Mon-Fri, 9am-noon Sat

With one of Rio's best foreign-language book collections, da Vinci also has a wide range of art and photography books, as well as coffee-table books about Rio's history and architecture. It's one floor down – follow the spiral ramp. There's a decent coffee shop nearby.

FARMERS MARKETS

The *feiras* (markets) that pop up in different locations throughout the week are the best places to shop for fruit and vegetables. For an authentic slice of homegrown Carioca commerce, nothing beats wandering through and taking in the action.

Cobal do Humaitá (Map pp78–9; ☎ 2266 1343; Rua Voluntários da Pátria 446, Botafogo; 🕑 7am-4pm Mon-Sat) The city's largest farmers market sells plenty of flowers, veggies and fruits; there are also cafés and restaurants on hand for those looking for a bit more.

Cobal de Leblon (Map p66; ☎ 2239 1549; Rua Gilberto Cardoso, Leblon; 🕑 7am-4pm Mon-Sat) Smaller than Humaitá's market, the Cobal de Leblon makes a fine setting for stopping to smell the flowers – or the *maracujá* (passion fruit) – before settling down to a meal at one of the open-air restaurants.

Copacabana Wednesday on Rua Domingos Ferreira, Thursday on Rua Belford Roxo and Rua Ronald de Carvalho, Sunday on Rua Décio Vilares.

Glória Sunday on Rua Augusto Seveiro.

Ipanema Monday on Rua Henrique Dumont, Tuesday on Praça General Osório and Friday on Praça NS da Paz.

Jardim Botânico Saturday on Rua Frei Leandro.

Leblon Thursday on Rua General Urquiza.

Urca Sunday on Praça Tenente Gil Guilherme.

LIVRARIA DA TRAVESSA

Map pp90–1 Books & Music

☎ 3231 8015; Travessa de Ouvidor 17, Centro; 🕑 9am-8pm Mon-Fri, 10am-1pm Sat

Livraria da Travessa, hands down, wins Centro's most-charming-bookstore award. The location, tucked off the narrow alley Travessa de Ouvidor, accounts for a large part of it, then there's the knowledgeable sales staff, the bistro, and the light falling just so across the shelves. A second Livraria da Travessa (Map pp90–1) on Av Rio Branco 44 has a decent café overlooking the store.

LIVRARIA IMPERIAL

Map pp90–1 Books & Music

☎ 2533 4537; Praça Quinze de Novembro 48, Centro; 🕑 9am-8pm Mon-Fri, 9.30am-2pm Sat

Bossa nova plays overhead at this charming bookstore-music shop. In addition to new books (including a selection of foreign-language titles), Livraria Imperial sells CDs covering bossa, samba and other styles.

TABACARIA AFRICANA

Map pp90–1 Cigars & Tobacco

☎ 2509 5333; Largo do Paço 38, Centro; 🕑 9am-5pm Mon-Fri

The sweet fragrance of pipe tobacco is embedded in the walls and furniture of this shop facing the Praça Quinze. Regulars sit at the table in front slowly drawing on the pick of the day while the afternoon drifts by, smoke like. In the back, the glass jars contain a variety of flavors and aromas. Let the shopkeeper put a mix together for you.

LOJA NOVO DESENHO

Map pp90–1 Home Decor

☎ 2524 2290; Av Infante Dom Henrique 85, Centro; 🕑 noon-6pm Tue-Fri, noon-7pm Sat & Sun

This 'Store of New Design' sells pure eye candy. Some of Rio's best modern designs are here (created by some of the country's best industrial designers). And you'll find whimsical two-dimensional vases, surreal clock faces and other clever works.

CASA OLIVEIRA Map pp90–1 Musical Instruments

☎ 2325 8109; Rua da Carioca 70, Centro; 🕑 10am-6pm Mon-Fri

One of several excellent music shops on Rua da Carioca, Casa Oliveira sells all the pieces that make up the rhythm section of Carnaval *baterias* (percussion sections). If *forró* (traditional, fast-paced music from the northeast) is more your speed, you can also purchase a variety of mandolins as well as accordions and electric guitars.

BERINJELA Map pp90–1 Music

☎ 2532 3646; Av Rio Branco 185, Centro

This is a favorite among music insiders for finding that old record or classic samba CD. Though not huge, the selection of used albums is decent, and the staff is friendly and helpful. It's hidden in a small shopping center, down a spiral ramp and just past Leonardo da Vinci bookshop.

EMPÓRIO MUSICALE Map pp90–1 Music

☎ 2252 9714; Rua Sete de Setembro, Centro; 🕒 10am-6pm Mon-Fri

This is an LP-lover's dream. You'll find bins and bins of old records covering the full spectrum of Brazilian music. You can unearth some gems of classic samba, *Música Popular Brasileira* (MPB) and funk. CD users have less to celebrate, with a rather paltry selection.

SUB & SUB Map pp90–1 Outdoor Gear

☎ 2509 1176; subsub.com.br; sobreloja (first flight up), Rua da Alfândega 98, Centro; 🕒 10am-6pm Mon-Fri

Sub & Sub has an array of gear for outdoor adventure: climbing and mountaineering, diving, snorkeling, camping and hiking. The knowledgeable staff can also recommend courses for those interested in learning a new craft.

UNIMAGEM Map pp90–1 Photography

☎ 2507 7745; Rua dos Andradas 29, Centro; 🕒 9am-6pm Mon-Fri, 9am-noon Sat

The choice of professional photographers in the city, Unimagem has a good selection of new and used cameras (SLRs, TLRs, point-and-shoot) as well as all the accessories (tripods, film, paper). It also runs a superb developing lab: black-and-white, color, slides and of course digital images. It can also provide a one-hour developing service for both slide and color film.

VERTICAL SHOPPING

Map pp90–1 Shopping Mall

☎ 2224 0697; Av Sete de Setembro 48, Centro; 🕒 9am-8pm Mon-Fri

This 1950s high-rise was transformed into a shopping center in 2002, giving Centro its own nine-story mall. Check out sexy beachwear in Farm and Totem Praia, shoes at Sollas and Via Mia and fashions at Juliana Faro.

EXPAND WINE STORE Map pp90–1 Wine

☎ 2220 1887; Av Erasmo Braga 299B, Centro; 🕒 9am-8pm Mon-Fri

This well-stocked wine shop is a great place to buy a few bottles while out exploring Centro. Chile, Argentina and 11 other countries are represented among the vintages. The 2nd floor has a wine bar where you can taste those velvety malbecs and merlots.

SANTA TERESA & LAPA

Stomping ground for Rio's bohemian crowd, Santa Teresa has a growing number of handicraft shops and vintage stores with some enticing restaurants and cafés that add to the appeal. In Lapa, you'll find Rua do Lavradio, the city's best antiques street. It's at its liveliest on the first Saturday of the month.

ALFONSO NUNE'S ANTIQUARIO

Map pp98–9 Antiques

☎ 2232 2620; Rua do Lavradio 60, Lapa; 🕒 9am-7pm Mon-Fri, 9am-3pm Sat

The old colonial edifice features an excellent selection of antiques – from tables and chairs to chandeliers and glassware. Discerning collectors will want to give the shop a good look over before proceeding to the other antique stores lining Lavradio.

CLOTHING SIZES

Women's clothing

Aus/UK	8	10	12	14	16	18
Europe	36	38	40	42	44	46
Japan	5	7	9	11	13	15
USA	6	8	10	12	14	16

Women's shoes

Aus/USA	5	6	7	8	9	10
Europe	35	36	37	38	39	40
France only	35	36	38	39	40	42
Japan	22	23	24	25	26	27
UK	3½	4½	5½	6½	7½	8½

Men's clothing

Aus	92	96	100	104	108	112
Europe	46	48	50	52	54	56
Japan	S		M	M		L
UK/USA	35	36	37	38	39	40

Men's shirts (collar sizes)

Aus/Japan	38	39	40	41	42	43
Europe	38	39	40	41	42	43
UK/USA	15	15½	16	16½	17	17½

Men's shoes

Aus/UK	7	8	9	10	11	12
Europe	41	42	43	44½	46	47
Japan	26	27	27½	28	29	30
USA	7½	8½	9½	10½	11½	12½

Measurements approximate only – try before you buy.

ARQUITETURA & DECORACÃO

Map pp98–9 Antiques

☎ 3970 0836; Rua do Lavradio 34, Lapa

One of Rua do Lavradio's most magical antique shops, with a small assortment of antiques ranging from heavy 1930s pieces to sleek, trim designs from the 1960s. Unfortunately, most of what's for sale is furniture, and you may have difficulty squeezing the Oscar Niemeyer *poltrona* (armchair) into your suitcase. Sharing the space is a small art gallery.

DO SECULO PASSADO

Map pp98–9 Antiques

☎ 2252 2770; Rua do Lavradio 106, Lapa

One of Lavradio's biggest antique shops, this place is packed with glass- and dishware, furniture, iron kettles, lamps, oil paintings and a wide variety of other displays that make for a fascinating glimpse into the past.

LA VAREDA

Map pp98–9 Handicrafts

☎ 2222 1848; www.lavareda.hpg.com.br in Portuguese; Rua Almirante Alexandrino 428, Santa Teresa; 🕑 10am-9pm Tue-Sun, 1-9pm Mon

On the *bonde* (tram) line near Largo do Guimarães, La Vareda stocks a colorful selection of handicrafts from local artists and artisans. Pottery, furniture, paintings, handmade dolls and tapestries cover the interior of the old store. You can also purchase stationery and prints highlighting historic Santa Teresa.

TRILHOS URBANOS

Map pp98–9 Handicrafts

☎ 2242 3632; Rua Almirante Alexandrino 402A, Santa Teresa; 🕑 10am-7pm Tue-Sat

Vying for attention near La Vareda, Trilhos Urbanos stocks a small but interesting assortment of handicrafts. Works by local artists and artisans are for sale – photographs, picture frames, paintings and works in metal.

PLANO B

Map pp98–9 Music & Tattoos

☎ 2507 9860; Rua Francisco Muratori 2A, Lapa; 🕑 10am-7pm Mon-Wed, 10am-10pm Thu & Fri, noon-10pm Sat & Sun

Only in Lapa will you encounter a place where you can pick through bins of old jazz records and new electronic mixes before stepping into the back room to get a tattoo down your arm, inspired perhaps by that old Elza Soares song playing overhead. Plano B also has a decent selection of CDs, and the young staff can advise – if samba-funk eludes you.

BRECHÓ ARTE 70

Map pp98–9 Thrift Shop

☎ 2221 3205; Rua Monte Alegre 337, Santa Teresa; 🕑 10.30am-9pm Tue-Sat, 2-9pm Sun

Brechó Arte 70 features several racks of secondhand clothes as well as the occasional antique from time to time. Depending on your luck, you can come across some good finds here. *Brechós,* incidentally, are secondhand stores, which come and go in this neighborhood.

BARRA DA TIJUCA & GREATER RIO

Barra da Tijuca is the kingdom of shopping malls, each offering something slightly different than the one next door – one even services its 4.8km of stores with a monorail.

CLUBE CHOCOLATE

Map pp60–1 Eclectic

☎ 3322 3733; store 202, São Conrado Fashion Mall, Estrada da Gávea 899, São Conrado; 🕑 noon-midnight Sun-Fri, 10am-midnight Sat

This innovative store is definitely not to be missed on any serious shopping itinerary. Amid a spacious, handsomely designed boutique you can browse through clothing designs of Marc Jacobs, Prada, Paul Smith and all the fashionable top Brazilian stylists. You can also have a bite at the French bistro or sample some of the latest CDs, books and gadgets.

BARRA SHOPPING

Map p108 Shopping Center

☎ 3089 1000; www.barrashopping.com.br in Portuguese; Av das Américas 4666, Barra da Tijuca; 🕑 10am-10pm Mon-Sat, 3-10pm Sun

Rio's largest mall (and one of the biggest in South America) is an easy place to shop away a few hours or days. Some 30 million shoppers pass through Barra's doors each year. Over 500 stores clutter the 4km-long stretch of stores, along with five movie screens, a children's parkland and a wealth of dining options.

RIO DESIGN CENTER

Map p108 Shopping Center

☎ 2461 9999; www.riodesign.com.br in Portuguese; Av das Américas 7770, Barra da Tijuca;

🕑 **10am-10pm Mon-Fri, 10am-8pm (stores), 11am-midnight (restaurants) Sat, 3-10pm Sun**
This architecturally rich center features a number of excellent home-furnishing stores selling designer lamps, vases, decorative pieces and furniture. It also has some very good restaurants and a few art galleries.

SÃO CONRADO FASHION MALL

Map pp60–1 Shopping Center

☎ **3083 0300; Estrada da Gávea 899, São Conrado;** 🕑 **10am-10pm**
Rio's most beautiful mall features all the big names – Armani, Versace, Louis Vuitton – and all of Brazil's most recognizable designers. It's located in the posh neighborhood of São Conrado, near the Hotel Intercontinental.

VIA PARQUE SHOPPING

Map p108 Shopping Center

☎ **2421 9222; www.shoppingviaparque.com.br in Portuguese; Av Ayrton Senna 3000, Barra da Tijuca;** 🕑 **10am-10pm Mon-Sat, 3-10pm Sun**
With 280 stores, six movie theaters and abundant restaurants, this is the heart of Rio's consumer culture. It's also home to one of the big concert arenas, Claro Hall.

EATING

top picks

What's your recommendation? www.lonelyplanet.com/rio-de-janeiro

EATING

If you haven't heard of Rio's excellent restaurants, you're in good company. Despite top-notch chefs, ethnically diverse cuisine and a rich bounty from farm, forest and sea, the city hasn't earned much of a culinary reputation abroad. Inside Brazil it's a different story, with Cariocas (residents of Rio) convinced that there's no place quite like home for sitting down to a bang-up meal – whether that entails mouth-watering steaks, coconut-flavored Afro-Brazilian stews or glistening slices of sashimi and plump sushi rolls.

It's easy to eat well in Rio, no matter what your budget or your dietary restrictions (although counting calories is daunting in this city of temptation). Fresh tropical fruit is the basic building block for a healthy meal. Most Cariocas (residents of Rio) start their mornings off with a stop at the local juice bar, where they can enjoy two or three dozen varieties of vitamin-filled elixirs, including Amazonian flavors like *açaí* (juice made from an Amazonian berry), *cupuaçu* (Amazonian fruit), *carimbola* (star fruit) and others. You'll also find the best restaurants make brilliant use of passion fruit, mango and other fruits. For a bit of caffeine, Cariocas opt for a *cafézinho,* short, black, strong and often quite sweet coffee.

At lunchtime, locals favor per-kilo restaurants, which range from simple, working-class affairs to sumptuous buffets lined with fresh salads, grilled meats, pastas, seafood dishes and a table packed with desserts. Like elsewhere, dinner is often as much about socializing as it is about eating, and the city has some magical settings for lingering over a long meal. You can dine at a sidewalk café overlooking the beach, book an outdoor table at a hidden spot high up in Santa Teresa or join the din of fellow diners in a traditional old-fashioned boteco, which are casual, open-sided bars scattered all over town.

Variety comes in many forms in Rio – which is not surprising given the large immigrant population. Lebanese, Japanese, Spanish, German, French and Italian cuisines are among the standouts, though there's an equally broad selection of regional Brazilian restaurants. Diners can sample rich, shrimp-filled *moqueca* (seafood stew cooked in coconut milk) from Bahia or tender *carne seca* (jerked meat) covered in *farofa* (manioc flour), a staple in Minas Gerais. Daring palates can venture north into Amazonia, enjoying savory *tacacá* (manioc paste, lip-numbing leaves of the vegetable *jambu,* and dried shrimp) or *tambaqui* (a large Amazonian fish) and other meaty fishes from the mighty Amazon. Cowboys and the *gaúcho* from the south bring the city its *churrascarias,* Brazil's famous all-you-can-eat barbecue restaurants where crisply dressed waiters bring piping-hot spits of fresh roasted meats to your table. Wherever you end up, try to pace yourself. Brazilian dishes are normally quite large – and some dishes are meant for two. When in doubt, ask the server to clarify.

Cafés, patisseries and ice-cream shops are also an integral part of the Rio experience. The leafy back streets of the Zona Sul (particularly restaurant-filled Ipanema) are great places to recharge with a cappuccino, a slice of chocolate torte or a creamy scoop of *sorvete* (ice cream). Juice bars whip up grilled sandwiches, and light bites like *pão de queijo* (cheese-filled rolls), but for the best assortment of snacks, plan a meal at the neighborhood boteco. *Salgados* (bar snacks) come in many satisfying, highly addictive, (and, yes unhealthy) varieties, like *bolinhos de bacalhau* (deep-fried codfish balls), *pasteis* (crispy pastries filled with meat or cheese) or *coxinhas* (pear-shaped cornmeal balls filled with chicken).

Those who'd like to get into the cuisine scene should check out *Eat Smart in Brazil* by Joan and David Peterson. It includes an overview of Brazil's culinary heritage and regional cuisines as well as recipes and a detailed glossary.

WHERE TO EAT

Ipanema and Leblon are the best places to browse for a memorable meal. There you'll find Rio's star chefs, beautifully set dining rooms and the fashion-conscious crowds that fill them. You'll also enjoy excellent meals in assorted Copacabana restaurants – though not in the most obvious places (not in the beachside strip for example). Other gems are hidden in the streets of Jardim Botânico, high up in Santa Teresa and along the narrow pedestrian lanes in Centro. For details on top streets for mealtime browsing, see boxed text, p131.

PRICE GUIDE

The price symbols in this chapter indicate the cost of a two-course meal for one person, excluding drinks.

$$$	over R$60
$$	R$25-60
$	under R$25

PRACTICALITIES

Opening Hours

Aside from juice bars, cafés and bakeries, few restaurants open for breakfast (those that do start serving around 7am). Cariocas don't typically order a sit-down meal until noon, the time when most places open. Restaurants in Centro typically open only during the week and only for lunch – usually from noon until 3pm. Restaurants in the Zona Sul, with its wealth of culinary options, attract larger dinner crowds than lunch ones, with restaurants filling up around 9pm or so. Typically, they don't close until midnight – and a few places stay open until 3am or 4am. On weekends, lunch is often the big meal of the day – Saturday being the traditional day to linger over *feijoada* (black beans and pork stew).

How Much?

Rio can be light or hard on the wallet, depending on where and what you eat. Juice bars are the cheapest; you can order a *misto quente* (toasted ham and cheese sandwich) and juice for around R$8. Pay-by-weight restaurants are also good value. These eateries vary in price and quality, but average about R$20 per kilo (a fairly full plate will cost R$14).

There is a vast array of midrange dining options; expect to pay between R$15 and R$25 for a main course. *Churrascarias* (traditional barbecue restaurants) offer all you can eat dining options – try to fast for at least six hours before going. Prices range from around R$30 to R$60 per person, with more food than you could possibly imagine (much less *eat*).

To experience the fruits of Rio's best chefs, head to Centro by day, where power-lunching executives enjoy masterfully prepared sushi, steak or duck confit in stately environments. By night, restaurants in Leblon and Ipanema (and a handful in Copacabana) compete for annual culinary prizes. A main course in any of these locations will cost upwards of R$40 and will have decent wine cellars that range beyond the Argentine and Chilean vintages at other places.

Booking Tables

Most restaurants accept reservations for both lunch and dinner, so call ahead to avoid a wait. Restaurants that don't accept reservations often have a bar where you can have a drink while you wait for a table.

Unfortunately, when you call to make a reservation, the person who answers the phone is not likely to speak English. Concierges are adept at booking seats for you, but if you're game, have a stab at Portuguese – Brazilians are usually flattered at the attempt.

Tipping

In restaurants, a 10% tip is usually included in the bill. When it isn't included – and your waiter will generally tell you if it's not – it's customary to leave 10%. If the service was exceptionally bad or good, adjust accordingly. Tipping in cafés and bars isn't common, but is always appreciated.

Groceries & Takeout

Open-air markets abound in the city. Juicy pineapples, mangos, papayas and other fruits make fine snacks for the beach. Some markets (p118) feature excellent regional cuisine – like Ipanema's Feira Hippie on Sunday with its Bahian vendors, and the northeastern restaurants at the Feira Nordestina.

Supermarkets provide another option for self-caterers. The city's most prominent supermarket chain, Zona Sul, is prevalent throughout Ipanema, Leblon and Copacabana. Zona Sul supermarket (p137) on Rua Dias Ferreira in Leblon is the best supermarket in Rio, with imported cheeses, fresh breads, deli items and salads, and wines and spirits. Nearby is Hortifruti (p137), an indoor fruit and vegetable market. Leblon's Garcia & Rodrigues (p133), which is also a restaurant, stocks a seductive selection of French and Italian wines, cheeses and other high-end deli items. The patisserie and ice-cream counters alone warrant a visit.

Downtown, the gleaming shelves at Lidador (p148) enable commuters to stock up on smoked meats, chocolates and other delicacies before they head off to the suburbs. Per-kilo places all have takeout containers, if you're in a hurry and simply want to grab something freshly cooked, while juice bars also accommodate takeout customers.

One needn't, however, even step off the sidewalks to find sustenance. Throughout town, you'll find vendors selling *agua de coco* (coconut water), available by the cup or by the liter. On the beach, you're never more than a stone's throw from drink stands; Copacabana also has shiny all-glass restaurant kiosks where you can get a full meal. Favorite drinks at these places are caipirinhas or beer *agua de coco,* served straight from the coconut. If you're frolicking in the waves and can't be bothered making the trek up the beach, just wait for the food to come to you. Vendors laden with heavy bags roam the beach till sundown, offering beer, soda, *globos* (a bag of puffed chips), maté (a tea-like drink) *sanduiches naturais* (sandwiches filled with ricotta cheese, chicken salad or tuna salad). Others offer *queijo coalho* (hot cheese), which will be cooked on a small coal-powered stove in front of you and served to you on a stick (with herbs if you prefer). You can also find vendors cooking *churrasco* (roasted meat) – also served on a stick, with or without *farofa*.

IPANEMA & LEBLON

Rio's best restaurants lie in the neighborhoods of Leblon and Ipanema. Here, along the tree-lined side streets abutting the major thoroughfares, you'll find a mix of trendy eateries, outdoor cafés and juice bars. Price and quality generally run high here, though the stylish new flavor of the month doesn't always live up to the hype.

ANTIQUARIUS Map p66 Portuguese $$$

☎ 2294 1049; Rua Aristídes Espínola 19, Leblon; mains R$60-95; ⏲ noon-2am

Serving without a doubt the city's best Portuguese cuisine, Antiquarius is a rewarding but pricey spot to celebrate old-world cuisine with an antique-filled dining room, top-notch service and lovingly prepared dishes. Some particular recommendations include the leg of lamb, the wild boar in red-wine sauce and the Portuguese favorite *bacalhau* (cod), elevated here to the sublime.

CAESAR PARK Map p64 Brazilian $$$

☎ 2525 2525; Av Vieira Souto 460, Ipanema; feijoada buffet R$75; ⏲ noon-6pm

Some of Rio's best *feijoada* is served at the Caesar Park Hotel on Saturday. The rich cuisine is expertly prepared, without a lot of extra fat, and you can sample nearly a dozen varieties of pork dishes. A live samba band lends a festive atmosphere to the feasting.

FASANO AL MARE Map p64 Seafood $$$

☎ 3202 4000; Av Vieira Souto 80, Ipanema; mains R$50-70; ⏲ noon-4pm & 7pm-1am

One of the most anticipated restaurant openings of recent years, the lavish Fasano Al Mare opened in 2007 and was hailed an instant success by Rio's media. Seafood features Italian accents and comes beautifully prepared in dishes like risotto with saffron and rock lobster, seared tuna and whole fish baked in salt. This is one place where reservations are essential.

TEN KAI Map p64 Japanese $$$

☎ 2540 5100; Rua Prudente de Morais 1810, Ipanema; mains R$40-70; ⏲ 7pm-1am Mon-Fri, 1pm-midnight Sat & Sun

In the top tier of the city's Japanese restaurants, Ten Kai serves mouth-watering sashimi and sushi, and maintains the strong culinary traditions of the East. The ambience is pure charm, with an artful interior lit by glowing paper lanterns.

CELEIRO Map p66 Salads $$

☎ 2274 7843; Rua Dias Ferreira 199, Leblon; per kg R$66; ⏲ 10am-5.30pm Mon-Sat

This casual spot on one of Leblon's main restaurant strips packs crowds in during lunchtime. Celeiro is mostly famed for its salad bar, though the small eatery serves excellent soups, pastries and quiches. Get there early to avoid the rush.

ZUKA Map p66 Eclectic $$

☎ 3205 7154; Rua Dias Ferreira 233, Leblon; mains R$40-60; ⏲ 7pm-1.30am Mon, noon-4pm & 7pm-1.30am Tue-Fri, 1.30pm-1.30am Sat & Sun

This trendy spot continues to draw crowds with its ever-inventive dishes. Tuna foie gras in thyme or the smoked duck with caramelized pineapple are excellent, though you'll want dessert – skewers of fruit in sake or chocolate soufflé.

GERO Map p64 Italian $$

☎ 2239 8158; Rua Aníbal de Mendonça 157, Ipanema; mains R$30-90; ⏲ noon-4.30pm & 7pm-1am Mon-Fri, noon-2am Sat, to midnight Sun

Elegance is the spice of choice at this handsome Ipanema favorite on posh Aníbal de Mendonça. Run by hotelier and restaurateur Rogério Fasano, Gero has some exquisite choices including tuna carpaccio, risotto with Tuscan sausage and the simple but delicious ravioli with tomato, mozzarella and basil.

PLATAFORMA Map p66 Churrascaria $$

☎ 2274 4022; Rua Adalberto Ferreira 32, Leblon; mains R$43-50; ⌚ noon until last customer
This restored *churrascaria* still draws a garrulous mix of politicians, artists and tourists. Dark, mellow woods in the dining room match the tones of the roast meats traveling from table to table. Also in this complex is the Bar do Tom, with live bossa nova, and downstairs is the Plataforma Show – the over-the-top Carnaval show for tourists.

ESPAÇO BRASA LEBLON Map p66 Churrascaria $$

☎ 2111 5700; Av Afrânio de Melo Franco 131, Leblon; per person R$50-60; ⌚ noon-1am
One of Rio's top *churrascarias*, Espaço Brasa features nearly 30 different types of meat as well as sushi, seafood and salads. The beautifully presented all-you-can-eat buffet is set in a dining room with tall ceilings and elegant table settings.

CASA DA FEIJOADA Map p64 Feijoada $$

☎ 2247 2776; Rua Prudente de Morais 10B, Ipanema; feijoada R$50; ⌚ noon-midnight
Admirers of Brazil's historic *feijoada* needn't wait until Saturday to experience the meaty meal. At this 15-year-old institution any day is fine to sample the rich black-bean and salted-pork dish. Served with the requisite orange slices, *farofa* and grated kale (cabbage), it goes nicely with a caipirinha.

CARLOTA Map p66 Eclectic $$

☎ 2540 6821; Rua Dias Ferreira 64, Leblon; mains R$40-60; ⌚ 7pm-midnight Tue-Fri, 1pm-midnight Sat & Sun
This award-winning restaurant has an intimate ambience that sits just right with the delicate cuisine. The small but ever-changing menu features elements from traditional Portuguese cooking (like the cod recipes) as well as Eastern influences (salmon sashimi, shiitake dishes). Regardless, inventive chef Carla Pernambuco always creates some memorable meals.

top picks

EAT STREETS

- **Rua Barão da Torre, Ipanema** This long, tree-lined street has stylish, time-tested favorites.
- **Rua Dias Ferreira, Leblon** A great street for serious culinary browsing, it is packed with award-winning eateries and ever-daring newcomers.
- **Rua Garcia D'Ávila, Ipanema** One of Ipanema's poshest locales, this is a choice destination for a light meal after window-shopping. Neighboring Rua Aníbal de Mendonça is the runner-up.
- **Rua Almirante Alexandrino, Santa Teresa** Perhaps Rio's most picturesque eat street, this one is lined with colorful restaurants offering sushi, pizza, Amazonian cuisine and everything in between.
- **Rua do Rosário, Centro** The eastern end of this old cobblestone street has an enticing selection of sidewalk cafés and bistros.

DA SILVA Map p64 Portuguese $$

☎ 2521 1289; Rua Barão da Torre 340, Ipanema; per kg R$38-45; ⌚ 11.30am-2am
Da Silva puts on a fine buffet for those who want to sample excellent Portuguese cuisine without all the fussiness. Lamb stew, pork tenderloin and delicate desserts all make regular appearances at the lunchtime self-serve per-kilo buffet – and on the nightly à la carte menu.

CAPRICCIOSA Map p64 Pizza $$

☎ 2523 3394; Rua Vinícius de Moraes 134, Ipanema; pizzas R$30-45; ⌚ 6pm-2am
Inside this trendy high-end pizzeria, you'll find delicious thin-crust pizzas employing the freshest ingredients. The price is high but so is the quality, and toppings aren't so much tossed onto the curst as they are artfully arranged. Among many flavorful combinations is the signature capricciosa (ham, bacon, an egg, artichoke hearts and mushrooms).

AZUL MARINHO Map p64 Seafood $$

☎ 2513 5014; Av Francisco Bhering, Praia do Arpoador, Ipanema; mains for two R$45-65; ⌚ noon-midnight
Below the Arpoador Inn, Azul Marinho serves an excellent range of seafood dishes, and the outdoor tables facing the ocean have the best beachside setting you'll find

FEIJOADA

As distinctively Carioca as Pão de Açúcar (Sugarloaf; p80) or Cristo Redentor (Christ the Redeemer; p85), the *feijoada completa* is a dish that constitutes an entire meal, which often begins with a caipirinha aperitif.

A properly prepared *feijoada* is made up of black beans slowly cooked with a great variety of meat – including dried tongue and pork offcuts – seasoned with salt, garlic, onion and oil. The stew is accompanied by white rice and finely shredded kale, then tossed with croutons, fried *farofa* (manioc flour) and pieces of orange.

Feijoada has its origins in Portuguese cooking, which uses a large variety of meats and vegetables; fried *farofa* (inherited from the Indians) and kale are also Portuguese favorites. The African influence comes with the spice and the tradition of using pork offcuts, which were the only part of the pig given to slaves.

Traditionally, Cariocas eat *feijoada* for lunch on Saturday (it's rarely served on other days). Among the top places to sample the signature dish are Caesar Park (p130), Galeto do Leblon (p134) and Casa da Feijoada (p131), which is one of the few places in Rio that serves *feijoada* daily. Vegetarians can sample tasty meat-free versions of *feijoada* at Vegetariano Social Club (p135) or Fontes (p136).

If you find yourself craving the dish after you return home, try your hand at making it.

Recipe

Ingredients

6 cups dried black beans
½kg smoked ham hocks
½kg Brazilian *lingüiça* (Brazilian sausage; substitute chorizo or sweet sausage)
½kg Brazilian *carne seca* or lean Canadian (loin-cut) bacon
1kg smoked pork ribs
The intrepid can add one each of a pork ear, foot, tail and tongue
2 bay leaves
3 garlic cloves, minced
1 large onion, chopped
3 tablespoons olive oil
4 strips smoked bacon
salt and black pepper
orange slices to garnish
rice, *farofa,* kale or collard greens to serve
hot sauce (optional) to serve

Preparation

After soaking beans overnight, bring them to a boil in 3L of water and then keep them on low to medium heat for several hours, stirring occasionally. Meanwhile, cut up the ham hocks, *lingüiça* and *carne seca* into 3cm or 4cm chunks, separate the pork ribs by twos and place them all in a separate pan full of water and bring to a boil. After the first boil, empty out the water and add the mixture, along with the bay leaves and salt and pepper, to the beans. As the pot simmers, in a separate pan sauté the garlic and onion in olive oil, adding in the smoked bacon. Take two ladles of beans from the pot, mash them and add to the frying pan. Stir around, cook for a few more minutes, then add frying-pan contents to the pot; this will thicken the mixture. Simmer for another two to three hours, until the beans are tender and the stock has a creamy consistency. Remove bay leaves and serve over rice with *farofa* and kale or collard greens. Garnish with fresh orange slices. Add hot sauce if desired, and be sure to enjoy with a cold caipirinha.

in the Zona Sul (there's no traffic between you and the sea, only sand). Try one of the *moquecas* (stew) or its famous whole fish baked in salt.

FRONTERA Map p64 Self-Serve $$

☎ 3289 2350; Rua Visconde de Pirajá 128, Ipanema; per kg R$35-38; ⏰ 11am-11pm

Run by a Dutch chef, Frontera offers more than 60 plates at its delectable lunch buffet, featuring a medley of French, Thai, Italian, Indian and other world flavors. It has a cozier atmosphere than most per-kilo places.

NAM THAI Map p66 Thai $$

☎ 2259 2962; Rua Rainha Guilhermina 95B, Leblon; mains R$30-50; ⏰ 7pm-1am Mon, 11.30am-4pm & 7pm-1am Tue-Fri, noon-1am Sat, to 11pm Sun

Thai cuisine is a rarity in Rio, which makes charming Nam Thai even more of a star.

The French colonial interior is a cozy setting for the eclectic Thai cooking. Favorites are squid salad and spicy shrimp curry with pineapple. No less intoxicating are Nam Thai's tropical drinks, like the *caipivodca de lychee* (lychee vodka caipirinha).

RÁSCAL Map p66 Self-Serve $$

☎ 3138 8503; Shopping Leblon, Av Afrânio de Melo Franco 290, Leblon; all-you-can-eat R$38-45

This popular São Paulo chain arrived in Rio in 2006 and quickly earned top marks for its fantastic lunch buffet. The huge spread of Italian cuisine includes salads, bruschetta, pizzas, pastas (six different kinds), along with a few juicy grill choices. At night Ráscal is à la carte.

NIK SUSHI Map p64 Japanese $$

☎ 2512 6446; Rua Garcia D'Ávila 83, Ipanema; all-you-can-eat R$29-42; 🕒 11.30am-midnight Tue-Sat, 1-11pm Sun

This simple but stylish Japanese restaurant has earned many loyal customers for its decent prices and delicately prepared dishes. Grilled items are available but are not as popular as the sushi – owing largely to the all-you-can-eat sushi lunches and dinners.

GARCIA & RODRIGUES Map p66 French $$

☎ 3206 4100; Av Ataúlfo de Paiva 1251, Leblon; mains R$28-50; 🕒 8am-midnight Sun-Thu, to 1am Fri & Sat

Serving French food with a Brazilian accent (like roast veal à la Pantanal), Garcia & Rodrigues remains popular with Gallic expats in the city. Its two floors provide an elegant dining experience, though you can also sit in the café in front if you simply want a quick bite. Behind the glass counters surrounding the tiled floor, you'll find breads and cheeses, a good wine selection, homemade ice cream and good-looking desserts.

ZAZÁ BISTRÔ TROPICAL
Map p64 French-Thai $$

☎ 2247 9101; Rua Joana Angélica 40, Ipanema; mains R$29-50; 🕒 7.30pm-midnight Sun-Wed, to 1.30am Fri & Sat

French-colonial decor and delicately spiced cuisine await those venturing inside this charming converted house in Ipanema. Inventive combinations like pumpkin and chestnut risotto or sesame-battered tuna with wasabi cream enhance the seductive mood inside. Upstairs, diners lounge on throw pillows, while candles glow along the walls. You can also dine on the porch out front – everything here is organic.

QUADRUCCI Map p66 Italian $$

☎ 2249 2301; Rua Dias Ferreira 233, Leblon; mains R$30-50; 🕒 noon-1am Mon-Sat, to 7pm Sun

Boasting a charming wooden patio, this Italian restaurant serves decent plates in a handsome but low-key setting. Start off with a tuna ceviche before moving on to tagliatelli with lamb and artichoke sauce or tortellini with basil pesto. Strudels and tortes finish off the proceedings nicely.

SUSHI LEBLON Map p66 Japanese $$

☎ 2512 7830; Rua Dias Ferreira 256, Leblon; mains R$25-40; 🕒 noon-4pm & 7pm-1.30am Mon-Sat, 1.30pm-midnight Sun

Leblon's top sushi destination boasts a Zen-like ambience with a handsome, dark wood sushi counter setting the stage for succulent cuisine. In addition to sashimi and sushi, you'll find grilled *namorado* (a type of perch) with passion fruit *farofa,* sea-urchin ceviche and refreshing sake to complement the meal.

OSTERIA DELL'ANGOLO Map p64 Italian $$

☎ 2259 3148; Rua Paul Redfern 40, Ipanema; mains R$25-50; 🕒 noon-4pm & 6pm until last customer Mon-Fri, 6pm until last customer Sat & Sun

Northern Italian cuisine is prepared and served with consummate skill. You'd be hard pressed to find fault with fresh pastas, seafood and much-lauded risottos – the squid risotto in ink sauce in particular. President Lula, among other notable visitors, once dined in the elegant but understated Osteria.

GULA GULA Map p64 Brazilian $$

☎ 2259 3084; Rua Henrique Dumont 87A, Ipanema; mains R$24-45; 🕒 noon-midnight

In a recent move to a cozy villa on Ipanema's western edge, Gula Gula continues to remain one Ipanema's culinary favorites – which means a lot in a neighborhood ever in search of the new. Quiches and salads are tops at this casual spot, but those in search of heartier fare can opt for grilled meats or other Brazilian dishes. Gula Gula is franchising fast, with locations in Centro (☎ 3852 1174; Rua Primeiro de Março 23A) and Leblon (☎ 2284 8792; Rua Rita Ludolf 87A) among other places.

BAZZAR Map p64 Eclectic $$

☎ 3202 2884; Rua Barão da Torre 538, Ipanema; mains R$26-40; ⏲ noon-midnight Mon-Thu, to 2am Fri & Sat, 10am-6pm Sun

Set on a peaceful, tree-lined street, this nicely designed restaurant serves a wide variety of cuisine, making it a good spot if you're not sure what you're in the mood for, but want something dazzling. Top choices are grilled *namorado* with whole-grain rice, citrus and pesto, and lamb with polenta and mushrooms. There's a smaller branch hidden on the second floor of Ipanema's Livraria da Travessa (☎ 2249 4977; Rua Visconde de Pirajá 572, Ipanema).

ARTIGIANO Map p64 Italian $$

☎ 2512 6107; Av Epitácio Pessoa 204, Ipanema; mains R$25-35; ⏲ 6pm-midnight Mon-Sat, noon-11pm Sun

Overlooking the Jardim de Alah, Artigiano is set in a picturesque villa with more than a hint of the old-world about it. Here, you will find an older, well-dressed crowd enjoying classic Italian fare, including some 20 superb varieties of handmade pasta amid the oil paintings and antique furnishings.

ALESSANDRO E FEDERICO
Map p64 Pizza $$

☎ 2522 5415; Rua Garcia D'Ávila 151, Ipanema; mains R$22-36; ⏲ 7pm-2am

Dominated by the wood-burning oven at center stage, this stylish two-story restaurant serves some of Ipanema's best thin-crust pizzas. You'll also find a large wine cellar and a well-dressed neighborhood crowd. Another Alessandro e Federico (☎ 2521 0828; Rua Garcia D'Ávila 134; ⏲ 9am-1am) on the same street specializes in fresh sandwiches and has an inviting front patio.

FELLINI Map p66 Self-Serve $$

☎ 2511 3600; Rua General Urquiza 104, Leblon; per kg R$37-45; ⏲ 11.30am-4pm & 7.30pm-midnight

One of Leblon's top buffet restaurants, Fellini has an enticing selection of dishes: salads, pastas, grilled fish and shrimp, a sushi counter and the hallowed roast-meat counter. Fellini's modest dining room attracts a mix of hungry patrons – tourists, neighborhood folk and the beautiful crowd included.

FRATELLI Map p66 Italian $$

☎ 2259 6699; Av General San Martin 983, Leblon; mains R$24-48; ⏲ 6pm-2am Mon-Fri, noon until last customer Sat & Sun

On a quiet street in Leblon, Fratelli's large glass windows frame families and young couples enjoying a fine neighborhood restaurant. It's the food, however, that ought to be on display: creamy linguini with *langosta* (lobster), polenta with porcini and Brie and plump tortellini all pair nicely with Fratelli's decent wine selection.

GALETO DO LEBLON Map p66 Brazilian $$

☎ 2294 3997; Rua Dias Ferreira 154, Leblon; mains R$20-36; ⏲ 11am-3am

One of the pioneers on this street, Galeto do Leblon has been around for over 35 years. Although a recent renovation has created an airy, modern feel, with glass windows around the outside, Galeto still serves the traditional Brazilian dishes that have made it such a neighborhood favorite over the years. On Saturday, stop in for excellent *feijoada*.

JUICE CO Map p66 Eclectic $$

☎ 2294 0048; Av General San Martin 889, Leblon; mains R$20-38; ⏲ noon-midnight

This stylish two-story restaurant serves much more than just tasty, freshly squeezed juices. In an überdesigned lounge-like setting, you can sample a wide range of fare – foccacia sandwiches, salads, risottos, grilled fish and roast meats, any of which can be paired nicely with one of 60 juice concoctions.

MIO Map p64 Italian $$

☎ 2521 2648; Rua Farme de Amoedo 52, Ipanema; mains R$24-32; ⏲ noon-2am

A mix of locals and *turistas* gather at this longtime Ipanema favorite for tasty traditional Italian dishes and excellent grilled seafood. A huge aquarium dominates the main dining room – though diners in the front patio will have their own glassed-in experience. There's also an impressive wine cellar (containing 700 vintages) and a humidor stocked with cigars.

KILOGRAMA Map p64 Self-Serve $$

☎ 2512 8220; Rua Visconde de Pirajá 644, Ipanema; per kg R$28; ⏲ 11am-11pm Mon-Sat, to 7pm Sun

A mix of young and old converge on this excellent lunch buffet during the day. There's a vague art-modern glow to the place, giving it a splash of style – which is a rarity among *a quilo* (per kilo) self-serve restaurants. Kilograma features lots of fresh fruits and salads, good cheeses, roast meats and sushi.

VIA SETE Map p64 Eclectic $$

☎ 2512 8100; Rua Garcia D'Ávila 125, Ipanema; mains R$24-40; noon-midnight

This restaurant on upscale Garcia D'Ávila serves a good selection of salads and sandwich wraps, as well as heartier fare like grilled tuna steak and a high-end cheeseburger (covered with mushrooms, thyme and a red-wine sauce). The pleasant front-side patio is a prime spot for sipping smooth tropical cocktails while practicing the discreet art of people-watching.

GAROTA DE IPANEMA Map p64 Brazilian $$

☎ 2523 3787; Rua Vinícius de Moraes, Ipanema; mains R$20-35; 11am-2am

A mix of tourists and neighborhood regulars pack the tables at the former bar where Tom Jobim and Vinícius de Moraes once held court. Although the food is fairly standard Brazilian fare, one dish stands out – the picanha Brasileira, a scrumptious skillet of sliced sirloin brought sizzling to your table. Wash it down with a few glasses of ice-cold *chope*, and you'll realize why Garotas have been springing up all over the city.

BRASILEIRINHO Map p64 Brazilian $$

☎ 2513 5184; Rua Jangadeiros 10, Ipanema; mains R$20-32; noon-midnight

Facing Praça General Osório, this simple eatery with its rustic charm serves a satisfying selection of traditional Mineiro cuisine. Traditional favorites include *tutu a mineira* (mashed black beans with mancioc), *carne seca* and passion fruit mousse for dessert. The *feijão* (beans) here are tops – not surprising given Brasileirinho is run by the same owners of Casa da Feijoada around the corner. It often has excellent multi-course lunch specials for under R$18.

DOCE DELÍCIA Map p66 Brazilian $$

☎ 2249 2970; Rua Dias Ferreira 48, Leblon; mains R$15-30; noon-11pm

Doce Delícia has a small but loyal following that is sold on the restaurant's innovative Eastern design concept. Restaurant-goers create their own salads from over 40 ingredients on the menu. Feeling daring? Go for the pumpkin, jerked meat and leeks. The only limit is your imagination, *cara*. There's a second branch in Ipanema (☎ 2259 0239; Rua Aníbal de Mendonça 55, Ipanema; noon-11pm).

VEGETARIANO SOCIAL CLUB

Map p66 Vegetarian $

☎ 2294 5200; Rua Conde Bernadotte 26L, Leblon; mains R$18-24; noon-5.30pm

Vegetarians interested in sampling Brazil's signature dish should visit this inviting spot on Saturday when tofu *feijoada* is served. The small menu changes regularly, and features salads, soups and *sucos* (juices), like rose-petal juice or guarana with mint and ginger. The café also serves organic wine.

CAFÉ SEVERINO Map p66 Café $

☎ 2239 5294; Rua Dias Ferreira 417, Leblon; mains R$15-24; 9am-midnight Mon-Sat, 10am-midnight Sun

In the back of the Argumento bookshop (p113), this charming café is a cozy place to hide away with a book or a new friend. In addition to coffees and lighter fare – sandwiches, salads and desserts – it's justly famed for its tasty crepes (try the salmon with Gruyère).

MEL & PIMENTA Map p64 Bistrô $

☎ 2227 1477; Rua Visconde de Pirajá 44B, Ipanema; mains R$9-24; 9am-7pm

This small, airy bistrô serves daily specials like tasty grilled fish and quiche with salad, which draw in the local lunch crowd. The tempting dessert case, however, means that any time is a good time to stop by for coffee and chocolate tart. You can also get a healthy breakfast here.

DELÍRIO TROPICAL Map p64 Salads $

☎ 3201 2977; Rua Garcia D'Ávila 48, Ipanema; salads R$12-16; 8am-10pm Mon-Sat, to 9pm Sun

Famed for its salads, Delírio Tropical serves 16 varieties each day along with a few soups and hot dishes (veggie burgers, grilled salmon) if you're famished. The open layout has a pleasant, casual feeling and there are two stories with big windows overlooking the street.

TALHO CAPIXABA Map p66 Sandwiches $

☎ 2512 8760; Av Ataúlfo de Paiva 1022, Leblon; mains R$12-24; 🕓 7am-9pm Mon-Sat, 8am-8pm Sun

This tiny deli and grocery store is one of the city's best spots to put together a takeout meal. In addition to pastas, salads and antipasti, you'll find some of the city's best sandwiches. At weekends, to accommodate the crowds, Talho Capixaba puts a few tables out on the sidewalk for customers to enjoy the tasty bites alfresco.

BIBI CREPES Map p66 Creperie $

☎ 2259 4948; Rua Cupertino Durão 81, Leblon; crepes R$10-15; 🕓 noon-1am

This small, open-sided restaurant attracts a young, garrulous crowd who come to enjoy the more than two dozen sweet and savory crepes available. There are plenty of straightforward options as well as creative choices like salmon with cream cheese. There are also decent salads – you choose up to 15 toppings. Come early to beat the lunchtime crowds. Bibi Crepes also has a branch in Copacabana (☎ 2513 6000; Rua Miguel Lemos 31).

NEW NATURAL Map p64 Vegetarian $

☎ 2287 0301; Rua Barão da Torre 167, Ipanema; lunch specials R$12; 🕓 7am-11pm

Featuring an excellent vegetarian lunch buffet, New Natural was the first health-food restaurant in the neighborhood. Fill up on fresh pots of soup, rice, veggies and beans without breaking the bank.

FONTES Map p64 Vegetarian $

☎ 2512 5900; Rua Visconde de Pirajá 605D, Ipanema; mains around R$12; 🕓 11am-10pm Mon-Sat, noon-8pm Sun

Hidden in a nondescript shopping plaza, this tiny, low-key restaurant is worth seeking out if you're after a decent vegetarian meal. The menu changes daily but features shiitake-filled manioc pastries, green salads, roasted eggplant and the like. On Saturday, the rich, smoked-tofu *feijoada* always draws a crowd.

KONI STORE Map p64 Japanese $

☎ 2521 9348; Rua Maria Quitéria 77, Ipanema; hand roll R$7-9; 🕓 noon-3am Mon-Wed, to 5am Thu-Sat, to midnight Sun

New in 2006, Koni is the current craze of Rio with a growing number of stands opening across town. The recipe is simple – *temaki* (a seaweed hand roll) stuffed with salmon, tuna, shrimp, roast beef or a combination – which can then be devoured at one of the tiny bistrô tables. It's stylish, tasty and cheap – a few reasons why you'll have to wait in line among club kids for a roll at 4am on a Friday night.

KURT Map p66 Patisserie $

☎ 2294 0599; Rua General Urquiza 117B, Leblon; pastries R$5-7; 🕓 8am-6pm Mon-Fri, to 5pm Sat

Entering a true patisserie should delight all of your senses, and Kurt does just that. The flaky strudels and palm-sized tortes with strawberries and kiwifruit lie illuminated behind the glass counter. The smell of cappuccino hangs in the air as classical music plays overhead. A few round tables then set the stage for the most rewarding sensory experience: tasting these delicate cakes and pastries.

UNIVERSO ORGÂNICO Map p66 Vegetarian $

☎ 3874 0186; store 105, Rua Conde Bernadotte 26, Leblon; juices R$6; 🕓 8am-7pm Mon, to 9.30pm Tue-Sat, 11am-8pm Sun

In the back of a small *galeria* (shopping center), Universo Orgânico whips up delicious fruit and veggie shakes, made with the fresh stuff. Try the carrot, ginger, apple and linseed combo and enjoy it with a veggie burger or savory non-meat *salgados*. The small grocery store sells organic goodies, and offers home-delivery.

CHAIKA Map p64 Fast Food $

☎ 2267 3838; Rua Visconde de Pirajá 321, Ipanema; mains R$8-24; 🕓 9am-1am

One of Ipanema's classics, this popular, low-key restaurant features a stand-up bar in front for quickly devoured hamburgers, pastries and sodas. The sit-down restaurant in the back offers a bigger menu – *panini*, salads and pancakes – and the staff will still bring your selection to you in a hurry.

MIL FRUTAS Map p64 Ice Cream $

☎ 2521 1384; Rua Garcia D'Ávila 134A, Ipanema; ice cream R$6-8; 🕓 10.30am-1am Mon-Fri, 9.30am-1am Sat & Sun

On chic Rua Garcia D'Ávila (next door to Rio's only Louis Vuitton store), Mil Frutas serves tasty ice cream that showcases fruits from the Amazon and abroad. *Jaca* (jackfruit), lychee and *açaí* are among the several dozen varieties – all of which are best enjoyed on the tiny shade-covered patio out front. There's another branch in Jardim Botânico (☎ 2511 2550; Rua JJ Seabra).

CAFEÍNA Map p64 Café $

☎ 2521 2194; Rua Farme de Amoedo 43, Ipanema; sandwiches R$8-12; 8am-11.30pm

In the heart of Ipanema, this inviting café (and its sidewalk tables) is a fine spot for having a cup of java while watching the city stroll by. In addition to strong coffee and a lively mixed crowd, you'll find sandwiches, salads and some very rich desserts.

ENVIADA Map p66 Café $

☎ 2512 1313; Rua Dias Ferreira 45, Leblon; desserts R$6-10; 11am-8pm

Step into this elegant café for heavenly chocolates, ice cream, cakes, teas and coffees. The setting is a cozy escape from the city with its old-fashioned tile floors, dainty chairs and tables, and broad pieces of artwork decorating the walls.

COLHER DE PAU Map p66 Patisserie $

☎ 2274 8295; Rua Rita Ludolf 90, Leblon; desserts R$6-8; 10am-7.30pm

Cakes and pies are displayed in such a way that their magnetic powers exert a force that would be foolish to resist. The branch at Ipanema (☎ 2523 3018; Rua Farme de Amoedo 39) also serves quiches, salads and sandwiches and is worth investigating.

ARMAZÉM DO CAFÉ Map p66 Café $

☎ 2259 0170; Rua Rita Ludolf 87B, Leblon; snacks R$4-8; 9am-midnight Sun-Thu, to 1am Fri & Sat

Dark-wood furnishings and the fresh-ground coffee aroma lend an authenticity to this Leblon coffeehouse. Connoisseurs rate the aromatic roasts much higher here than neighboring Cafeína. It also serves waffles, snacks and desserts.

SORVETE BRASIL Map p64 Ice Cream $

☎ 2247 8404; Rua Maria Quitéria 74C, Ipanema; per scoop R$3.50-5.50; 10am-10pm

A delightful pit stop on a sunny day in Ipanema, Sorvete Brasil scoops up more than 50 different ice-cream flavors including Amazonian *cupuaçu,* lychee, star fruit and guava.

EMPÓRIO ARABE Map p66 Middle Eastern $

☎ 2512 7373; Av Ataúlfo de Paiva 370, Leblon; savory pies R$2.30-5; noon-8pm Mon-Sat

There are only a few tables inside this tiny restaurant in Leblon, but most people stop by just long enough to down a quick bite from the counter facing the sidewalk. Triangular pies filled with chicken, spinach or ricotta make for a speedy snack on your way back from the beach.

BIBI SUCOS Map p66 Juice Bar $

☎ 2259 4298; Av Ataúlfo de Paiva 591, Leblon; juice R$4-6; 9am-1am

Among Rio's countless juice bars, Bibi Sucos is a long-standing favorite. You'll find over 40 different varieties, and a never-ending supply of the favorite *açaí*. Sandwiches will quell greater hunger pangs.

POLIS SUCOS Map p64 Juice Bar $

☎ 2247 2518; Rua Maria Quitéria 70, Ipanema; juices R$3-6; 7am-midnight

One of Ipanema's favorite spots for a dose of fresh-squeezed vitamins, this juice bar facing the Praça Nossa Senhora (NS) de Paz has dozens of flavors, and you can pair those tangy beverages with sandwiches or *pão de queijo*.

ZONA SUL SUPERMARKET Map p66 Supermarket

☎ 2259 4699; Rua Dias Ferreira 290, Leblon; 24hr, 7am Mon-midnight Sun

A Rio institution for 44 years, Zona Sul supermarket has branches all over the city. The one in Leblon is the best of the bunch, with fresh-baked breads, imported cheeses, olives, French Bordeaux, prosciutto and many other delicacies.

HORTIFRUTI Map p66 Fruit Market

☎ 2512 6820; Rua Dias Ferreira 57, Leblon; 8am-8pm Mon-Sat, to 2pm Sun

Leblon's popular indoor produce market features a wide variety of fruits and vegetables, as well as a small juice bar.

GÁVEA, JARDIM BOTÂNICO & LAGOA

One of the big draws here is the collection of open-air restaurants around the peaceful Lagoa Rodrigo de Freitas. On warm evenings live music fills the air as diners eat, drink and enjoy the views across the water. The hotspots for cuisine and live music are the Parque dos

Patins on the west side and Parque do Cantagalo on the east side.

Gávea has a handful of dining and drinking spots around Praça Santos Dumont, while Jardim Botânico's thickest concentration of eateries is on Rua JJ Seabra and Rua Pacheco Leão.

OLYMPE Map pp70–1 Eclectic $$$

☎ 2539 4542; Rua Custódio Serrão 62, Lagoa; mains R$44-82; 🕑 7.30pm-midnight Mon-Thu & Sat, noon-4pm & 7pm-midnight Fri

One of Rio's best chefs, Claude Troisgros continues to dazzle guests with unforgettable meals at his award-winning restaurant. Originally from France, Troisgros mixes the old-world with the new in dishes like heart-of-palm salad with fresh octopus and red snapper covered with foie gras and asparagus tempura. The setting is a lovely house on a quiet tree-lined street.

QUADRIFOGLIO Map pp70–1 Italian $$

☎ 2294 1433; Rua JJ Seabra 19, Jardim Botânico; plates R$42-60; 🕑 noon-3.30pm & 7.30pm-midnight Mon-Thu, noon-3.30pm & 7.30pm-1am Fri, 7.30pm-1am Sat, noon-5pm Sun

A charming Italian spot famed for exotic raviolis like its *ravioli de maça ao creme e semente de papoula* (apple ravioli with cream and poppy-seed sauce), Quadrifoglio has long been a neighborhood favorite – ever since it opened.

NAKOMBI Map pp70–1 Japanese $$

☎ 2246 1518; Rua Maria Angélica 183, Jardim Botânico; mains R$35-55; 🕑 7pm-midnight

Another São Paulo transplant that opened in Rio in 2007, Nakombi quickly become a favorite for its excellent sushi and its over-the-top design. Inside the airy, 700-sq-meter multilevel interior, you'll find hundreds of Buddhas encased in the walls and floor, a mini waterfall and an upstairs with a retractable roof and a DJ booth. The focal point is the kombi (minivan), from which comes the dozens of fine combinations (it's also the source of the restaurant's name: before opening restaurants, visionary Paulo Barossi prepared and served his rolls from his mobile sushi bar).

ESCOLA DO PÃO Map pp70–1 Bistrô $$

☎ 2294 0027; Rua General Garzon 10, Jardim Botânico; brunch R$48; 🕑 5pm-midnight Tue-Sat, 9am-1pm Sat & Sun

In a converted colonial mansion, this beautifully decorated restaurant serves delightful gourmet fare including grilled chicken with shiitake mushrooms, grilled trout and four different risottos. On weekends, Cariocas come from near and far to enjoy the weekend brunch, the highlights of which are the tasty fresh-baked breads and pastries.

LULU Map pp70–1 Italian $$

☎ 2294 7830; Rua Visconde de Carandaí 2, Jardim Botânico; mains R$35-50

On a quiet tree-lined corner in Jardim Botânico, this stylish three-story restaurant serves contemporary Italian cuisine with flair. The excellent pastas are made in-house (try the goat cheese and eggplant), while heartier palates might opt for the chef's osso buco, fresh fish of the day with polenta or duck confit. On clear nights, reserve a table on the top-floor patio for idyllic views over the neighborhood.

00 (ZERO ZERO) Map pp70–1 Brazilian $$

☎ 2540 8041; Planetário da Gávea, Av Padre Leonel Franca 240, Gávea; mains from R$30; 🕑 8pm until late

Housed in Gávea's planetarium, 00 is a sleek restaurant-lounge that serves Brazilian cuisine with Asian and Mediterranean overtones. Jerked beef and leek-tapioca rolls or filet mignon with puree of *arracacha* (a root vegetable that is something of a cross between carrot and celery) are best enjoyed on the open-air veranda. After dinner, have a few cocktails and stick around: some of Rio's best DJs spin at parties here (p169).

BRAZ Map pp70–1 Pizza $$

☎ 2535 0687; Rua Maria Angélica 129, Jardim Botânico; pizzas R$28-43; 🕑 7pm-midnight

The much-touted pizzeria from São Paulo won a huge Carioca following after it opened in Rio in 2007. Perfect crusts and super-fresh ingredients are two of the components that make Braz the best pizza place in town. This is no secret, so arrive early and plan on having a few quiet *chopes* on the front patio before scoring that table.

GUIMAS Map pp70–1 Eclectic $$

☎ 2259 7996; Rua José Roberto Macedo Soares 5, Gávea; mains R$25-35; 🕑 noon-1am

RIO'S CULINARY STAR: CLAUDE TROISGROS

One of Rio's most venerated chefs, Claude Troisgros hails from a long line of French gastronomes. Born in Roanne, France, Claude came to Brazil in the late '70s, when his father (creator of Roanne's three-star Michelin restaurant Troisgros) asked him if he wanted to go to Rio. After gaining experience at Le Pre Catelan, Claude went out on his own, quickly gaining a following for his then unknown restaurant among Rio's epicures. Since then, he's earned the reputation as Rio's – and probably Brazil's – best chef, having cooked for a number of distinguished clients – including the Clintons when they were last in town. In 2007, he again earned the accolades: he was named chef of the year by the Quatro Rodas guide, *Veja* and *Gula* magazines and *O Globo* newspaper. Wanting to get to the culinary heart of the matter, Lonely Planet got in touch with Troisgros who shared his thoughts on cooking, eating and Rio's dining scene.

I heard that when you came to Rio, you were planning to stay for just two years. What made you stay longer? I fell in love with the Brazilian people, the country and felt that I could make my professional life here, delving into the fruits, spices and vegetables of Brazil.

What are some of the things that excite you about Brazilian cooking? What ingredients do you most like working with? I love to incorporate Brazilian flavors into my French techniques. The most exciting ingredients for me are passion fruit, *jabuticaba* (a grape-like fruit), Chinese okra, taro root, *yuca, cupuaçu* and *açaí* (juice made from an Amazonian berry), coconut, dried meat, giant shrimp, *batata baroa* (a distant relative of the parsnip), *surubim* (a river fish) and tapioca.

What are some of your favorite dishes – both to prepare and to eat? Some of my favorite things to cook are grouper with caramelized bananas, and crepe soufflé with passion fruit. As for eating, I love the Brazilian coconut stew *moqueca* and *carne seca com abobora* (fried dried meat with pumpkin).

Do you cook much at home? I like to cook at home for friends, making things like risotto, roasted fish or meat, and pastas. Sometimes I go out, and it's always to the same places: Azumi (p140), Roberta Sudbrack, Osteria dell'Angolo (p133) and 66 Bistro.

How do you think the dining scene has changed since you first moved to Rio? Of course the scene has changed a lot. When I arrived in 1979, there was no butter or cream and people drank whisky or sweet German wine. Today you can find anything in Brazil, with high quality products available, incredible fruits, good wines. Brazil now has excellent and creative chefs, who are cooking for more discerning customers. There's an incredible evolution underway in the way people are thinking about traditional Brazilian cooking.

Any tips for visitors who are unfamiliar with Brazilian cooking? A few things: when you have a caipirinha, always ask the barman to cut the lime fresh. Always have caipirinha with *cachaça* (rather than vodka, sake or something else). Do not forget to have the traditional *feijoada* experience on Saturday at lunchtime. Have a traditional dinner at a boteco in Lapa, and if you have time go to Bira (p149) in Barra de Guaratiba – it's incredible.

An interview with Claude Troisgros, chef

A classic Carioca boteco with a creative flair, Guimas has been going strong for almost 20 years. Trout with leeks or the honey-roast duck with pear rice go nicely with the superfine *caipivodcas* (caipirinhas made with vodka instead of *cachaça*). The small but cozy open-air restaurant attracts a more colorful mix of diners as the night progresses.

ARAB DA LAGOA

Map pp70–1 Middle Eastern $$

☎ 2540 0747; Parque dos Patins, Av Borges de Medeiros, Lagoa; platter for 2 R$45; 🕑 10am-1am Sun-Thu, to 2.30am Fri & Sat

One of the lake's most popular outdoor restaurants, serving traditional Middle Eastern specialties like hummus, baba ghanoush, tabbouleh, kibbe and tasty thin-crust pizzas. The large platters for two or more are good for sampling the tasty varieties. During the day, it's a peaceful refuge from the city, while at night you can hear live samba, *choro* (romantic, intimate samba) or jazz from 9pm (cover charge R$5).

BRASEIRO DA GÁVEA

Map pp70–1 Brazilian $$

☎ 2239 7494; Praça Santos Dumont 116, Gávea; mains R$18-30; 🕑 11am-1am Mon-Thu, to 3am Fri & Sat

This family-style eatery serves up large portions of its popular steak with *farofa,* pot roast or fried chicken. On weekends, the open-air spot fills with the din of conversation and the aroma of fresh *chope* drifting by. A younger crowd takes over at night and into the early morning.

CAFÉ DU LAGE Map pp70–1 Cafe $

☎ 2226 8125; off Rua Jardim Botânico 414, Jardim Botânico; light lunch R$7-12; 🕒 9am-10.30pm Mon-Fri, 9am-5pm Sat & Sun

Inside the lush Parque Lage, this beautifully sited café serves tasty sandwiches, salads and other light fare. On weekends, it's a popular gathering spot for young families who come for the brunch (R$17), which features fresh breads and jams, fruits, juices and the like.

COPACABANA & LEME

Rio's most visited neighborhood has an enormous variety of restaurants, from award-winning dining rooms to charming old bistros from the 1950s, as well as creperies, *churrascarias,* sushi bars and other ethnic haunts. In general, you will encounter less experimentation here, but if you're looking for excellent traditional cuisine – both Brazilian and international – you will find plenty of delectable options in Copacabana.

The restaurant strip along Av Atlântica has fine views of the seaside, but generally unexceptional food. Things get seedy here at night, and if you're looking for an escort, you're in the right spot. If you're looking for good cuisine, however, go elsewhere. The narrow roads crisscrossing Av NS de Copacabana all the way from Leme to Arpoador contain many fine establishments – and many mediocre ones. Do some exploring, trust your instincts and *bom proveito* (happy eating).

LE PRÉ CATALAN Map pp76–7 French $$$

☎ 2525 1232; Level E, Sofitel Rio de Janeiro, Av Atlântica 4240, Copacabana; mains from R$60; 🕒 7.30-11pm Mon-Sat

Le Pré Catalan is often rated Rio's best traditional French restaurant, with exquisitely prepared dishes under the watch of award-winning chef Roland Villard. Most diners select the three-course *prix-fixe* (fixed-price) menu (R$140), which changes every two weeks. The modern, stylish dining room has elegant views of Copacabana beach.

CIPRIANI Map pp76–7 Italian $$$

☎ 2545 8747; Copacabana Palace Hotel, Av Atlântica 1702, Copacabana; mains R$50-80; 🕒 12.30-3pm & 7pm-1am Mon-Sat, 12.30-4pm & 7pm-1am Sun

On a candlelit patio beside the Palace's pool, Cipriani serves fine northern Italian cuisine to a well-dressed, largely non-Brazilian crowd. Signature dishes such as the gnocchi, the sirloin with port sauce, and the smoked scallops all meet their mark. For dessert, tiramisu and chocolate mousse are both good options. The dress code is once again in force, so leave your Havaianas at home.

SIRI MOLE & CIA
Map pp76–7 Brazilian $$$

☎ 2267 0894; Rua Francisco Otaviano 50, Copacabana; mains R$46-80; 🕒 7pm until last customer Mon, noon until last customer Tue-Sun

Understated elegance is the key to Siri Mole & Cia's longstanding success – both in ambience and in the perfectly prepared seafood. Among the favorites are *moqueca de siri mole* (spicy, soft-shell-crab stew), *acarajé* (spicy shrimp-filled croquettes) and the grilled fish.

AZUMI Map pp76–7 Japanese $$

☎ 2541 4294; Rua Ministro Viveiros de Castro 127, Copacabana; meals R$30-60; 🕒 7pm-midnight Tue-Thu & Sun, to 1am Fri & Sat

Some claim Azumi is the bastion of traditional Japanese cuisine in the city. This laid-back sushi bar certainly has its fans – both in the Nisei community and from abroad. Azumi's *sushiman* (sushi chef) masterfully prepares delectable sushi and sashimi, though tempuras and soups are also excellent. Be sure to ask what's in season.

DON CAMILLO Map pp76–7 Italian $$

☎ 2225 5126; Av Atlântica 3056, Copacabana; mains R$30-50; 🕒 noon-2am

One of the few decent restaurants on the Copa strip, this handsomely appointed Italian restaurant has flavorful pastas and lasagnas, as well as some excellent seafood dishes. Antique tile floors, distressed wood beams and black-and-white photos make a nice setting for the dining. For something a little different try risotto with mushrooms followed by profiteroles.

MISS TANAKA Map pp76–7 Japanese $$

☎ 2275 3589; Av Atlântica 974, Leme; mains R$30-50; 🕒 noon-1am

Much to the delight of Leme residents, this former Jardim Botânico mainstay moved into the neighborhood in late 2007. The marvelously whimsical interior is like a paean to the gods of kitsch with hanging flower chandeliers, shelves lined with dolls and Buddhas and wallpaper that's pure eye candy. The cuisine is no less delightful, with delicious appetizers and mouth-watering sushi.

ATLÂNTICO Map pp76–7 Eclectic $$

☎ 2513 2485; Av Atlântica 3880, Copacabana; mains R$30-45; 7pm-2am

Named after the road and ocean that fronts it, Atlântico, with its loud electronica and moody lighting can't quite decide whether it's a restaurant or a bar. The sleek contemporary dining room was opened in 2007 and serves seafood with a twist; standout selections include crusted tuna with shrimp sauce and salmon with a flight marinade.

SÃO SEBASTIÃO Map pp76–7 Eclectic $$

☎ 2541 5585; Rua Gustavo Sampaio 361, Leme; mains R$26-45; 1-4pm & 7pm-midnight Mon-Sat

This hidden gem has brought a dash of style to Leme since its opening in 2002. In an artfully decorated bistro, Chef Pedro Prado prepares beautiful French and Italian dishes that don't neglect the flavors of the tropics. Salmon with passion fruit, steak tartare, shrimp salad and ceviche are among the eclectic choices. Live jazz some nights add to the appeal.

PONTINHO Map pp76–7 Brazilian $$

☎ 2257 1676; Rua Décio Vilares 360, Copacabana; mains R$25-45; 7am-midnight Mon-Sat, 9am-6pm Sun

Tucked away on a peaceful corner of Copacabana, Pontinho is a traditional open-sided boteco serving sizzling platters of *picanha* (thin cut of rump steak), grilled chicken, omelets and other satisfying dishes to a neighborhood crowd. On your way to this untouristy spot, be sure to take a stroll past the leafy Praça Edmundo Bittencourt.

AMIR Map pp76–7 Middle Eastern $$

☎ 2275 5596; Rua Ronald de Carvalho 55C, Copacabana; meals R$25-45; noon-11pm Sun-Thu, to midnight Fri & Sat

A cozy air pervades this small, casual restaurant near the beach. As you step inside, you'll notice the handsomely dressed waiters in embroidered vests, and heavenly aromas wafting from the kitchen. Delicious platters – hummus, *kaftas* (spiced meat patty), falafel, kibbe and salads – are the best way to experience Amir's riches.

LE BLÉ NOIR Map pp76–7 Creperie $$

☎ 2287 1272; Rua Xavier da Silveira 15A, Copacabana; mains R$24-48; 7pm-1am Wed-Thu & Sun, to 2am Fri & Sat

Flickering candles and subdued conversation make this restaurant a real date-pleaser. Le Blé Noir offers over 50 different varieties of crepe, and pairs rich ingredients like shrimp and artichoke hearts or Brie, honey and toasted almonds. Call for a reservation or wait and enjoy a cocktail on the patio.

CAPRICCIOSA Map pp76–7 Pizza $$

☎ 2255 2598; Rua Domingos Ferreira 187, Copacabana; mains R$30-45; 6pm-2am

This stylish spot serves excellent thin-crust pizzas. See p131.

COPA CAFÉ Map pp76–7 Eclectic $$

☎ 2235 2947; Av Atlântica 3056, Copacabana; mains R$22-44; 7pm-2am Tue-Sun

This stylish new two-story restaurant facing Copacabana beach brings some much-needed life to the aging restaurant strip along Av Atlântica. The black wood floors, white bar stools, trim open layout and ambient electronic music make a nice setting for fresh fish, steak and high-end burgers.

SHIRLEY Map pp76–7 Spanish $$

☎ 2275 1398; Rua Gustavo Sampaio 610, Leme; mains for two R$46-60; 11am-12.30am

The aroma of succulent paella hangs in the air as waiters hurry to and from the kitchen, bearing platefuls of fresh seafood. Shirley is currently the only Spanish restaurant in town, and attracts a local following in its small Leme dining room. In addition to paella, the mussel-vinaigrette appetizer or the octopus and squid in ink are also recommended.

LA TRATTORIA Map pp76–7 Italian $$

☎ 2255 3319; Rua Fernando Mendes 7A, Copacabana; mains R$18-38; noon-1am

Old photos, simple furnishings, hearty dishes and the constant din of conversation have made this trattoria a neighborhood favorite for over 30 years. Shrimp dishes are the Italian family's specialty – they've won over many diners with their *espaguete com camarão e óleo tartufado* (spaghetti with shrimp and truffle oil).

CARRETÃO Map pp76–7 Churrascaria $$

☎ 2542 2148; Rua Ronald de Carvalho 55, Leme; all-you-can-eat R$27; 🕑 11.30am-midnight

It's all about the meat at this decent but inexpensive *churrascaria* in Leme. With several branches throughout the city, including an Ipanema Carretão (☎ 2267 3965; Rua Visconde de Pirajá 112), this popular chain serves up consistently good cuts – and heaps of them. There's also a small salad bar, and you can order sides from the menu at no added charge.

LA FIORENTINA Map pp76–7 Italian $$

☎ 2543 8465; Av Atlântica 458A, Leme; mains R$18-30; 🕑 noon-2am

One of Leme's classic Italian restaurants, La Fiorentina attracted Rio's glitterati in the '60s. Today, its beach-facing outdoor tables draw a loyal, mostly neighborhood crowd, who come to feast on the 15 different flavors of pizza and a well-stocked bar.

ARATACA Map pp76–7 Amazonian $$

☎ 2548 6624; Rua Domingos Ferreira 41D, Copacabana; mains R$20-35; 🕑 10am-9pm

The casual, no-nonsense Arataca serves the exotic cuisine of the Amazon. While there's better *tacacá* on offer in Rio (Flamengo's Tacacá do Norte, p145, is the city's best), Arataca is a handy spot to grab a savory bowl of the soup. There's also *pirarucu* (a kind of fish), *pato no tucupi* (roast duck flavored with garlic) or *vatapá* (seafood dish with a thick sauce made from manioc paste, coconut and dendê oil), all of which go nicely with real guarana juice.

GALERIA 1618 Map pp76–7 Bistrô $

☎ 2295 1618; Rua Gustavo Sampaio 840, Leme; mains R$17-28; 🕑 9am-11pm

Equal parts bookstore, art gallery and bistro, the quaint Galeria 1618 opened in 2006 under the guidance of two French expats. As well as quiches, coffee, juices and desserts, the chef prepares excellent daily specials – risotto with shrimp, grilled tuna etc.

TRAITEURS DE FRANCE
Map pp76–7 French $

☎ 2548 6440; Av NS de Copacabana 386B, Copacabana; mains R$12-32; 🕑 10am-8pm Mon-Sat to 6pm Sun

Step into this pleasant café and restaurant for an escape from the busy traffic. In front, you'll find a variety of tempting baked goods, perfect for a quick takeout for the beach, while the restaurant in the back offers salmon crepes, quiches, and grilled meats. You can also opt for lunch specials (R$13 to R$18).

CONFEITARIA COLOMBO
Map pp76–7 Café $

☎ 3201 4049; Forte de Copacabana, Praça Coronel Eugênio Franco, Copacabana; mains R$14-26; 🕑 10am-8pm Tue-Sun

Far removed from the hustle and bustle of Av Atlântica, this handsome café offers truly magnificent views of Copacabana beach. At the outdoor tables, you can sit beneath shady palm trees, enjoying cappuccino, salads, quiche or crepes as young soldiers from the fort file past. To get there, you'll have to pay admission (R$2) to the Forte de Copacabana (Copacabana fort; p77), but it's well worth the price. In Centro there's also a Confeitaria Colombo (p147) that is worth a visit.

YONZA Map pp76–7 Creperie $

☎ 2521 4248; Rua Miguel Lemos 21B, Copacabana; crepes R$12-18; 🕑 1pm-midnight Tue-Fri, 6pm-midnight Sat & Sun

Surfboards and Japanese anime superhero posters create the ambience at this creperie in an otherwise empty stretch of Copacabana. A young crowd flocks here at night to fill up on crepes. The simple *queijo e tomate* (cheese and tomato) does just fine.

CERVANTES Map pp76–7 Brazilian $

☎ 2275 6147; Av Prado Júnior 335B, Copacabana; sandwiches R$12-16; 🕑 noon-4am Tue-Thu, to 5am Fri & Sat, to 3am Sun

A Copacabana institution, the late-night Cervantes gathers a broad mix of Cariocas who come to feast on Cervantes' trademark meat and pineapple sandwiches. Its waiters are famed for their fussiness, along with their quickness to the tap when your *chope* runneth dry. Around the corner (Rua Barato Ribeiro 7), Cervantes' stand-up boteco serves up tasty bites in a hurry.

BAKERS Map pp76–7 Patisserie $

☎ 3209 1212; Rua Santa Clara 86B, Copacabana; sandwiches R$8-12; 🕑 9am-8pm

One of the best places for flaky croissants, banana Danishes, strudels and other fresh-baked treats. There are also deli sandwiches (try the turkey breast and provolone cheese).

BOTAFOGO & URCA

Botafogo generally has a better drinking than dining scene, though there are some top picks hidden in these old streets. Urca, largely untouched by commercial development, has only a few choices.

YORUBÁ Map pp78–9 Bahian $$

☎ 2541 9387; Rua Arnaldo Quintela 94, Botafogo; mains for 2 R$80-95; ⏲ 7-11pm Wed-Fri, noon-6pm Sat & Sun

Yorubá looks as if it's always prepared for the imminent arrival of an *orixá* (spirit or deity). Leaves lie scattered across the floor as candle flames flicker on the walls. Young waiters in red aprons stand at attention while something mystical transpires in the kitchen. Plates here are simply heavenly: plump shrimp and rich coconut milk blend to perfection in *bobó de camarão,* and the *moqueca* is simply outstanding.

ADEGA DO VALENTIM

Map pp78–9 Portuguese $$

☎ 2541 1166; Rua da Passagem 178, Botafogo; mains R$30-50; ⏲ noon-midnight

Bacalhau in 12 ways is the specialty at this old-fashioned Portuguese restaurant. Jocular old waiters also serve other favorites: baked rabbit, roast suckling pig, octopus, the list goes on…

GAROTA DA URCA Map pp78–9 Brazilian $$

☎ 2541 8585; Rua João Luís Alves 56, Urca; mains R$20-40; ⏲ 11am until last customer

Overlooking the small Praia da Urca, this neighborhood restaurant serves standard Brazilian fare at decent prices. The weekday lunch specials are good value, and you can enjoy views over the bay from the open-air veranda. By night, a more garrulous crowd meets here for steak and *chope*.

MIAM MIAM Map pp78–9 Contemporary $$

☎ 2244 0125; Rua General Goés Monteiro 34, Botafogo; mains R$22-30; ⏲ 8pm-1am Mon-Sat

Exposed brick walls and a mishmash of retro furnishings set the scene for dining in style at Botafogo's newest culinary darling. Miam Miam, which is French for yum-yum, opened in 2006 under the guidance of chef Roberta Ciasca, who trained at Paris' famous Le Cordon Bleu. Here, she serves up her own brand of 'comfort food', which means bruschetta with pesto and tapenade, endive salad with gorgonzola, pepper crusted tuna with lentil ragout and many other unique (and yes, yummy) dishes. Don't miss the creative cocktail menu or the desserts.

EMPORIUM PAX Map pp78–9 Brazilian $

☎ 2559 9713; 7th fl, Praia de Botafogo 400, Botafogo; mains R$16-30; ⏲ noon-midnight

One of many eateries at Botafogo Praia Shopping (p120), Emporium Pax is a more polished affair than the adjoining food court and offers spectacular views of Pão de Açúcar and Baía de Guanabara. As well as salads, pastas and tasty desserts, the lunch buffet draws in the shopping and film-goers.

CAFÉ BOTÂNICO Map pp78–9 Café $

☎ 2535 2465; Rua Capitão Salomão 14B, Botafogo; mains R$15-25; ⏲ 9am-7pm Mon-Fri, 8am-2.30pm Sat

This letter-box-sized café and bistro serves tasty bites, like goat cheese quiche, pumpkin soup and homemade sandwiches. Don't neglect the tasty pie and cake selection.

LIVRARIA PREFÁCIO Map pp78–9 Café $

☎ 2527 5699; Rua Voluntários da Pátria 39, Botafogo; mains R$12-24; ⏲ 10am-10pm Mon-Fri, 2-10pm Sat & Sun

In the back of the small, arts-oriented bookshop of the same name, this café, with its exposed brick walls and atmospheric lighting, makes the perfect hideaway on those rare rainy days. The menu features bruschetta, salads, sandwiches – vegetarian, *croque monsieur* (toasted ham and cheese sandwich) – and desserts, and the café fills with diners killing time before catching a film at the cinema next door. The café hosts occasional book signings and art openings.

FLAMENGO & LARANJEIRAS

The traditional neighborhood of Flamengo has a mix of longtime local favorites and stylish newcomers. Rua Marquês de Abrantes is one of the best streets in which to wander and see old and new vying for attention.

Laranjeiras sees very few tourists and although there's not much of a restaurant scene, the neighborhood has several charming options, well worth seeking out for those wanting to get off the beaten path.

PORCÃO RIO'S Map p84 — Churrascaria $$$

☎ 2554 8535; Av Infante Dom Henrique, Flamengo; all-you-can-eat R$68; 🕑 11.30am-midnight Sun-Thu, to 1am Fri & Sat

Set in the Parque do Flamengo with a stunning view of Pão de Açúcar, Porcão Rio's has been gradually moving up the charts in the *churrascaria* ratings. Some claim it's the best in the city; others are content just to go for the view. Whatever the case, you're in for an eating extravaganza. Call a few days in advance to book that table by the window.

RESTAURANTE KIOTO Map p84 — Japanese $$

☎ 2556 9880; 3rd fl, Rua Ministerio Tavares Lira 105, Flamengo; all-you-can-eat R$35; 🕑 7pm-midnight

Hidden on a street behind Largo do Machado this simple, well-concealed restaurant is worth seeking out when craving a sushi feast that won't break the bank. There's an enormous variety of rolls at the buffet, and you can take pride in dining in a restaurant known to only a handful of Cariocas.

INTIHUASI Map p84 — Peruvian $$

☎ 2225 7653; Rua Barão do Flamengo 35D, Flamengo; mains R$27-42; 🕑 noon-3pm & 7-11pm Tue-Sat, noon-5pm Sun

A welcome newcomer to Flamengo – and one of Rio's only Peruvian restaurants – Intihuasi is a small, sweetly decorated spot serving excellent ceviches, seafood soups and other classic dishes from the Andes. Wash those tamales down with a pisco sour or Inka Cola.

SENAC BISTRÔ Map p84 — Brazilian $$

☎ 3138 1540; Rua Marquês de Abrantes 99, Flamengo; mains $22-36; 🕑 noon-4pm Tue-Sun, 7pm-midnight Tue-Sat

On the bottom floor of an old mansion built 100 or so years ago, Senac serves tasty plates of seared tuna, shrimp *moqueca* and other Brazilian specialties. In spite of the splendid exterior, the decor inside is a bit lacking. The chocolate cake, however, makes up for any ambience issues. It comes warm and oozing decadence.

CHURRASCARIA MAJÓRICA Map p84 — Churrascaria $$

☎ 2285 6789; Rua Senador Vergueiro 11, Flamengo; mains from R$26; 🕑 noon-midnight Tue-Thu, to 1am Fri & Sat

A true *gaúcho* (person from Rio Grande do Sul) would chuckle at the kitschy cowboy accoutrements inside this restaurant. He'd shut his trap, however, once his plate of steak arrived. Meat is very serious business at Majórica, and if you're seeking an authentic *churrascaria* experience, look no further.

LUIGI'S Map p84 — Italian $$

☎ 2205 7343; Rua Senador Corrêia 10, Laranjeiras; mains R$25-35

Well off the beaten path, Luigi's is a casual Italian restaurant set in an old villa in Laranjeiras. Join neighborhood regulars for a drink on the small covered courtyard in front before venturing inside for homemade gnocchi with gorgonzola, fresh mushroom and tomato tagliatelle or risotto with seafood.

LAMAS Map p84 — Brazilian $$

☎ 2556 0799; Rua Marquês de Abrantes 18A, Flamengo; mains R$20-40; 🕑 8am-2.30am Sun-Thu, to 4am Fri & Sat

This classic Brazilian restaurant opened in 1874, and has fans from all over. In spite of the mileage, dishes here hold up well, and those omniscient waiters in starched white coats will tell you what's hot in the kitchen. You can't go wrong with grilled *lingüiça* or filet mignon with garlic.

HIDEAWAY Map p84 — Pizzeria $

☎ 2285 0921; Rua das Laranjeiras 308, Laranjeiras; mains R$20-25; 🕑 6pm-midnight Tue-Thu & Sun, 6pm-4am Fri-Sat

Aptly named, Hideaway is secreted inside a converted 19th-century house. The all-glass ceiling (with lush greenery framing the outside) and minimalist design give a contemporary polish to the place. Although there are better places to eat pizza, Hideaway remains a current favorite for the good vibe – particularly in the small lounge adjoining the restaurant – and the live jazz and MPB *(Música Popular Brasileira)* nights, which are currently on Tuesday.

ESPAÇO RIO CARIOCA Map p84 — Bistrô $

☎ 2225 7332; Rua Leite Leal, Laranjeiras; mains R$20-25

Espaço Rio Carioca, which opened in 2007, is yet another symbol of Laranjeiras' ongoing revitalization. Above a ground-level bookstore, the airy café and bistro serves tasty salads, cheese plates (a rarity in Rio), wines by the glass and handsomely prepared sandwiches. There's also an outdoor patio that makes a fine vantage point for observing this peaceful stretch of Rio (note the row houses next door – Rio's first). The space hosts live music and other cultural events throughout the week.

BELMONTE Map p84 Brazilian $

☎ 2552 3349; Praia do Flamengo 300, Flamengo; mains R$9-20; ⏲ 7am until last customer

One of the classic botecos in Rio, Belmonte is a vision of Rio from the '50s. Globe lights hang overhead as patrons steel their nerves with *cachaça* or *chope* from the narrow bar. Meanwhile, unhurried waiters make their way across the intricate tile floors, carrying plates of trout or steak sandwiches. This hugely successful chain is now widespread across Rio.

TACACÁ DO NORTE Map p84 Amazonian $

☎ 2205 7545; Rua Barão do Flamengo 35R, Flamengo; tacacá R$8; ⏲ 9am-10pm Mon-Sat, to 7pm Sun

In the Amazonian state of Pará, people order their *tacacá* late in the afternoon from their favorite street vendor. The dish is usually served from a gourd bowl. In Rio, you don't have to wait until the sun is setting. The fragrant soup of manioc paste, *jambu* (a Brazilian vegetable) leaves, and fresh and dried shrimp isn't for everyone. But then again, neither is the Amazon. For the faint of heart, this simple lunch counter also offers fruit juices and a handful of daily specials like *pirarucu* from Amazônia.

CATETE & GLÓRIA

Rio's working class neighborhoods are dotted with inexpensive juice bars and lunch counters – making this a good area for those eating on a dime. Most places are along Rua do Catete, with a couple of standouts hidden along the back streets.

CASA DA SUÍÇA Map p87 Swiss $$

☎ 2509 3870; Rua Cândido Mendes 157, Glória; fondues R$46-56; ⏲ noon-3pm & 7pm-midnight Mon-Fri, 7pm-1am Sat, noon-4pm & 7-11pm Sun

Tucked inside the Swiss Embassy, this cozy restaurant serves top-notch steak tartare, though it specializes in flambés and fondues. The Casa da Suíça creates an almost tangible aura of sensuality – perhaps due to those open fires flaring inside. After dinner, you can hear live music at the St Moritz bar.

NANQUIM Map p87 Self-Serve $$

☎ 2556 5119; Rua do Pinheiro 10, Flamengo; per kg R$44; ⏲ noon-3.30pm Mon-Fri, 6-10pm Sat & Sun

Hidden inside the Instituto dos Arquitetos on a quiet street, this inviting restaurant functions as a self-serve at lunchtime with an à la carte menu at night. Risotto, pastas, seafood, quiche and salads are among the options. The 19th-century building is a mix of rustic and modern, with designs and sketches by Oscar Niemeyer adorning the walls. A second branch in Jardim Botânico (☎ 3874 0015; Rua Jardim Botânico 644) offers the same mix of contemporary design and good food.

ESTAÇÃO REPÚBLICA Map p87 Self-Serve $$

☎ 2225 2650; Rua do Catete 104, Catete; per kg R$32; ⏲ 11am-midnight Mon-Sat, to 11pm Sun

Estação's buffet table is a neighborhood institution, featuring an extensive selection of salads, meats, pastas and vegetables. It's easy to indulge without breaking the bank. Sundays are family affairs here.

TABERNA DA GLÓRIA Map p87 Brazilian $$

☎ 2265 7835; Rua do Russel 32A, Glória; mains R$20-30; ⏲ 11.30am-1am Sun-Thu, to 2am Fri & Sat

On a small plaza in the heart of Glória, this large outdoor eatery serves decent Brazilian staples, and in abundance – most dishes here serve two. The *feijoada* on Saturday still draws crowds, and if you're not up for a big meal, appetizers and ice-cold *chope* are a good way to enjoy the open-air ambience.

CATETE GRILL Map p87 Self-Serve $

☎ 2285 3442; Rua do Catete 239, Catete; per kg R$18-28; ⏲ 11am-midnight Mon-Sat, to 11pm Sun

One of the newer restaurants in Catete, the Catete Grill has won over the neighborhood with its excellent buffet – served all day. It also offers ice creams – *a quilo* of course.

CENTRO & CINELÂNDIA

Rio's busiest neighborhood has everything from greasy lunch counters to French bistros, with ethnic and vegetarian fare, juice bars and *churrascarias*. Most restaurants open only for lunch on weekdays. Many pedestrian-only areas throughout Centro (like Rua do Rosário) are full of restaurants, some spilling onto the sidewalk, others hidden on upstairs floors, all of which make restaurant-hunting something of an art. Areas worth exploring include Travessa do Comércio just after work, when the restaurants and cafés fill with chatter; another early-evening gathering spot is Av Marechal Floriano, full of snack bars specializing in fried sardines and beer. Cinelândia, just behind the Praça Floriano, features a number of open-air cafés and restaurants.

CAIS DO ORIENTE Map pp90–1 Eclectic $$

☎ 2203 0178; Rua Visconde de Itaboraí 8, Centro; mains R$42-50; 🕑 noon-4pm Mon, to midnight Tue-Sat

Brick walls lined with tapestries stretch high to the ceiling in this almost-cinematic 1870s mansion. Set on a brick-lined street, hidden from the masses, Cais do Oriente blends West with East in dishes like sesame tuna. On Friday and Saturday nights, live bands perform in the restaurant (R$20 cover; see p164).

RESTAURANTE ALBAMAR

Map pp90–1 Seafood $$

☎ 2240 8378; Praça Marechal Âncora 186, Centro; mains around R$40; 🕑 11.30am-6pm Tue-Sun

The green gazebo structure perched over water offers excellent views of the Baía de Guanabara and Niterói. The seafood has its fans, but it's not nearly as outstanding as the view. The *peixe brasileira* (fish in coconut milk) is one of the most popular dishes.

ATRIUM Map pp90–1 Brazilian $$

☎ 2220 0193; Paço Imperial, Praça Quinze de Novembro 48, Centro; mains R$30-45; 🕑 11.30am-3.30pm Mon-Fri

A stately dining room in the Paço Imperial, Atrium serves power-lunching business execs and those simply wanting a taste of decadence. The lamb with rosemary and mushroom risotto would have brought a smile to the face of Dom Pedro I (who once gazed out these same windows a little less than 200 years ago).

DA SILVA Map pp90–1 Portuguese $$

☎ 2524 1010; 4th fl, Av Graça Aranha 187, Centro; all-you-can-eat R$36; 🕑 noon-4pm Mon-Fri

Hidden inside the Clube Ginástico Português, this large, simply decorated restaurant spreads one of Rio's best lunch buffets. Portuguese in flavor, like its sister the Ipanema Da Silva (p131), Da Silva in Centro has beautiful salads, steaks and seafood, along with an enormous variety of addictive *bacalhau* dishes and dozens of other dishes that change daily.

CBF Map pp90–1 Portuguese & Spanish $$

☎ 2232 3215; Praça Tiradentes 83, Centro; mains R$25-40; 🕑 11am-midnight Mon-Sat

Located on the west side of the historic Praça Tiradentes, CBF opened in 2007, breathing much new life into a tired neighborhood. Despite the newness, CBF is an atmospheric place and a top choice for enjoying delicious *bacalhau* dishes, scrumptious paellas and a host of other Iberian favorites. After dining with friends at the large picnic tables, you will be well-placed to explore the nearby samba clubs in Lapa.

BAR LUIZ Map pp90–1 German $$

☎ 2262 6900; Rua da Carioca 39, Centro; mains R$20-35; 🕑 11am-11.30pm Mon-Sat

Bar Luiz first opened in 1887, making it one of the city's oldest *cervejarias* (pubs). A festive air fills the old saloon as diners get their fill of traditional German cooking (potato salad and smoked meats), along with ice-cold drafts – including dark beer – on tap.

ARTE TEMPERADA Map pp90–1 French $$

☎ 2253 2589; rear entrance of Casa França-Brasil, Rua Visconde de Itaboraí 78, Centro; mains R$20-30; 🕑 11am-4pm Mon-Fri

Hidden in a tiny alley behind the Casa França-Brasil, this charming restaurant serves delicious Franco-Brazilian cuisine without the fuss. Some top choices are the crepes, the bouillabaisse, and the chicken breast served with passion fruit sauce and polenta. You can also opt for the two-course plate of the day.

ATELIÊ ODEON Map pp90–1 Brazilian $

☎ 2240 0746; Praça Floriano, Cinelândia; mains R$18-25; 🕑 noon-10pm Mon-Fri

Next to the art-house cinema of the same name, the Ateliê Odeon serves up decent Brazilian fare on its open-air terrace to a festive crowd. Ateliê opens onto the Praça Floriano, which is a lively gathering spot on weekday evenings. At weekends, it stays opens during film screenings next door.

CONFEITARIA COLOMBO

Map pp90–1 Patisserie $

☎ 2232 2300; Rua Gonçalves Dias 34, Centro; desserts/mains from R$6/24; 🕑 8am-8pm Mon-Fri, 10am-5pm Sat

Stained-glass windows, brocaded mirrors and marble countertops create a lavish setting for coffee or a meal. Dating from the late 1800s, the Confeitaria Colombo serves desserts befitting the elegant decor. The restaurant overhead serves traditional Brazilian cuisine for those wanting to further soak up the splendor. There's also a Confeitaria Colombo (p142) in Copacabana.

CEDRO DO LÍBANO Map pp90–1 Lebanese $

☎ 2224 0163; Rua Senhor dos Passos 231, Centro; mains R$14-26; 🕑 11am-5pm

White plastic chairs and tables covered by white tablecloths might make you feel like you stumbled into someone's wedding reception at this dining spot in the heart of Saara. But in fact, the white decorating in this 70-year-old Lebanese institution has more to do with the purity of the Lebanese cooking: kibbe, *kaftas*, lamb – all tender portions of perfection.

RANCHO INN Map pp90–1 French $

☎ 2263 5197; 2nd fl, Rua do Rosário 74, Centro; mains R$14-26; 🕑 11.30am-3.30pm Mon-Fri

Exposed brick and tall windows lend a vaguely Parisian air to this charming lunchtime spot. In addition to offerings like *caprese raviolini* (tomato and mozzarella ravioli) and snapper with basil and almonds, the salads and quiches are *muito gostoso* (very tasty).

TEMPEH Map pp90–1 Vegetarian $

☎ 2232 8007; 2nd fl, Rua Primeiro de Março 24, Centro; per kg R$22; 🕑 lunch Mon-Sat

Don't be intimidated by the new-age music. This is one of Centro's best vegetarian restaurants, serving a wide assortment of flavorful dishes, including soups, pastas, veggie burgers, tabouli, fried yucca, soba noodles, vegan sushi and desserts. The old colonial walls add to the charm.

top picks

BRAZILIAN

- Espírito Santa (p148) Heavenly *tambaqui* and other Amazonian cuisine – the best this side of the Rio Amazonas.
- Juice Co (p134) Rio's best *suco*, served without sugar.
- Caesar Park (p130) Rio's best Saturday *feijoada*.
- Porcão Rio's (p144) The best *churrasco* with stunning views to match those juicy cuts.
- Yorubá (p143) Serving delectable *moqueca* and Bahian cuisine fit for the gods.
- Fellini (p134) Best per-kilo restaurant (lunch or dinner).
- Bracarense (p153) Best appetizers.

BRASSERIE ROSÁRIO Map pp90–1 French $

☎ 2518 3033; Rua do Rosário 34, Centro; mains from R$18; 🕑 8am-8pm Mon-Fri, 10am-5pm Sat

Set in a handsomely restored 1860s building, this atmospheric bistro has a hint of Paris about it. The front counters are full of croissants, *pain au chocolat* (chocolate croissant) and other baked items, while the restaurant menu features roast meats and fish, soups, baguette sandwiches and the like. Old American jazz plays overhead.

BEDUÍNO Map pp90–1 Middle Eastern $

☎ 2524 5142; Av Presidente Wilson 123, Centro; mains R$14-24; 🕑 6am-midnight Mon-Fri

You'll always find a lunchtime crowd at this low-key restaurant east of Cinelândia. Reliably good food and excellent prices are Beduíno's keys to success, with 30 different traditional Middle Eastern dishes to choose from. Favorites include grilled *kafta*, lamb stew, and rice and lentils.

BISTRÔ DO PAÇO Map pp90–1 Self-Serve $

☎ 2262 3613; Paço Imperial, Praça Quinze de Novembro 48, Centro; mains R$10-24; 🕑 11am-7.30pm Mon-Fri, noon-7pm Sat & Sun

On the ground floor of the Paço Imperial, this informal restaurant offers a tasty assortment of quiches, salads, soups and other light fare. Save room for the delicious pies and cakes.

CAFÉ DO RODRIGUES Map pp90–1 Café $

☎ 3231 8015; Travessa de Ouvidor 17, Centro; lunch R$12-20; 9am-8pm Mon-Fri, 10am-1pm Sat

Inside the charming Centro branch of the Livraria da Travessa bookstore (p122), Café do Rodrigues is a suitable setting for philosophical conversation when the world – or the humidity – has worn you down. Browse for books, then peruse your finds over a *torta do palmito* (heart-of-palm quiche), a hearty soup or a flavorful salad.

CASA CAVÉ Map pp90–1 Patisserie $

☎ 2221 0533; Rua Sete de Setembro 137, Centro; pastries from R$4; 9am-7pm Mon-Fri, to 1pm Sat

Set with attractive tile floors and marble tabletops, this simple, historic coffeehouse (c 1860), lures in passersby with its glass shop windows full of tempting desserts. Inside, diners gather at the long, narrow counter, sipping hot coffee served by bustling waitstaff.

LIDADOR Map pp90–1 Liquor Store & Deli $

☎ 2533 4988; Rua da Assembléia 65, Centro; 9am-8pm Mon-Fri

Gleaming bottles stretch high to the ceiling of this well-stocked liquor cabinet. Founded in 1924, Lidador also sells a range of smoked meats, chocolates and imported goods. A tiny area in the back serves as an informal pub.

SANTA TERESA & LAPA

Great views, a diverse crowd and a scenic atmosphere among late 19th-century buildings all set the stage for a great night out in bohemian Santa Teresa. Most restaurants are within a short stroll of Largo do Guimarães. Although Lapa is known more for its samba than its cuisine, more and more restaurants are opening in the area, catering to the young crowds headed to the dance halls.

APRAZÍVEL Map pp98–9 Brazilian $$

☎ 2508 9174; Rua Aprazível 62, Santa Teresa; mains around R$40; noon-1am Tue & Thu-Sat, 1-6pm Sun

Hidden on a windy road high up in Santa Teresa, Aprazível offers beautiful views and a lush garden setting. Brazilian fare with a twist showcases plates of succulent quail and salmon with mango chutney. Wednesday night is dedicated to live *choro* (R$10 cover). This place is a bit out of the way, so take a taxi (and have your map handy, as drivers don't always know this place).

ESPÍRITO SANTA Map pp98–9 Amazonian $$

☎ 2508 7095; Rua Almirante Alexandrino 264, Santa Teresa; mains R$27-36; noon-6pm Sun & Wed, to midnight Thu-Sat

One of our Santa Teresa's best new restaurants, Espírito Santa is set in a beautifully restored mansion in Santa Teresa. Take a seat on the back terrace with its sweeping views or inside the charming, airy dining room, and feast on rich, expertly prepared meat and seafood dishes from the Amazon.

SOBRENATURAL Map pp98–9 Seafood $$

☎ 2224 1003; Rua Almirante Alexandrino 432, Santa Teresa; mains for 2 R$45-70; noon-midnight

The exposed brick and old hardwood ceiling set the stage for feasting on the *frutas do mar* (seafood). Lines gather on weekends for the grilled fish and *moqueca*. During the week, stop by for the tasty lunchtime specials.

MANGUE SECO CACHAÇARIA Map pp98–9 Bahian $$

☎ 3852 1947; Rua do Lavradio 23, Lapa; mains for two R$40-60; 11am-11pm Tue-Thu, 11am-2am Fri & Sat

Part of the Rio Scenarium empire, Mangue Seco is a popular spot for grabbing a meal or a drink before doing the Lapa samba circuit. The menu has a mix of seafood and Bahian fare, with hearty *moquecas* and *bobó de camarão* (shrimp pastries) among the most popular dishes. There's live music Thursday to Saturday nights, and an upstairs bar that stocks over 100 different types of *cachaça*.

NOVA CAPELA Map pp98–9 Portuguese $$

☎ 2252 6228; Av Mem de Sá 96, Lapa; mains R$18-50; 11am until last customer

Like Bar Brasil next door, Nova Capela dates from the beginning of the 20th century. It stays open late into the evening, and fills with a noisy mix of artists, musicians and party kids. Legendarily bad-tempered waiters serve up big plates of traditional Portuguese cuisine. The *cabrito* (goat) is among the best examples of this dish you'll encounter in Rio.

SANSUSHI Map pp98–9 Japanese $$

☎ **2224 4658; Rua Almirante Alexandrino 382, Santa Teresa; meals R$20-40; 7pm-midnight Tue-Fri, 1pm-midnight Sat, to 8pm Sun**

This tiny sushi spot on Santa Teresa's main strip attracts a loyal local following with its delectable sushi and sashimi (36 varieties) as well as teriyaki and other hot dishes.

BAR BRASIL Map pp98–9 German $$

☎ **2509 5943; Av Mem de Sá 90, Lapa; mains R$20-40; 11.30am-11pm Mon-Fri, to 4pm Sat**

According to legend, this German restaurant went by the name Bar Adolf until WWII. Although the name has been Brazilianized, the cuisine is still prepared in the same tradition as it was back before the war. Sauerkraut, wursts, lentils and an ever-flowing tap quench the appetites and thirsts of the sometimes-rowdy Lapa crowd.

MIKE'S HAUS Map pp98–9 German $$

☎ **2509 5248; Rua Almirante Alexandrino 1458A, Santa Teresa; mains R$20-34; noon-midnight Tue-Sun**

Mike's Haus has German pub atmosphere with traditional cooking and cold glasses of imported Weizenbier. Although plates are small here, the place remains a popular gathering spot for expats and Cariocas on Friday and Saturday night.

BAR DO MINEIRO Map pp98–9 Brazilian $$

☎ **2221 9227; Rua Paschoal Carlos Magno 99, Santa Teresa; mains R$18-32; 11am-2am Tue-Thu, to 4am Fri & Sat, to 8pm Sun**

Photographs of old Rio cover the walls of this old school boteco in the heart of Santa Teresa. Lively crowds have been filling this spot for years to enjoy traditional Minas Gerais dishes. *Feijoada* is tops on Saturday. Other good anytime dishes include *carne seca* and *lingüiça*. Strong caipirinhas will help get you in the mood.

SANTA ARTE Map pp98–9 Eclectic $

☎ **2242 9366; Rua Pascoal Carlos Magno 103A, Santa Teresa; mains R$16-25; closed Tue**

Near the heart of Santa Teresa, this colonial charmer is the setting for tasty and inventive contemporary cuisine. World music plays overhead as diners enjoy grilled eggplant sandwiches, seafood pasta and, the most popular dish, a poppy-seed crusted salmon served on mashed plantains. At night, the place is at its liveliest, with occasional live music and a fair bit of pedestrian traffic outside.

ENCONTROS CARIOCAS Map pp98–9 Pizza $

☎ **2221 0028; Av Mem de Sá 77, Lapa; pizzas R$14-30; 6pm-5am Wed-Sun**

This late-night pizza parlor is a good place to stop in while exploring Lapa's live music scene. Featuring a wide variety of ingredients (such as shiitake mushrooms, sun-dried tomatoes and jerked beefs), Encontras Cariocas serves tasty pies amid an atmosphere of old-fashioned charm – high wooden ceilings, brick walls and warm lighting.

SANTA SCENARIUM Map pp98–9 Brazilian $

☎ **3147 9007; Rua do Lavradio 36, Lapa; mains R$16-25; 11.30am-midnight**

Angels, saints and other sacred images adorn the exposed brick walls of this marvelously atmospheric restaurant on Lapa's antique row. Grilled meats and other Brazilian staples are on offer at lunchtime, while at night, Cariocas gather for cold beer, appetizers and sandwiches (like the popular filet mignon on ciabatta). There's live music most nights.

JASMIN MANGO Map pp98–9 Café $

☎ **2242 2605; Rua Pascoal Carlos Magno 143, Santa Teresa; mains R$15-30; 10am-11pm**

Well placed beside the *bonde* (tram) stop on Largo do Guimarães, Jasmin Mango is a charming spot to linger over sandwiches, quiches, pastas, pizzas and desserts. The airy patio attached to the tiny café is a particularly fine spot for taking in the street scene.

BARRA DA TIJUCA & WEST OF RIO

Other parts of Rio offer some of the city's more rustic dining experiences. Outside the city limits one can find open-air spots overlooking the coast – beautiful views complemented by fresh seafood.

BIRA Map p108 Seafood $$$

☎ **2410 8304; Estrada da Vendinha 68A, Barra de Guaratiba; mains for 2 R$95-120; noon-6pm Thu-Fri, to 8pm Sat & Sun**

Splendid views of Baía de Marambaia await diners who make the trek to Bira, about

45 minutes outside the city. On a breezy wooden deck, diners can partake in the flavorful, rich seafood emerging from the kitchen. *Moquecas,* sea bass, shrimp, crab-meat pastries – all are prepared with doting tenderness.

TIA PALMIRA Map p108 Seafood $$$

☎ 2410 8169; Caminho do Souza 18, Barra de Guaratiba; prix-fixe lunch R$60; 🕑 11.30am-5pm Tue-Fri, to 6pm Sat & Sun

On weekends, Cariocas feast on seafood at this simple open-air eatery overlooking the coast. A venerable destination for 40 years, Tia Palmira keeps its fans coming back for its exquisite seafood *rodízio* (all-you-can-eat barbecue dinner). Plate after plate of *vatapá,* crabmeat, grilled fish, shrimp pastries and other fruits of the sea come to your table until you can eat no more.

BARREADO Map p108 Seafood $$

☎ 2442 2023; Estrada dos Bandeirantes 21295, Vargem Grande; mains for 2 R$58-88; 🕑 noon-11pm Thu-Sat, noon-8pm Sun

In a lush setting west of Barra, this rustic spot serves fresh Brazilian seafood with a wildly eclectic twist. Meals are prepared in the wood-burning oven, and pumpkin is the serving vehicle of choice. You can order it filled with rich delicacies like shrimp with *catupiry* (a kind of cheese), scampi, or lobster and mango. For those who'd rather save the pumpkins for Halloween, *vatapá* and roast meats are also excellent choices.

DRINKING

top picks

- **Bar Urca** (p156)
- **Boteco Casual** (p158)
- **Braseiro da Gávea** (p154)
- **Champanharia Ovelha Negra** (p157)
- **Copa Café** (p155)
- **Da Graça** (p155)
- **Devassa** (p153)
- **Jobi** (p153)
- **Londra** (p154)
- **Palaphita Kitch** (p155)

What's your recommendation? www.lonelyplanet.com/rio-de-janeiro

DRINKING

Blessed with those deliciously warm nights, Rio de Janeiro has some enticing nightspots that make good use of the tropical setting. On nearly any evening of the year (unless it's raining) you'll find Cariocas (residents of Rio) drinking up the views at open-air bars on the lake, enjoying spontaneous gatherings at sidewalk cafés and heading to the corner pub to catch a game. For an insight into Rio's drinking culture, familiarize yourself with one of the great sociocultural icons of the city – the *boteco*. These casual, open-sided bars are scattered all over town, and draw in a broad cross-section of society. You'll find young and old, upper class and working class, men and women, black and white mixing over ice-cold *chope* (draft beer) or caipirinhas (cane-liquor cocktails), swapping the latest gossip as bow-tied waiters move deftly among the crowd. Just as most Cariocas have a favorite team, nearly every local also has a favorite *boteco* to call his or her own. These range from hole-in-the-wall joints where canned beer is handed out to drinkers slouched over plastic tables, to classic, wood-paneled bar rooms, with murals on the walls, expertly mixed drinks and a history dating back several generations. Wherever you go in the city, you'll find food is an important part of the experience, as Cariocas rate bars not just on the drinks and the vibe but on the menu as well.

In addition to *botecos*, there are other options when you're ready to head out for the night. Rio has stylish lounges with electronic music and the usual beautiful crowd. There are also flirty college hangouts, hotel bars with a view and a ragged assortment of bohemian haunts. For those seeking a bit of flash, Leblon and Ipanema are good options – though Leblon boasts classic watering holes, too. You'll find a more youthful bar scene in Gávea and Jardim Botânico, while a good place for a date is at one of the Lagoa kiosks. Copacabana has a mix of brash newcomers and old favorites, while Botafogo is famed for its low-key bars. Centro's colorful, open-air spots are great options on weeknights, when the narrow, colonial streets make a picturesque setting for a few drinks. You'll find similarly atmospheric digs in Santa Teresa. At the opposite end of the spectrum is Barra da Tijuca, home to large entertainment complexes with bars, discos and restaurants all housed in one shopping-mall-like structure.

For a pub crawl through one of Rio's best *boteco*-filled neighborhoods, see p68.

HOW MUCH?

In *botecos* and most casual places, a draft beer will set you back about R$3.50 to R$4, with cocktails running about R$7. The prices rise at fancier spots and can top out at R$18 for a cocktail at Rio's swankiest spots.

Most bars will add in a 10% service charge to the bill, as is done for restaurants.

IPANEMA & LEBLON

Ipanema has a mix of stylish and classic bars, with a 20- and 30-something crowd common to most. For drinking al fresco, you'll find peacefully set tables along the east side of Praça General Osório. Leblon has even more bars, with venerable *botecos* and a few lounges as well. A particularly good place to wander is toward the west end of Av General San Martin. For a pub lover's tour of Rio, see p68.

ACADEMIA DA CACHAÇA Map p66

☎ 2239 1542; Rua Conde de Bernadotte 26G, Leblon; noon-1am Sun-Thu, to 2am Fri & Sat

Although *cachaça* (cane liquor) has a bad reputation in some parts, here the fiery liquor is given a respect it nearly deserves. Along with tasty, inexpensive meals, this pleasant indoor-outdoor spot serves dozens of varieties of *cachaça,* and you can order it straight, with honey and lime, or disguised in a fruity caipirinha. For a treat (and/or a bad hangover), try the passion-fruit *batida* (*cachaça* and passion-fruit juice).

BAR D'HOTEL Map p66

☎ 2172 1100; 2nd fl, Marina All Suites, Av Delfim Moreira 696, Leblon; 6pm-2am

The waves crashing on the shore are just part of the background of this texture-rich bar overlooking Ipanema beach. The narrow bar is like a magnet for the style set, who gather in the intimate space to enjoy tropical drinks to the backdrop of sea and ambient electronic music.

BRACARENSE Map p66

☎ 2294 3549; Rua José Linhares 85B, Leblon; 🕑 7am-midnight Mon-Sat, 9am-10pm Sun

Opened in 1948, Bracarense is a classic Carioca watering hole, famous for its simple, unpretentious ambience and its heavenly *salgados* (bar snacks). A steady stream of neighborhood regulars enjoys over 20 varieties of the snacks (try the *aipim com camarão* – cassava with shrimp) to the accompaniment of icy-cold *chope*.

COBAL DO LEBLON Map p66

☎ 2239 1549; Rua Gilberto Cardoso, Leblon; 🕑 closed Mon

Leblon's flower-and-produce market features a number of open-air bars and restaurants. A vibrant, youthful air pervades this place, and it's a major meeting spot in the summer.

CONVERSA FIADA Map p66

☎ 2512 9767; Av Ataúlfo de Paiva 900B, Leblon; 🕑 noon-2am

'Conversa Fiada,' which can mean chit-chat or nonsense depending on the context, is an apt title for this lively Leblon bar. With its deep-red walls, an open-sided setting and a laid-back crowd it's earned a place among the top neighborhood *botecos*.

DEVASSA Map p66

☎ 2259 8271; Rua General San Martin 1241, Leblon; 🕑 5pm-5am

Serving perhaps Rio's best beer, Devassa makes its own creamy brews, before offering them up to festive crowds at its two-floor *chopperia* (beer hall). Top picks: *sarará* (wheat beer), *ruiva* (pale ale) and *mulatta* (a mix of dark and light beer with a shot of coffee). An occasional *Música Popular Brasileira* (MPB) band adds to the din on the upstairs level.

EMPÓRIO Map p64

☎ 2267 7992; Rua Maria Quitéria 37, Ipanema; 🕑 noon-2am

A young mix of Cariocas and gringos stirs things up over cheap cocktails at this battered old favorite in Ipanema. A porch in front overlooks the street – a fine spot to stake out when the air gets too thick with cigarette smoke or bad '80s music.

ESPELUNCA CHIC Map p64

☎ 2247 8609; Rua Maria Quitéria 46, Ipanema; 🕑 noon-3am

A popular newcomer on the Rio scene, Espelunca is a friendly bar that has *boteco* charm – open-sided, wood tables, minimal decor and waiters bustling about under trays of *chope* and piping hot appetizers, including tasty mini-*moquecas* (seafood stew).

GAROTA DE IPANEMA Map p64

☎ 2523 3787; Rua Vinícius de Moraes 49, Ipanema; 🕑 11am-2.30am

During its first incarnation, this small, open-sided bar was called the Bar Veloso. Its name and anonymity disappeared once two scruffy young regulars – Tom Jobim and Vinícius de Moraes – penned the famous song here that changed history (and the name of the street, too). Today, you'll find plenty of tourists here, but little inspiration aside from the ice-cold *chope*.

GUAPO LOCO Map p66

☎ 2294 2915; Rua Rainha Guilhermina 48, Leblon; 🕑 7pm-midnight Mon, to 4am Tue-Fri, noon-4am Sat, to midnight Sun

This colorful Mexican restaurant and bar is one of Leblon's livelier spots for the under-30 crowd. Things get rowdier as the night progresses, helped along no doubt by the wide variety of tequilas on hand. Guapo Loco also serves decent quesadillas, tacos and fajitas if hunger strikes after working the tiny dance floor.

JILÓ Map p66

☎ 2274 6841; Av General San Martin 1227, Leblon; 🕑 6pm-2am Mon-Fri, noon-2am Sat & Sun

This lively open-sided bar opened in 2005, adding a splash more color to an already festive street. Creamy *chope,* a tasty appetizer menu and the inviting, informal ambience have paved the way for its popularity, with the bar and its sidewalk tables packed on weekend nights.

JOBI Map p66

☎ 2274 0547; Av Ataúlfo de Paiva 1166, Leblon; 🕑 9am until last customer

A favorite since 1956, Jobi has served a lot of beer in its day, and its popularity hasn't waned. The unadorned *botequim* (bar with table service) still serves plenty; grab a seat by the sidewalk and let the night unfold. If hunger beckons, try the tasty appetizers (the jerked beef and the codfish croquettes are tops).

LONDRA Map p64

☎ 3202 4000; Av Vieira Souto 80, Ipanema; 🕒 7pm-2.30am Mon-Sat

Rio's glammiest bar is inside the newly opened Hotel Fasano, and offers a vision of decadence matched by few of the city's nightspots. The cozy space, designed by Philippe Starck, has an enchantingly illuminated bar, leather armchairs and divans, and a DJ spinning a good mix of world electronica. As you might imagine, the crowd is pure A-list, the cocktails are pricey (R$15 to R$26), and unless you're a model (or have one draped on your arm), prepare for a long wait at the door.

LORD JIM Map p64

☎ 2259 3047; Rua Paul Redfern 63, Ipanema; 🕒 6pm-2am Mon-Thu, 6pm-3am Fri, 1pm-3am Sat & Sun

Something of a novelty for Cariocas, Lord Jim is one of several English-style pubs scattered about the Zona Sul. Darts, English-speaking waiters and all the requisite expat beers – Guinness, Harps, Bass, Foster's etc – are on hand to complete the ambience. The pub hosts quiz nights on Wednesday.

PIZZARIA GUANABARA Map p66

☎ 2294 0797; Av Ataulfo de Paiva 1228, Leblon; 🕒 noon-3am

One of the pillars of Baixo Leblon, this popular drinking spot serves lousy pizza – but that hasn't stopped patrons from packing this place at all hours of the night. Expect simple ambience and a young, flirtatious, beer-drinking crowd.

SHENANIGAN'S Map p64

☎ 2267 5860; Rua Visconde de Pirajá 112A, Ipanema; 🕒 6pm-3am Mon-Fri, 2pm-3am Sat, to 2am Sun

Overlooking the Praça General Osorio, Shenanigan's is a fairly recent addition to Ipanema's growing pub scene. And it's no small success: through the smoke hanging overhead, the beautiful wait staff shuttles between tables *packed* full of Cariocas and sunburnt gringos. The exposed brick walls, pool table and mix of spoken languages all contribute to the dark and pubby ambience Shenanigan's aims for.

TÔ NEM AÍ Map p64

☎ 2247 8403; Rua Farme de Amoedo 57, Ipanema; 🕒 noon-3am)

On one of Ipanema's livelier streets, this popular fairly new watering hole attracts a fun, very mixed crowd to its indoor and outdoor tables. Caipirinhas and *chope* are the drinks of choice, and there are excellent appetizers and light fare on hand.

GÁVEA, JARDIM BOTÂNICO & LAGOA

Gávea has one of Rio's liveliest young drinking spots – an area called Baixo Gávea, near Praça Santos Dumont. The bars here almost always draw in a crowd, with imbibers spilling onto the plaza most nights. Jardim Botânico has a youthful population that comes out en masse to the bars along Rua JJ Seabra. Meanwhile, the lakeside kiosks offer a more sedate experience, with couples gathering for live music to the backdrop of Lagoa and Christ the Redeemer.

BAR LAGOA Map p64

☎ 2523 1135; Av Epitácio Pessoa 1674, Lagoa; 🕒 6pm-2am Mon, noon-2am Tue-Sun

With a view of the lake, Bar Lagoa is one of the neighborhood's classic haunts. Founded in 1935, this open-air spot hasn't changed all that much since then: the bar still has surly waiters serving the excellent beer to ever-crowded tables, and in spite of its years, a youthful air pervades.

BRASEIRO DA GÁVEA Map pp70–1

☎ 2239 7494; Praça Santos Dumont 116, Gávea; 🕒 10am-1am, to 3am Fri & Sat

In an area more commonly referred to as Baixo Gávea, Braseiro da Gávea is one of several bars in the area responsible for the local residents' chronic lack of sleep. A mixed crowd celebrates here most nights, with patrons spilling onto the facing Praça Santos Dumont.

CAROLINE CAFÉ Map pp70–1

☎ 2540 0705; Rua JJ Seabra 10, Jardim Botânico; 🕒 6pm-3am Sun-Thu, to 4am Fri, 7pm-4am Sat

A mix of couples and groups of friends out for the night (pre- or post-clubs) fills Caroline Café most nights of the week. The sexy young crowd milling around the tables inside and out makes this place a bit sceney at times.

DA GRAÇA Map pp70–1

☎ 2249 5484; Rua Pacheco Leão 780, Jardim Botânico; 🕑 6pm-1.30am Tue-Thu, noon-1.30am Fri & Sat

The colorful Da Graça is one of Jardim Botânico's liveliest bars. The decor is festive and kitsch: rising up to the tall ceilings are walls draped with shimmery fabric, and brightly hued lamps decorate the entrance. On weekends, the sidewalk tables and the inside of the bar gather a loud but fun crowd.

DRINK CAFÉ Map pp70–1

☎ 2239 4136; Parque dos Patins, Av Borges de Medeiros, Lagoa; live-music charge US$2; 🕑 5pm-2am Mon, 9am-2am Tue-Sun

One of a handful of lively, open-air restaurants along the lake, the Drink Café is one of the most charming spots to hear live jazz and bossa nova. Besides the peaceful setting and decent tunes, Drink Café has a small menu featuring German specialties.

JOTA BAR Map pp70–1

☎ 3874 6835; Rua Jardim Botânico 595, Jardim Botânico; 🕑 6pm-2am

This sleek, trim bar features DJs most nights (beginning at 10pm), a young, fairly hip crowd and a talented group of bartenders. If Jota Bar doesn't suit, you'll find several other decent bars just around the corner.

PALAPHITA KITCH Map pp70–1

☎ 2227 0837; kiosk 20, Av Epitâcio Pessoa, Lagoa; 🕑 6pm-3am

A great spot for a sundowner, Palaphita Kitch is an open-air, thatched-roof wonderland with rustic bamboo furniture, flickering tiki torches, and a peaceful setting on the edge of the lake. This is a popular spot with couples, who come for the creative (and pricey) cocktails and the fine views.

SATURNINO Map pp70–1

☎ 3874 0064; Rua Saturnino de Brito 50, Jardim Botânico; 🕑 6pm-2am Sun-Wed, to 3am Thu-Sat

Another newcomer to the scene, Saturnino was quick to become a neighborhood favorite. In a large room with high ceilings and touches of tropical decor, the stylish 20-something crowd mingles over *chope* and fruity cocktails (that could use a touch more alcohol). The open-sided patio in front is a particularly fine vantage point for people-watching.

SKY LOUNGE Map pp70–1

☎ 2219 3133; Av Borges de Medeiros 1426, Lagoa; 🕑 9pm-3am Wed-Sat

This beautifully designed lounge is a stylish but informal place for a drink, with a glass rooftop lending an open feel to the place. DJs spin house and techno to a young Zona Sul crowd. The open-air patio is a particularly enticing in the moonlight.

COPACABANA & LEME

Although there's been some suggestion of recovery in recent years, Copacabana is generally not the place to go out drinking. Av Atlântica has plenty of open-air bars and restaurants, but it's mostly tourists filling the sidewalk tables, and things get rather seedy as the evening progresses. The best places here are the high-end hotel bars, some of which have million-dollar views. Another good option if you want food with your beer is the classic Cervantes (p142).

ALLEGRO BISTRÔ MUSICAL Map pp76–7

☎ 2548 5005; www.modernsound.com.br; Modern Sound records, Rua Barata Ribeiro 502, Copacabana; 🕑 9am-9pm Mon-Fri, to 8pm Sat

This small café and drinking spot in Copacabana features live music most days. See p119 for more details.

COPA CAFÉ Map pp76–7

☎ 2235 2947; Av Atlântica 3056, Copacabana; 🕑 7pm-2am Tue-Sun

One of Copacabana's best new bars, Copa Café has sleek contemporary design, a satisfying menu and plenty of tasty drink concoctions. See also p141.

COPACABANA PALACE POOLSIDE BAR Map pp76–7

☎ 2548 7070; Copacabana Palace hotel, Av Atlântica 1702, Copacabana; 🕑 noon-11pm

Even if you can't swing the overpriced rooms, you can still soak up some of the

COCKTAILS FOR CARIOCAS

One of the great gifts to the cocktail industry is the caipirinha, which is near universally loved – or feared – in Rio.

The ingredients are simple – *cachaça* (cane liquor), lime, sugar and crushed ice – but a well-made caipirinha is a work of art. The key component here is the high-proof (40% or so) cane spirit (also known as *pinga* or *aguardente*) which is produced and consumed throughout the country. The production of *cachaça* is as old as slavery in Brazil, with the first distilleries growing up with the sugar plantations – first to satisfy local consumption and then to export to Africa in exchange for slaves.

Other ways to experience *cachaça* are to mix with fresh fruit juices to make *batidas* (often served as frothy, half-frozen cocktails) or, if it's a particularly fine label (the best *cachaças* generally come from Minas Gerais), to drink it straight. Those who've had their fill of cane spirits might prefer the *caipirosca* or *caipivodcas*, which replace the *cachaça* with vodka.

Despite the widespread love affair with the caipirinha, *chope* (*shoh*-pee; draft beer) is also extremely popular in the city. This pale blond pilsner is lighter than and far superior to canned or bottled beer, and it's served ice cold in most bars, which is perhaps one reason why Cariocas are the largest consumers of *chope* in the country.

decadence that the Palace delivers. The poolside bar offers dozens of sumptuous libations on a lovely outdoor terrace, a setting suitable for young duchesses and weary travelers alike. If you're looking for something more stately, head inside to the elegant piano bar (open 4pm to midnight).

ESPELUNCA CHIC Map pp76–7

☎ 2236 4090; Rua Bolívar 17A, Copacabana; 11am-2am

This inviting new drinking spot attracts a good mix of neighborhood locals, much like its sibling in Ipanema (p153).

HORSE'S NECK Map pp76–7

☎ 2525 1232; Sofitel Rio de Janeiro, Av Atlântica 4240, Copacabana; 5pm-1am

Formerly a British-style pub, this place has been reborn as a creature from Africa, with leopards being the animal of choice when it comes to the print on seat cushions and wall hangings. Just like before, it's still a peaceful place to grab a drink, with an inviting balcony overlooking the ocean.

SINDICATO DO CHOPP Map pp76–7

☎ 2523 4644; Av Atlântica 3806, Copacabana; 11am-3am

A Copacabana institution, this open-air bar looks out on the wide avenue, with the beach in the background. Owing to its breezy location, it attracts a wide mix of people, all playing a part in Copa's inimitable street theater. The food isn't so hot here, but the beers are icy cold and the ocean is, well, right there. A second Sindicato do Chopp, on Av Atlântica 514 in Leme, also overlooks the beach.

SKYLAB BAR Map pp76–7

☎ 2525 1500; 30th fl, Rio Othon Palace, Av Atlântica 3264, Copacabana; 7pm-midnight

It's all about the view at this bar in the Rio Othon Palace. From 30 floors up, the coastline unfolds, allowing a glimpse of the *cidade maravilhosa* (marvelous city) at its most striking.

BOTAFOGO & URCA

Botafogo is the place to go for lively, authentic Carioca bars, with fun, mixed crowds and little of the pretense you might encounter in bars further south. Rua Visconde de Caravelas is a good place to browse the pub scene. Untouched Urca remains fairly nightlife-starved, though it does have several excellent open-air spots, including Praia Vermelha p80) for live samba.

BAR URCA Map pp78–9

☎ 2295 8744; Rua Cândido Gaffré 205, Urca; 6pm-midnight Mon-Sat 6-9pm Sun

This simple neighborhood bar and restaurant has a marvelous setting near Urca's bayside waterfront. At night, young and old crowd along the seaside wall as waiters bring cold drinks and appetizers.

BOTEQUIM Map pp78–9

☎ 2286 3391; Rua Visconde de Caravelas 184, Botafogo; 11.30am-1am Sun-Thu, to 2am Fri & Sat

Another of Botafogo's great neighborhood bars, Botequim is an old-school, down-at-the-heels watering hole serving a friendly crowd. The menu has plenty of appetizers and more substantial dishes if you need something to accompany those *chopes*.

CHAMPANHARIA OVELHA NEGRA

Map pp78–9

☎ 2226 1064; Rua Bambina, Botafogo; ⌚ 5-11pm Mon-Fri

One of Rio's best happy-hour scenes, Ovelha Negra draws a mix of locals who come for the lively conversation and the 40 different varieties of champagne and *prosecco* (Italian sparkling white wine) – the specialties of the house. It's a tiny bar, opened in 2005, but with a classic *boteco* feel.

COBAL DO HUMAITÁ Map pp78–9

Rua Voluntaírios da Pátria, Botafogo

A large farmers market on the western edge of Botafogo, the Cobal transforms into a casual nightspot when the sun goes down, complete with live music and open-air eating and drinking.

DRINKERIA MALDITA Map pp78–9

☎ 2527 2456; Rua Voluntários da Pátria 10, Botafogo; ⌚ 6pm-4am Tue-Sun

Brought to you by the folks of Casa da Matriz (p169) this hipster-loving bar opened in 2007 and remains a top draw of Botafogo. Indoors features pop art and band posters, with DJs spinning rock anthems on the turntables. There are also dozens of tables out on the sidewalk – a fine setting for one of 32 creative elixirs from the enticing cocktail menu.

ESPÍRITO DO CHOPP Map pp78–9

☎ 2266 5599; Cobal do Humaitá, Rua Voluntários da Pátria 446, Botafogo; ⌚ 9am-2.30am Sun-Wed, to 4am Thu-Sat

One of many open-air venues in the Cobal, Espirito do Chopp fills up its plastic tables most nights with a festive, low-key crowd. The beer flows in abundance here, and there's always music nearby – either here or at one of the neighboring bars.

GAROTA DA URCA Map pp78–9

☎ 2541 8585; Rua João Luís Alves 56, Urca; ⌚ 11am until last customer

A neighborhood crowd gathers over *chope* and *salgados* in the evening at this low-key spot. See p143.

O PLEBEU Map pp78–9

☎ 2286 0699; Rua Capitão Salomão 50, Botafogo; ⌚ 8.30am-4am Mon-Sat, 8am-8pm Sun

In the liveliest stretch of Botafogo, O Plebeu is a handsome but unpretentious two-story bar with tables spilling onto the sidewalk and a second-floor balcony. Neighborhood regulars pack this place, drawn by ice-cold beer (served in bottles), codfish balls and the low-key garrulous crowd.

FLAMENGO, LARANJEIRAS & COSME VELHO

Very few tourists find their way to the bars in Flamengo, which are mostly low-key neighborhood hangouts popular around happy hour. Rua Marquês de Abrantes is the best street to take in the scene, with bars and restaurants attracting a drinking crowd. Laranjeiras is best known for Rua Alice, which sports a couple of traditional *botecos* as well as the excellent nightspot Casa Rosa. A short taxi ride from there is the pizzeria and nightclub Hideaway (p144) and in the opposite direction, the jazz bar Clan Café (p164).

BELMONTE Map p84

☎ 2552 3349; Praia do Flamengo 300, Flamengo; ⌚ 7am until last customer

One of Flamengo's ultra-classic *botecos*, Belmonte serves up well-chilled *chope* until late into the night. See p145 for more details.

BAR DO SERAFIM Map p84

☎ 2225 2843; Rua Alice 24A, Laranjeiras

On a lively stretch of Rua Alice, the Bar do Serafim is a small, simple, convivial *boteco* serving tasty Portuguese appetizers and plenty of *chope*. It's been around since 1944 and remains an institution (and popular happy-hour spot) among neighborhood regulars.

CENTRO & CINELÂNDIA

Rio's working stiffs have some fine choices when it comes to joining the happy-hour fray. One of the most magical settings for a sundowner is along the historic Travessa do Comércio. The sidewalk tables on this narrow, cobbled lane pack on weekday nights, particularly as the weekend nears (Thursday is always a good bet). These places see a bit of action during the day on Saturday (several restaurants along Rua do Rosario serve

BAR BITES

If you're heading home from the beach and can't be bothered with a sit-down meal, go Carioca and grab a few appetizers and a *chope* at a neighborhood bar. Known by many names – *petiscos, tira-gostos* or *salgados* – these satisfying snacks come in many shapes and sizes and are available at most bars. Here are some items you are most likely to find:

Batida A strong mixed drink made with *cachaça* and fruit juice, usually passion fruit or lime.
Bolinhos de aipim Deep-fried cassava balls, sometimes served with shrimp and other treats baked inside.
Bolinhos de bacalhau Deep-fried codfish balls.
Bolinhos de queijo Crispy deep-fried cheese balls.
Caipirinha The national drink of Brazil; a strong mixed drink made with limes, sugar and *cachaça*.
Chope Light pilsner draft beer.
Coxinha Pear-shaped cornmeal balls filled with fried chicken or beef.
Misto quente A hot ham-and-cheese sandwich.
Pão de queijo A slightly gooey cheese bread, baked into bite-sized biscuits; the biscuits are so popular in Brazil that a whole franchise was launched on their success (naturally named Pão de Queijo).
Pasteis Crispy pastries filled with meat, chicken, shrimp or cheese (often the mild catupiry).

feijoada – black bean and pork stew), but close the rest of the weekend. Another choice after-work spot is Praça Floriano, with its handful of bars. Blues lovers should also check out the curious Banca do Blues (p162).

AMARELINHO Map pp90–1

☎ 2240 8434; Praça Floriano 55, Cinelândia; 🕑 11am until last customer

Easy to spot by its bright *amarelo* (yellow) awning, Amarelinho has a splendid setting on the Praça Floriano. Waiters serve plenty of *chope* here, wandering among the crowded tables, with the Teatro Municipal in the background. Amarelinho is a popular lunch spot but packs even bigger crowds for that oh-so-refreshing after-work brew.

ATELIÊ ODEON Map pp90–1

☎ 2240 0746; Praça Floriano, Cinelândia; 🕑 noon-10pm Mon-Fri

A lunch and after-work crowd gathers at this pleasant open-air bistro on the edge of Praça Floriano. See p146 for more details.

BAR LUIZ Map pp90–1

☎ 2262 6900; Rua da Carioca 39, Centro; 🕑 11am-11.30pm Mon-Sat

Well over 100 years old, this saloon and dining spot serves some of the city's best brew. See p146 for more details.

BOTECO CASUAL Map pp90–1

☎ 2232 0250; Travessa do Comércio 26, Centro; 🕑 noon-midnight Mon-Fri, noon-5pm Sat

Hidden in a narrow lane leading off Praça Quinze de Novembro, Boteco Casual is one of several charming open-air bars on the colonial Travessa do Comércio. The scenic lane is a popular meeting spot and a festive air arrives at workday's end as Cariocas fill the tables spilling onto the street.

ESCH CAFÉ Map pp90–1

☎ 2507 5866; Rua do Rosário 107, Centro; 🕑 noon-10pm Mon-Fri

The smoky twin of the Leblon Esch Café (p164), this Esch offers the same selection of Cuban cigars from its humidor. Its dark-wood interior features stuffed leather chairs and a decent food-and-cocktail menu, and jazz one night a week (Thursday from 7pm to 9pm).

SANTA TERESA & LAPA

Two of Rio's most atmospheric neighborhoods are still rough around the edges, so take care when visiting here. Lapa is at its wildest during the weekends, with Cariocas from all over the city heading to the neighborhood's samba clubs (p165). Santa Teresa's bar scene is sprinkled along the main street near Largo do Guimarães, though Largo das Neves, with its tiny plaza and open-sided bars, is also a draw. Take a taxi when visiting these neighborhoods at night.

ADEGA FLOR DE COIMBRA Map pp98–9

☎ 2224 4582; Rua Teotônio Regadas 34, Lapa; 🕑 noon-2am Mon-Sat, noon-6pm Sun

In the same building that was once the home of Brazilian painter Cândido Portinari, the Adega Flor de Coimbra has been a bohemian haunt since it opened in 1938. Back in its early days, leftists, artists and intellectuals drank copiously at the slim, old bar looking out on Lapa. Today, it draws a mix of similar types, who drink wine and sangria with Adega's tasty *bolinhos de bacalhau* (codfish croquettes) or *feijoada*.

ANTONIO'S Map pp98–9

☎ 2224 4197; Av Mem de Sá 88, Lapa; 🕙 4pm-5am

This new spot in Lapa has lots of old-school charm with its hanging lamps, wrought-iron trimwork and simple wooden tables (with a few seats on the sidewalk for taking in the street scene). Plenty of other drinking spots are nearby, if you fee like wandering.

ARMAZÉM SÃO THIAGO Map pp98–9

☎ 2232 0822; Rua Áurea 26, Santa Teresa; 🕙 11am-11pm Mon-Sat, to 6pm Sun

Part grocer, part bar, this hole-in-the-wall drinking establishment features a few stand-up tables and a counter. It doesn't look like much, and the neighborhood regulars would probably say it isn't – between sips of their beers – which is part of its charm. The crowds pack this place on weekends, with revelers spilling onto the sidewalks.

BAR DO MINEIRO Map pp98–9

☎ 2221 9227; Rua Paschoal Carlos Magno 99, Santa Teresa; 🕙 11am-2am Tue-Thu, to 3am Fri & Sat, to midnight Sun

Famous for its Minas Gerais cuisine, Bar do Mineiro is one of Santa Teresa's most traditional *botecos* – and an excellent place for a drink while catching up on the local gossip. See p149 for more details.

BOTECO DO GOMES Map pp98–9

☎ 2531 9717; Rua do Riachuelo 62, Lapa; 🕙 7am-midnight

A fairly new addition to Lapa, the Boteco do Gomes has the classical look of an old-time bar with brick walls, art-deco light fixtures, and tile floors. Patrons are a mix of musicians, students and Lapa hangabouts, who gather for a quick drink at stand-up tables in front or at the roomier tables in back.

CAFÉ NEVES Map pp98–9

☎ 2221 4863; Largo das Neves 11, Santa Teresa; 🕙 6pm until last customer Tue-Sat

Small but charming, Café Neves is one of Santa Teresa's gems. It faces out onto Largo das Neves, with the occasional tram rattling by in the early evening. The open-sided bar draws a vibrant mix as the weekend nears.

CHOPERIA BRAZOOKA Map pp98–9

☎ 3474 3363; Rua Mem de Sá 70, Lapa; 🕙 6pm-2am Tue-Wed, 6pm-5am Thu-Sat

A popular new addition to Lapa, this three-story beer house has lots of nooks and crannies where you can while away the night over ice-cold drafts and tasty finger foods. The 20- and 30-something crowd packs this place, so arrive early to score a table.

GOIA BEIRA Map pp98–9

☎ 2232 5751; Largo das Neves 13, Santa Teresa; 🕙 6pm-midnight Sun-Thu, 7.30pm-2am Fri & Sat

Another handsome bar on Largo das Neves, Goia Beira is a small, intimate spot serving a range of tasty *cachaças*. The open-air scene gets lively on weekends, with an occasional band playing out on the square.

MIKE'S HAUS Map pp98–9

☎ 2509 5248; Rua Almirante Alexandrino 1458A, Santa Teresa; 🕙 11.30am-midnight Mon-Sat

This German-style pub attracts a mix of expats and Cariocas on weekend nights. It's a bit off the beaten path, so plan on sticking around a while before moving on. See p149 for more details.

TABERNA DO JUCA Map pp98–9

☎ 2221 9839; Av Mem de Sá 65, Lapa; 🕙 noon-2am Sun-Thu, noon-6am Fri & Sat

A staple of Lapa's hard-drinking scene, this classic-looking spot attracts a diverse bunch – old artists, shop owners, musicians, prostitutes and the odd ones you can't pin down – and the crowd tends to get more colorful as the night progresses.

TUMBAO DE MALEVO Map pp98–9

☎ 2242 9434; Rua Paschoal Carlos Magno 121, Santa Teresa; 🕙 4pm-midnight Thu-Sun

High up above the street, this casual, open-air café attracts an eclectic neighborhood crowd and serves as the backdrop to rotating art exhibitions and the occasional live samba show or experimental theater event. In addition to beer and cocktails, Tumbao serves sandwiches and other light bites.

NIGHTLIFE

top picks

NIGHTLIFE

The city that gave the world samba, bossa nova and baile funk offers dozens of ways to spend a sleepless night among the Cariocas (residents of Rio). Music is the lifeblood of Rio, with few places in the world rivaling its dynamism. You'll find samba clubs, jazz bars, dance halls, lounges and nightclubs all churning out that addictive Brazilian sound. In general, Cariocas prefer live bands over DJs, with many places around the city to hear the latest talent (though Lapa is the headquarters of the music scene). While there are fewer nightclubs, these certainly have their supporters – and hardcore partiers often end their night on a dance floor after catching live music elsewhere.

As with bar-goers, there are a few different subcultures (models and modelizers, surfers, hipsters and hippies) within the nightlife circuit, though there's plenty of crossover between groups. The well-heeled crowd from the Zona Sul for instance tends to favor high-end nightclubs in Gávea and Barra, while an alternative crowd heads to the clubs in Botafogo. Lapa's mix of bars and dance halls attracts a more diverse mix of people from all backgrounds who have little in common aside for a love of samba.

Venues come and go – and the best parties are often one-off events in unique spots – so it helps if you can get the latest from a local source. If you can read a bit of Portuguese, pick up the *Veja Rio* insert in *Veja* magazine, which comes out each Sunday. Thursday and Friday editions of *O Globo* and *Jornal do Brasil* also have extensive entertainment sections. Rio Festa (www.riofesta.com.br) lists the top picks for shows, clubs and happy-hours each week.

MUSIC & DANCE

Rio has a world-class music scene. Samba, jazz, bossa nova, *Música Popular Brasileira* (MPB), rock, hip-hop, reggae, electronic music and the fusions among them are a big part of the picture. Brazil's many regional styles – *forró* (traditional Brazilian music from the northeast), *chorinho* (romantic, intimate samba) and *pagode* (relaxed and rhythmic samba) – are also a part of the scene.

Venues range from megamodern concert halls seating thousands to intimate samba clubs in edgy neighborhoods. Antiquated colonial mansions, outdoor parks overlooking the city, old-school bars, crumbling buildings on the edge of town and hypermodern lounges facing the ocean are all part of the mix.

LIVE MUSIC

Although straight-up bossa nova isn't much in fashion today in Rio, jazz has been growing in popularity, and there's even a dedicated newsstand where you can catch live blues once or twice a week. Those looking to dance should check out samba clubs (p165). For more information on Brazilian music, see p34.

ALLEGRO BISTRÔ MUSICAL Map pp76–7

☎ 2548 5005; www.modernsound.com.br; Modern Sound, Rua Barata Ribeiro 502, Copacabana; admission free; ⌚ store 9am-9pm Mon-Fri, to 8pm Sat

This small café in Copacabana's music store Modern Sound (p119) features live music most nights of the week. Jazz and MPB groups play to a mix of Cariocas, predominantly aged 30 and up. Most groups play from 5pm to 9pm, though Allegro periodically becomes a lunchtime venue (1pm to 5pm). The more popular groups attract a large audience, with people spilling out into the store. Reservations are available if you want to be sure to snag a table.

ASA BRANCA Map pp98–9

☎ 2224 9358; Av Mem de Sá 17, Lapa; admission R$10-20; ⌚ 10pm-3am Thu-Sun

Near the Arcos da Lapa, Asa Branca attracts lovers of *forró* to its large, smoky dance floor. Recently renovated, this is one of the mainstays of Lapa, with a slightly older crowd packing in on weekends. In addition to some of the best *forró* in the city, the club also hosts samba and MPB.

BANCA DO BLUES Map pp90–1

☎ 2517 3310; Av Rio Branco 311, Centro

A rather nondescript *banca* (newspaper stand) by day transforms into a serious jam fest for blues bands certain nights of the week. It's a great street scene, with folding chairs, vendors selling beer and the clash of electronically amplified chords firing up the blues-loving crowd. The schedule changes,

SAMBA SCHOOLS & SHOWS

Starting in September (in preparation for Carnaval) most big samba schools open their weekly rehearsals to the public. An *escola de samba* (samba school) is a professional troupe that performs in the samba parade during Carnaval. These are large dance parties, not specific lessons in samba, although you may learn to samba at some of them. They typically charge between R$5 and R$20 at the door, and you'll be able to buy drinks. Many samba schools are in the favelas (shanty towns), so use common sense when going.

Following is a list of samba schools, contact information and rehearsal days – they all get incredibly packed as Carnaval approaches. The best ones for tourists are generally Salgueiro and Mangueira. It's always best to confirm if there is going to be a rehearsal. A decent website for checking times and reading up on other Carnaval-related activities is www.rio-carnival.net.

Beija-Flor (☎ 2791 2866; www.beija-flor.com.br in Portuguese; Praçinha Wallace Paes Leme 1025, Nilópolis; 🕑 9pm Thu)

Caprichosos de Pilares (☎ 2592 5620; www.caprichosos.com.br in Portuguese; Rua Faleiros 1, Pilares; 🕑 10pm Sat)

Grande Rio (☎ 2775 8422; www.granderio.org.br in Portuguese; Rua Almirante Barroso 5-6, Duque de Caixas; 🕑 10pm Fri)

Imperatriz Leopoldinense (☎ 2560 8037; www.imperatrizleopoldinense.com.br in Portuguese; Rua Professor Lacê 235, Ramos; 🕑 8pm Sun)

Mangueira (Map pp60–1; ☎ 2567 4637; www.mangueira.com.br in Portuguese; Rua Visconde de Niterói 1072, Mangueira; 🕑 10pm Sat)

Mocidade Independente de Padre Miguel (☎ 3332 5823; Rua Coronel Tamarindo 38, Padre Miguel; 🕑 10pm Sat)

Porta da Pedra (☎ 3707 1518; www.gresuportadapedra.com.br; Av Lúcio Tomé Feteiro 290, São Gonçalo; 🕑 10pm Fri)

Portela (☎ 2489 6440; www.gresportela.com.br in Portuguese; Rua Clara Nunes 81, Madureira; 🕑 10pm Fri)

Rocinha (Map pp60–1; ☎ 3205 3303; www.academicosdarocinha.com.br in Portuguese; Rua Bertha Lutz 80, São Conrado; 🕑 10pm Sat)

Salgueiro (Map pp60–1; ☎ 2238 9226; www.salgueiro.com.br in Portuguese; Rua Silva Teles 104, Andaraí; 🕑 10pm Sat)

Tradição (☎ 3350 5668; Estrada Intendente Magalhães 160, Campinho; 🕑 8pm Fri)

Unidos da Tijuca (☎ 2263 9836; www.unidosdatijuca.com.br in Portuguese; Clube dos Portuários, Rua Francisco Bicalho 47, Cidade Nova; 🕑 10pm Sat)

Vila Isabel (☎ 2578 0077; www.gresunidosdevilaisabel.com.br in Portuguese; Av Blvd 28 de Setembro 382, Vila Isabel; 🕑 11pm Sat)

Viradouro (☎ 2628 7840; www.unidosdoviradouro.com.br in Portuguese; Av do Contorno 16, Barreto, Niterói; 🕑 10pm Sat)

so call before making the trip. At the time of writing, bands were playing on Friday night, starting at about 7pm or 8pm.

BECO DO RATO Map pp98–9

☎ 2508 9574; Rua Joaquim Silva 11, Lapa; admission free; 🕑 7pm-2am Thu-Sat

One of Lapa's classic samba spots, this tiny bar has excellent live groups playing to a cheerful crowd. The outdoor seating and informal setting are an unbeatable mix. Marcio, the friendly owner, hails from Minas Gerais; to get the night started, ask him for a tasty *cachaça* (cane liquor) from his home state. Friday night is particularly good to catch live samba.

BIP BIP Map pp76–7

☎ 2267 9696; Rua Almirante Gonçalves 50, Copacabana; admission free; 🕑 6.30pm-1am

For years, Bip Bip has been one of the city's favorite spots to catch a live *roda de samba* (informal samba played around a table). Although the ambience isn't much to speak of – just a storefront with a few battered tables – as the evening progresses, the tree-lined neighborhood becomes the backdrop to serious, improvised jam sessions with music and revelers spilling out onto the sidewalk. The schedule at the time of writing was samba on Sunday, *chorinho* on Tuesday and bossa nova on Wednesday. The music usually begins around 8pm.

CAIS DO ORIENTE Map pp90–1

☎ 2233 2531; Rua Visconde de Itaboraí 8, Centro; admission R$20-30

On the 2nd floor of this 1870s mansion in Centro, jazz, bossa nova and MPB groups perform throughout the year. Most shows happen on Friday or Saturday night; call or stop in to see what's on. Most shows start around 10pm. There's also a restaurant; see p146.

CLAN CAFÉ Map p84

☎ 2558 2322; Rua Cosme Velho 564, Cosme Velho; admission free; 6pm-1am Tue & Wed, to 1.30am Thu & Fri, 1pm-2am Sat

Set against the hillside of Corcovado, the unmarked door of Clan Café hides a large open-air patio covered with abundant greenery. Slow-paced waiters shuffle between the many tables as talented musicians fill the air with sound. Tuesday belongs to *chorinho,* while MPB rules on Wednesday, and jazz on Saturday. The music starts around 9pm.

ESCH CAFÉ Map p66

☎ 2512 5651; Rua Dias Ferreira 78, Leblon; noon until last customer

Billing itself as the House of Havana, Esch offers a blend of Cuban cigars and jazz. The dark-wood interior combined with the well-dressed over-30 crowd will probably make you feel like you're stepping into a Johnnie Walker photo shoot. Groups perform throughout the week – weekdays around 7pm, weekends around 2pm.

FAR UP Map pp78–9

☎ 2266 5599; Cobal do Humaitá, Rua Voluntários da Pátria 446, Botafogo; admission R$5-15; 9pm-2am Tue-Thu, to 5am Fri & Sat

Featuring live music most nights of the week, Far Up is a good destination if you're hanging out in Botafogo. The program leans toward rock and MPB, although the Tuesday night karaoke session mixes things up.

HIDEAWAY Map p84

☎ 2285 0921; Rua das Laranjeiras, Laranjeiras; 6pm-2am Mon-Thu, to 4am Fri & Sat

This fairly recent restaurant in Rio hosts live jazz and MPB concerts (at the time of writing, Tuesday night – but call for the latest schedule) and the food isn't half bad. See p144 for more details.

MAZE INN Map p87

☎ 2558 5447; www.jazzrio.info; Casa 66, Rua Tavares Bastos 414, Catete; admission R$15; 10pm-3am 1st Fri of month

Also known as the 'Casa do Bob' after owner Bob Nadkarni, this once-a-month event is well worth attending if you're in town. It's set in the guesthouse (p198) of the same name high up in Tavares Bastos (Rio's safest favela). Your R$15 buys you a night of live jazz (usually a trio) and more importantly those fantastic views over the city.

PARQUE DAS RUINAS Map pp98–9

☎ 2252 1039; Rua Murtinho Nobre 169, Santa Teresa; admission free

This scenic park overlooking downtown has live jazz concerts throughout the year. Music ranges from jazz to regional Brazilian. Schedules change regularly, but there are often events on Sunday afternoon.

PRAIA VERMELHA Map pp78–9

☎ 2275 7292; Praça General Tibúrcio, Urca; cover R$5-10; 11.30am-midnight

Perched over the beach of the same name, Praia Vermelha has gorgeous views of Pão de Açúcar looming overhead. By night, jazzy MPB bands play from 6pm onward, making for an enviable open-air setting. The food, unfortunately, is less spectacular. Steer clear of the limp pizzas and stick to beer and cocktails.

SACADURA Map pp90–1

☎ 2233 0378; Rua Sacadura Cabral 147, Gamboa; admission free; 8pm-2am Tue-Sat

A new addition to Rio's nightlife, Sacadura is located a few doors down from Trapiche Gamboa (p168) in an otherwise fairly deserted stretch of Gamboa. It offers a mix of MPB, samba-rock and jazz in a big open venue with exposed masonry and dim lighting.

Despite the loud rock pounding from onstage, the crowd was fairly staid when last we stopped by. It's located north of Centro – take a taxi.

SEVERYNA Map p84

☎ 2556 1296; Rua Ipiranga 54, Laranjeiras; admission free; 🕒 11.30am-2am

At night this broad, simple dining hall (c 1950) forms the backdrop to northeastern rhythms. Large percussive groups perform *xote* (a 2/4 dance style derived from the polka), *forró* and *chorinho*, among other styles, to a sometimes-packed house. Shows begin at 8.30pm.

TEATRO RIVAL PETROBRAS Map pp90–1

☎ 2524 1666; www.rivalbr.com.br in Portuguese; Rua Álvaro Alvim 33, Cinelândia; admission R$15-30

Near Praça Floriano, this 450-seat hall has become a popular spot for some of the city's up-and-coming groups as well as veteran musicians. Four or five nights a week, Teatro Rival hosts MPB, *pagode*, samba, *chorinho* and *forró* groups. Tickets for events here can be purchased through Ticketronics (p174).

VINÍCIUS PIANO BAR Map p64

☎ 2523 4757; Rua Prudente de Morais 34, Ipanema; admission R$10-30

Billing itself as the 'temple of bossa nova,' Vinícius Piano Bar has been an icon in the neighborhood since 1989. The indoor/outdoor tables make a fine setting to listen to decent bossa nova – although it's mostly tourists filling those seats since bossa nova isn't very popular anymore among Cariocas.

Samba Clubs

Gafieiras (dancehalls) have risen from the ashes of a once-bombed-out neighborhood and reinvigorated it with an air of youth and song. The neighborhood in question is Lapa, and after years of neglect it has reclaimed its place as Rio's nightlife center. In the '20s and '30s, Lapa was a major destination for the bohemian crowd, who were attracted to its decadent cabaret joints, brothels and *gafieiras*. Today, its vintage buildings hide beautifully restored interiors set with wide dance floors. Although not all the places mentioned here are in Lapa – and not all of them can be technically classed as *gafieiras* either – they all reconnect with that great samba sound.

CARIOCA NIGHTS

One of Rio's best summer-long parties is the annual Noites Cariocas, featuring a mix of Brazilian and international stars playing before a festive, dance-loving crowd. In recent years performers like Jorge Benjor, Gilberto Gil and Marcelo D2 have all played. The event kicks off in mid-November and runs through early February, with concerts held on Friday and Saturday night from about 10pm to 4am. Locations change from year to year, with past *noites* taking place atop Pão de Açúcar and more recently at the Pier Mauá, just north of Centro. Admission is typically around R$80. See the Noites Cariocas website (http://oinoites cariocas.oi.com.br in Portuguese) for more details.

BAR DA LADEIRA Map pp98–9

☎ 2539 0216; Rua Paschoal Carlos Magno 99, Santa Teresa; 🕒 8pm-3am Wed-Sat; admission R$10-20

Just around the corner from the Arcos da Lapa, this early 1900s house was recently converted into a live samba joint. The large space with its multiple rooms has a small dance floor, a pool table and plenty of little nooks and crannies. The samba bands get going around 9pm.

CARIOCA DA GEMA Map pp98–9

☎ 2221 0043; Av Mem de Sá 79, Lapa; admission R$10-20; 🕒 6pm-2am Mon-Wed, to 3am Thu & Fri, 9pm-4am Sat

Although it's now surrounded by clubs, Carioca da Gema was one of Lapa's pioneers when it opened in 2000. This small, warmly lit club still attracts some of the city's best samba bands, and you'll find a festive, mixed crowd filling the dance floor most nights. Current favorites are Monday and Friday.

CASA ROSA Map p84

☎ 2557 2562; Rua Alice 550, Laranjeiras; admission R$15-20; 🕒 11pm-5am Fri & Sat, 7pm-2am Sun

In the first decades of the 20th century, Casa Rosa was one of the city's most famous brothels in Rio's red-light area. Times have changed somewhat and today the demure Pink House is one of Rio's best nightspots. It has a large outdoor patio between several dance floors, where different bands play throughout the night. Surprisingly, there's also a thrift shop here, open until about 3am. The rest of the party keeps going until dawn. Saturday is the best night

SAMBA DA MESA *Carmen Michael*

On Friday night, Rio's samba community congregates in front of the faded colonial facades of Rua do Mercado under a canopy of tropical foliage to play *samba da mesa* (literally, samba of the table). On the worn cobblestones, a long table stands, altar like. Around it the musicians sit and the crowd gyrates, paying homage to their favorite religion. *Samba da mesa* in Rio today is a grassroots movement of musicians and appreciators passionately committed to keeping their music on the street and in an improvised form.

It typically involves a table, at least one *cavaquinho* (small, ukulele-like instrument) player, an assortment of *tambores* (drums) and any number of makeshift instruments like Coke cans, knives and forks that will make a rattle. The standard of the music can be outstanding, and it is not uncommon to catch sight of a samba *bamba* (big-name samba performer) keeping the beat for the group or belting out one of its tunes. Depending on which bohemians have blown through for the night, you might even catch a duel, where two singers will pit their wits against each other in a battle of rhymes. It is a challenge of the intellect, and the topics include everything from love to poverty to the opponent's mother. Even if you speak some Portuguese, you probably won't understand the slang and local references, but the delight of the crowd is infectious.

Street samba has taken a battering from the commercialization of music and space, the rising popularity of funk in the favelas and the police clampdown on 'noise pollution' in public spaces. However for those still interested in a little piece of bohemian Rio, there are several established places that support free, improvised street music. On Friday night, Rua do Mercado and Travessa do Comércio near Praça Quinze in Centro attract the younger radical chic set. On Sunday and Tuesday night, Bip Bip (p163), a tiny bar in Copacabana, caters for hard-core *sambistas* (samba dancers). If you're around on December 2, Dia de Samba (Samba Day), then you can join the samba train bound for Otavio Cross with the rest of Rio's samba community. The musicians disembark in the dusty backstreets of this working-class suburb, which is transformed every year into a labyrinth of makeshift bars and stages that host a 24-hour marathon of *samba da mesa*.

Impromptu street gatherings in Rio are more elusive at other times and finding them can sometimes resemble the mad scramble of trying to locate an illegal rave in the Western world. But it's an unforgettable experience if you find one. There are few fixed places for these parties, and they move from one week to the next. The *bairro* (neighborhood) of Lapa, in particular Rua Joaquim Silva, generally has something going on, but if not, keep your ears open for the unmistakable sound of the *samba bateria* (percussive-style samba) – follow that sound and you will find a party. Pay heed to the local etiquette: ensure you do not talk over the music, don't use cameras with a flash, and don't sit down unless you are a contributing musician.

to go, though Casa Rosa's new Sunday *roda de samba* party also draws its fans – a good mix of Cariocas.

CENTRO CULTURAL CARIOCA Map pp90–1

☎ 2252 6468; www.centroculturalcarioca.com.br in Portuguese; Rua do Teatro 37, Centro; 🕑 7pm-2am Mon-Fri, 8.30pm-3am Sat

This handsomely restored 19th-century building hosts excellent samba bands on weekends, and is a good option for those wanting to escape the Lapa crowds. The scene here is much more staid, making it a good choice for couples.

CLUBE GUANABARA Map pp78–9

☎ 2295 2597; Av Repórter Nestor Moreira 42, Botafogo; admission R$10; 🕑 10pm-2am Wed

Located on the edge of Guanabara Bay, this laid-back space provides a great setting for live samba and *choro*. Musicians gather around a few plastic tables, while young and old dance and mingle over tall bottles of Skol beer. Best of all is the pier at the end of the club, where you can take a break from the music and get an eyeful of the city coastline.

DEMOCRÁTICUS Map pp98–9

☎ 2252 4611; Rua do Riachuelo 91, Lapa; admission R$15-30; 🕑 10pm-3am Wed-Sat

Murals line the foyer walls of this 1867 mansion. The rhythms filter down from above. Follow the sound up the marble staircase and out into a large hall filled with tables, an enormous dance floor and a long stage covered with musicians. A wide mix of Cariocas gathers here to dance, revel in the music and soak up the splendor of the samba-infused setting. If you come to just one *gafieira* in Lapa, Democráticus is a good choice.

ESTRELA DA LAPA Map pp98–9

☎ 2507 6686; Av Mem de Sá, Lapa; admission R$15-25; 🕑 6pm-1am Wed & Thu, to 3am Fri, 7pm-3am Sat

One of Lapa's latest installments, this handsome samba club is set in a restored 19th-century mansion. Estrela da Lapa has an eclectic music scene and hosts bands playing *choro,* blues and hip-hop. Shows begin at 9pm, followed by a DJ who keeps the dance floor going until late.

ESTUDANTINA CAFÉ Map pp90–1

☎ 2507 8067; Praça Tiradentes 79, Centro; admission R$10-15; 🕒 11pm-3.30am Thu-Sat

This old dance hall packs large, older crowds on the weekend, there to enjoy the excellent samba bands. The open-air veranda provides a nice spot to cool off if you've danced yourself into a sweat.

LAPA 40 GRAUS Map pp98–9

☎ 3970 1338; Rua Riachuelo 97, Lapa; admission R$20-30; 🕒 10pm-3am Tue-Sat

Lapa's newest venture is an impressive multistory samba club with tables for lounging on the first floor, pool tables on the second floor, and the stage and dancing on the top floor. It's a few doors down from Democráticus, and at research time was the hot new place for hearing top samba bands.

LAPA CAPADÓCIA Map pp98–9

☎ 2224 8638; Av Gomes Freire 773, Lapa; admission R$10; 🕒 7pm-3am Wed-Sat

Watched over by an enormous statue of São Jorge (St George, an important saint/deity in the Afro-Brazilian pantheon), Lapa Capadócia opened its doors in 2007 and offers a combination of live music, tasty appetizers and ever-flowing *chope* (draft beer) to small, chatty crowds. There's an outdoor space in the back (that may eventually host a small creperie) and an upstairs, though overall the place feels small and intimate.

MANGUE SECO CACHAÇARIA Map pp90–1

☎ 3852 1947; Rua do Lavradio 23, Lapa; admission R$10-20; 🕒 11am-3pm Mon, to 1am Tue-Sat

Set in a street lined with a mix of antique shops and bars, the two-story Mangue Seco has a casual bar and restaurant on the first floor and a *cachaçaria* (*cachaça* bar) on the 2nd floor. Sample over 100 different brands of the fiery stuff while listening to live *choro,* bossa nova or samba bands (starting at 8pm Tuesday to Thursday, and 10pm Friday and Saturday).

MISTURA CARIOCA Map pp98–9

☎ 2221 6833; Av Gomes Freire 791, Lapa; admission R$12-18; 🕒 7pm-3am Tue-Sat

Another classic samba club in Lapa, Mistura Carioca has two levels, with the band playing to a crowded first floor, and a quiet upper level, where you can look down on the band and dancers below. Big glass chandeliers add to the old-time charm.

RIO SCENARIUM Map pp98–9

☎ 3852 5516; www.rioscenarium.com.br in Portuguese; Rua do Lavradio 20, Lapa; admission R$15-30; 🕒 6.30pm-2am Tue-Thu, 7pm-3am Fri & Sat

One of the city's loveliest nightspots, Rio Scenarium has three floors, each lavishly decorated with antiques. Balconies overlook the stage on the 1st floor, with dancers keeping time to the jazz-infused samba, *choro* or *pagode* filling the air. Rio Scenarium has had much press outside of Brazil, and today it has a local-to-foreigner ratio of 50:50.

SACRILÉGIO Map pp98–9

☎ 2222 7345; Av Mem de Sá 81, Lapa; admission R$12-20; 🕒 7pm-1am Tue-Thu, to 3am Fri, 9pm-3am Sat

Next door to Carioca da Gema (p165), Sacrilégio is another major spot for catching live bands in an intimate setting. The outdoor garden makes a fine spot for imbibing a few cold *chopes* while the music filters through the windows. In addition to samba, Sacrilégio hosts *choro, forró* and MPB bands.

SEMENTE Map pp98–9

☎ 9781 2451; Rua Joaquim Silva 138, Lapa; admission R$15; 🕒 8pm-2am Sun-Thu

One of the few places in Lapa that holds court on Sunday and Monday nights, Semente has longevity. Although the place has closed and reopened a few times, Semente was one of the first places in Lapa to bring samba back to the city. Its current incarnation is small and intimate, with good bands and a crowd that comes for the music rather than all the Lapa mayhem (hence, the place is closed Friday and Saturday nights).

TEATRO ODISSÉIA Map pp98–9

☎ 2224 6367; Av Mem de Sá 66, Lapa; admission R$10-20; 🕒 9pm-3am Tue-Sat

This newly opened three-story Lapa club features live music shows and DJs, with a relaxed area upstairs if you need a break from the sounds. You'll find plenty of samba, and MPB and rock make an occasional appearance at the club.

BAILE FUNKS *Tom Phillips*

It's long past midnight and the streets in the Zona Norte community of Cidade Alta are filling. The sports hall is crammed with local youths – there for the community's weekly *baile* (literally a dance or ball). On stage the DJ hammers out a blend of Rio's bass-heavy funk music, around him a troupe of dancers wiggle simultaneously through impossibly complex moves. Security men from the neighborhood's resident drug gang – the Comando Vermelho – hover around the dance floor, in case of trouble.

Bailes sprung out of the Carioca favelas (shanty towns) during the 1970s, and since then their popularity has skyrocketed. Some 100,000 people attend parties like this each weekend in and around the city – in nightclubs, sports centers and on street corners.

The *baile's* increasing profile has been accompanied by controversy. Many criticize the music's sexually explicit lyrics, which they say encourage underage sex and violence against women.

The movement's infamy is compounded by its ties to the drugs trade – many of the parties are funded by Rio's *traficantes* (drug traffickers), keen to ingratiate themselves with locals.

These days the music is undeniably part of the mainstream, with the city's wealthy *playboyzada* (playboys) dancing alongside people from the favela. Rio's politicians are even trying to regulate the parties for the first time. Tour guides like Be a Local (p225) have begun to include the *bailes* on their itineraries. Most tours visit the Castelo das Pedras venue, which holds some 10,000 people.

TRAPICHE GAMBOA Map pp90–1

☎ 2516 0868; www.trapichegamboa.com.br in Portuguese; Rua Sacadura Cabral 155, Gamboa; admission R$12-20; 🕑 7pm-1am Tue-Thu, to 3.30am Fri, 9pm-3.30am Sat

Easily one of the city's most charming spots to hear live samba, Trapiche Gamboa opened in 2004 in a multistory colonial edifice in Gamboa and has tile floors, a friendly mixed crowd and decent appetizers. It's a casual affair, with samba musicians gathering around a table on the ground floor, and dancers spilling out in front of them. Grab a seat on one of the upper floors for prime viewing of the action below. It's located north of Centro, and is best reached by taxi (R$25 from the Zona Sul).

BIG VENUES

In addition to small bars and clubs, Rio has a few large concert halls that attract Brazilian stars like Gilberto Gil and Milton Nascimento, as well as well-known international bands visiting Rio on world tours. Citywide music festivals include October's Tim Festival (p22) and Noites Cariocas, held on summer weekends (December to February). In addition to the venues listed here, during the warmer months concerts sometimes take place on the beaches of Copacabana, Botafogo, Barra da Tijuca and more often the Marina da Glória.

CANECÃO Map pp78–9

☎ 2105 2000; www.canecao.com.br in Portuguese; Av Venceslau Brás 215, Botafogo

Near the Rio Sul Shopping (p121), Canecão holds big-venue music concerts – rock, MPB, hip-hop – throughout the year. Tickets are available at Ticketronics outlets (p174) or at the Canecão box office (cash only).

CIRCO VOADOR Map pp98–9

☎ 2533 5873; www.circovoador.com.br in Portuguese; Rua dos Arcos, Lapa; admission R$15-45

In a curvilinear building behind the Arcos da Lapa, this brand-new theater hosts a wide range of music. The acoustics here are excellent, and after a show you'll find plenty of other musical options in the area. Check the website to see what's on. You can also take classes in *capoeira* (Afro-Brazilian martial arts), dance and yoga.

CITIBANK HALL Map p108

☎ 0300-789 6846; Av Ayrton Senna 3000, Barra da Tijuca

Rio's largest concert house tends to change names every few years, but continues to host top international and Brazilian bands. As well as music shows, Citibank Hall stages ballets, operas and an occasional circus. The hall, which seats around 6000, is in the Via Parque Shopping Center (p125) in Barra. Purchase tickets through Ticketmaster (p174).

FUNDIÇÃO PROGRESSO Map pp98–9

☎ 2220 5070; www.fundicao.org; Rua dos Arcos 24, Lapa; admission R$10-30

This former foundry in Lapa hides one of Rio's top music and theater spaces. A diverse range of shows is staged here, which include big-name acts like Manu Chao and Caetano Veloso as well as theater, video arts and ballet. The foundation is one of Lapa's premier arts institutions, and you can study dance, *capoeira* and circus arts here.

NIGHTCLUBS

Rio has some great places to shake your *bunda* (booty). DJs pull from the latest house, drum 'n' bass and hip-hop favorites as well as more uniquely Brazilian combinations like electro-samba and bossa-jazz. In addition to local DJs, Rio attracts a handful of vinyl gurus from São Paulo, New York and London to spin at bigger affairs. Flyers advertising dance parties and raves (pronounced *hah*-vees) can be found in some boutiques in Ipanema and Leblon, and in the surf shops in Galeria River (p119) by Praia Arpoador. Most clubs give a discount if you've got a flyer. You'll also save money if you're female. Men pay about 50% more than women for club entrance.

00 (ZERO ZERO) Map pp70–1

☎ 2540 8041; Planetário da Gávea, Av Padre Leonel Franca 240, Gávea; admission R$20-45; ⏲ 10pm-4am Fri & Sat, 7pm-2am Sun

Housed in Gávea's planetarium, 00 is a restaurant by day, sleek lounge by night. A mix of Cariocas joins the fray here, though they mostly tend to be a fashion-literate, Zona Sul crowd. Playground, 00's Sunday party, has quite a following among house fans – gay and straight. In addition to rotating parties, the club also hosts CD-release parties.

BARONNETI Map p64

☎ 2522 1460; Rua Barão da Torre 354, Ipanema; admission R$15-30; ⏲ 11pm-5am Tue-Sun

One of Ipanema's only nightclubs, Baronneti has a sleek and trim interior with a choice of two dance floors. Given its prime Zona Sul location, you'll find a young, well-heeled crowd here. Eclectic DJs and fruity cocktails keep the fans returning again and again.

BUNKER Map pp76–7

☎ 3813 0300; Rua Raul Pompéia 94, Copacabana; admission R$10-25; ⏲ 11.30pm-3am Thu-Sun

Featuring big parties throughout the week, Bunker is one of Copacabana's big draws. Its three rooms have different music and you'll find an eclectic mix of Cariocas and tourists against the backdrop of hip-hop, acid jazz, rock, trance and deep house – among other selections. Weekends get crowded – come early and stake out a spot before the masses converge (around 1am).

CASA DA MATRIZ Map pp78–9

☎ 2266 1014; www.casadamatriz.com.br in Portuguese; Rua Henrique de Novaes 107, Botafogo; admission R$10-25; ⏲ 11.30pm-5am Mon & Thu-Sat

Artwork lines this space in Botafogo. With numerous rooms to explore (lounge, screening room, dance floors) this old mansion embodies the creative side of the Carioca spirit. Check the website for party listings.

CINE LAPA Map pp98–9

☎ 3239 0488; matrizonline.oi.com.br in Portuguese; Av Mem de Sá 23, Lapa; admission R$10-20

In the heart of Lapa, this newly revamped space serves up a steady diet of rock, with punk, psychedelic, Brit pop and straight-up classic rock. Live bands sometimes take the stage, and the two-floor space also has a small cinema (seating 40), and plans for club events and art events throughout the year.

CLUB SIX Map pp90–1

☎ 2510 3230; Rua das Marrecas 38, Lapa; admission R$10-40; ⏲ 11pm-6am Fri & Sat

Near the Arcos da Lapa, Club Six is a huge industrial space housing three dance floors, five bars and a number of spots for lounging scattered about the building. It's a top pick for dancing, with DJs spinning house, hip-hop, trance and MPB till daybreak.

FOSFOBOX Map pp76–7

☎ 2548 7498; Rua Siqueira Campos 143, Copacabana; admission R$10-25; ⏲ 11pm-4am Wed-Sat, 10pm-3am Sun

This subterranean club is hidden under a shopping center near the metro station. Good DJs spin everything from funk to glam rock, and the crowd here is one of the more eclectic in the club scene.

MELT Map p66

☎ 2249 9309; Rua Rita Ludolf 47, Leblon; admission R$20-40; ⏲ 10pm-4am Mon & Thu-Sat, 11pm-4am Tue & Wed

The Melt club gathers a young, attractive crowd in its candlelit downstairs lounge, sipping brightly colored elixirs. Upstairs, DJs break beats over the dance floor, with the occasional band making an appearance.

GAY RIO *Dan Littauer*

As one of the world's most exciting cities, Rio has been attracting queers since the beginning of the 20th century. Gay balls date as far back as the 1930s, and Carnaval celebrations have long given gays a chance to dress up, dance and meet. The gay balls have become an institution – the most famous is Gala Gay at Scala, a fabulous *festa* (party) that attracts worldwide attention and is televised live throughout Brazil. Turma OK, the second-longest-running gay and lesbian club in the world, is still alive and kicking in Rio. Indeed, Rio has been a mecca for gay and lesbian tourists since the 1950s. At that time, the place to see and be seen was the beach right in front of Copacabana Palace (still a gay beach, which now attracts an older crowd), while nights were spent in the clubs of Copacabana and Centro.

Nowadays the GLBT (gay, lesbian, bisexual, transgender) scene, especially for visitors, is in Ipanema, with the gay beach (at the end of Rua Farme de Amoedo; look for the rainbow flag) at center stage. Rua Farme de Amoedo, where the girl of Ipanema has been brushed aside by muscle boys (humorously nicknamed 'barbies'), is the queerest street in Rio.

Having said all this, the Carioca definition and idea of a 'gay friendly' area is very different from, say, the Castro, Old Compton St or the Marais where there are clearly demarcated areas for GLBT businesses. Rainbow flags are still a rarity in Rio, and people prefer mixing to exclusivity. Remember that most of the 30-something crowd grew up beneath a dictatorship that was not exactly gay friendly, and it's only the younger generation that is beginning to openly assert its sexual identity.

Nightlife

For all the latest parties about town, check out www.gbrazil.com. Here's a quick rundown of our top nightlife picks:

Monday This is among the quieter evenings in town as Cariocas recover from weekend partying. If you've just arrived, spend time on Rua Farme de Amoedo; Bofetada is a good choice of venue. Girls can head to La Girl for a decent line up of DJs.

Tuesday One option is to hang around Posto 6 bars and then move on to Le Boy's Xtravaganza, the best party in town on Tuesday. If you're not in the mood for dancing, head to the open-air bars around Lapa, where, on steamy summer nights, the area hosts many pre-Carnaval parties – all of them gay friendly.

Wednesday You can take in the ambient music at the Copa or at Copa Café (p141), followed by a drag show at Le Boy. If you want just to relax, opt instead for one of Rio's lounges or restaurants, including Bar d'Hotel (p152), Zazá Bistrô Tropical (p133), Gero (p130) and 00 (Zero Zero; p138).

Thursday A great night to go out: around midnight, leave Rua Farme de Amoedo and walk one block to Galeria Café. You can have a drink at the bar outside or go straight to the excellent party inside, where DJs spin '70s and '80s records. Another option is Dama de Ferro, for excellent house music. In Copacabana, top choices for '80s music are Le Boy or the Copa. Girls can check out La Girl.

Friday This is the day for Lapa, a queer-friendly neighborhood with a fabulous atmosphere. After checking out the street party on Rua Joaquim Silva, you have many choices: for a fun, trashy night, Cabaret Casanova puts on a hilarious drag show. You can also go to Star Club, to the Buraco da Lacraia party that plays almost every imaginable musical style. The club also has a pool table, karaoke and pub. If you'd rather stay in the Zona Sul then try Le Boy, Galeria Café, Dama de Ferro, Fosfobox or the Copa. If you prefer a mature crowd, head to La Cueva.

Saturday Hang around Baixo Leblon, a gay-friendly, bohemian part of Leblon with lots of bars and restaurants that stay open late. This is usually the best night for partying. Try Galeria Café with its groovy house tunes or Dama de Ferro for the country's best funk, electro and house DJs. Fosfobox attracts lovers of electronic music. Le Boy has its biggest night. Head to La Girl for a girls' night.

Sunday Hang out at the beach, where you'll see seemingly every Carioca enjoying the seaside. Afterward, go to Rua Farme de Amoedo and spend time at Bar Bofetada (which incidentally translates as 'big slap in your face'!) with the barbies. The best club tonight is 00 (Zero Zero, p138), where you can also enjoy a yummy dinner and relax in the lounge. Le Boy is popular with the barbies on this night.

Venues

Bar Bofetada (Map p64; ☎ 2227 6992; Rua Farme de Amoedo 87A, Ipanema) This place is frequented by gay guys enjoying a glass of beer after the beach. It's a good place to watch the boys doing the catwalk up and down Rua Farme de Amoedo.

Cabaret Casanova (☎ 2221 6555; Av Mem de Sá 25, Lapa; Fri & Sat) This is one of Rio's oldest clubs, featuring a good mixed crowd, drag queens and slightly trashy music.

Casa da Lua (Map p64; ☎ 2247 4652; Rua Barão da Torre 240A, Ipanema) This lesbian bar is in a leafy part of Ipanema and serves great drinks.

Cine Ideal (☎ 2252 3460; www.cineideal.com.br in Portuguese; Rua da Carioca 62, Centro; Fri & Sat) An old movie theater, and now an electronic music club, Ideal has an outdoor terrace with views of old Rio.

Copa (☎ 2256 7412; www.thecopa.com.br; Rua Aires Saldanha 13A, Copacabana; Fri & Sat) This restaurant, bar and dance club is a relaxed hangout, attracting an 'intellectual' crowd of guys and girls aged 30 and up.

Dama de Ferro (Map p64; ☎ 2247 2330; www.damadeferro.com.br in Portuguese; Rua Vinícius de Moraes 288, Ipanema; Tue-Sat) This club boasts one of the best electronic-music scenes in town but no one goes until very late (we're talking sunrise late).

Fosfobox (Map pp76–7; ☎ 2548 9478; www.fosfobox.com.br in Portuguese; basement level, loja 22A, Rua Siqueira Campos 143, Copacabana; Tue-Sun) This small underground club has live alternative bands, a mixed crowd and easygoing ambience.

Galeria Café (Map p64; ☎ 2523 8250; www.galeriacafe.com.br; Rua Teixeira de Mello 31, Ipanema; Thu-Sat) This bar with a very mixed crowd has lovely decor.

La Cueva (☎ 2521 4999; www.boatelacueva.com; basement, Rua Miguel Lemos 51, Copacabana; Tue-Sun) This small club caters mostly for bear crowds and the more mature on weekends, but throws great parties on weekdays, especially Tuesday.

La Girl (Map pp76–7; ☎ 2247 8342; www.lagirl.com.br in Portuguese; Rua Raul Pompéia 102, Copacabana; Mon, Fri & Sat) This lesbian club has a great atmosphere.

Le Boy (Map pp76–7; ☎ 2513 4993; www.leboy.com.br in Portuguese; Rua Raul Pompéia 102, Copacabana; Tue-Sun) Open since 1992, Le Boy is Rio's gay temple. There are theme nights with drag shows and go-go boys. Girls pay more to get in.

Space Club (☎ 2434 0984; Av Sernambetiba 5750, Barra da Tijuca; Fri & Sat) Cool club in the west part of the city, with beautiful boys and tribal music.

Star Club (Buraco Da Lacraia; ☎ 2242 0446; Rua André Cavalcante 58, Lapa; Thu-Sat) This wicked place has entertained people for over 12 years. You'll find glamorous and trashy visitors, bizarre drag shows, karaoke, a dark room and other attractions.

Turma OK (Rua do Resende 43, Centro; Thu & Fri) The oldest club in South America has lots of trashy music (and we mean that in the kindest way) and attracts people from all over Rio – and the rest of the world. Not surprisingly, it gets very animated around Carnaval time.

The Week (Map pp90–1; ☎ 2253 1020; Rua Sacadura Cabral 154, Centro; Sat) Rio's newest and currently best gay dance club has a spacious dance floor, excellent DJs and lots of go-go boxes.

NUTH Map p108

☎ 3153 8595; www.nuth.com.br in Portuguese; Av Armando Lombardi 999, Barra da Tijuca; admission men R$40-70, women R$20-30; 9pm-4am

This club is one of the city's favorite dance spots, despite its location in Barra. Expect a friendly, well-dressed crowd grooving to DJs spinning electro-samba, house and hip-hop. If you don't like the venue, or the price tag, there are other bars and restaurants nearby.

PISTA 3 Map pp78–9

☎ 2266 1014; Rua São João Batista 14, Botafogo; admission R$10-30; midnight-4am

Brought to you by the same owners of nearby Casa de Matriz, Pista 3 is another good dance spot, with notable DJs spinning a wide mix of rock, electronica and funk. It has two floors, one for dancing, one for lounging (complete with pool table, and area for drinking and snacking).

THE ARTS

top picks

- **Theatro Municipal** (p175)
- **Espaço SESC** (p175)
- **Centro Cultural Oi Futuro** (p174)
- **Sala Cecília Meireles** (p175)
- **Odeon BR** (p176)

THE ARTS

Although most visitors don't come to Rio for the ballet, the city does have some attractions for lovers of the arts. Dance, theater, classical music, performance art and opera have their small but loyal Carioca (residents to Rio) following. Cinema, on the other hand, is a bigger deal, with Rio being one of the leading film centers in Latin America.

Rio has produced a number of successful dance troupes, including the contemporary Companhia de Dança Deborah Colker, which spends much of its time touring abroad. A homegrown talent you might catch in town is the Cia de Dança Dani Lima, an avant-garde troupe that weaves provocative pieces together through dance and aerial gymnastics. Also keep an eye out for the Lapa-based Intrépida Trupe, whose talented acrobat/dancers bring surreal works to the stage. There aren't any spaces dedicated solely to dance, and performances can take place at many of the venues listed in this chapter. Rio's biggest dance festival, Festival Panorama de Dança (p22) is held in late October and early November. For classical dance, try to see a production by the Ballet do Theatro Municipal, which puts on highly professional performances at Rio's most venerable theater.

There's a long history of theater in Brazil, with literary greats from the 19th century, including the highly imaginative Carioca Machado de Assis, giving vision to the stage. Talents from the 20th century, like the great Nelson Rodrigues and more recently Gerald Thomas, have kept the flame alive, and you can still see some of their work on Rio's stages. There are more than two dozen theaters in town. Unfortunately, if you don't speak Portuguese you may not get a lot out of an evening at the theater.

In the classical music scene, Rio has several symphony orchestras and irregular appearances by chamber groups and soloists. The best venues are the Sala Cecília Meireles, with its excellent acoustics, and the magnificent Theatro Municipal. You might also attend a performance at the Centro Cultural Banco do Brasil or the Fundação Eva Klabin Rapaport (p73), both of which host orchestral works periodically.

Important classical festivals include Música no Museu (Music in the Museum; www.musicanomuseu.com.br), with numerous free concerts held throughout the year in Rio's museums. Música nas Igrejas (Music in the Churches; www.musicanasigrejas.com.br in Portuguese) brings listeners into Rio's gilded churches, with 20 or so performances held in different churches during the year.

Tickets & Reservations

TICKETMASTER

☎ 0300 789 6846; www.ticketmaster.com.br in Portuguese; 🕑 9am-8pm Mon-Sat

This international company sells tickets to shows at Citibank Hall (p168) in Barra da Tijuca and the Theatro Municipal (p94) in Centro. Tickets can be purchased over the phone or online (you'll need Portuguese) and at Modern Sound (p119).

TICKETRONICS

☎ 0300 789 3350; www.ticketronics.com.br in Portuguese; Modern Sound, Rua Barata Ribeiro 502, Copacabana; 🕑 9am-9pm Mon-Fri, to 8pm Sat

Tickets for a wide range of shows, concerts and dance performances can be purchased through Ticketronics either over the phone (Portuguese only) or through a distributor like Modern Sound (p119).

PERFORMING ARTS

The city's theaters and concert halls generally stage more than one type of event, with classical concerts, plays, dance performances, recitals, author readings and the odd samba concert (this is Rio after all) filling up the calendar at the same venue.

ARTE SESC CULTURAL CENTER Map p84

☎ 3138 1020; Rua Marquês de Abrantes 99, Flamengo

Housed in one of Flamengo's old mansions, Arte Sesc has occasional classical recitals throughout the year. It also hosts panel discussions on various art and cultural topics.

CENTRO CULTURAL OI FUTURO Map p87

☎ 3131 3060; www.oifuturo.org.br; Rua Dois de Dezembro 63, Catete

This hyper-modern cultural center and gallery space also stages dance performances and concerts. The fare here generally steers well clear of the mainstream. See also p86.

ESPAÇO BNDES Map pp90–1

☎ 2277 7757; Av República do Chile 100, Centro

Weekly concerts are held at this Centro venue throughout the year. Featuring a mix of popular and classical music, BNDES in the past has featured musicians exploring symphonic pop, and experimental groups playing samba-jazz.

ESPAÇO SESC Map pp76–7

☎ 2547 0156; www.sescrj.org.br in Portuguese; Rua Domingos Ferreira 160, Copacabana

Hosting an excellent assortment of theater and dance performances, Espaço SESC is a bulwark of the Copacabana arts scene. The repertoire tends toward the experimental and avant-garde, particularly during annual dance and theater festivals.

SALA CECÍLIA MEIRELES Map pp98–9

☎ 2224 3913; Largo da Lapa 47, Lapa; ticket office 1-6pm

Lapa's splendid early-20th-century gem hosts orchestral concerts throughout the year. Lately, the repertoire has included contemporary groups, playing both *choro* (romantic, intimate samba) and classical music. Concerts start at 7.30pm.

TEATRO CARLOS GOMES Map pp90–1

☎ 2232 8701; Rua Pedro I, 22, Centro

Facing the Praça Tiradentes, the large Teatro Gomes stages avant-garde dance shows and experimental theater. The theater seats 600; tickets for events here can be purchased through Ticketronics (opposite).

TEATRO DO CENTRO CULTURAL BANCO DO BRASIL Map pp90–1

☎ 3808 2000; Rua Primeiro de Março 66, Centro

In addition to its exhibitions, this large cultural center in downtown Rio has two stages and a cinema. Film, dance and musical events are often coordinated with current exhibits.

TEATRO DO LEBLON Map p66

☎ 2274 3536; Rua Conde Bernadotte 26, Leblon

This nicely located theater shows a mix of drama, cutting-edge and children's performances on three different stages. In the same complex is a bookstore, cafés and a range of eating/drinking spots.

TEATRO LAURA ALVIM Map p64

☎ 2267 1647; Av Vieira Souto 176, Ipanema

Across from the beach in Ipanema, this small center stages plays and hosts classical and other live-music styles. It also has art openings, a cinema and an enticing atrium café.

TEATRO NELSON RODRIGUES Map pp98–9

☎ 2262 5483; Av República do Chile 230, Centro

Inside the wildly modernist 1970s-era Caixa Cultural complex, you'll find one of Brazil's best stages for dance and theater. Also onsite are several art galleries, a lunchtime bistro, gardens and a koi pond.

THEATRO MUNICIPAL Map pp90–1

☎ 2299 1711; Praça Floriano, Cinelândia

This gorgeous art-nouveau theater provides the setting for Rio's best opera, ballet and symphonic concerts. Tickets are available at the box office or at Ticketronics (opposite). The theater seats 2400, and sight lines are generally quite good.

CINEMA

There's plenty of variety at Rio's many cinemas. The market here is remarkably open to foreign and independent films, documentaries and avant-garde cinema. This isn't to say that mainstream Hollywood films are in short supply. The latest American blockbusters get ample airtime at movie megaplexes, while cultural centers, museums and old one-screen theaters offer a more diverse repertoire. Films are shown in the original language with Portuguese subtitles. On weekends, popular shows often sell out, so buy your ticket early. Prices range from R$14 to R$18 per ticket, with matinee prices Monday through Thursday. For extensive listings and times pick up a copy of *O Globo, Jornal do Brasil* or *Veja Rio*.

CASA DA CULTURA LAURA ALVIM Map p64

☎ 2267 1647; Av Vieira Souto 176, Ipanema

Facing the beach, the charming Laura Alvim cultural center screens foreign (of the non-Hollywood variety) and independent flicks. Its small screening room seats 72.

RIO DE JANEIRO INTERNATIONAL FILM FESTIVAL

The Rio film fest is one of the biggest in Latin America, with more than 300 films shown at some 35 theaters in Rio, and occasional screenings at the Marina da Glória and other open-air spots around town. In past years, the two-week festival has attracted over 300,000 viewers. It runs from the last week of September to the first week of October, with top prizes handed out in the form of iconic Troféus Redentores (Redeemer Prizes); small, slightly abstract, gold statues shaped like Christ the Redeemer. Although there's a wide variety of international fare screened here, the festival often sets the stage for the success of Brazilian films aimed at wide release. On rare occasions, a film is seen by millions before it's even screened at the festival. In 2007, for instance, the movie *Tropa de Elite* (Elite Squad; p38) premiered at the festival, but before it appeared an unfinished cut of the film was stolen in production and leaked over the internet. It became a bootleg sensation, with more than three million viewers watching the pirated copy before it ever hit the big screen. This didn't stop it from becoming the highest grossing Brazilian film of the year (some cynics even suggested the filmmakers were responsible for the leak as a means of generating controversy and publicity).

For more on the festival, including films and locations, check the multilingual www.festivaldorio.com.br.

CASA FRANÇA-BRASIL Map pp90–1

☎ 2253 5366; Rua Visconde de Itaboraí, Centro

Housed in the Casa França-Brasil (p93), this small 53-seat theater shows French films and an occasional independent classic.

CINE SANTA TERESA Map pp98–9

☎ 2507 6841; www.cinesanta.com.br; Rua Paschoal Carlos Magno 136, Santa Teresa

This small, single-screen theater (seating just 46) is nicely located on Largo do Guimarães. Befitting the art-loving hood, the cinema screens a selection of independent and Brazilian films.

ESPAÇO MUSEU DA REPÚBLICA Map p87

☎ 3826 7984; Museu da República, Rua do Catete 153, Catete

The screening room in the dramatic Museu da República (p86) shows films you aren't likely to encounter elsewhere. The focus is world cinema – both contemporary and classic films.

ESPAÇO UNIBANCO DE CINEMA Map pp78–9

☎ 3221 9221; Rua Voluntários da Pátria 35, Botafogo

This two-screen cinema in Botafogo shows a range of films – Brazilian, foreign, independent and the occasional Hollywood film. It has a lovely café inside, as well as a used record-and-book shop with a number of works focusing on the film arts.

ESTAÇÃO BOTAFOGO Map pp78–9

☎ 2226 1988; Rua Voluntários da Pátria 88, Botafogo

One block from Espaço Unibanco, this small three-screen theater shows a mix of Brazilian and foreign films. The small café in front is a good place to grab a quick *cafézinho* (small black coffee) before the movie.

ESTAÇÃO IPANEMA Map p64

☎ 2540 6445; Rua Visconde de Pirajá 605, Ipanema

On the 1st floor of a small shopping complex in Ipanema, Estação Ipanema screens popular contemporary films from Brazil and abroad. Its single theater seats 140.

ESTAÇÃO PAÇO Map pp90–1

☎ 2529 4829; Paço Imperial, Praça Quinze de Novembro 48, Centro

This small, one-room screening theater (seating 64) in the Paço Imperial doesn't offer much in the way of state-of-the-art cinema viewing. However, the excellent selection of foreign and independent films makes up for the technological shortcomings.

ODEON BR Map pp90–1

☎ 2262 5089; Praça Mahatma Gandhi 5, Cinelândia

Rio de Janeiro's landmark cinema is a remnant of the once flourishing moviehouse scene that gave rise to the name Cinelândia. The restored 1920s film palace shows independent films, documentaries and foreign films, and hosts the gala for prominent film festivals. It also hosts worthwhile monthly events like movie marathons (11pm to 6am) on the first Friday of the month. Next door, Ateliê Odeon (p146) opens around weekend screenings.

ROXY Map pp76–7

☎ 3221 9292; Av Nossa Senhora de Copacabana 945, Copacabana

Copacabana's only cinema is a good retreat when the weather sours. The Roxy shows the usual films on wide release.

TEATRO LEBLON Map p66

☎ 3221 9292; Av Ataúlfo de Paiva 391, Leblon

Leblon's popular theater has two screens showing the latest Hollywood releases.

UCI – NEW YORK CITY CENTER Map p108

☎ 2432 4840; New York City Center, Av das Americas 5000, Barra da Tijuca; 🕒 1-10pm Mon-Fri, 11am-midnight Sat & Sun

UCI – New York City Center is Brazil's largest megaplex, featuring 18 different screening rooms complete with large, comfortable chairs and stadium seating. Films are screened constantly (every 10 minutes on weekends).

SPORTS & ACTIVITIES

top picks

- **Hang gliding** Soar above the sea and city on a tandem hang-gliding flight (p183)
- **Rock climbing** Climb to the summit of Pão de Açúcar (p181)
- **Hiking** Walk past waterfalls hidden in the tropical rain forest inside the city limits (p183)
- **Dancing** Learn the steps at a private dance class (p185) to prepare for those late Lapa nights

What's your recommendation? www.lonelyplanet.com/rio-de-janeiro

SPORTS & ACTIVITIES

When it comes to the pursuit of sport, Cariocas (residents of Rio) seem to be ruled by the sun, spilling out of doors on lovely days for pick-up games of soccer, volleyball and *futevôlei* (volleyball played without using the hands). Runners, cyclists and power-walkers take to the streets, as hikers and rock-climbers head for the hills and surfers make for the beach.

Those who'd rather sit than spin can head to the stadium (or the pub) for the big game. Like other Brazilians, Cariocas are addicted to football, with every man, woman and child expected to profess their undying devotion to one team or another by about the age of five. *Futebol* games are an intense spectacle – as much because of the crazed fans as the teams out on the field. The rivalries are particularly intense when Rio's club teams – Botafogo (black-and-white-striped jerseys), Flamengo (red jerseys with black hoops), Fluminense (red, green and white stripes) and Vasco da Gama (white with a black sash) – play each other. Professional club competitions are held year-round and the games can be played on any day of the week (though Saturday, Sunday and Wednesday are favorites). An excellent book on Brazil's great sport, and its relationship to culture, religion and politics, is *Futebol: The Brazilian Way of Life* (2002) by Alex Bellos. For results, schedules and league tables visit www.netgol.com.

On the national level, Brazilians have proven that they are among the world's best footballers, having produced scores of brilliants players and winning the World Cup five times.

While the nation has a fairly one-track mind when it comes to professional sports, Brazilians have distinguished themselves in other arenas. They dominate in auto racing, for instance. Brazilian drivers have won more Formula One world championships than any other nationality, a fact that probably won't surprise anyone who rents a car for the weekend. The greatest racer, three-time world champion Ayrton Senna, was almost canonized after his death.

Tennis also has its following, helped along by Gustavo 'Guga' Kuerten who was once ranked number one in the world and won the French Open three times between 1997 and 2001. Basketball (with three Brazilian players in the NBA), volleyball (both men's and women's teams are ranked number one in the *Federation Internationale de Volleyball's* world ranking) and even professional bull riding have their Brazilian stars.

Amid such a sporting nation, there are plenty of ways to join the fray. Rio's lush mountains and glimmering coastline cry out for action, and you can hone your game – whether it be volleyball, soccer or *frescobal* (played with wooden racquets and a rubber ball) – without ever leaving that sparkling shoreline. Nearby, palm-lined paths set the stage for jogging, hiking, walking and cycling. While the mountain backdrops are fine to gaze at, they are also the setting for some of the city's unique adventures: you can climb up them, hang-glide down from them or go hiking in the forests that surround them. For something a little different, sign up for a dance class, go scuba diving off the islands near Rio, book a fishing trip or stretch those sunburned gams at a yoga class. And for those who'd rather take their sport sitting down, there's always Maracanã (below), the world's largest football stadium.

SPECTATOR SPORTS

HORSE RACING

JOQUEI CLUBE Map pp70–1

☎ 3534 9000; www.jcb.com.br in Portuguese; Jardim Botânico 1003, Gávea; ⏲ 6.15-11pm Mon, 4-11pm Fri, 2-8pm Sat & Sun

One of the country's loveliest racetracks, with a great view of the mountains and Corcovado, the Joquei Clube (Jockey Club) seats 35,000 and lies on the Gávea side of the Lagoa Rodrigo de Freitas opposite Praça Santos Dumont. Local race fans are part of the attraction – it's a different slice of Rio life.

Tourists are welcome in the members' area, which has a bar overlooking the track. Races are held on Monday, Friday, Saturday and Sunday. The big event is the Brazilian Grand Prix (the first Sunday in August).

FOOTBALL

MARACANÃ FOOTBALL STADIUM

Map pp60–1

☎ 2299 2941; Av Maracanã, São Cristóvão; admission R$20-100; Ⓜ Maracanã

Nearly every Brazilian child dreams of playing in Maracanã, Rio's enormous shrine to soccer. Matches here rate among the most exciting in the world, and the behavior of the fans is no less colorful. The devoted pound huge samba drums as their team takes the field, and if things are going badly – or very well – fans are sometimes driven to sheer madness. Some detonate smoke bombs in team colors, while others launch beer bottles, cups full of urine or dead chickens into the seats below. Enormous flags spread across large sections of the bleachers as people dance in the aisles (known to inspire a goal or two).

Games take place year-round and can happen any day of the week. Rio's big four clubs are Flamengo, Fluminense, Vasco da Gama and Botafogo. Although buses run to and from the stadium, the metro is safer and less crowded on game days. The stadium has color-coded seating, with tourists and more sedate folk generally sitting in the somewhat isolated white section, and rowdier flans flocking to the green and yellow sections or the wildest blue section on the lowest level. Those who want the best views at any price opt for the *especial* seats, which run R$100 a seat. The ticket price is R$20 to R$30 for most games. For more information on the stadium, see p104.

OUTDOOR ACTIVITIES

Climb, hike, surf or hang glide your way across Rio's enticing landscapes and seascapes. For those seeking more than just a taste of the outdoors, take a class and become an expert in your sport of choice. For other organized activities – walking tours, boat trips, fishing excursions, helicopter rides and favela (shanty town) tours – see p224.

CLIMBING

Rio is the center of rock climbing in Brazil, with 350 documented climbs within 40 minutes of the city center. Climbing in Rio is best during the cooler months of the year (April to October); during the summer, the tropical sun heats up the rock to ovenlike temperatures and turns the forests into saunas. People do climb during the summer, but usually only in the early morning or late afternoon when it's not so hot.

A number of agencies offer climbing and hiking tours. Rio also has several well-organized climbing clubs, which have weekly meetings. The clubs, which welcome outsiders, also have something of a social component for those interested in mingling with Cariocas. Safety-conscious outfitters typically charge R$150 for a full-day climbing excursion.

CENTRO EXCURSIONISTA BRASILEIRA Map pp90–1

CEB; ☎ 2252 9844; www.ceb.org.br in Portuguese; 8th fl, Av Almirante Barroso 2, Centro; 🕓 office 2-6pm Mon-Fri, meetings 7pm Thu

Founded in 1919, CEB sponsors day hikes and weekend treks (with camping). It also arranges trips further out, such as two-week hikes across Ushuaia in Southern Argentina. The club plans its activities at its weekly meeting, a good spot to have a chat with the laid-back enthusiasts. Its office is open during the week for people who want to stop in, say hello and take a look at the bulletin board, which lists upcoming excursions – as does the website.

CLUBE EXCURSIONISTA CARIOCA Map pp76–7

CEC; ☎ 2255 1348; www.carioca.org.br in Portuguese; Ste 206, Rua Hilário de Gouveia 71, Copacabana; 🕓 meetings 8.30pm Thu

Although CEC is 50 years old, it's still going strong. Typically, CEC arranges hikes and technical climbs, although from time to time it organizes rappelling and rafting. The club is also involved in preservation and education efforts, and offers five-week courses on basic mountaineering.

CRUX ECOADVENTURE

☎ 3474 1726, 9392 9203; www.cruxecoaventura.com.br

This highly reputable outfit offers a range of climbing excursions and other outdoor adventures. The most popular is the ascent up Pão de Açúcar, which isn't as impossible as it looks. Guides are very safety-conscious and have years of experience. Other possibilities include rappelling down waterfalls, full-day hikes through Floresta da Tijuca, and biking and kayaking trips.

DIVING

CALYPSO

☎ 2542 8718, 9939 5997; www.calypsobrasil.com.br; AS Divers, Rua da Alfândega 97, Centro

Calypso offers courses (up to Dive Master) in waters near Rio. The company also offers excellent excursions for certified divers to Arraial do Cabo and Angra dos Reis, among other spots. Those looking to do diving further afield should consider one of Calypso's affordably priced excursions to Fernando Noronha, a lovely island in the northeast. You can get more information at its associated store, AS Divers. Classes are held at the Clube de Regatas Guanabara (Av Reporter Nestor Moreira 42, Botafogo).

DIVE POINT Map p66

☎ 2239 5105; www.divepoint.com.br; Shop 5, Av Ataúlfo de Paiva 1174, Leblon

Scuba divers can rent equipment or take classes from Dive Point. It also offers diving courses, and dive tours around Rio's main beaches and Ilha Cagarras (the island in front of Ipanema), as well as the premier dive spots in Angra dos Reis, Búzios.

MAR DO RIO Map p87

☎ 2225 7508; www.mardorio.com.br in Portuguese; Marina da Glória, Av Infante Dom Henrique, Glória

One of several dive operators in the Marina da Glória, Mar do Rio offers two-tank dives (US$70) on Saturday and Sunday, departing at 8.30am and returning at 2.30pm. It also offers night dives twice a month. Less-experienced divers can opt for one of the courses, including a five-day PADI-certified basic course (US$375).

OUTDOORS WITH MARCELO CASTRO: BIG ADVENTURES IN TROPICAL RIO

One of Rio's top guides, Marcelo Castro has been leading rock climbing, rappelling and other adventure tours for more than 10 years. He's also an integral member of the Associação Carioca de Turismo de Aventura (ACTA), an organization devoted to ensuring that adventure outfits maintain rigorous standards (particularly in safety) in their operations. In addition to founding the adventure outfit Crux Ecoaventura, he also has a partnership with the Municipal Tourism Agency, providing qualification courses and workshops to help other guides improve their skills and understand the market better. Lonely Planet sat down with Castro for a chat about rock climbing and his favorite ways to spend a sun-drenched afternoon in Rio.

How did you first get into rock climbing? I was a skateboarder till I got an injury and had to quit the flips and hard impacts for a while. For therapy, I started mountaineering on Sugarloaf, back in 1996. Six months later I was already on technical multi-pitch rock climbing. Meeting the older guys in Urca neighborhood, the largest urban rock-climbing center in the world, I was exposed to a brand new horizon: the steep granite routes of Rio and their astonishing views from the summit. Once you start rock climbing, you always want to feel that feeling of freedom again.

How would you describe the climbing in Rio? Rock climbing in Rio started almost 100 years ago, when Carioca climbers founded the Brazilian Excursionist Center (CEB; p181) in 1919. At this time, all the traditional climbers came from Rio. Later on, many other rock-climbing associations around Brasil started to grow, and the sport expanded. Today, it's no longer just men climbing. Women are also present on Rio de Janeiro's granite walls, and it's quite common to see two women climbing together, sharing the lead on the route. The sport is developing really quickly and some of our best climbers now are under 18 years old.

What are some of your favorite climbs around Rio? Corcovado and Sugarloaf have a very nice range of climbing routes; they are must-go places to climb. There is also the Morro Dois Irmãos cliff facing Ipanema. If you go out of town, Dedo de Deus in Teresópolis and Pedra Maria Comprida in Petrópolis are good options to beat the weekend crowds and find cooler temperatures – both are less than 90 minutes away from Rio.

In Rio, what are your favorite adventure trips to organize? Some of our finest adventure trips are mountaineering to the top of the Sugarloaf, rappelling down the Feiticeira waterfall in Ilha Grande, hiking up the Tijuca Peak inside Tijuca National Park, and doing the two-hour Corcovado hike to the Christ Redeemer Statue; I also like kayaking in Guanabara Bay.

With the growing number of adventure outfits in Rio, how do you recommend travelers find a good, safe, experienced guide? First of all, you should check with ACTA (www.actarj.com.br) or Ministério do Turismo (abeta.com.br) to find which adventure tours companies are meeting the new Brazilian Standards for Adventure Tourism (ABNT) guidelines. Always asks for information during the reservation process; ask if they provide the equipment, if they have bilingual tour guides and find out if they know about the ABNT standards and the best practices.

An interview with Marcelo Castro, rock climber and adventure-tour guide

FISHING

MARLIN YACHT TOURS Map p87

☎ 2225 7434; l; www.marlinyacht.com.br; Marina da Glória, Av Infante Dom Henrique, Glória

Those who have their own equipment should look into hiring a boat. The Marina da Glória has a number of outfits, although Marlin Yacht Tours has the largest fleet.

UNIVERSIDADE DA PESCA

☎ 3971 7211; www.upesca.com.br in Portuguese; Rua do Bispo 94, ste 1207, bloco 2, Rio Comprido

Universidade da Pesca offers a wide range of fishing tours – from day trips around Baía de Guanabara and Ilha Cagarras to week-long adventures in the Amazon. Trips include instructors and multilingual guides.

HANG GLIDING

If you weigh less than 100kg (about 220lb) and have a spare R$250 to spend, you can do the fantastic hang glide off 510m Pedra Bonita – one of the giant granite slabs that tower above Rio – onto Pepino beach in São Conrado. No experience is necessary. We've been assured that the winds are very safe here and the pilots know what they are doing. Guest riders are secured in a kind of pouch that is attached to the hang glider.

Naturally, hang-gliding flights are one of those activities that are at the mercy of weather and wind conditions. During summer you can usually fly on all but three or four days a month, and conditions during winter are even better. If you fly early in the day, you will have more flexibility to accommodate unforeseen weather delays. You should also ensure that your flight lasts as long as possible; try to get a guarantee of at least seven to 10 minutes (anything under six minutes is unacceptable), and 15 minutes is ideal.

The price of the flight includes pick-up and drop-off from your hotel. Travel agents can book tandem flights, but they add their own fee; to cut out the middle-men, call direct.

ASSOCIAÇÃO BRASILEIRO DE VÔO LIVRE

☎ 3322 0266; www.abvl.com.br in Portuguese; Av Prefeito Mendes de Moraes, São Conrado

If you've had a taste of hang gliding and think you've found your calling, the Associação Brasileiro de Vôo Livre (Brazilian Association of Hang Gliding) offers classes in the sport.

CLUBE ESPORTIVO ULTRALEVES

☎ 2441 1880; Av Embaixador Abelardo Bueno 671, Jacarepaguá; 🕑 8am-sunset Tue-Sun

Ultra-leve (ultralight) flights are more comfortable than hang gliders, but you have to listen to the motor. Trips leave from the Aeroclube do Jacarepaguá. The club has some long-range ultralights that can stay up for more than two hours. Courses are available.

JUST FLY

☎ 2268 0565, 9985 7540; www.justfly.com.br

Paulo Celani is a highly experienced tandem flyer with over 6000 flights to his credit. His fee includes picking you up from and dropping you off at your hotel.

SUPERFLY

☎ 3322 2286, 9982 5703; www.riosuperfly.com.br; Casa 2, Estrada das Canoas 1476, São Conrado

Founder Ruy Marra has more than 25 years of flying experience and is an excellent tandem glider pilot. Regarded as one of the best in Rio, Ruy is also the person to see if you want to paraglide (gliding with a special parachute).

TANDEM FLY

☎ 2422 6371, 2422 0941; www.riotandemfly.com.br

Three experienced pilots run this flight outfit, and they'll arrange pick up and drop off at your hotel. They also give lessons for those wanting to learn how to fly solo.

HIKING

Rio is good for hiking and offers some outstanding nature walks. Visitors can hike one of the many trails through Floresta da Tijuca (p105) or head to one of the three national parks within a few hours of the city.

In recent years there's been a boom in organized hikes around the city, including hikes through wilderness areas around Corcovado, Morro da Urca and Pão de Açúcar, and of course Tijuca. It's advisable to go with a guide for a number of obvious reasons – getting lost and getting robbed being at the top of the list. Group outings can also be a great way to meet Cariocas.

RIO ADVENTURES

☎ 2705 5747; www.rioadventures.com; hiking/climbing/rafting tours from R$50/125/150

Offering a range of outdoor activities, Rio Adventures leads hikes through Tijuca

top picks

HIKES

Ringed with tropical rainforest, Rio has plenty of inspiring places in which to get a dose of the tropic's natural wonders. Here's a rundown of the city's best hikes, courtesy of Juliana Botafogo of Tangará Ecological Hikes (below).

- Corcovado Heavy hike to one of Rio's icons, with lovely views. It's steep, but highly rewarding.
- Pedra Bonita Easy hike along a sunny trail; there's not much vegetation, but the views are worth it. You'll see part of Alto da Boa Vista and all of São Conrado, plus the islands off Rio's coast.
- Pedra da Gávea Heaviest hike in Rio, but the sacrifice is worth it. Some rock-climbing skills needed.
- Primatas Waterfall Easy hike less than one hour from Jardim Botânico. Gorgeous trail, interesting vegetation and a chance to spot monkeys.
- Tijuca Peak Moderate hike to the highest place in the city: simply breathtaking views.

National Park, including short treks up Pico Tijuca and Pedro Bonito. It also offers sightseeing tours, rock climbs (Pão de Açúcar, Corcovado and Pico da Tijuca), rafting excursions (to Paraibuna River, 175km northwest of Rio) and parachuting and paragliding trips. It employs experienced guides, who speak Portuguese, English and Spanish among other languages.

RIO HIKING

☎ 2552 9204; www.riohiking.com.br; full-day tour R$125-150

This popular outfit offers hiking trips ranging from easy to strenuous and covering a variety of terrains around Rio. Favorite treks include hikes up Pedra da Gávea and ascending Pão de Açúcar. You can also arrange kayaking, diving, river rafting and numerous other adventure sports here.

TANGARÁ ECOLOGICAL HIKES

☎ 2252 8202, 9656 1460; www.tangarapasseios.com.br in Portuguese; per person R$20-40

Popular with a mix of Brazilians and foreigners, Tangará offers scheduled hiking trips, including climbs up Pedra da Gávea, ascents through rain forest to the top of Corcovado and hikes to waterfalls hidden in Horto (near Jardim Botânico). Hikes take place on Saturday and Sunday. Unlike pricier organized tours, transport isn't provided, so you'll have to take a bus or taxi to the designated meeting place. Call or check the website for the latest scheduled trips.

PADDLE BOATING

Those who've always dreamed of paddling a swan boat around the Zona Sul's largest lake can do just that on the Lagoa Rodrigo de Freitas. Paddle-boat hire (Map pp70–1; R$20 per half hour) is available on weekends on the east shore near the Parque do Cantagalo.

VOLLEYBALL & OTHER BEACH SPORTS

Volleyball is Brazil's second-most popular sport (after football). A natural activity for the beach, it's also a popular spectator sport on TV. A local variation of volleyball you'll see on Rio's beaches is *futevôlei* – played without using hands. Good luck!

Usually played on the firm sand at the shoreline, *frescobal* involves two players, each with a wooden racquet, hitting a small rubber ball back and forth as hard as possible.

ESCOLINHA DE VÔLEI Map p64

☎ 9702 5794; Ipanema beach

Those interested in improving their volleyball game – or just meeting some Cariocas – should pay a visit to Pelé de Ipanema. Pelé, who speaks English, has been hosting volleyball classes for 10 years. Lessons are in the morning (from about 6.30am to 9am) and in the afternoon (2pm to 9pm), ranging from one to two hours. He currently charges around R$50 for the month and you can come as often as you like. Look for his large Brazilian flag on the beach near Rua Garcia D'Ávila. Pelé's students are a mix of Cariocas and expats, who then meet for games after honing the fundamentals.

WALKING, JOGGING & CYCLING

Splendid views and the sounds of the ever-present ocean nearby are just two of the features of the many good walking and jogging paths of the Zona Sul. The Parque do Flamengo (p83) has plenty of paths stretching between city and bay. Further south the Lagoa Rodrigo de Freitas (p73) has a 7.5km track for cyclists, joggers and rollerbladers. At the lakeside Parque do Cantagalo you can rent bicycles, tricycles or quadricycles (around R$20 per hour). The favorite option is the seaside path from Leme to Barra da Tijuca. Sunday is the best day to go, as the road is closed to traffic but open to the city's many outdoor enthusiasts.

Closed to bicycles but open to walkers and joggers is the Pista Cláudio Coutinho, between the mountains and the sea at Praia Vermelha in Urca. It's open from 7am until 6pm daily.

See p215 for bike-rental information.

HEALTH & FITNESS

DANCING

Given samba's resurgence throughout the city, it's not surprising there are a number of places where you can learn the moves. You can also find places to study *forró* (dance accompanied by the traditional, fast-paced music from the northeast), salsa and even the tango. A dance class is a good setting to meet other people while getting those two left feet to step in time.

CASA DE DANÇA CARLINHOS DE JESUS Map pp78–9

☎ 2541 6186; www.carlinhosdejesus.com.br in Portuguese; Rua Álvaro Ramos 11, Botafogo

At this respected dance academy in Botafogo, Carlinhos and his instructors offer evening classes in samba, *forró*, salsa and tango. On some Friday nights, open dance parties for students and guests are held. One of Botafogo's colorful bloco parties, Dois Pra Lá, Dois Pra Cá (p52) begins from here during Carnaval.

CENTRO CULTURAL CARIOCA Map pp90–1

☎ 2252 5751; www.centroculturalcarioca.com.br in Portuguese; Rua Sete de Setembro 237, Centro; 🕑 11am-8pm Mon-Fri

The cultural center offers one-hour classes in samba, ballroom dancing and the sensual lambada. Most classes meet twice a week and cost around R$65 for a month-long course. The large dance hall hosts parties on Friday at which samba bands perform.

FUNDIÇÃO PROGRESSO Map pp98–9

☎ 2220 5070; www.fundicao.org in Portuguese; Rua dos Arcos 24, Lapa

This cultural center offers a wide range of courses, including classes in dancing (African styles, as well as salsa, tango and samba). Those seeking something different can sign up for classes in percussion, acrobatics (run by the respected dance-theater-circus outfit Intrépida Trupe) or *capoeira* (Afro-Brazilian martial arts). Courses are typically around R$135 for the month.

NÚCLEO DE DANÇA RENATA PEÇANHA Map pp90–1

☎ 2221 1011; Rua da Carioca 14, Centro

A large upstairs spot on the edge of Lapa, this dance academy offers classes in *forró*, salsa, zouk (a slow and sensual dance derived from the lambada) and samba. Twice-weekly classes cost about R$65 per month.

DAY SPAS

Surprisingly for a city devoted to looking good, Rio doesn't have many spa options.

SPA MARIA BONITA Map p64

☎ 2513 4050; www.spamariabonita.com.br in Portuguese; Level P, Rua Prudente de Morais 729, Ipanema

Although better known for its largest spa in Friburgo, Maria Bonita does offer a full range of treatments for those who'd rather not trek out to the countryside. Options at the Ipanema branch include aromatherapy baths, deep tissue massage, shiatsu and acupuncture.

GYMS

Many hotels in Rio feature small workout centers with, perhaps, an adjoining sauna, but for those looking for a more intensive workout there are other options.

BODY TECH Map p66

☎ 2529 8898; Rua General Urquiza, Leblon; 🕑 6am-11pm Mon-Fri, 9am-9pm Sat, 9am-2pm Sun

Body Tech has gyms all over the Zona Sul, which offer a full range of services: swimming pool, free weights and cardio machines and classes such as dance, gymnastics and spinning. The best of the bunch is the three-story Leblon branch, but there are also a couple of Body Techs in Ipanema on Rua Barão de Torre 577 (Map p64) and on Rua Gomes Carneiro 90 (Map p64), and one in Copacabana (Map pp76–7) on Av NS de Copacabana 801.

CAPOEIRA

The only surviving martial art native to the new world, *capoeira* was invented by Afro-Brazilian slaves about 400 years ago. In its original form, the grappling martial art developed as a means of self-defense against the slave owners. Once the fighting art was discovered, it was quickly banned and *capoeira* went underground. The slaves, however, continued to hone their fighting skills; they merely did it out of sight, practicing secretly in the forest. Later the sport was disguised as a kind of dance, allowing them to practice in the open. This is the form that exists today.

Capoeira, which is referred to as a *jogo* (game), is accompanied by hand clapping and the plucking of the *berimbau* (a long, single-stringed instrument). Initially the music was used to warn fighters of the boss' approach; today it guides the rhythm of the game. Fast tempos dictate the players' exchange of fast, powerful kicks and blows, while slower tempos bring the pace down to a quasi dance. The *berimbau* is accompanied by the *atabaque* (floor drum) and a *pandeiro* (Brazilian tambourine).

The movements combine elements of fighting and dancing, and are executed (at least by the highly skilled) as fluid and circular, playful and respectful. *Capoeira's* popularity has spread far beyond Brazil's borders (there's even a *capoeira* club in Serbia). You can see musicians and spectators arranged in the *roda de capoeira* (*capoeira* circle) at the weekly Feira Nordestina (p103) in São Cristóvão.

Those interested in taking classes can try one of the following:

Associação Centro de Capoeira Angola (☎ 9954 3659, 2558 8015; www.ccarj.com; Rua do Catete 164, Catete; per class/month R$25/90) A new *capoeira* center in Catete.

Casa Rosa (☎ 8874 8804; www.casarosa.com.br; Rua Alice 550, Laranjeiras; classes R$30-100) The popular music space in Laranjeiras offers both weekly classes and private lessons.

Fundição Progresso (☎ 2220 5070; www.fundicao.org; Rua dos Arcos 24, Lapa) This major arts and music center offers classes in a wide range of fields, including *capoeira*.

YOGA

Yoga's popularity is on the rise in Rio, with a growing number of places where you can hone your sun salutations. Those around on Sunday can take a free class at 10am in Parque da Catacumba (Map pp70–1) in front of Lagoa Rodrigo de Freitas. At most places, your first class is free.

BLYSS YÔGA Map p64

☎ 2513 0005; www.blyss.com.br; ste 211, Rua Visconde de Pirajá 318, Ipanema

Near Praca Nossa Senhora da Paz, this peaceful center offers a full schedule of morning, afternoon and evening classes in Vinyasa and Hatha yoga.

SIVANANDA CENTER Map pp78–9

☎ 2266 4896; www.yogasivananda.com.br; Rua das Palmeiras 13, Botafogo

A branch of the respected international organization, this Sivananda Center has a good mix of beginner and advanced classes, as well as well as a free meditation class on Friday evening.

SLEEPING

top picks

- **Hotel Fasano** (p188)
- **Ipanema Plaza** (p189)
- **Ritz Plaza Hotel** (p190)
- **Porto Bay Rio Internacional** (p193)
- **Portinari Design Hotel** (p194)
- **Mama Ruisa** (p199)
- **Castelinho 38** (p199)
- **Cama e Café** (p200)
- **Maze Inn** (p198)
- **Rio Hostel** (p200)

SLEEPING

Rio has some excellent lodging options, including newly opened boutique hotels along the beach, trendy hostels and cozy B&Bs. The majority of hotel rooms are in high-rises in the Zona Sul (Copacabana has scores of options), though you'll also find elegant hotels, bohemian guesthouses and budget favorites in offbeat neighborhoods. Many guestrooms received a makeover for the 2007 Pan American Games, but Rio still has its share of sadly neglected spaces. It's wise to shop around.

For those unfamiliar with Rio, here's our two cents' worth on where to stay: if you want to be in the heart of the action and don't mind paying for it, stay in Ipanema or Leblon, with beautiful beaches, and excellent restaurants, shopping and nightlife. If you don't want to pay a premium for those neighborhoods, opt for busier Copacabana. Here you'll find more (including some less-expensive) lodging options, and you'll still be near the beach, and a short taxi ride or possibly a walk to Ipanema; you'll also have access to the metro, which is handy for zipping to other neighborhoods. If you're not in Rio for the beaches or simply want an alternative take on things, take a peak at Santa Teresa's colonial guesthouses. This historic hood has culture, some unique overnight options, and good restaurants and cafés. It's also close to the unrivaled music scene of Lapa. Neighborhoods along the metro line (Botafogo, Flamengo and Catete) generally have much cheaper options than the beachside southern neighborhoods; and for those who want the beach, and nothing but the beach, there's Barra, which is laid-back but far from the rest of Rio (meaning you'll need a car or boatloads of patience to endure those long bus or taxi rides).

Wherever you stay, try to reserve ahead. Hotel rates are about 30% higher during the summer months (December through February) and many places book up. Prices double or triple for New Year's Eve and Carnaval, and most places, including hostels, will only book in four-day blocks around these holidays.

Keep in mind that many hotels add a combined 15% service and tax charge. The cheaper places don't generally bother with this.

Places are listed in each neighborhood by price, from most- to least-expensive.

IPANEMA & LEBLON

These elegant neighborhoods have much allure: stay here and you'll be a short stroll from lovely beaches, top-notch restaurants and a vibrant nightlife scene. Although many more hotels litter the beaches of Leme and Copacabana, there are abundant lodging options here, including boutique hotels, serviced apartments, hostels and plenty of cookie-cutter high-rises as well. Prices here are generally much higher than elsewhere, though it's still possible to find affordable – if rather modest – lodging.

HOTEL FASANO Map p64 Hotel $$$

☎ 3202 4000; www.fasano.com.br; Av Vieira Souto 80, Ipanema; d/ste from R$1064/2211;

Rio's loveliest new hotel opened in 2007 to much fanfare with its brilliant rooms, decadent seafood restaurant and über-stylish bar. Designed by Philippe Starck, the Fasano has 91 rooms set with Egyptian cotton sheets, goose down pillows, plasma TV screens (with DVD players) and artful design touches. The best rooms have balconies overlooking the crashing waves of Ipanema beach, which lies just across the road from the hotel. Views from the rooftop pool are truly breathtaking – as are the room rates.

MARINA ALL SUITES

Map p66 Boutique Hotel $$$

☎ 2172 1001; www.marinaallsuites.com.br; Av Delfim Moreira 696, Leblon; ste R$730-1165;

Marina All Suites has beautifully decorated rooms, doting service and all the creature comforts you can imagine. As per the

BOOK ACCOMMODATION ONLINE

For more accommodation reviews and recommendations by Lonely Planet authors, check out www.lonelyplanet.com/hotels. You'll find the true, insider lowdown on the best places to stay. Reviews are thorough and independent. Best of all, you can book online.

name, it's all suites here, meaning you'll have between 420 and 800 sq ft between the comfy bedroom and living room in which to stretch out. The best rooms in the oceanfront hotel have splendid views of the shoreline, and other attractions are the trendy Bar D'Hotel (p152), the lovely top-floor pool and the onsite cinema that you can rent out.

CAESAR PARK Map p64 Hotel $$$

☎ 2525 2525; www.caesar-park.com; Av Vieira Souto 460, Ipanema; d from R$610;

The Caesar Park breathes opulence; it's apparent from the moment you catch sight of a classical pianist playing in the foyer. The rooms are sizable, with a warm, cozy feel and have artwork on the walls, flat-screen TVs and high-speed internet connections. The best rooms have enviable ocean views.

SOL IPANEMA Map p64 Hotel $$$

☎ 2525 2020; www.solipanema.com.br; Av Vieira Souto 320, Ipanema; d from R$505;

Occupying a prime plot of real estate facing Ipanema beach, the tall, slender Sol Ipanema features rooms decorated in warm hues, with dark wood furnishings and good lighting. Standard rooms are roughly the same size as the deluxe rooms, though the latter face the ocean, meaning you can hear the waves crashing on the shore as you drift off to sleep.

IPANEMA HOTEL RESIDÊNCIA

Map p64 Serviced Apartments $$$

☎ 3125 5000; www.ipanemahotel.com.br; Rua Barão da Torre 192, Ipanema; d from R$450;

Set on one of Ipanema's lovely tree-lined streets, this high-rise hotel has large apartments, with kitchen units, lounge areas and pleasantly furnished bedrooms. Each apartment is furnished differently, so try looking at a few before committing.

VISCONTI Map p64 Serviced Apartments $$$

☎ 2125 3540; www.promenade.com.br; Rua Prudente de Morais 1050, Ipanema; ste from R$440;

The Visconti has stylish modern suites (wood floors, stuffed leather furniture, modular lamps) with living-dining rooms, balconies and bedrooms. It's on a residential, tree-lined street a block from the beach.

PRICE GUIDE

Most prices are for double rooms, except for hostels with only dorm beds, in which case the price is for one person in a dorm bed.

$$$	over R$350
$$	R$150 to R$350
$	under R$150

MARINA PALACE

Map p66 Hotel $$$

☎ 2172 1001; www.hotelmarina.com.br; Av Delfim Moreira 696, Leblon; d standard/deluxe/ste from R$418/448/570;

Occupying a privileged position overlooking Praia do Leblon, the 26-story Marina Palace has a range of rooms, the best of which have a trim, contemporary look with artwork on the walls, sizable beds, flat-screen TVs, and DVD and CD players. At the bottom end of the scale you'll find similar features but darker carpeting (a tad worn) and poorer lighting. Deluxe rooms face the ocean and add more space to the equation. The Marina has top-notch service and a top-floor bar and restaurant with 360-degree views.

IPANEMA PLAZA Map p64 Hotel $$$

☎ 3687 2000; www.ipanemaplazahotel.com; Rua Farme de Amoedo 34, Ipanema; d from R$400;

A top choice in Ipanema, the 18-story Plaza features nicely decorated rooms with tile floors, a muted color scheme and sizable windows to let in the tropical rays. You'll also find broad, comfortable beds, spacious bathrooms (all with tubs) and a lovely rooftop pool. Some rooms overlook the ocean, while others face the outstretched arms of Cristo Redentor.

IPANEMA TOWER Map p64 Hotel $$$

☎ 2247 7033; www.ipanematower.com; Rua Prudente de Morais 1008, Ipanema; ste from R$400;

Along one of Ipanema's main thoroughfares, the all-suites Ipanema Tower has large, fully furnished apartments with pressed-wood floors, a balcony (some with ocean views), small kitchen, living room and bedroom. While the furnishings are far from opulent, they're cozy enough, with a decent kitchen table and a few pieces of modern artwork on the walls.

RITZ PLAZA HOTEL

Map p66 Serviced Apartments $$

☎ 2540 4940; www.ritzhotel.com.br; Av Ataúlfo de Paiva 1280, Leblon; d R$300-330, apt R$400;

The newly renovated Ritz Plaza is a stylish hotel in one of Rio's most desirable areas. Here you'll find top-notch service, handsome, spacious rooms and a relaxed atmosphere that gives the place a boutique feel. The one- or two- bedroom suites all have kitchen units, balconies – some with partial ocean views – art on the walls, good lighting and spotless bedrooms. It's good value considering the high quality of the rooms, the proximity of the beach (three blocks) and the draw of the neighborhood (the city's top restaurants pack the street behind the hotel).

MONSIEUR LE BLOND

Map p66 Serviced Apartments $$$

☎ 3722 5000; www.redeprotel.com.br in Portuguese; Av Bartolomeu Mitre 325, Leblon; ste from R$370;

A five-minute walk from Praia de Leblon, Monsieur Le Blond combines the service of a hotel with the convenience of an apartment. The colorful accommodations are all comfortably furnished with small kitchens, combined living-dining areas and balconies – some with fine views. The pool, which gets direct sunlight only part of the day, makes a fine place for sunbathing and mingling with the mostly Brazilian clients.

HOTEL PRAIA IPANEMA Map p64 Hotel $$$

☎ 2141 4949; www.praiaipanema.com; Av Vieira Souto 706, Ipanema; d from R$360;

With a view of Ipanema beach, this popular 16-story hotel offers trim, comfortable rooms, each with a balcony. The design is sleek and modern, with off-white tile floors, recessed lighting and artwork on the walls. Stretch out on the molded white lounge chairs next to the rooftop pool. The bar has a view, and there's a small fitness center.

SHERATON Map p66 Hotel $$

☎ 2274 1122; www.sheraton-rio.com; Av Niemeyer 121, Vidigal; d from R$350;

The Sheraton is a true resort hotel, with large, peaceful grounds. Every room has a balcony, facing either Leblon and Ipanema or verdant greenery. The rooms are nicely furnished in a cozy, contemporary style, and if you stay out here you'll enjoy a nearly private beach in front, tennis courts, swimming pools and a good health club. The main drawback is that it's a bit far from the action.

PARTHENON QUEEN ELIZABETH

Map p64 Hotel $$

☎ 3222 9100; www.accorhotels.com.br; Av Rainha Elizabeth 440, Ipanema; d from R$350;

This hotel offers trim and tidy suites, with pressed-wood floors, big windows and light, muted colors. Some rooms have balconies, and the upper two floors (eight and nine) have slightly better views (though you still won't see the ocean). There's also a pool, which is unfortunately surrounded by tall buildings.

EVEREST RIO Map p64 Hotel $$

☎ 2525 2200; www.everest.com.br; Rua Prudente de Morais 1117, Ipanema; d from R$320;

Another of Ipanema's elegant high-rise hotels, the Everest Rio features nicely decorated rooms (ranging from small to spacious), professional service and an enviable location. All the rooms have carpeting, large windows that let in plenty of light and modernized bathrooms with bathtubs. Deluxe here means more space (the view is the same) and a queen-size bed.

MAR IPANEMA Map p64 Hotel $$

☎ 3875 9190; www.maripanema.com.br; Rua Visconde de Pirajá 539, Ipanema; d from R$315;

This is a decent midrange option in Ipanema. The rooms feature a trim, modern design with decent beds, good lighting, tidy wooden floors and an inviting color scheme. The downside is the lack of a view, which is hardly relevant if you plan to spend your day out enjoying the city.

LEBLON OCEAN HOTEL RESIDÊNCIA

Map p66 Serviced Apartments $$

☎ 2158 8282; Rua Rainha Guilhermina 117, Leblon; apt from R$250;

This all-suites hotel has a range of spacious, simply furnished suites, all with kitchen units and small balconies. There's also a small indoor pool and sauna, and Rio's best restaurants (and a handful of bars) are just outside the door. The only catch is that you have to book a minimum of five days.

ARPOADOR INN Map p64 Hotel $$

☎ 2523 0060; www.arpoadorinn.com.br; Rua Francisco Otaviano 177, Ipanema; d R$228-468;

LONG-TERM RENTALS

If you're planning to stay in Rio for longer than a few nights, you might consider renting an apartment. There are a number of agencies dedicated to tracking down short-term hires for foreigners, and it's a fairly straightforward affair booking one. As is the case for hotels, prices rise during Carnaval and New Year's, with places booking up far in advance. Nightly rates range from R$100 to R$500 and up.

Aurélio Rio Guide (Map p64; ☎ 9223 9945; www.aurelioriog uide.com; Suite 1912, Rua Visconde de Pirajá 550, Ipanema) Aurélio rents Ipanema and Copacabana apartments, as well as a gorgeous house in Búzios.

Blame it on Rio 4 Travel (Map pp76–7; ☎ 3813 5510; www.blameitonrio4travel.com; Rua Xavier da Silveira 15B, Copacabana) This popular agency rents many types of apartments; it also rents cell phones and provides many other services.

Candida Botafogo (☎ 2247 7079; candidabotafogo@hotmail.com) Candida rents several lovely apartments located in a villa in Ipanema.

Copacabana Holiday (Map pp76–7; ☎ 2542 1525; www.copacabanaholiday.com.br; Rua Barata Ribeiro 90A, Copacabana) Specializing in Copacabana, this agency rents apartments for a minimum of three days.

Fantastic Rio (Map pp76–7; ☎ 2543 2667; www.fantasticrio.hpg.ig.com.br; Apt 501, Av Atlântica 974, Leme) Multilingual Peter Corr of Fantastic Rio rents a range of apartments from modest one-bedrooms to spacious four-bedrooms with beach views.

Rio Apartments (Map p64; ☎ 2247 6221; www.rioapartments.com; Suite 301, Rua Farme de Amoedo 76, Ipanema) Offers a wide selection of apartments in the Zona Sul, and offers a range of services.

Overlooking Praia do Arpoador (Arpoador beach), this six-story hotel is the only one in Ipanema or Copacabana that doesn't have a busy street between it and the beach. The rooms are small and basic, but the 'deluxe' rooms have glorious ocean views.

IPANEMA SWEET

Map p64 Serviced Apartments $$

☎ 8277 4815; soniacordeiro@globo.com; Rua Visconde de Pirajá 161, Ipanema; apt from R$220;

Modern, furnished apartments with kitchen, lounge and balcony (no view) are good value here. All rooms are different, but the best have cozy touches like an Oriental carpet, artwork or stylish furniture. Guests also have access to two outdoor pools, a sauna and a laundry. The mix of Brazilians and international visitors who stay here consistently rate the place highly.

IPANEMA FLAT HOTEL RESIDÊNCIA

Map p64 Serviced Apartments $$

☎ 2523 1292; fax 2287 9844; Rua Gomes Carneiro 137, Ipanema; d from R$200;

This place is suffering from a bad case of style envy: cheaply furnished rooms are seriously short on style and just aching to get some. Still, the simple apartments have kitchens, balconies (no view) and bland but clean bedrooms at reasonable prices for the area.

HOTEL VERMONT Map p64 Hotel $$

☎ 3202 5500; hoteisvermont@uol.com.br; Rua Visconde de Pirajá 254, Ipanema; d from R$190;

One of the few second-rate hotels in Ipanema, the Hotel Vermont offers guests no-frills accommodations. Although the place received a slight makeover in recent years, the rooms are nothing fancy – clean but not spotless, with tile floors and elderly bathrooms.

IPANEMA INN Map p64 Hotel $$

☎ 2523 6092; www.ipanemainn.com.br; Rua Maria Quitéria 27, Ipanema; d R$180-270;

Ipanema Inn is a simple hotel with nice touches. The pleasant rooms have wood-block prints on the walls, off-white tile floors and modern bathrooms with big tubs. *Superiores* (front-facing rooms) don't have ocean views, but if you lean far enough out the window, you get a glimpse of the glistening sea. Ipanema Inn has friendly, multilingual staff.

YAYA HOTEL Map p64 Hotel $$

☎ 3813 3912; www.yayario.com; Rua Farme de Amoedo 135, Ipanema; s/d/tr R$143/208/242;

For an alternative to high-rise hotels, Yaya (opened in 2007) is an excellent option. The eight private rooms are handsomely decorated with pressed-wood floors, artwork on the walls and a trim, fresh appearance. The

AIRPORT ACCOMMODATIONS

There are two hotels at the international airport. The better of the two is the Rio Luxor Aeroporto (☎ 2468 8998; www.luxor-hotels.com.br; s/d R$323/360). Situated on the 3rd floor of the airport, the 64 rooms here are comfortably furnished, with cable TV, modern bathrooms and 24-hour room service. There's also a bar in the hotel. The Hotel Pousada Galeão (☎/fax 3398 3848; d from R$185) is on the 1st floor of international arrivals. Rooms are small but comfortably furnished – lots of dark wood in the interior.

downside: rooms share four bathrooms. There's a small lounge for relaxing, and the location is superb.

HOTEL SAN MARCO Map p64 Hotel $

☎ 2540 5032; www.sanmarcohotel.net; Rua Visconde de Pirajá 524, Ipanema; s/d from R$140/155;

Like the Vermont up the road, it's all about location if you stay at the San Marco. A coffin-sized elevator carries you up to the rooms, which are small, dark and cramped, with faded green duvets and tile floors. The beach, however, is just two blocks away.

MARGARIDA'S POUSADA Map p64 Hotel $

☎ 2239 1840; margaridacarneiro@hotmail.com; Rua Barão da Torre 600, Ipanema; s/d/apt from R$80/120/250;

For those seeking a smaller, cozier atmosphere than the high-rise hotels can provide, this excellently located Ipanema guesthouse is a good option. You'll find a dozen pleasant, simply furnished rooms scattered about the low-rise building, with a bigger private apartment available for rent in a building nearby.

HOSTEL HARMONIA Map p64 Hostel $

☎ 2523 4905; www.hostelharmonia.com; Casa 18, Rua Barão da Torre 175, Ipanema; dm R$45;

Run by three Swedes, Hostel Harmonia is one of the best choices on Ipanema's hostel row, with a good traveler vibe to the place. The lounge and private rooms have attractive two-toned wood floors, and quarters are clean and nicely maintained with six beds in each room.

MANGO TREE Map p64 Hostel $

☎ 2287 9255; www.mangotreehostel.com; Rua Prudente de Morais 594, Ipanema; dm/d R$45/140;

In a handsome villa in Ipanema, this popular hostel opened in 2007, offering spruce little rooms with two-toned wood floors and a good traveler vibe. The front porch provides open-air space for unwinding, and there's also a lounge/TV room and a small backyard.

IPANEMA BEACH HOUSE Map p64 Hostel $

☎ 3202 2693; www.ipanemahouse.com; Rua Barão da Torre 485, Ipanema; dm/d R$45/140;

The Ipanema Beach House is one of Rio's best-looking hostels. It's set in a converted two-story house with six- and nine-bed dorms (in the form of three-tiered bunk beds). There are private rooms, indoor and outdoor lounge spaces, a small bar and a beautiful pool.

LIGHTHOUSE HOSTEL Map p64 Hostel $

☎ 2522 1353; www.thelighthouse.com.br; No 20, Rua Barão da Torre 175, Ipanema; dm/d R$45/120;

Along with a handful of other budget spots on this quiet lane, the Lighthouse has an easy-going vibe and clean, simple rooms that attract a good mix of backpackers. Accommodations consist of eight-bed dorm rooms and one private double (with a fold-out sofa to sleep three).

WAVE HOSTEL Map p64 Hostel $

☎ 2227 6458; wavehostel@yahoo.com.br; No 5, Rua Barão da Torre 175, Ipanema; dm R$45;

Popular with surfers and a youthful, laid-back crowd, the intimate Wave Hostel has wood floors and well-maintained common areas. Because of its size, if you want to snag a bed in one of the four-bed dorms, book early.

LEMON SPIRIT HOSTEL Map p66 Hostel $

☎ 2294 1853; www.lemonspirit.com; Rua Cupertino Durão 56, Leblon; dm/d/tr R$40/140/160;

Leblon's first hostel, Lemon Spirit boasts an excellent location one block from the beach. The dorm rooms are clean and simple with not much decor. There's also a tiny courtyard in front, and the attractive bar in the lobby is a good spot for meeting other travelers over caipirinhas (cane-liquor cocktails).

TERRASSE HOSTEL Map p64 Hostel $

☎ 2247 6130; www.terrassehostel.com; Rua Farme de Amoedo 35, Ipanema; dm/s/tw/d R$40/60/100/130;

New in 2007, Terrasse Hostel is a small, narrow hostel with basic rooms and not much in the way of atmosphere. It is, however, brilliantly located on one of Ipanema's best streets, with good cafés, bars and of course the beach just steps from the door.

CHE LAGARTO IPANEMA Map p64 Hostel $

☎ 2512 8076; www.chelagarto.com; Rua Paul Redfern 48, Ipanema; dm R$37-45, d R$120-130;

Part of a small empire of hostels in the Zona Sul, Che Lagarto's Ipanema branch is a popular budget spot for those young travelers who want to be close to the beach. It's a five-story hostel, with basic rooms and not much common space – aside from the pricey bar on the 1st floor.

RIO HOSTEL – IPANEMA Map p64 Hostel $

☎ 2287 2928; www.riohostelipanema.com; Casa 1, Rua Canning 18, Copacabana; dm/d R$37/130;

An excellent edition to the backpacker scene, the friendly Rio Hostel is set in a small villa on a peaceful stretch of Ipanema. A good mix of travelers stay here, enjoying the clean rooms, the airy top-floor deck with hammocks and the small front veranda. The same owners operate the respected Santa Teresa hostel (p200) of the same name.

COPACABANA & LEME

Rio's tourist district has more hotels than any other neighborhood in town. Av Atlântica is lined with high-rise lodging, while backstreets offer similar options at slightly lower prices. Copacabana caters to all styles and budgets: backpackers, business travelers, families and horny teenagers all find their way here.

COPACABANA PALACE Map pp76–7 Hotel $$$

☎ 2548 7070; www.copacabanapalace.com.br; Av Atlântica 1702, Copacabana; d from R$665;

Rio's most famous hotel, the Palace has hosted heads of state, rock stars and other prominent personalities (Queen Elizabeth once stayed here, as did the Rolling Stones). The dazzling white facade dates from the 1920s, when it became a symbol of the city. Today it hosts a range of rooms, from deluxe rooms to spacious suites with balconies. Despite the price tag, some rooms could use some upkeep. There's a lovely pool, excellent restaurants and fine service.

SOFITEL RIO DE JANEIRO

Map pp76–7 Hotel $$$

☎ 2525 1232; www.sofitel.com; Av Atlântica 4240, Copacabana; d from R$520;

One of Rio's most expensive hotels, the French-owned Sofitel does its best to dazzle visitors. The excellent service, comfortable rooms, two lovely pools and beachfront location have earned many fans. All of the rooms have balconies and are tastefully furnished. Deluxe rooms and suites have ocean views.

PESTANA RIO ATLÂNTICA

Map pp76–7 Hotel $$$

☎ 2548 6332; www.pestana.com; Av Atlântica 2230, Copacabana; d from R$410;

Beautifully located along Copacabana beach, the Pestana has excellent amenities, decent service and a wide range of rooms. The best have wood floors, balconies and a bright, modern design scheme. Rooms at the lower end are carpeted, rather bland and too small to recommend.

PORTO BAY RIO INTERNACIONAL

Map pp76–7 Hotel $$$

☎ 2546 8000; www.riointernacional.com.br; Av Atlântica 1500, Copacabana; d/ste from R$390/790;

The Rio Internacional had a total overhaul in 2004, which transformed it into one of Copacabana's top beachfront hotels. The rooms have a light and airy feel, and are painted in cool, elegant tones (mint is a favorite). Large white duvets, light hardwoods, stylish furnishings and simple artwork all complement each other nicely. Big windows let in lots of natural light, and most rooms have balconies.

RIO GUESTHOUSE Map pp76–7 Hotel $$

☎ 2521 8568; www.rioguesthouse.com; Rua Francisco Sá 5, Copacabana; d R$330-462;

On the top floors of a high-rise overlooking Copacabana beach, this small guesthouse offers excellent rooms in a cozy setting, topped only by the warm welcome you'll receive throughout your stay. Inside this split-level penthouse you'll find antique furnishings, colorful artwork and an outdoor patio with gorgeous views over Copacabana.

OLINDA OTHON CLASSIC

Map pp76–7 Hotel $$

☎ 2159 9000; www.othon.com.br; Av Atlântica 2230, Copacabana; d standard/deluxe/ste R$330/455/530;

Set in a handsome, white building overlooking Copacabana beach, the Olinda Othon is indeed a classic. Its marble lobby, complete with chandeliers, Oriental carpets and grand piano, has an old-world charm, although its rooms are modern. The best of the bunch face the ocean and are worth the extra *reais*.

DESIGN HOTEL PORTINARI

Map pp76–7 Hotel $$

☎ 3222 8800; www.hotelportinari.com.br; Rua Francisco Sá 17, Copacabana; d from R$310;

This stylish 13-story hotel demonstrates real design smarts. The rooms have tile floors, artful lighting and big windows, and each floor is decorated in a different style. The top-floor restaurant is set with tropical plants and boasts fine views through the floor-to-ceiling windows.

MERCURE ARPOADOR Map pp76–7 Hotel $$

☎ 2113 8600; www.accorhotels.com.br; Rua Francisco Otaviano 61, Copacabana; s/d from R$300/350;

top picks

HOTEL BARS

- **Londra** (Hotel Fasano; p154) Attracts a pure A-list crowd, mingling over cocktails in the lovely Philippe Starck-designed lounge.
- **Poolside Bar** (Copacabana Palace; p155) The elegant, old-world setting at the bar is among the best features of this grand dame.
- **Azul Marinho** (Arpoador Inn; p131) Boasting unobstructed views of Ipanema beach, this restaurant-café is a fine spot for a sundowner.
- **Bar D'Hotel** (Marina All Suites; p152) A trendy Zona Sul crowd gathers over cocktails to the backdrop of waves crashing on Ipanema beach.
- **Horse's Neck** (Sofitel; p156) Grab a *cerveja* (beer) inside the wildly decorated bar or step onto the terrace for splendid views of Copacabana beach.

This dapper all-suites hotel is nicely located in Arpoador, giving easy access to both Ipanema and Copacabana. Suites have sleek white leather sofas that open into beds, modern kitchenettes, TVs with a stereo and a DVD player, ambient lighting and comfortable bedrooms. All rooms have balconies, although there's no view. Rates are lower on weekends.

OURO VERDE HOTEL Map pp76–7 Hotel $$

☎ 2543 4123; www.dayrell.com.br; Av Atlântica 1456, Copacabana; d from R$270;

Ouro Verde is set in an attractive 1950s building overlooking Copacabana beach. Unlike the majority of hotels along this strip, the Ouro Verde aims for an old-world aesthetic, with spacious, classically appointed rooms and common areas. Superior rooms have balconies (overlooking either the beach or Corcovado); on the downside, the carpets are a little worn, and the whole place could use an update.

COPACABANA HOTEL RESIDÊNCIA

Map pp76–7 Serviced Apartments $$

☎ 2548 7212; www.copahotelresid.com.br; Rua Barata Ribeiro 222, Copacabana; d from R$250;

The Copacabana Hotel Residência is a fine choice for those seeking a bit more space. The clean, well-maintained suites all have small kitchen units and lounge rooms with good natural lighting. Keep in mind that busy Barata Ribeiro is awfully noisy; try to snag a top-floor apartment.

MARTINIQUE COPA HOTEL

Map pp76–7 Hotel $$

☎ 2195 5200; www.windsorhoteis.com.br; Rua Sá Ferreira 30, Copacabana; d from R$240;

Near the Ipanema end of Copacabana, the Martinique Copa is an all-glass high-rise with clean, comfortable, somewhat small rooms with good beds that are a fair value for the neighborhood. It's just 30m to the beach, and the hotel spreads a fine breakfast buffet.

HOTEL DEBRET Map pp76–7 Hotel $$

☎ 2522 0132; www.debret.com; Av Atlântica 3564, Copacabana; d R$222-263;

Boasting fine views of Copacabana beach, the Debret has a range of rooms that vary in quality from fair to fairly cramped. It has a cozy lobby and simply furnished rooms with pressed-wood floors. The corner rooms are the best, with plenty of light, twin armchairs and a tiny desk. By all means pay extra for rooms with the ocean view; they're among the best you'll find at this price.

ROYAL RIO PALACE Map pp76–7 Hotel $$

☎ 2122 9292; www.royalrio.com; Rua Duvivier 82, Copacabana; s/d R$220/273;

Not far from the beach, this shiny glass-and-steel high-rise (opened in 2004) offers comfortable, modern lodging and decent amenities. The rooms are very well maintained, and boast wood floors, a nice design aesthetic and sizable windows. Upper category rooms have saunas (quite unusual for Rio), and there's a pleasant top-floor pool.

SOUTH AMERICAN COPACABANA HOTEL Map pp76–7 Hotel $$

☎ 2227 9161; www.southamericanhotel.com.br; Rua Francisco Sá 90, Copacabana; d from R$215;

Solid value for its trim, modern rooms, this 13-story hotel is nicely located within a short stroll to both Copacabana and Ipanema beaches. Rooms are set with pressed-wood floors, colorful bedspreads and a touch of artwork on the walls.

MAR PALACE Map pp76–7 Hotel $$

☎ 2132 1500; www.hotelmarpalace.com.br; Av NS de Copacabana 552, Copacabana; d R$210;

On Copacabana's busiest road, this sleek glass-and-steel high-rise building hides trim, modest-sized rooms with faux-wood floors and large windows overlooking the street. There's a tiny pool and a sauna on the top floor, as well as a workout room with views of Cristo Redentor.

HOTEL ASTORIA COPACABANA Map pp76–7 Hotel $$

☎ 2545 9090; www.astoria.com.br; Rua República do Peru 345, Copacabana; d from R$210;

Yet another of Copacabana's glass-and-steel high-rises, this 11-story hotel has small, clean rooms with tile floors and east-facing windows that let in a decent amount of sunlight. Cheery duvets add some color to the otherwise cookie-cutter design. The pool is small but fine enough for a refreshing dip during the day.

RIO ROISS HOTEL Map pp76–7 Hotel $$

☎ 3222 9950; rioroiss.com.br; Rua Aires Saldanha 48, Copacabana; s/d from R$207/288;

This friendly low-key place received a recent makeover giving new carpets and flat-screen TVs to its pleasant rooms. For added space and bigger windows, opt for a corner room (any room ending in 2).

COPACABANA PRAIA HOTEL Map pp76–7 Hotel $$

☎ 2522 5646; www.copacabanapraiahotel.com.br; Rua Francisco Otaviano 30, Copacabana; s/d R$200/220;

The 11-story Copacabana Praia is set in Arpoador, within walking distance of both Ipanema and Copacabana beaches. Rooms are a mixed bag, and the best are spacious with faux-wood floors, solid furnishings and partial beach views. The simplest rooms are small with carpeting.

REAL PALACE HOTEL Map pp76–7 Hotel $$

☎ 2101 9292; www.realpalacehotelrj.com.br; Rua Duvivier 70, Copacabana; s/d R$194/230;

Set on a quiet street a few blocks from Copacabana's famous beach, this simple 13-story hotel has small, sparsely furnished rooms. Tiles (of the faux-wood variety) cover the clean-swept floors, and the rooms all get decent light. There's a small rooftop pool, though it lies in shadows for most of the day.

AUGUSTO'S COPACABANA Map pp76–7 Hotel $$

☎ 2547 1800; www.augustoshotel.com.br; Rua Bolívar 119, Copacabana; s/d/tr R$189/210/262;

Augusto's is a straightforward hotel with fair prices. The rooms have a light and airy feel, and the bathrooms are modern. Some rooms have balconies, although the only way you'll see the ocean is to step onto them and look to the right. The biggest rooms end in 1 or 8.

ACAPULCO Map pp76–7 Hotel $$

☎ 3077 2000; www.acapulcohotel.com.br; Rua Gustavo Sampaio 854, Leme; s/d from R$185/205;

The Acapulco hotel lies just a short stroll (one block) from the immortalized Copacabana beach, and its recent renovations have made it an attractive and fairly priced option. Most rooms have a neat look about them with pressed-wood floors and colorful duvets and curtains.

APA HOTEL Map pp76–7 Hotel $$

☎ 2548 8112; www.apahotel.com.br; Rua República do Peru 305, Copacabana; s/d R$165/178;

The Apa would be one of Copacabana's most stylish hotels were the year 1973. Unfortunately, times have changed, but the anointed style of Apa's 52 rooms lives on. Here you'll find tile floors, balconies (in most rooms), decent lighting and reasonable prices.

ATLANTIS COPACABANA HOTEL

Map pp76–7 Hotel $$

☎ 2521 1142; www.atlantishotel.com.br in Portuguese; Rua Bulhões de Carvalho 61, Copacabana; s/d from R$160/180;

On the border between Copacabana and Ipanema, Atlantis's rooms are short on style and cheaply furnished, though ongoing renovations may improve things. Rooms above the 9th floor generally have fine views, and there's a modest pool and sauna on the roof.

HOTEL VILAMAR

Map pp76–7 Hotel $$

☎ 3461 5601; www.hotelvilamarcopacabana.com.br; Rua Bolívar 75, Copacabana; s/d from R$160/180;

The 15-story Hotel Vilamar is set on a quiet street in Copacabana. Inside this fair-priced place, you'll find inviting rooms with pressed-wood floors, cheery duvets and big windows affording decent natural light.

HOTEL SANTA CLARA Map pp76–7 Hotel $

☎ 2256 2650; www.hotelsantaclara.com.br; Rua Décio Vilares 316, Copacabana; d front/back R$150/140

Along one of Copacabana's most peaceful streets, this simple three-story hotel has some charming, old-fashioned features, and it's a nice alternative to the high-rises found elsewhere in the neighborhood. The upstairs rooms are best, with wood floors, antique bed frames, a writing desk and a balcony.

ORLA COPACABANA

Map pp76–7 Boutique Hotel $

☎ 2525 2425; www.orlahotel.com.br; Av Atlântica 4122, Copacabana; d R$140-304;

The Spanish-owned Orla Copacabana has attractive, understated rooms, but the beach-facing location is the real draw. The standards are too dark and cramped to recommend, so it's not worth staying here unless you book one of the chic deluxe rooms with that desirable ocean view.

RESIDENCIAL APARTT

Map pp76–7 Serviced Apartments $

☎ 2522 1722; www.apartt.com.br; Rua Francisco Otaviano 42, Copacabana; s/d R$121/198;

This old-fashioned all-suites hotel doesn't have much charm about it, but the price and location are excellent. Basic one-bedroom suites have small kitchen units, a gloomy lounge room (with cable TV) and a bedroom with adequate natural lighting. Breakfast is included in the price (served until 1pm).

HOTEL TOLEDO Map pp76–7 Hotel $

☎ 2257 1990; www.hoteltoledo.com.br; Rua Domingos Ferreira 71, Copacabana; s/d R$120/140

A block from the beach, the Toledo offers low prices for those who don't need many creature comforts. The rooms have either tile floors or worn green carpeting, and range from small to large (the best are spacious with tall ceilings). The overall look is dated, but it's a fair value.

RIO ROCKERS Map pp76–7 Hostel $

☎ 3511 2221; www.riorockers.com.br; Rua Tonelero 376, Copacabana; dm/d from R$38/100;

Rio Rockers is an HI hostel set in a small, converted house on a busy road and offers simple dorm rooms (with six or eight beds) and one private double. It's a popular place, but there isn't much common space apart from the café/breakfast area on the first floor.

CHE LAGARTO Map pp76–7 Hostel $

☎ 2256 2776; www.chelagarto.com; Rua Anita Garibaldi 87, Copacabana; dm R$36-40, d R$110-130;

A current favorite among young backpackers, Argentine-owned Che Lagarto attracts a festive crowd that gathers over the pool table or at the patio bar for beer and caipirinhas most nights. It's a good place for meeting fellow partiers.

RIO BACKPACKERS Map pp76–7 Hostel $

☎ 2236 3803; www.riobackpackers.com.br; Travessa Santa Leocádia 38, Copacabana; dm/d R$35/100;

Young backpackers flock to this popular, three-story hostel in Copacabana. Although the rooms are a bit small, the house has plenty of choice spots in which to relax and meet other travelers.

EDIFICIO JUCATI

Map pp76–7 Hostel & Serviced Apartments $

☎ 2547 5422; www.edificiojucati.com.br; Rua Tenente Marones de Gusmão 85, Copacabana; dm/s/d/tr R$30/100/120/140

A few steps away from a small park, on a tranquil street, this unsigned hostel gathers its share of budget travelers with some of the cheapest beds in Copacabana. You'll also find large, simply furnished apartments with kitchen units at excellent prices.

MELLOW YELLOW Map pp76–7 Hostel $

☎ 2547 1993; www.mellowyellow.com.br; Rua General Barbosa Lima 51, Copacabana; dm R$30-45, d R$100-110

Copacabana's biggest hostel, Mellow Yellow attracts young travelers willing to endure basic accommodations in exchange for a party atmosphere. There's a bar, many lounge areas and a patio with spa. The hostel also hosts barbecue nights regularly. Dorm rooms have anywhere from four to 24 beds; the cheapest lack air-conditioning.

BAMBOO RIO Map pp76–7 Hostel $

☎ 2236 1117; www.bamboorio.com; Rua Lacerda Coutinho 45, Copacabana; dm R$30-39, d R$110-120;

Yet another hostel set in a former villa, Bamboo Rio is a friendly, comfortable hostel with tidy dorm rooms (sleeping from five to 12), ample lounge space, a tiny pool and an inviting bar area. Overall, it's a nice choice for Copacabana, with a good traveler vibe.

WALK ON THE BEACH HOSTEL

Map pp76–7 Hostel $

☎ 2545 7500; www.walk-on-the-beach.com; Rua Dias da Rocha 85, Copacabana; dm R$27-37;

Set in an unsigned two-story villa on one of Copacabana's rare quiet streets, this friendly hostel offers good-value dorm rooms (each with six to 12 beds). It's a friendly place with a lounge room and a small bar, but not much ambience; they could use some new mattresses.

BOTAFOGO & URCA

Botafogo and Urca are among the least-explored neighborhoods by foreign visitors. There aren't many accommodations in the area, but there are abundant opportunities to experience authentic Rio – its tree-lined streets, old-school *botecos* (neighborhood bars) and hidden restaurants – if you do stay here.

EL MISTI Map pp78–9 Hostel $

☎ 2226 0991; www.elmistihostel.com; Praia do Botafogo 462, Casa 9, Botafogo; dm/s/d from R$29/80/100;

Located along Botafogo's hostel row, El Misti is a popular budget spot among Brazilian and foreign travelers for its cheap dorm rooms (with triple bunk beds) and lively atmosphere. It's a short walk to the Botafogo metro station.

FLAMENGO

One of Rio's oldest neighborhoods, Flamengo attracts visitors who are seeking a more authentically Carioca (resident of Rio) experience – its neighborhood feel, traditional bars and youthful inhabitants add to the charm. Prices here are lower than in Copacabana or Ipanema. Keep in mind that although Flamengo is now the waterfront, the bay is too polluted for swimming. Although there aren't many options in Flamengo proper, nearby Catete (below) offers decent accommodation giving speedy access to the neighborhood.

HOTEL PAYSANDU Map p84 Hotel $

☎ 2558 7270; www.paysanduhotel.com.br; Rua Paissandu 23, Flamengo; s/d R$109/121;

Set on a quiet street lined with imperial palm trees, the Paysandu is an affordable although still-decent option in Flamengo. The hotel's best rooms feature high ceilings, good natural light and space to stretch out.

CATETE & GLÓRIA

Aside from the historic Glória hotel, this area is largely a budget destination, with battered guesthouses within a short walk of the Catete metro station. If you don't mind roughing it, you'll be able to take advantage of the city's cheapest accommodations, but don't expect much in the way of ambience.

GLÓRIA Map p87 Hotel $$$

☎ **2555 7373; www.hotelgloriario.com.br; Rua do Russel 632, Glória; d from $350;**

A grand 1920s hotel, Glória still retains the aura of its past. There are red-carpet hallways, old paintings, antique fixtures and a liberal use of brass throughout the palatial hotel. Note that the hotel has two distinct wings: the old one with aging but atmospheric rooms (some in a sorry state), and the new wing with trim, modern, fairly bland rooms. At the very top end, you'll find antique-filled rooms with wood floors, marble bathrooms and glorious views of the bay.

FLAMENGO PALACE Map p87 Hotel $$

☎ **2557 7552; hotelflamengopalace.com.br; Praia do Flamengo 6, Flamengo; s/d R$154/176;**

Trapped in the '70s, the Flamengo Palace has bare rooms with simple furnishings and an odd touch here and there – like wooden-framed oval mirrors and wild curtain patterns. *Luxo* rooms have excellent views of the bay but are noisier.

IMPERIAL HOTEL Map p87 Hotel $

☎ **2556 5212; www.imperialhotel.com.br; Rua do Catete 186, Catete; d R$135-150;**

The Imperial Hotel wins the award for longest hallway. The attractive white building has only three stories but goes back endlessly to reveal a crop of recently renovated rooms and suites. Some rooms are too dark for our taste, while others have better natural lighting and that all-important Jacuzzi tub.

HOTEL INGLÊS Map p87 Hotel $

☎ **2558 3052; www.hotelingles.com.br; Rua Silveira Martins 20, Flamengo; d R$125-155;**

Boasting a colonial facade, Hotel Inglês has a range of simple rooms, the best with high ceilings and windows overlooking the leafy Parque do Catete. Rooms in back are too cramped to recommend.

BEIJA FLOR HOTEL Map p87 Hotel $

☎ **2285 2492; Rua Ferreira Viana 20, Flamengo; s/d R$100/110;**

This recently remodeled hotel has clean rooms with tile floors and modern bathrooms. On the downside, some rooms lack decent ventilation (opening onto an air shaft). It's on a quiet street within walking distance of the metro.

MAZE INN Map p87 Hotel $

☎ **2558 5547; www.jazzrio.info; Casa 66, Rua Tavares Bastos 414, favela Tavares Bastos; s/d from R$80/100**

Set in favela Tavares Bastos, one of Rio's safest favelas (shanty towns), the Maze Inn is a fantastic place to overnight – for those looking for an alternative view of Rio. The eight double rooms are uniquely decorated with original artworks (for sale) by English owner Bob Nadkarni, while the veranda offers stunning views of the bay and Pão de Açúcar.

HOTEL FERREIRA VIANA Map p87 Hotel $

☎ **2205 7396; Rua Ferreira Viana 58, Flamengo; s/d R$55/75;**

Not the nicest place in the area but this place is at least cheap. Your *reais* will buy you a small, dark room with tile floors and thin mattresses. Some rooms are better than others so take a peek before committing.

HOTEL RIAZOR Map p87 Hotel $

☎ **2225 0121; hotelriazor1@hotmail.com; Rua do Catete 160, Catete; s/d R$55/70;**

The lovely colonial facade of the Riazor hides battered quarters short on style. The equation is very simple here: bed, bathroom, TV, air-conditioning, and a door by which to exit the room and explore the city. You'll find a mix of travelers and lost souls at Hotel Riazor.

CATETE HOSTEL Map p87 Hostel $

☎ **3826 0522; www.catetehostel.com.br; Casa 1, Rua do Catete 92, Catete; dm/d from R$28/80**

On a quiet lane off busy Rua do Catete, this large hostel offers pleasant, simple dorm rooms with tile floors (nine beds in each) as well as private rooms, some with verandas. There's a large lounge area, a kitchen and all the other backpacker essentials.

SANTA TERESA & LAPA

In the last few years, Santa Teresa has enjoyed something of a renaissance, with a growing number of galleries, restaurants and handsome new guesthouses opening their doors. Travelers who stay here will be far from the beaches, but the trade-off is that you're in the heart of Rio's Montmartre. More than a few travelers who've passed through here have fallen for the atmospheric hood and ended up staying far longer than they originally intended.

LOVE AMONG THE CARIOCAS

Living in such a crowded city, Cariocas (residents of Rio) sometimes have a terrible time snatching a few moments of privacy. For those living with their parents or sharing a tiny apartment with roommates, an empty stretch of beach, a park bench or a seat in the back of a café are all fine spots to steal a few kisses, but for more…progressive action, Cariocas take things elsewhere – to the motel, aka the *love* motel.

Love motels aren't so much a Carioca oddity as they are a Brazilian institution. They are found in every part of the country, usually sprouting along the outskirts of cities and towns. Some are designed with lavish facades – decked out to resemble medieval castles, Roman temples or ancient pyramids – while others blend more discreetly into the surrounding landscape. Regardless of the exteriors, the interiors are far removed from the 'less is more' design philosophy. Mirrors cover the ceiling while heart-shaped, vibrating beds stretch beneath them. Rose-tinted mood lights, Jacuzzis, televisions loaded with porn channels, dual-headed showers and a menu on the bedside table featuring sex toys that guests can order to the room – all these come standard in most love motels. Such places scream seediness in the West. In Brazil, however, they're not viewed as anything out of the ordinary. People need a place for their liaisons – they might as well have a laugh and a bit of fun while they're at it. The motels are used by young lovers who want to get away from their parents, parents who want to get away from their kids and couples who want to get away from their spouses. They are an integral part of the nation's social fabric, and it's not uncommon for Cariocas to host parties in them.

Most motels rent rooms by the hour, though some give discounted prices for four-hour blocks or offer lunchtime specials. In Rio many of them are out on the roads that lead to the city, such as Av Brasil in the Zona Norte and Av Niemeyer between Leblon and São Conrado. There are a few, however, scattered about Centro, Flamengo and Botafogo.

The quality of the motels varies, reflecting their popularity across social classes. The most lavish are three-story suites with a hot tub beneath a skylight on the top floor, a sauna and bathroom on the 2nd floor, and the garage underneath (allowing anonymity). They come standard with all the other mood-enhancement features mentioned earlier. For the best suites, expect to pay upwards of R$400 for eight hours and more on weekends. Standard rooms cost quite a bit less, and Cariocas claim that an equally fine time can be had there.

For those interested in checking out this cultural institution, there are a number of motels in the Zona Sul, particularly along Av Niemeyer just west of Leblon, including:

Shalimar (☎ 3322 3392; www.hotelshalimar.com.br; Av Niemeyer 218, Vidigal; r for 6 hr from R$42)

Sinless (☎ 2512 9913; www.sinless.com.br; Av Niemeyer 214, Vidigal; r for 6 hr from R$42)

Vips (☎ 2507 2037; www.vipsmotel.com.br; Av Niemeyer 418, Vidigal; ste for 8 hr from R$90).

SOLAR DE SANTA Map pp98–9 Hotel $$$

☎ 2221 2117; www.solardesanta.com; Ladeira do Meireles 32, Santa Teresa; house per night R$2000;

This marvelous colonial mansion has beautifully designed rooms with wood floors and colorful details. Rooms open onto a veranda with splendid views through the lush foliage out front to the downtown. The whole place (four rooms and one bungalow) plus staff is available for rent, and can accommodate up to 13 guests.

MAMA RUISA Map pp98–9 Hotel $$$

☎ 2242 1281; www.mamaruisa.com; Rua Santa Cristina 132, Santa Teresa; d from €230 (R$630);

Santa Teresa's loveliest new boutique hotel, Mama Ruisa aims for bohemian chic in its seven spacious, uniquely designed guestrooms. Every whim is catered for in this inspiring converted colonial mansion, and guests can opt for massages, private tours or just enjoy the spectacular view over the bay from the swimming pool.

CASTELINHO 38 Map pp98–9 Hotel $

☎ 2252 2549; www.castelinho38.com; Rua Triunfo 38, Santa Teresa; s/d from R$120/150

Opened as a guesthouse in 2006, Castelinho offers a range of spacious rooms with high ceilings, wood floors and a light, airy design. It's set in a mid-19th century mansion and has an outdoor terrace with a garden and lounge space.

CASA ÁUREA Map pp98–9 B&B $

☎ 2242 5830; www.casaaurea.com.br; Rua Áurea 80, Santa Teresa; s/d from R$110/140

Set on a quiet street, this handsome two-story house has been converted into a simple guesthouse with cozy rooms. It's within a short walking distance of the *bonde* (tram) as well as the neighborhood's best restaurants and bars. Casa Áurea's best feature is the large, private garden beside the house.

CAMA E CAFÉ Map pp98–9 B&B $

☎ 2221 7635; www.camaecafe.com in Portuguese; Rua Progresso 67, Santa Teresa; d R$95-190;

Run by three young local entrepreneurs dedicated to rejuvenating the area, Cama e Café is a bed-and-breakfast network that links travelers with local residents. There are several dozen colonial houses to choose from, with accommodations ranging from modest to lavish – indeed the best rooms are antique-filled suites set inside castle-like mansions with verandas and lush gardens.

HOTEL MARAJÓ Map pp98–9 Hotel $

☎ 2224 4134; Rua Joaquim Silva 99, Lapa; s/d from R$45/55

Near all the nightlife action of Lapa, this basic hotel rents simple, no-nonsense rooms to travelers on a budget. While Marajó isn't winning any design awards, the functional, inexpensive digs make it a find.

RIO HOSTEL Map pp98–9 Hostel $

☎ 3852 0827; www.riohostel.com; Rua Joaquim Murtinho 361, Santa Teresa; dm R$37, d R$100-120;

The Rio Hostel provides travelers with a home away from home. The spacious lounge, backyard patio with pool, Ping-Pong room and kitchen for guests all add to the charm of this Santa favorite. The rooms are clean, and there are attractive private double rooms, including a small chalet behind the pool. The hostel overlooks downtown Rio and lies along the *bonde* line. It can be a bit tricky to find – if you reach Curvelo Sq (the first major *bonde* stop), you've gone too far. Disembark and walk 200m back down the hill.

CASA MANGO MANGO Map pp98–9 Hotel $

☎ 2508 6440; www.casamangomango.com; Rua Joaquim Murtinho 587, Santa Teresa; dm R$35, d without/with bathroom R$120/168

In an atmospheric Victorian mansion, this friendly guesthouse has comfortable, spacious rooms, and a lush garden and patio. Excellent breakfasts are served.

POUSADA FAVELINHA Map pp98–9 Hostel $

www.favelinha.com; Rua Antonio Joaquim 13, Morro do Pereirão da Silva; dm/d R$35/75

Located in the Favela Pereirão da Silva, Pousada Favelinha has four double rooms and a five-bed dorm room, all with balconies that have stunning views over the city to Pão de Açúcar. There's also a terrace, a lounge and lots of insider info from the welcoming Brazilian-German owners. While the Pereirão da Silva is one of Rio's more peaceful favelas, this place isn't for everyone – some love it, some don't. To get there, take the *bonde* to Colegio Asunção (Rua Almirante Alexandrino 2024) and enter the favela through the school grounds.

SAMBA VILLA HOSTEL Map pp98–9 Hostel $

☎ 2232 4607; www.sambavilla.com.br; Rua Evaristo da Veiga 147, Lapa; dm R$19;

Probably the cheapest place to stay in Rio, Samba Villa has clean, basic dormitories above a popular bar operated by the same owners. There's free internet, lots of helpful tips on making the most of your stay, and some of Rio's best bars are just a short stroll from the hostel.

BARRA DA TIJUCA & WEST OF RIO

Very few foreign travelers stay in the neighborhoods west of Leblon, as it's a real hassle getting around unless you have a car. The advantages however, are being close to some of Rio's best beaches – which get wilder the further west you go.

CASA DEL MAR Map p108 Hotel $$

☎ 2158 6999; www.promenade.com.br; Av Sernambetiba 5740, Barra da Tijuca; ste from R$250;

This lovely all-suites hotel features stylish, modern furnishings spread between the living-dining area and the bedroom. The location is excellent and the pool enticing.

PRAIA LINDA Map p108 Hotel $$

☎ 2494 2186; www.hotelpraialinda.com.br; Av Pepê, Barra da Tijuca; d from R$230;

Facing the Praia do Pepê, if you're staying in Barra this is a decent value, with clean and comfortable rooms, and excellent beach and ocean views.

EXCURSIONS

EXCURSIONS

Although most travelers have a hard time tearing themselves away from Rio, fabulous beaches, mountain getaways and rain-forest-covered islands are just a short drive from town. Whether you seek adventure or an idyllic retreat, you'll find countless options in the relatively small state of Rio de Janeiro.

On sunny weekends, Cariocas (residents of Rio) craving a relaxing beach holiday head east to Búzios (p209). Once a remote fishing village, the town lies on a peninsula with pretty beaches and scores of elegant *pousadas* (guesthouses), top-notch restaurants and a lively bar scene. Surfers and those wanting a more sedate experience might detour to Saquarema or the sleepy beach town of Arraial do Cabo.

West of Rio lies the beautiful coastline of the Costa Verde (Green Coast), where lush mountains meet the sea, with hundreds of islands and beaches in the area. The star attraction here is peaceful Paraty (p204), an old gold-mining town with handsomely preserved cobblestone streets and jewel-box churches. Antique-filled *pousadas* now occupy some of the colonial buildings, with an assortment of spots for fine dining. It's particularly popular with couples seeking a romantic getaway.

This coastline is also home to Ilha Grande (p207), a hilly car-free island, with dozens of beaches and more than 100km of hiking trails amid Mata Atlântica (Atlantic rain forest). The seaside town of Vila do Abraão, with its mellow vibe, is an excellent intro to island life.

Cariocas with a yearning for the mountains have a few options. Just north of Rio stands the imperial city of Petrópolis (p211). Its palaces, cathedral, and European-style gardens and boulevards lie beneath the jagged mountains of Serra dos Órgãos, one of the great climbing meccas of Rio. In addition to rock climbing, visitors can raft in mountain streams and hike through the nearby national park.

Further out, in the northwest corner of the state is Brazil's oldest national park, the Parque Nacional de Itatiaia, where stark high-country plateaus and rocky spires intermingle with lush, low-country jungle. Bordering the park, the towns of Visconde de Mauá (p213) welcome visitors with rustic cabins, rushing streams and fresh-grilled trout.

BEACHES & ISLANDS

Though no longer the 'undiscovered' paradise that it was in the 1960s, Búzios (p209) still has gorgeous beaches. Some are easy to reach, while others require a hike. By night, the bayside promenade offers plenty of nightlife diversions with its outdoor restaurants and bars. Scenic beaches also lie near Paraty (p204), while Arraial do Cabo (p210) and surfer-favorite Saquarema (p210) draw their share of visitors. Ilha Grande (p207) also has striking beaches, several of which rank among Brazil's prettiest.

NATIONAL PARKS

Breathe in the fresh mountain air and hike the trails of Rio state's untamed national parks. North of Rio, the peaks of the Parque Nacional da Serra dos Órgãos (p213) make an impressive backdrop to treks in the area. Four hours northwest of Rio, the Parque Nacional de Itatiaia (p214) is packed with waterfalls, clear blue lakes and dramatic peaks.

TOWNS

In a cool mountain climate, Petrópolis (p211), with its canals, landscaped parks and city squares, has a European air. Its palaces and museums are good places to discover Brazil's imperial epoch. For a window into Brazil's early settlement days, strike out for Paraty (p204), a perfectly preserved colonial town, with much history hidden inside its churches and 18th-century townhouses. Northwest of Rio, the villages of Visconde de Mauá (p213) and its surroundings are set in a lush alpine area, with idyllic streams, waterfalls, and cozy chalets scattered along country lanes.

DRIVES

The Costa Verde (accessible via BR 101 west) provides the setting for one of the country's most spectacular drives. The panoramic road hugs the coast's edge as it winds its way past lush peaks, beaches and colonial settlements. The prettiest stretches run some 150km from Mangaratiba (111km west of Rio) to Paraty.

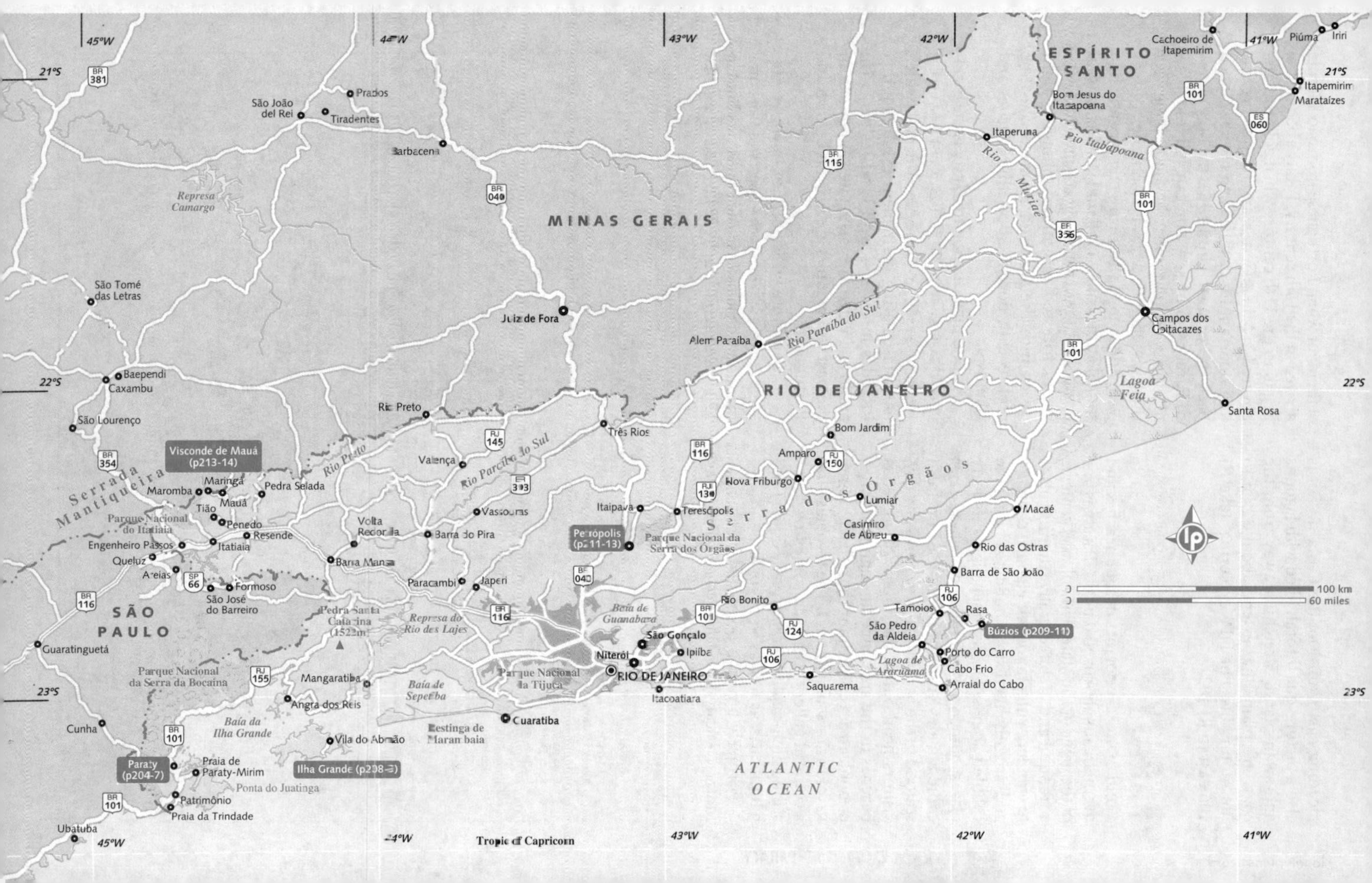

MINAS GERAIS
RIO DE JANEIRO
ESPÍRITO SANTO
SÃO PAULO
ATLANTIC OCEAN
Juiz de Fora
Barbacena
São João del Rei
Tiradentes
Prados
São Tomé das Letras
Baependi
Caxambu
São Lourenço
Visconde de Mauá (p213-14)
Maringá
Maromba
Mauá
Tião
Penedo
Pedra Selada
Resende
Itatiaia
Parque Nacional do Itatiaia
Engenheiro Passos
Queluz
Formoso
São José do Barreiro
Guaratinguetá
Cunha
Paraty (p204-7)
Praia de Paraty-Mirim
Ponta do Juatinga
Patrimônio
Praia da Trindade
Ubatuba
Parque Nacional da Serra da Bocaina
Baía da Ilha Grande
Angra dos Reis
Mangaratiba
Vila do Abraão
Baía de Sepetiba
Cuaratiba
Barra Mansa
Volta Redonda
Barra do Pira
Vassouras
Valença
Rio Preto
Três Rios
Paracambi
Japeri
Represa do Rio des Lajes
Petrópolis (p211-13)
Itaipava
Teresópolis
Parque Nacional da Serra dos Órgãos
Serra dos Órgãos
Nova Friburgo
Amparo
Bom Jardim
Lumiar
Casimiro de Abreu
Baía de Guanabara
São Gonçalo
Niterói
RIO DE JANEIRO
Ipiíba
Itacoatiara
Parque Nacional da Tijuca
Rio Bonito
Saquarema
Lagoa de Araruama
São Pedro da Aldeia
Tamoios
Rasa
Búzios (p209-11)
Porto do Carro
Cabo Frio
Arraial do Cabo
Barra de São João
Rio das Ostras
Macaé
Santa Rosa
Lagoa Feia
Campos dos Goitacazes
Além Paraíba
Rio Paraíba do Sul
Rio Muriaé
Rio Itabapoana
Itaperuna
Bom Jesus do Itabapoana
Cachoeiro de Itapemirim
Piúma
Iriri
Itapemirim
Marataízes
Represa Camargo
Serra da Mantiqueira
Tropic of Capricorn
100 km
60 miles

Heading east from Rio, the Costa do Sol is also a picturesque littoral, filled with lagoons and swampland. Stretching away from the coast are plains that extend about 30km to the mountains. For DIY exploring, take RJ 106 east to RJ 102.

PARATY

Amid a landscape of picturesque beaches and dramatic jungle-covered peaks, Paraty is one of the gems of Rio state. The colonial center is a tranquil and architecturally stunning place to wander, with photogenic colonial churches and brightly hued stone buildings lining the cobbled streets. On summer nights its leafy plazas, outdoor restaurants and open-air cafés come alive as visiting crowds feast on fresh seafood to the backdrop of live music. By day, visitors head out to the dozens of gorgeous beaches in the area, hike through rain forest or book an adventure tour (horseback riding, kayaking or scuba diving). The town also has a colorful gallery scene and some fine shops selling high-quality *cachaça* (cane liquor) and handicrafts, as well as works of art.

Formerly a region populated by Guianás Indians, Paraty first emerged as a European settlement when Portuguese from São Vicente arrived in the 16th century. Paraty's boom time began in the 17th century when gold was discovered in Minas Gerais, and the port became an important link as the riches were shipped back to Portugal. Until 1954, the only access to Paraty was by sea. You can still find a few old-timers around town who fondly remember the days when Paraty was so remote.

In addition to the town's culinary and historical attractions, you'll find striking natural beauty in the surrounding countryside, with steep, forested mountains plunging right down into the sea, and a varied coastline replete with dozens of pristine beaches and islands.

A good introduction to Paraty is the excellent Casa da Cultura (☎ 3371 2325; Rua Dona Geralda 177; admission R$5; 🕒 10am-6.30pm Wed-Mon), which has a fascinating permanent exhibition that includes interviews with local residents (in audio and video format), as well as relics from the past. All exhibits are in both English and Portuguese.

A 20-minute walk north of town, Forte Defensor Perpétuo (🕒 9am-noon & 2-5pm Wed-Sun) commands a fine view over the bay. It was built in 1703 (and rebuilt in 1822) to defend against

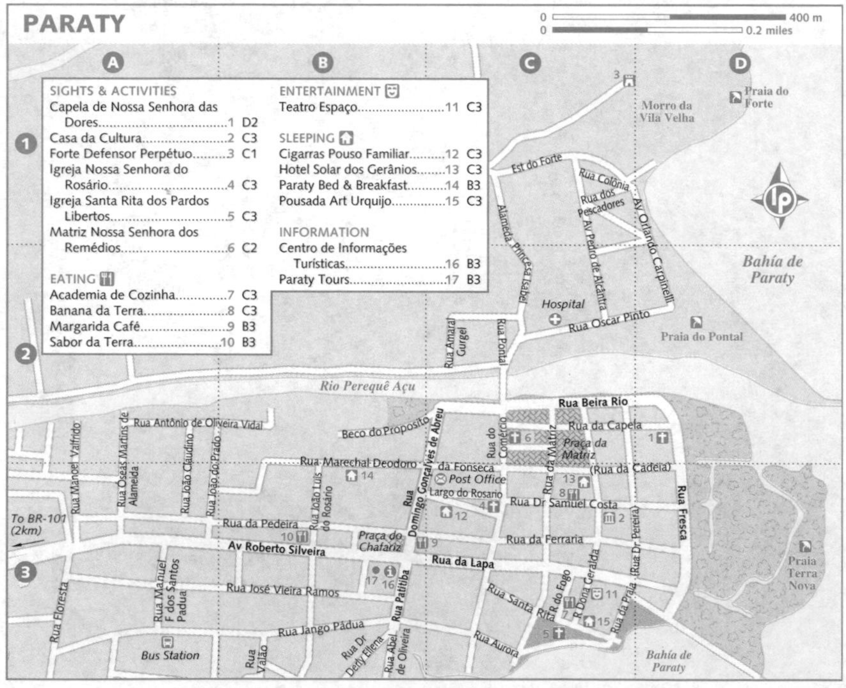

PARTYING IN PARATY

The city by the sea has a calendar packed full with colorful festivals. Among the biggest events is Paraty's Festa do Divino Espírito Santo, which features all sorts of merrymaking that revolves around the *fólios* (musical groups that go door to door, singing and joking). The vibrant festival begins nine days before Pentecostal Sunday (the seventh Sunday after Easter).

Festas Juninas are held throughout June, when the town becomes the stage for music, street parties and folk dancing such as the *xiba* (a circle clog dance) and the *ciranda* (a *xiba* with guitar accompaniment). The final festival is on June 29 with a maritime procession to Ilha do Araújo, one of the islands near Paraty. From Friday to Sunday on the third weekend in August, Paraty hosts its popular Festa da Pinga (*pinga* is a more polite term for *cachaça,* the fiery sugarcane spirit). Local distilleries are on hand to dazzle (or at least intoxicate) festival goers with their rare spirits.

The Festival Literária Internacional de Parati (www.flip.org.br), launched in 2003, brings authors from around the world to Paraty for five days each July. The opening concert features big names in Brazilian music.

The Festa de Nossa Senhora (NS) dos Remédios takes place on September 8, with street processions and religious celebrations.

The city also attracts a crowd to its Carnaval, when revelers cover themselves in mud and dance wildly through the streets.

New festivals keep springing up each year, including festivals of photography and video art, gastronomy and seafood. See www.paraty.com.br/eventos.asp (in Portuguese) for a full list.

pirate raids on the gold pipeline that ran to Minas Gerais. The fort, located on the Morro da Vila Velha (the hill past Praia do Pontal) also houses an arts center.

A visit to the town's old churches provides a glimpse of the complexities of 18th-century life: two were built for whites, one for blacks and a fourth for freed mulattos (persons of mixed black and white ancestry).

Built by slaves in 1725, the Igreja Nossa Senhora do Rosário (cnr Rua Samuel Costa & Rua do Comércio; admission R$2; 9am-noon & 2-5pm Tue-Sat, 9am-3pm Sun) served as the city's black parish. Its two wooden, gilt-trimmed side altars showcase the talents of early 19th-century wood-carvers. Note also the black St Benedict holding the Christ child to the left of the altar, the stone pulpit carved into the wall, and the pineapple-like chandelier base in the roof – a symbol of prosperity. An old burial ground lies beneath the church floorboards.

Overlooking the lush Praça da Matriz, the Matriz Nossa Senhora dos Remédios (cnr Rua da Matriz & Rua da Capela; admission R$2; 9am-noon & 1.30-5pm Wed-Sat, 9am-3pm Sun) is a fine stone church with handsome tiled floors, wedding cake-style alcoves and a row of glass-encased saint figures peering down at would-be worshippers. Paraty's settlement began around the time builders first erected the church. In 1646, the benefactor Maria Jácome de Melo donated the land between the rivers on two conditions: that a chapel dedicated to Our Lady be built and that no harm come to the Indians residing there. Sadly, the second demand was ignored.

Freed mulattos worshipped in the Igreja Santa Rita dos Pardos Libertos (Rua Santa Rita; admission R$2; 9am-noon & 1.30-3pm Wed-Sun). It houses a tiny museum of sacred art and some fine woodwork on the doorways and altars.

Facing the sea, the small, white Capela de Nossa Senhora das Dores (Rua Dr Pereira) gathered the colonial white elite. Dating from 1800 but renovated in 1901, the church hides a fascinating cemetery in the inner courtyard. It opens only sporadically.

Paraty has 65 islands and 300 beaches in its vicinity. The first beach you'll reach walking north of town (just across the canal) is Praia do Pontal, which can get a little murky at times. A handful of open-air restaurants line its shore. The cleaner and relatively secluded Praia do Forte lies a quick walk north from there. Another 2km further north is Praia

TRANSPORTATION: PARATY

Distance from Rio 261km

Direction West

Travel Time Four hours

Car From the Zona Sul, head north on Av D Infante Henrique, which follows the curve of the bay as it eventually links up with Av Presidente Kubitschek. Look for signs to merge onto Av Brasil; this turns into BR 101, which leads all the way out to Paraty.

Bus Costa Verde buses (R$40) depart eight times daily between 6am and 9pm from Novo Rio bus station in Rio.

DETOUR: A QUICK DIP

Paraty's resplendent natural setting makes for some fine exploring. Gorgeous beaches lie within a 30-minute drive and a one-hour boat ride, and most are surrounded by green mountains with deep blue seas lapping at the shore. Two of the best beaches are Praia de Paraty-Mirim, 27km east of Paraty, where there are a few *barracas* (food stalls) on the beach, and Praia da Trindade, with calm seas that reflect the lush vegetation surrounding it. If you'd prefer to hike into the forest, visit a waterfall and take a dip in a natural swimming hole, there's the nearby Parque Nacional da Serra da Bocaina. This national park has rich plant and animal life, but with the park's limited infrastructure it's hard to see much of this. For a short visit, head west out of Paraty about 15km along the Paraty–Cunha road (Estrada Paraty Cunha), which winds its way uphill. Stop at the Cachoeira do Tobogã (look for signs: it's a brief hike off the Paraty–Cunha road) where you can go for a swim.

On your way back to Paraty, at the 7km marker on the road, stop at the lovely Vila Verde (☎ 3371 7808; Paraty-Cunha road; mains R$18-32; 11am-6pm Tue-Sun low season, 11am until last customer daily high season), which serves homemade pastas, risottos and smoked salmon as well as good desserts and coffee. The restaurant is beautifully landscaped – a small brook trickles through the property, surrounded by lots of greenery.

do Jabaquara, a spacious beach with great views, shallow waters and a small restaurant overlooking the sand.

For visits to the less accessible sands, schooner tours depart daily, making stops at several beaches; book through Paraty Tours (below). An alternative is to hire one of the small motorboats at the port. Local boatmen know some great spots in the region and will happily take you for the right price (plan on R$40 per hour).

INFORMATION

Centro de Informações Turísticas (☎ 3371 1222; www.paraty.com.br; Av Roberto Silveira; 9am-9pm) Distributes good maps of the area (as does Paraty Tours, next door) and maintains updated information on hotels and restaurants in the area.

Paraty Tours (☎ 3371 1327; www.paratytours.com.br; Av Roberto Silveira 11; 9am-8pm) One of several tour companies in town, Paraty Tours is a good source of information and offers a range of tours (including schooner tours), and kayaking, biking, horse riding and diving trips. It's at the colonial end of town. It also rents bikes.

EATING

Academia de Cozinha (☎ 3371 6468; Rua Dona Geralda 288; dinner R$170) Mixing theater and haute cuisine, the Academia de Cozinha stages cooking shows in Portuguese and English. Guests learn about the regional cuisines, watch chef Yara Castro Roberts in action, then enjoy the fruits of her labor. The price of dinner includes cocktails, wine, desserts and a wide variety of other fare.

Banana da Terra (☎ 3371 1725; Rua Dr Samuel Costa 198; mains R$40-52) One of Paraty's most elegant options, Banana da Terra serves delectable oven-baked fish dishes. Try the seafood, vegetables and saffron rice served in banana leaves, and follow it with banana pastry with ginger ice cream.

Margarida Café (☎ 3371 2441; Praça do Chafariz; mains R$16-30; noon-midnight) This charming restaurant serves tasty seafood dishes and wood-fired pizzas, which you can enjoy in the spacious lounge area or inner courtyard. Live music most nights.

Sabor da Terra (☎ 3371 2384; Av Roberto Silveira 180; per kg R$20; 11am-10pm) Paraty's best per-kilo is just outside the historic center and spreads a buffet table of salads, grilled meats, seafood dishes, pastas, risottos and regional fare.

SLEEPING

Pousada Arte Urquijo (☎ 3371 1362; www.urquijo.com.br; Rua Dona Geralda 79; d from R$340;) Artist-owner Luz Urquijo rents out six beautiful, uniquely designed guest rooms in this boutique guesthouse. All rooms are set in a handsomely restored 18th-century mansion, and some of the rooms have balconies and sea views. There is also a stylish bar and a swimming pool.

Cigarras Pouso Familiar (☎ 3371 1497; www.paraty.com.br/cigarras; Largo do Rosario 7; d from R$150) Decorated with colorful lamps and run by a retired professor, this elegant colonial building retains the feel of a family home. Some rooms have kitchenettes, and there's a veranda with views of the facing square.

Hotel Solar dos Gerânios (☎ 3371 1550; www.paraty.com.br/geranio in Portuguese; Praça da Matriz 2; s/d from R$60/80) This colonial hotel overlooking the Praça da Matriz features wood and ceramic sculptures, heavy rustic furniture and *azulejos* (Portuguese tiles). Some rooms have balconies, so check a few before committing.

Paraty Bed & Breakfast (☎ 3371 7041; paratybedbreakfast@hotmail.com; Rua Marechal Deodoro 519; s/d from R$40/60) A short walk from the historic district, Paraty Bed & Breakfast is excellent value for its clean rooms with tile floors and trim wood furnishings. It's owned by a British expat.

ENTERTAINMENT

Teatro Espaço (☎ 3371 1575; Rua Dona Geralda 327; puppet-show admission R$50; 9pm Wed & Sat) For years the Teatro Espaço has been garnering praise for its famous puppet theater. The performances are staged by the Grupo Contadores de Estórias, who present powerful, wordless theater (with musical accompaniment) with their lifelike puppets.

ILHA GRANDE

The fabulous Ilha Grande is a pristine island of tropical scenery and gorgeous beaches among sheltered bays, brooks and waterfalls. Virgin Atlantic rain forest still blankets the hillsides and the guttural cry of howler monkeys can be heard on parts of the island.

Ilha Grande owes its pristine condition to its unusual history. Before the Portuguese arrival, the island was home to the Tupinambá Indians whose trails around the island are still in use. Once Europeans reached Brazil, Ilha Grande became a shelter for pirates and smugglers from the 16th to the 18th centuries. The island was also the site of a prison (Lazareto), first built at Abraão Bay and later moved to Dois Rios, a tiny settlement on the south side. The latter was demolished in 1994 (you can still see the ruins), and since then tourism has fast become the island's chief source of income.

Vila do Abraão is the principal village, and the starting point for many adventures. From here, you can take schooner tours to gorgeous beaches such as Praia Lopes Mendes (which often tops charts listing the world's most beautiful beaches), Saco do Céu, Lagoa Azul and Lagoa Verde. Schooner companies organize regular trips to points around the island, with daily departures to Lopes Mendes. You can also reach the beach via a forest trail by heading east of Vila do Abraão.

There are numerous hikes you can do from Vila do Abraão. One excellent day hike

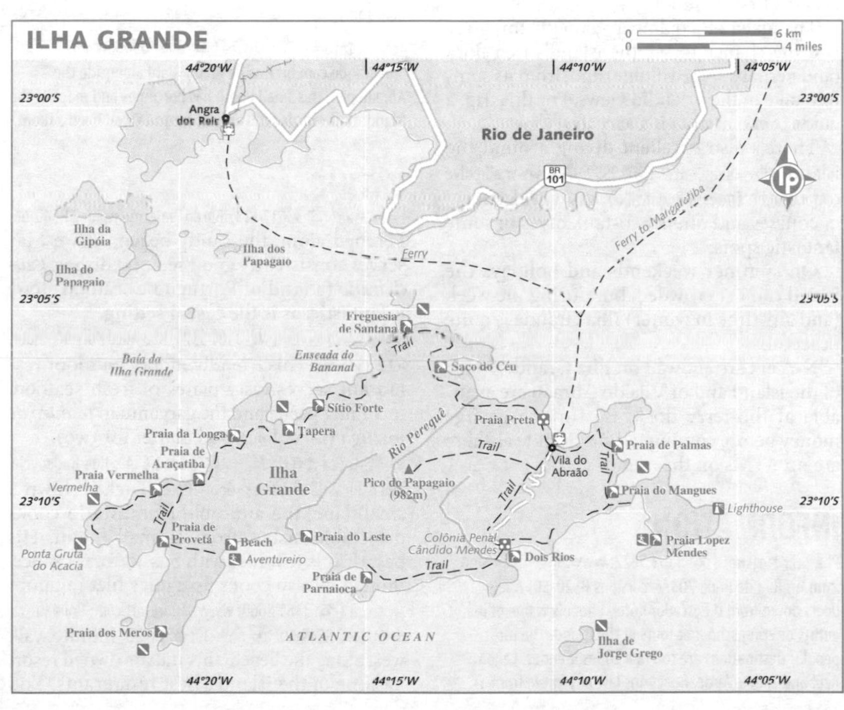

TRANSPORTATION: ILHA GRANDE

Distance from Rio 150km

Direction West

Travel Time Two hours to Mangaratiba or 2½ hours to Angra dos Reis, and then a 90-minute ferry ride.

Car From the Zona Sul, head north on Av D Infante Henrique, which follows the curve of the bay as it goes north to Centro and eventually links up with Av Presidente Kubitschek. Look for signs to merge onto Av Brasil. This turns into BR 101, which leads all the way out to Mangaratiba or Angra. Both places offer long-term parking near the dock for around R$15 per day.

Ferry Once you reach either Mangaratiba or Angra, catch the ferry to Vila do Abraão. Boats from Mangaratiba depart at 8am and return at 5.30pm daily. From Angra, boats depart at 3.30pm Monday to Friday and 1.30pm Saturday, Sunday and bank holidays; they return to Angra at 10am daily. A one-way ferry ride costs R$6 Monday to Friday and R$15 Saturday and Sunday. Ferry schedules fluctuate, so it's wise to confirm the times when making a reservation at your hotel.

Bus Costa Verde buses depart every 45 minutes between 5am and 9pm from the main Novo Rio bus station to either Mangaratiba (R$17) or Angra (R$32). Make sure you verify ferry connections to avoid getting stuck overnight in Angra or Mangaratiba.

(13km, or about six hours return trip) takes you over the top of the island to a gorgeous beach framed by two rivers (Dois Rios). This is also the site of the prison ruins and a ghost-like town. You'll find several simple eateries here that serve inexpensive lunches. A shorter walk north from Abraão leads to Praia Preta, where you can see the ruins of Lazareto, the island's first prison.

The hike to Pico do Papagaio (982m) gives you the chance to see the island's rich flora (and perhaps some wildlife) and, from its summit, take in the splendid views. For this trip, a guide is essential as it's easy to get lost.

There's also excellent diving around the island. Elite Dive Center (☎ 9999 9789; www.elitedivecenter.com.br; Travessa Buganville) has a wide range of courses and offers two-tank dives in some fantastic spots.

On summer weekends and holidays the island can get crowded, but during the week (and any time in winter) Ilha Grande is quite peaceful.

No cars are allowed on Ilha Grande. Maps of the island and of Vila do Abraão are available at the ferry dock. Be sure to change money before coming to Ilha Grande as there are no ATMs on the island.

INFORMATION

Phoenix Turismo (☎ 3361 5822; www.phoenixturismo.com.br; Rua da Praia 703; excursions R$20-50) A few doors down from O Pescador hotel, Phoenix is one of many outfits offering schooner tours of the island. The most popular destinations are to Praia Lopes Mendes, Lagoa Azul and Lagoa Verde. Boat trips last anywhere from a half- to a full day; you can order lunch on the boat and rent snorkeling gear.

Sudoeste SW Turismo (☎ 3361 5516; www.sudoestesw.com.br; Rua da Praia 647) Next door to O Pescador hotel, Sudoeste has excellent Portuguese/English-speaking guides available for hikes around the island – from day climbs up Pico do Papagaio to five-day camping treks around the island. You can also rent kayaks or book private boat tours.

Tourist Information Office (☎ 3361 5508; www.ilhagrande.com.br; Rua da Praia) Right alongside the Abraão pier, this small booth has brochures and maps of the island; staff can also call around for you if you need a room.

EATING

Lua e Mar (☎ 3361 5113; Rua da Praia; mains for 2 R$40-66) Perched along the sandy beach, Lua e Mar serves consistently good seafood dishes. *Caldeirado* (a kind of Portuguese seafood stew) is fantastic, as is the casual setting.

Corsário Negro (☎ 3361 5321; Rua Alice Kury 90; mains for 2 R$45-60) This friendly indoor-outdoor restaurant serves tasty plates of fresh seafood, including paella and the gargantuan *tesouro de tortuga* (mixed seafood platter for two).

Restaurant Dom Mario (☎ 3361 5349; Rua Buganville; mains for 2 R$45-60; 6pm-10pm) Tucked down a small lane, the amicable Dom Mario cooks delectable dishes from a small menu. His best dish is fish filet with passion-fruit sauce, though he also cooks up a juicy filet mignon.

Sagu (☎ 3361 5660; www.saguresort.com; Praia Brava; mains for 2 R$45-60; 6pm-10pm) A 20-minute walk west along the beach, this Italian-owned resort has one of the island's best restaurants. You can enjoy traditional old-world fare and fresh seafood while dining on a deck overlooking the sea.

SLEEPING

Asalem (☎ 3361 5602; www.asalem.com.br; s/d R$235/280) A 25-minute walk east of Abraão, this idyllic *pousada* is surrounded by lush scenery. All of the rooms have terraces overlooking the sea, with a sleeping loft upstairs and a lounge with hammock on the first level.

Naturalia (☎ 3361 9583; www.pousadanaturalia.net; Praia do Abraão 149; s/d from R$100/140) A 10-minute walk east of the dock, this pleasant *pousada* has handsome rooms, each with wood floors, lovely sea views and a hammock in which to while away the afternoon.

Pousada Manaca (☎ 3361 5404; www.manaca.ilhagrande.org; Praia do Abraão; d from R$150) Nicely located facing the beach, this cozy guesthouse has just seven rooms (three with beach views and balconies). Rooms are small but nicely designed. Like Naturalia, Manaca uses solar energy panels.

O Pescador (☎ 9943 5226; www.opescadordailha.com.br; Rua da Praia; d R$160-190) Cozily furnished rooms and an excellent restaurant make a great combination at this charming spot overlooking the beach.

BÚZIOS

Búzios is a lovely beach resort on a jutting peninsula scalloped by 17 beaches. It was a simple fishing village until the early 1960s, when it was 'discovered' by Brigitte Bardot and her Brazilian boyfriend. Today, Búzios has much more to offer than just its spectacular natural setting. The village has boutiques, elegant restaurants, open-air bars and lavishly decorated B&Bs. Many foreign-owned (especially Argentinean) *pousadas* and restaurants have sprouted along the peninsula's shores, and a mix of international travelers adds to the jumble of languages you'll hear on the streets.

Búzios is not a single town but rather three settlements on the peninsula: Ossos, Manguinhos and Armação de Búzios.

The main village of Armação de Búzios has two main streets running through it. The posh Rua das Pedras hugs the shoreline, with waterfront *pousadas*, bars and restaurants lining the stone-paved street. Rua das Pedras turns into Orla Bardot as it heads north. Rua Turibe Farias, just behind Rua das Pedras, has a number of good boutiques, ice-cream parlors and a pleasant square (Praça Santos Dumont) that becomes a sceney gathering spot at night.

Sparkling white-sand beaches are the daytime attraction in Búzios, with over a dozen within a short drive from the center. To get an overview of the area, take a schooner tour, or rent a buggy and explore the area on your own. In general, the southern beaches are trickier to get to, but they're prettier and have better surf. The northern beaches are closer to the towns and more sheltered.

Boasting a long stretch of sand and good surf, Geribá remains one of the most popular beaches. Lively restaurants and bars lie scattered along the shore and sun-seekers pack the sands. A bit calmer and less developed is the small Ferradurinha (Little Horseshoe), just east of Geribá. Continuing counterclockwise you'll find Ferradura, another horseshoe-shaped beach that's popular with windsurfers. Next are Lagoinha, a rocky beach with rough water, and Praia da Foca and Praia do Forno, both of which have colder water than

TRANSPORTATION: BÚZIOS

Distance from Rio 176km

Direction East

Travel Time 2½ hours

Car From the Zona Sul, head north to the Rio–Niterói bridge (toll R$3.20). After passing the toll, take RJ 101 in the direction of Rio Bonita. After reaching Rio Bonito, take BR 124 (Via Lagos Hwy; toll R$7-10) west. Stay on this highway until it ends, then continue east another 7km until you reach an Ipiranga gas station at the entrance of São Pedro da Aldeia. Take a left at the gas station and then a right onto BR 106 in the direction of Macaé/Búzios. After another 14km you will reach the Atéque Enfim gas station. Turn right and stay on this road until you reach Búzios. For those who'd rather take the slower, scenic route, a coastal road runs from Itacoatiara out to Cabo Frio then north.

Bus From Novo Rio bus station, Viação 1001 (☎ 4004 5001; fare R$24) buses depart seven times daily. The trip takes three hours. Alternatively, take an hourly bus to Cabo Frio and transfer to Búzios.

DETOUR: COASTAL SPOTS

Along the way from Rio to Búzios, there are a number of scenic beaches, surfing spots and fishing villages.

Follow the directions for getting to Búzios (ie take the Rio–Niterói bridge and turn off at Rio Bonito). Turn onto RJ 124 at Rio Bonito (the Via Lagos Hwy) and continue for 23km until you reach the turnoff for Saquarema. This small community lies about 100km east of Rio de Janeiro, and enjoys long stretches of open beach, bordered by lagoons and mountains. The town still has a somnolent air to it, though on weekends it attracts a large surfer crowd thanks to waves of up to 3m. A number of beaches lie near the town, including the popular Barra Nova and Praia da Vila. About 3km north of Saquarema is Praia Itaúna, a good spot that hosts an annual surfing contest during the first two weeks of October.

From Saquarema continue east along the coastal road for another 60km and you'll reach Arraial do Cabo, a moderate-sized village with beaches that compare to the finest in Búzios. Unlike Búzios, however, Arraial is a sleepy, somewhat blue-collar town. Discovered a few centuries ago by Amerigo Vespucci, Praia dos Anjos has beautiful turquoise water, but a little too much boat traffic for safe swimming. It also has a Museum of Oceanography (Praia dos Anjos; 9am-noon & 1-4.30pm Tue-Sun). Aside from Praia dos Anjos, the most popular beaches in Arraial do Cabo are Praia do Forno, Praia Brava and Praia Grande.

The Gruta Azul (Blue Cavern), on the southwestern side of Ilha de Cabo Frio, is another beautiful spot. Be alert to the tides: the entrance to the underwater cavern isn't always open. There are lots of dive operators running tours here, including Sandmar (2622 5703; www.sandmar.com.br).

Ten kilometers north of Arraial do Cabo lies Cabo Frio, which sits between the Canal do Itajuru on one side and the ocean on the other. It's a bit overdeveloped by tourism, but there is some lovely landscape nearby. East of town, along a scenic road, is the Praia do Forte with bleached white sand and a backdrop of low scrub, cacti and grasses. At the northern end of Praia do Forte is a stone fortress, Forte São Mateus (10am-4pm Tue-Sun), which was built in 1616 and served as a stronghold against pirates.

The sand dunes around Cabo Frio are one of the region's most interesting features. The dunes facing the excellent surfing spot of Praia do Peró lie 6km north of town in the direction of Búzios. Praia do Peró is near Ogivas and after Praia Brava and Praia das Conchas. The Pontal dunes of Praia do Forte stretch from the Forte São Mateus to Morro de Miranda (Miranda Hill), while the Dama Branca (White Lady) sand dunes are on the road to Arraial do Cabo. The dunes can be dangerous due to robberies, so talk to locals before heading out.

the other beaches. Praia Olho de Boi (Bull's Eye) has the unique distinction of being named after Brazil's first postage stamp. It's a pocket-sized beach reached by a little trail from the long, clean beach of Praia Brava, which lies to the west.

João Fernandinho and João Fernandes are good locations for snorkeling, as are the topless beaches of Azedinha and Azeda. Praia dos Ossos, Praia da Armação, Praia do Caboclo and Praia dos Amores are pretty to look at, but are not ideal for sunbathing as they can get crowded with boats just offshore, which won't leave you with much privacy. Praia da Tartaruga is quiet and pretty. Praia do Gaucho and Manguinhos are town beaches further along the coastal strip.

Although the best choice of restaurants and nightlife is in Armação de Búzios, some travelers prefer to stay at the beach (Geribá is a top choice), while others opt for Ossos. At the northernmost tip of the peninsula, this is the oldest and most attractive village, with a harbor and yacht club, and a few hotels and bars. Manguinhos, at the isthmus, is the busiest and most commercial village, and is probably the least enticing option. There's also Rasa, northwest along the coast, where Brazil's political dignitaries and CEOs come to relax.

Owing to Búzios' charm and popularity with Cariocas, prices rise substantially on holidays (especially New Year's Eve and Carnaval).

INFORMATION

Búzios Trolley (2623 4733; www.buziostrolley.com.br; Orla Bardot 550, Armação de Búzios; tours from R$30) This outfit runs a variety of excursions, including a daily two-hour open-sided bus tour that visits 12 of the peninsula's beaches. You can also book rafting tours, and trips by glass-bottomed catamaran.

GusCar (2623 8225; www.guscar.com.br in Portuguese; Estrada da Usina 444, Armação de Búzios) GusCar rents buggies and cars for around R$100 per day.

Queen Lory (2623 1179; www.queenlorytours.com.br; Rua João Fernandes 89, Ossos; tours from R$40) This outfit offers daily 2½- and five-hour schooner tours to Ilha Feia, Tartaruga and João Fernandinho.

Secretaria de Turismo (2623 6200; www.buziosturismo.com; Praça Santos Dumont, Búzios; 9am-9pm)

Pick up a map of the beaches in the area at this tourist-information office, which is one block from Rua das Pedras. Another branch (☎ 0800 249 999, open 24 hours) is at the entrance to Búzios.

EATING & DRINKING

Sushi Jardin (☎ 2623 6898; Praça dos Ossos 1358, Ossos; mains R$40-60; 🕓 6pm-midnight Tue-Sun) Set in a cozy candlelit sculpture garden, this new spot has tempting seafood concoctions to complement traditional Japanese fare.

Sawasdee (☎ 2623 4644; Orla Bardot 422, Armação de Búzios; mains from R$42) One of the best Thai restaurants in the state, Sawasdee showcases fresh seafood in its mouth-watering dishes. Start off with a *kaipilychia* (lychee and cane-liquor cocktail).

Cigalon (☎ 2623 0932; Rua das Pedras 199, Armação de Búzios; mains R$34-60) You'll find decadent French cuisine and lovely views at this romantic beachside spot in the center of town.

Restaurante David (☎ 2623 2981; Rua Turíbio de Farias 260, Armação de Búzios; mains R$35-45) Still going strong after three decades, David's serves enjoyable seafood dishes at little wooden tables with checkered tablecloths.

SLEEPING

Casas Brancas (☎ 2623 1458; www.casasbrancas.com.br; Morro do Humaitá 10, Armação de Búzios; d from R$600; 🏊) Set on a hill, the Mediterranean-style Casas Brancas has bay views, spacious rooms (some with balconies and living rooms), a swimming pool and a lovely patio. Full spa services.

Zen-do Pousada (☎ 2623 1542; Rua João Fernandes 60, Ossos; d from R$150) This sweet little guesthouse has just three rooms. The upstairs unit is especially bright and cheery, with a balcony overlooking the spacious backyard.

Brigitta's Guesthouse (☎ 2623 6157; www.brigittas.com.br; Rua das Pedras 131, Armação de Búzios; s/d from R$90/120) Overlooking the water, this charming guesthouse is one of at least a dozen *pousadas* along this strip. Brigitta's has just four cozy rooms, lending it the feel of a B&B. There's an excellent restaurant attached.

PETRÓPOLIS

An attractive mountain retreat with a decidedly European air, Petrópolis is a favorite weekend getaway for Cariocas. Horse-drawn carriages still clatter through the streets, and the city's small bridges and canals, manicured parks and old-fashioned lampposts add to its charm. The city makes a fine place for strolls and taking in the museums, and is an excellent starting point for exploring the picturesque countryside of this region.

Emperor Dom Pedro I first came across the lovely setting on a journey from Rio to Minas Gerais. It was little more than farmland in the 1830s, but Dom Pedro liked the scenery so much that he decided to buy some land. Although he abdicated the throne and returned to Portugal, the land passed to his son, Dom Pedro II, who built a summer retreat here. By the 1840s, the whole court had jumped on the bandwagon, and a palace rose against the mountains. With mansions and a looming

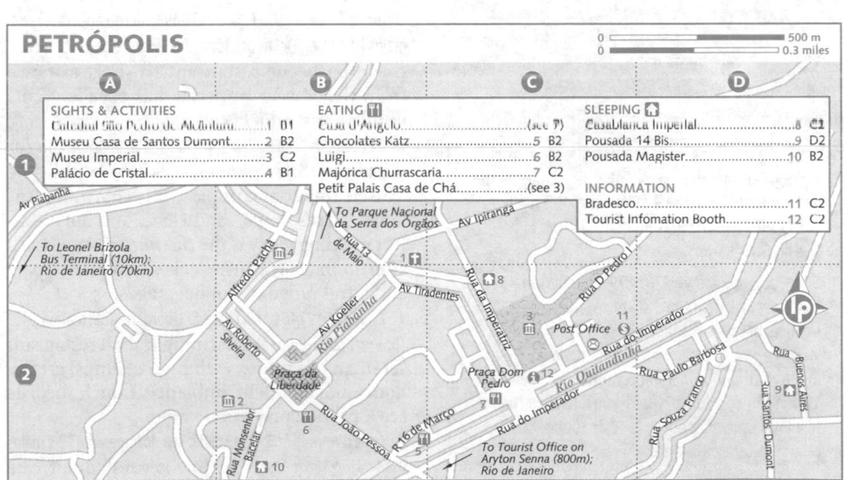

cathedral, Petrópolis earned the nickname 'Imperial City.'

Downtown Petrópolis is a living museum that provides a window into the past. One of the city's gems is the neoclassical Museu Imperial (☎ 2237 8000; Rua da Imperatriz 220; admission R$8; 11am-5.30pm Tue-Sun), which served as the home away from home for Dom Pedro II and his wife, Dona Teresa, when the humidity (and mosquitoes) in Rio became unbearable. The lavish, faithfully preserved building features exhibits from the royal collection, including a 1.7kg crown covered with 639 diamonds and 77 pearls.

North of the Museu Imperial, the Catedral São Pedro de Alcântara (☎ 2242 4300; Rua São Pedro de Alcântara 60; admission free; 8am-noon & 2-6pm Tue-Sun) houses the tombs of Dom Pedro II, Dona Teresa and their daughter Princesa Isabel. From the steps of the cathedral you'll have fine views of most of the region, with the spires of the town set against the mountains.

Another eye-catching sight in Petrópolis is the Palácio de Cristal (☎ 2247 3721; Rua Alfredo Pachá; admission free; 9am-5.30pm Tue-Sun), which was built for Princesa Isabel in France and brought to the country in 1884. It houses a greenhouse, just as it did back then, and features fountains and lush greenery in front.

Following the imperial era, in the late 19th century Petrópolis became a center for intellectuals and artists, nurturing the talents of Austrian writer Stefan Zweig, composer Rui Barbosa and Santos Dumont, the inventor, architect and writer often dubbed the 'father of Brazilian aviation' for his early flights (he also invented the wristwatch). You can learn more about the man by touring the small, fascinating home that he designed himself at the Museu Casa de Santos Dumont (☎ 2247 3158; Rua do Encanto 22; admission R$5; 9.30am-5pm Tue-Sun).

Some uncommonly charming château-like restaurants lie near Petrópolis, but you'll need a car to visit them as the best places are outside of the city center. If you're just around for the day, you can easily explore the historic center on foot, though with its crisp, calm nights and surplus of cozy cottages and B&Bs, Petrópolis makes a great overnight trip. If you visit, keep in mind that most museums close on Monday.

TRANSPORTATION: PETRÓPOLIS

Distance from Rio 68km

Direction North

Travel Time 1½ hours

Car: Take the Linha Vermelha Hwy from Rio. After passing signs for the international airport, be on the lookout for BR 040; you'll merge onto this highway (also called Rodovia Washington Luís) and follow the signs to Petrópolis.

Bus: Fácil/Única (☎ 2263 8792; per person R$14) buses departs from Novo Rio bus station every 20 minutes between 5.15am and 7pm. For the best views be sure to leave well before sundown. Buses arrive at Leonel Brizola station in Bingen, some 10km from downtown, where you'll have to change to a local Esperança bus (bus 10 or 100) or taxi to reach the Centro Histórico.

INFORMATION

Bradesco (Rua do Imperador 268; 10am-5pm Mon-Fri) It has an ATM.

Rios Brasileiros Rafting (☎ 2243 4372; www.rbrafting.com.br in Portuguese) Rios organizes rafting, rappelling and hiking adventures around the area. Portuguese- and English-speaking guides are available. The guides will pick you up from your hotel.

Tourist Information Booth (☎ 2246 9377; Praça dos Expedicionários; 9am-5pm) Stocks brochures and maps, and can recommend hotels in the area. There's also a good information office at the obelisk on the way into town from Rio.

Trekking Petrópolis (☎ 2235 7607; www.rioserra.com.br/trekking) Organizes hikes, mountain-biking, rafting and bird-watching trips through Mata Atlântica rain forest.

EATING

Majórica Churrascaria (☎ 2242 2498; Rua do Imperador 754; mains R$24-36; noon-10pm Tue-Sun) This *churrascaria* (barbecue restaurant), a short distance from the Museu Imperial, has excellent cuts of meat, served à la carte.

Petit Palais Casa de Chá (☎ 2237 8000; Av Imperatriz 220; afternoon tea R$20; noon-7pm Tue-Sun) Within the Museu Imperial complex, this charming teahouse serves soups, sandwiches and full meals. Its crowning glory is the *chá imperial* – a lavish afternoon tea featuring cakes, croissants, pâté and a full range of hot beverages.

Luigi (☎ 2246 0279; Praça da Liberdade 185; mains R$15-30; 11am-10pm) A charming Italian restaurant set in an old house with high ceilings, creaky floors and candlelit ambience. Lunch specials are a particularly good value.

Casa d'Angelo (☎ 2242 0888; Rua do Imperador 700; mains R$14-24; 8am-1am) This low-key restaurant, café

DETOUR: MOUNTAIN TOWNS

The lush greenery of the mountains makes a lovely setting for a scenic drive, but if you'd like to see the greenery from the inside, head to Parque Nacional Da Serra Dos Órgãos (admission R$3; 8am-5pm main entrance). The national park has extensive trails through Mata Atlântica rain forest and has a variety of rich plant and animal life. Dedo de Deus (God's Finger), Cabeça de Peixe (Fish Head) and Verruga do Frade (Friar's Wart) are among the more imaginative trail names. Unfortunately, most of the trails are unmarked and off the extents of available maps. Those interested in hiking or climbing one of the peaks should inquire at Rios Brasileiros Rafting (opposite) in Petrópolis.

Those wanting a short hike (and a picnic) can take the 3.5km walking trail, visiting the waterfalls, natural swimming pools, tended lawns and gardens. There are two entrances to the park, both on BR 116. The one closer to Teresópolis offers more facilities.

Another village in the mountains is Nova Friburgo, which has good hotels and restaurants, as well as many lovely natural attractions: woods, waterfalls, trails, sunny mountain mornings and cool evenings. Do be aware that it gets chilly and rainy during the winter months, from June to August.

The area around Nova Friburgo was first settled by families from the Swiss canton of Friburg. During the Napoleonic wars, Dom João encouraged immigration to Brazil. At the time, people were starving in Switzerland, so in 1818 around 300 families packed up and headed for Brazil. The passage overseas was grueling and many families died en route. Those who survived settled in the mountains and established the small village of Nova Friburgo in the New World.

A tourist information office (☎ 2543 6307; Praça Dr Demervel B Moreira; 8am-8pm) is in the center of town. Scout out the surrounding area from Morro da Cruz (1800m), which is accessible by chairlift (9am-6pm Sat, Sun & holidays); the chairlift station is in the center at Praça Teleférico. Alternatively, there's Pico da Caledônia (2310m), offering fantastic views and launching sites for hang gliders. It's a 6km uphill hike, but the view is worth it.

From Nova Friburgo you can hike to Pedra do Cão Sentado, explore the Furnas do Catete or visit the mountain towns of Bom Jardim (23km northeast on BR 116) or Lumiar (25km east of the turnoff at Muri, which is 9km south of Nova Friburgo). In Lumiar, hippies, cheap pensions, waterfalls, walking trails and white-water canoe trips abound.

and bar is a Petrópolis institution, where regulars amble in for a *cafezinho* (coffee – short, black, strong and usually quite sweet) or a beer at all hours. It's especially worth visiting on Saturday, when they serve a tasty and inexpensive *feijoada* (black bean and pork stew).

Chocolates Katz (☎ 2237 0447; Rua do Imperador 912; desserts R$4) This lovely coffee shop and patisserie makes a fine stop for a cappuccino and chocolate torte.

SLEEPING

Pousada Magister (☎ 2242 1054; www.pousadamagister.com.br; Rua Monsenhor Bacelar 71; d R$165-210) Near the Casa de Santos Dumont, this century-old mansion offers has attractive, bright rooms with wood floors and trim furnishings.

Pousada 14 Bis (☎ 2231 0946; www.pousada14bis.com.br; Rua Buenos Aires 192; s/d from R$85/140) One of Petrópolis' most charming hotels, the Pousada 14 Bis has handsome rooms with wooden floors and large windows overlooking the street or onto the pleasant garden out the back.

Casablanca Imperial (☎ 2242 6662; www.casablancahotel.com.br in Portuguese; Rua do Imperatriz 286; s/d from R$145/180) The Casablanca Imperial is a grand old dame near the Museu Imperial. Its 50 rooms are a mixed bag, but the best feature high ceilings, old shutters, long bathrooms with tubs, and antique furnishings.

VISCONDE DE MAUÁ

Set in the Itatiaia, a region of charming country towns, wandering steams and lush forests, Visconde de Mauá is actually made up of three small villages (Mauá, Maringá and Maromba) scattered a few kilometers apart along the Rio Preto. The chief reason for coming is to soak up the lovely, peaceful setting, best enjoyed from one of the cozy chalets in the region. It's a perfect spot to unwind. Picturesque walks along quiet lanes lie just outside your door.

Although the scenery is undoubtedly new-world tropics, there's an element of the old-world in Itatiaia. It was first settled by Swiss and German immigrants in the early 20th century. (Nearby Penedo, with its saunas, was settled by the Finns.) Visconde de Mauá lies roughly halfway between Rio and São Paulo, in the alpine Serra da Mantiqueira.

Hikes in the area include walks to waterfalls. The Santa Clara Cachoeira, the nicest in the area, is a 6km walk north of Maringá on the Ribeirão Santa Clara. Trails on either side of the falls pass through bamboo groves.

DETOUR: PARQUE NACIONAL DE ITATIAIA

One of Brazil's loveliest national parks is a short drive from Visconde de Mauá. The Parque Nacional do Itatiaia contains virgin rain forest, breathtaking mountain trails and plenty of idyllic rivers, lakes and waterfalls in which to splash about. It's also packed with wildlife, including some 400 bird species as well as monkeys, sloths and many other rain forest creatures. There are numerous trails in the park ranging from hour-long hikes to multiday treks. A recommended day hike (six hours) is the Tres Picos hike, an uphill route that leads past the refreshing Rio Bonito before continuing on to a fantastic lookout point. At the main park entrance, 7km north of the BR 116, you can pick up trail maps at the Visitors Centre (park entrance R$3; 10am-4pm).

To get there from Visconde de Mauá head back to BR 116, take a right and look for the signed turnoff to the right another 6km further on.

You'll find a natural pool in the Rio Preto between Visconde de Mauá and Maringá. Reach it by turning left just before the bridge.

Beyond Maromba, you can take a 2.5km walk out of town (follow the signs) to Cachoeira do Escorrega, where a naturally formed water slide slants into a chilly swimming hole. If you continue along the same road and take the first left at the fork you'll reach Cachoeira Veu de Noiva, another beautiful waterfall.

INFORMATION

Tourist Information Hut (3387 1283; 9am-noon & 1-8pm Tue-Sun) At the entrance to the village of Mauá, this small booth can provide information in Portuguese.

www.viscondedemaua.com.br (in Portugese) A good website with information about the region.

TRANSPORTATION: VISCONDE DE MAUÁ

Distance from Rio 152km

Direction Northwest

Travel Time 3½ hours

Car Take Av Brasil north to BR 116. Take BR 116 west to Resende, where you'll see signs pointing north to Visconde de Mauá. The last 10km is unpaved.

Bus From Novo Rio bus station, Cidade do Aço (2253 8471; www.cidadedoaco.com.br in Portuguese) buses depart Friday at 7.35pm for Maromba (R$41, 4½ hours). They return on Sunday at 4pm. Another option is to catch a more frequent Cidade do Aço bus to the transport-hub town of Resende (2¼ hours, R$25), and an onward bus (R$5, two hours, three to four daily) to Visconde de Mauá.

EATING

Agua Viva (3387 1594; Estrada Maringá/Moromba 7km; meals from R$11; 11am-10pm Fri-Wed) This place serves trout and *mineiro* (Minas Gerais cuisine) food in a delightful riverside location. Outdoor seating and hammocks allow you to relax to the sound of rushing water during and after the meal. The owner speaks some English.

Filho da Truta (3387 1527; www.ofilhodatruta.com.br; Vale do Pavão; meals from R$20; 11am-11pm) Run by an enterprising couple of Lebanese–French descent, this restaurant has won national acclaim for its 37 different trout recipes. The attached *pousada* (guesthouse) has doubles starting at R$85 (or R$115 with three meals a day).

SLEEPING

Olho d'Agua (3387 1386; www.olhodaguamaua.com.br in Portuguese; Maringá; d R$130-210) In the heart of Maringá's shopping district, Olho d'Agua has seven free-standing chalets, set amid peaceful gardens. Each is handsomely decorated in bright colors, and most have little decks strung with hammocks; several also have huge spa bathtubs and fireplaces. The onsite restaurant is excellent.

Pousada Moriá (3387 1505; www.pousadamoria.com.br in Portuguese; Estrada da Maromba; d R$140, with whirlpool tub R$250;) This idyllic hideaway is opposite the Cachoeira do Escorrega. Chalets all have electric blankets and fireplaces, there's a DVD library and the onsite restaurant serves trout and fondue. Breakfast is served in a glass-walled cabin or out on the deck overlooking the waterfall.

TRANSPORTATION

AIR

Many international flights pass through São Paolo before arriving in Rio at the Aeroporto Internacional Antonio Carlos Jobim (commonly called Galeão) on Ilha do Governador (Governor's Island). TAM (www.tam.com.br) and Varig (www.varig.com) are Brazil's biggest international carriers. (Varig, however, is in a perilous financial state, and slashing many of its flights.)

Airlines

Aerolineas Argentinas (AR; ☎ 2103 4200; www.aerolineas.com.ar)

Air Canada (AC; ☎ 04111-3254 6600; www.aircanada.ca)

Air France (AF; ☎ 4003 9955; www.airfrance.com)

Alitalia (AZ; ☎ 0800-704 0206; www.alitalia.com)

American Airlines (AA; ☎ 0300 789 7778; www.aa.com)

Avianca (AV; ☎ 2220 7697; www.avianca.com)

British Airways (BA; ☎ 4004 4440; www.britishairways.com)

Continental Airlines (CO; ☎ 2531 1850; www.continental.com)

COPA (CM; ☎ 0800-771 2672; www.copaair.com)

Delta Airlines (DL; ☎ 4003 2121; www.delta.com)

Gol (G3; ☎ 0800-701 2131; www.voegol.com.br)

Iberia (IB; ☎ 2282 1336; www.Iberia.com)

Japan Airlines (JL; ☎ 04111-3175 2270; www.jal.com)

KLM (KL; ☎ 4003 9966; www.klm.com)

Lan Chile (LA; ☎ 2240 9388; www.lanchile.com)

Lufthansa (LH; ☎ 04111-6445 2499; www.lufthansa.com)

Penta (5P; ☎ 0300-789 2029)

South African (SA; ☎ 04111-3065 5115; www.flysaa.com)

Spanair (JK; ☎ 0800-550 002; www.spanair.com)

Suriname Airways (PY; ☎ 04191-3210 6284)

Swissair (LX; ☎ 04111-3049 2720; www.swiss.com)

TAM (KK; ☎ 0800-570 5700; www.tam.com.br)

TAP Air Portugal (TP; ☎ 2131 7771; www.flytap.com)

United Airlines (UA; ☎ 2217 1951; www.united.com)

Varig (RG; ☎ 04111-4003 7000; www.varig.com.br)

THINGS CHANGE...

The information in this chapter is particularly vulnerable to change. Check directly with the airline or a travel agent to make sure you understand how a fare (and ticket you may buy) works and be aware of the security requirements for international travel. Shop carefully. The details given in this chapter should be regarded as pointers and are not a substitute for your own careful, up-to-date research.

Airports

Rio's Galeão international airport (Map pp60–1) is 15km north of the city center on Ilha do Governador. Aeroporto Santos Dumont (Map pp90–1), used by some domestic flights, is by the bay, in the city center, 1km east of Cinelândia metro station.

Departure Tax

The international departure tax from Brazil is US$36. This has probably been included in the price of your ticket, but if it's not, you have to pay it in cash (either in US dollars or *reais*) at the airport before departure.

BICYCLE

Although traffic can be intimidating on Rio's roads, the city has many kilometers of bike paths along the beach, around Lagoa and along Parque do Flamengo. You can rent bikes from a stand along the west side of Lagoa Rodrigo de Freitas for R$10 per hour. Other places to rent bikes include the following:

Ciclovia (Map pp76–7; ☎ 2275 5299; Av Prado Júnior 330, Copacabana; per hr/day R$8/50)

Consuelo (Map pp76–7; ☎ 2513 0159, 8811 5552; Av Atlântica near Posto 4, Copacabana; per hr R$10) In addition to having a pick-up service on Copacabana beach, this place delivers to all hotels in the Zona Sul.

Special Bike (Map p64; ☎ 2521 2686; Rua Visconde de Pirajá 135B, Ipanema; per hr/day R$15/45; ⏰ 9am-7pm Mon-Fri, to 2pm Sat)

BOAT

Rio has several islands in the bay that you can visit by ferry; another way to see the city is by taking the commuter ferry to Niterói. Niterói's

CLIMATE CHANGE & TRAVEL

Climate change is a serious threat to the ecosystems that humans rely upon, and air travel is the fastest-growing contributor to the problem. Lonely Planet regards travel, overall, as a global benefit, but believes we all have a responsibility to limit our personal impact on global warming.

Flying & Climate Change

Pretty much every form of motorized travel generates CO_2 (the main cause of human-induced climate change) but planes are far and away the worst offenders, not just because of the sheer distances they allow us to travel, but because they release greenhouse gases high into the atmosphere. The statistics are frightening: two people taking a return flight between Europe and the US will contribute as much to climate change as an average household's gas and electricity consumption over a whole year.

Carbon Offset Schemes

Climatecare.org and other websites use 'carbon calculators' that allow travelers to offset the level of greenhouse gases they are responsible for with financial contributions to sustainable travel schemes that reduce global warming – including projects in India, Honduras, Kazakhstan and Uganda.

Lonely Planet, together with Rough Guides and other concerned partners in the travel industry, support the carbon offset scheme run by climatecare.org. Lonely Planet offsets all of its staff and author travel.

For more information check out our website: www.lonelyplanet.com.

main attraction is the Museu do Arte Contemporânea (p106), but many visitors board the ferry just for the fine views of downtown and the surrounding landscape. The ferry costs R$4.60 return and leaves every 15 to 30 minutes from Praça Quinze de Novembro (Map p90–1) in Centro. Faster, more comfortable catamarans run every 20 minutes from 7am to 8pm and cost R$11 return. See p104 for more information on the following trips.

Ilha de Paquetá (Map pp90–1; ☎ ferries 2533 6661, hydrofoils 2533 7524) The regular ferry takes 70 minutes and costs R$8 return on weekdays (R$15 return on weekends). The more comfortable hydrofoil takes only 25 minutes and costs R$16, but was out of commission at time of research. The ferry service goes from 5.30am to 11pm, leaving every two to three hours.

Ilha Fiscal (Map pp90–1; ☎ 3870 6992; fare R$8; ⌚ departs 1pm, 2.30pm & 4pm Thu-Sun except on the 2nd weekend of each month) Boats depart from the Espaço Cultural da Marinha three times a day from Thursday to Sunday and include a guided tour of the Palácio da Ilha Fiscal (p104). It's a short ride (15 minutes).

BUS

City Bus

By far the most widespread form of transport is the city bus. You'll see them traveling at breakneck speeds around hairpin curves or clogged in stifling traffic jams at rush hour. There are hundreds of lines crisscrossing the city, with the most useful for visitors coursing along the corridors between Leblon and Copacabana. Every bus has its destination written on the front and on the side, and if you see the bus for you, hail it by sticking your arm straight out (drivers won't stop unless flagged down).

Board the bus from the front, and pay the collector sitting toward the front. Conveniently enough, the collector can usually make change. After paying, go through the turnstile and take your seat. You'll exit through the rear. Most buses cost around R$1.90 to R$2.30.

Rio buses have a bad reputation in the international media as the setting for robberies, bombings and indiscriminate violence (the 2002 documentary film *Bus 174* didn't help matters much). In truth, such acts are rare and usually limited to outer-suburban areas where tourists aren't likely to travel. Do keep an eye on your belongings while riding, and don't travel by bus at night; taxis are generally a safer option.

Long-Distance Bus

Buses connect Rio with cities and towns all over the country. Most arrive and depart from the loud Novo Rio Rodoviária (Novo Rio bus station; Map pp60–1; ☎ 3213 1800; www.novorio.com.br in Portuguese; Av Francisco Bicalho 1, São Cristóvão), which lies about five minutes by bus northwest of the city center. The people at the Riotur desk on the bus station's ground floor can provide information on transportation and lodging.

The other Rio bus station is the Menezes Cortes Rodoviária (Menezes Cortes bus terminal; Map pp90–1; ☎ 2299 1380; Rua São José 35, Centro), which handles services to some destinations in Rio de Janeiro state, such as Petrópolis and Teresópolis. You can catch buses to these two destinations from Novo Rio as well.

If you arrive in Rio by bus, it's a good idea to take a taxi to your hotel, or at least to the general area where you want to stay. Traveling on local buses with all your belongings is a little risky. A small booth near the Riotur desk at Novo Rio bus station organizes the yellow cabs out front. Excellent buses leave every 15 minutes or so for São Paulo (six hours). Most major destinations are serviced by very comfortable *leito* (executive) buses leaving late at night.

It's a good idea to buy a ticket a couple of days in advance if you can, especially if you want to travel on a weekend or during a Brazilian holiday period. Some agencies in the city sell tickets for some (but not all!) of the bus lines. In Ipanema, try Paxtur (Map p64; ☎ 2523 1000; store 114, Rua Visconde de Pirajá 303), which charges a nominal fee (R$3.50) per ticket.

CAR

Driving & Parking

In the city itself, driving can be a frustrating experience even if you know your way around. Traffic snarls and parking problems do not make for an enjoyable holiday. If the bus and metro aren't your style, there are plenty of taxis. However, if you do drive in the city, it's good to know a couple of things: At night, Cariocas (residents of Rio) don't always stop at red lights, because of the small risk of robberies at deserted intersections. Between 10pm and 6am, cars slow at red lights and then proceed if no one is around. Another thing to know is that if you park your car on the street, it's common to pay the *flanelinha* (parking attendant) a few *reais* (usually R$2) to look after it. Some of the *flanelinhas* work for the city, others are 'freelance,' but regardless, it's a common practice throughout Brazil.

Rental

Renting a car is relatively cheap, but gasoline is expensive. If you don't mind the expense, it's a great way to explore some of the remote beaches, mountain towns and national parks near Rio. Getting a car is fairly simple as long as you have a driver's license, a credit card and a passport. To rent a car you must be at least 25 years old. Ideally, you should have an international driver's permit, which you'll need to pick up from your home country. In reality, rental-car companies accept any driver's license – it's the cops who will want to see an international driver's permit.

Prices start around R$100 per day for a car without air-conditioning, but they go down a bit in the low season. There is a bit of competition between the major agencies, so it's worth shopping around. If you are quoted prices on the phone, make sure they include insurance, which is compulsory.

Car-rental agencies can be found at either airport or scattered along Av Princesa Isabel in Copacabana. At the international airport, Hertz (☎ 3398 4377), Localiza (☎ 3398 5445) and Unidas (☎ 3398 3452) provide rentals. In Copacabana, among the many are Hertz (Map pp76–7; ☎ 2275 7440; Av Princesa Isabel 500) and Localiza (Map pp76–7; ☎ 2275 3340; Av Princesa Isabel 150).

GETTING INTO TOWN

The most economical way of reaching the international airport is to take the Real Auto Bus (☎ 0800-240 850), known locally as the *frescão*. These relatively safe, air-conditioned buses go from the international airport (outside the arrivals floor of terminal one or the ground floor of terminal two) to Novo Rio bus station (Av Rio Branco, Centro), Aeroporto Santos Dumont, southward through Glória, Flamengo and Botafogo and along the beaches of Copacabana, Ipanema and Leblon to Barra da Tijuca (and vice versa). The buses run every 20 to 30 minutes, 5.20am to 12.10am, and will stop wherever you ask. Fares are around R$6. You can transfer to the metro at Carioca station.

Heading to the airports, you can catch the Real Auto Bus in front of the major hotels along the main beaches, but you have to look alive and flag it down.

Comun (standard) taxis from the international airport are generally safe, though there are occasional robberies reported. Radio taxis are safer, but more expensive. You pay a set fare at the airport. A yellow-and-blue *comun* taxi should cost around R$30 to R$35 to Ipanema if the meter is working. A radio taxi costs around R$80.

Many hotels and hostels also arrange airport transport, typically charging around R$60.

METRÔ-ÔNIBUS

A convenient way to reach the metro is via Metrô-Ônibus (metro buses; www.metrorio.com.br) – modern, silver buses that make limited stops as they shuttle passengers to and from metro stations. For most destinations, a one-way *metrô na superficie* (surface metro) ticket costs as much as a metro ride (R$2.40) but includes both the bus ride and the metro ride (hold onto your ticket). Although there are growing numbers of these buses on Rio's streets, the most useful one for travelers staying in Leblon, Ipanema and southern Copacabana is the metro bus marked 'Gávea'. This will take you to and from the Copacabana metro station Siqueira Campos. If you're entering the metro and plan on connecting to a bus, be sure to request *metrô + metrô na superficie* tickets at the booth; otherwise, you'll just receive single-use metro tickets.

Catch the metro bus on the following streets:

To Metro	From Metro
Rua Padre Leonel França (Gávea)	Metro station Siqueira Campos
Praça Antero de Quental (Leblon)	Av Rainha Elizabeth 234 (Copacabana)
Av Ataúlfo de Paiva 19 (Leblon)	Praça General Osório (Ipanema)
Rua Visconde de Pirajá 259 (Ipanema)	Rua Prudente de Morais 814 (Ipanema)
Rua Visconde de Pirajá 25 (Ipanema)	Rua Prudente de Morais 1800 (Ipanema)
Rua Francisco Sá 51 (Copacabana)	Praça Antero de Quental (Leblon)
Metro station Siqueira Campos	Rua Marquês de São Vicente 22 (Gávea)
	Rua Padre Leonel França (Gávea)

If you're going from the metro to Gávea or Jardim Botânico, disembark at Botafogo station and catch the integrated metro bus from there. Stops are at Cobal do Humaitá, Rua Maria Angélica (near Rua Jardim Botânico 164), the Hospital da Lagoa (Rua Jardim Botânico 518), the edge of the botanical gardens (Rua Jardim Botânico 728), Praça Santos Dumont, Gávea Trade Center (Marquês de São Vicente 124) and PUC (Av Rubens Berardo 175).

You can also go to Barra by metro bus. It costs R$3.25 and departs from Siqueira Campos station, with stops at Posto 9 (Ipanema beach), Posto 12 (Leblon beach), São Conrado Fashion Mall, Praia do Pepino (São Conrado), Shopping Downtown, Barra Shopping and Casa Shopping, among other stops.

METRO

Rio's subway system (www.metrorio.com.br) is an excellent way to get around. It's open from 5am to midnight Monday through Saturday, and 7am to 11pm on Sunday and holidays. During Carnaval the metro operates non-stop from 5am Saturday morning until 11pm on Tuesday. Both lines are air-conditioned, clean, fast and safe. The main line goes from Cantagalo (a station that opened in 2007) in Copacabana to Saens Peña, connecting with the secondary line to Estácio (which provides service to São Cristóvão, Maracanã and beyond). The main stops in Centro are Cinelândia and Carioca. More stations are planned in the coming years, and the city will eventually integrate Ipanema into the transport system by 2009 or 2010 with a station at Praça General Osorio.

You can buy a selection of one-way, round-trip or 10-ride tickets. An *unitário* (basic single) costs R$2.40, and there's no discount for *duplo* (round-trip) or multiple-ride tickets. Free subway maps are available from most ticket booths.

MINIVAN

Minivans (Cariocas call them *vans)* are an alternative form of transportation in Rio and usually much faster than buses. They run along Av Rio Branco to the Zona Sul as far as Barra da Tijuca. On the return trip, they run along the coast almost all the way into the center. They run frequently, and cost between R$2 and R$4.50. They do get crowded, and are not a good idea if you have luggage.

TAXI

Rio's yellow-and-blue taxis are prevalent throughout the city. They're fairly inexpensive and provide a good way to zip around. Unfortunately, they aren't completely safe and hassle-free. A few rare cases have been reported of people being assaulted and robbed by taxi drivers. A much more common problem is fare inflation. Many of the taxi drivers who hang around the hotels are sharks, so it's worth walking a block or so to avoid them.

Make sure the meter works. If it doesn't, ask to be let out of the cab. Meters have a flag that switches the tariff; this should be in the number-one position (80% fare), except on Sunday, holidays, between 9pm and 6am, when driving outside the Zona Sul and during December.

The flat rate is around R$4, plus around R$1 per kilometer. Radio taxis are 30% more expensive than regular taxis, but safer.

Most people don't tip taxi drivers, but it's common to round up the fare.

A few radio-taxi companies include Centraltáxi (☎ 2195 1000), Coopertrama (☎ 2209 9292), JB (☎ 2178 4000) and Transcoopass (☎ 2209 1555).

TRAIN

The suburban train station, Estação Dom Pedro II (Central do Brasil; Map pp60–1; ☎ 2111 9494; Praça Cristiano Ottoni, Av Presidente Vargas, Centro) is one of Brazil's busiest commuter stations. To get there, take the metro to Central station and head upstairs. This is the train station that was featured in the Academy Award-nominated film *Central do Brasil* (Central Station).

TRAM

Rio was once serviced by a multitude of *bondes* (trams), with routes throughout the city. The only one still running is the Santa Teresa tram, known locally as the *bondinho*. It's still the best way to get to this neighborhood from downtown.

The bonde station (Map pp90–1; Rua Lélio Gama 65) in Centro is best reached by traveling via Rua Senador Dantas and taking a turn west into Rua Lélio Gama. At the top of the small hill, you'll find the station. *Bondes* (R$0.60) depart every 30 minutes. The two routes currently open have been in operation since the 19th century. Both travel over the Arcos da Lapa (p100) and along Rua Joaquim Murtinho before reaching Largo do Guimarães (p100; Rua Almirante Alexandrino) in the heart of boho Santa Teresa. From there, one line (Paula Matos) takes a northwestern route, terminating at Largo das Neves (p100). The longer route (Dois Irmãos) continues from Largo do Guimarães uphill and southwest before terminating near the water reservoir at Dois Irmãos.

Although a policeman often accompanies the tram as a potential deterrent, the favelas (shanty towns) down the hillsides still make this a high-crime area. Go, by all means, but don't take any valuables with you. See p97 for more details.

DIRECTORY

ACCOMMODATIONS

Accommodation listings in the Sleeping chapter (p188) are organized by neighborhood, and arranged by price, from most expensive to cheapest within each neighborhood. In Rio, the average double room with bathroom costs about R$200, with seasonal variations (highest in summer, from December to February). Over New Year's Eve and during Carnaval, every place in town will double or triple their prices, and most will require minimum stays of four days.

See our price guide on p189 for an indication of the standard price range for top-end, midrange and budget accommodations.

We've quoted standard rates, but booking online may save you cash. Numerous websites allow you to peruse listings and make reservations online, including www.lonelyplanet.com and www.ipanema.com.

BUSINESS HOURS

Office hours in Rio are from 9am to 6pm, Monday to Friday. Most shops and government services (such as the post offices) are open from 9am to 6pm Monday to Friday, and from 9am to 1pm on Saturday.

Because many Cariocas (residents of Rio) have little free time during the week, Saturday mornings are often spent shopping. Shops are usually open weekdays from 9am to 6pm and on Saturday from 9am to 1pm. Stores in the large shopping malls are open from 10am to 10pm Monday through Saturday and on Sundays from 3pm to 10pm.

Banks, always in their own little world, generally open from 9am or 10am to 3pm or 4pm Monday to Friday. Currency-exchange places often open an hour after that, when the daily dollar rates become available.

CHILDREN

Brazilians are very family-oriented, and many hotels let children stay free, although the age limit varies. Baby-sitters are readily available and most restaurants have high chairs.

Don't forget Lonely Planet's *Travel with Children,* by Cathy Lanigan, gives a lot of good tips and advice on traveling with kids in the tropics.

See p75 for more details on sights and activities for children.

CLIMATE

Rio lies only a few dozen kilometers north of the Tropic of Capricorn, so it has a classic tropical climate. In summer (December to February), Rio is hot and humid; temperatures around 100°F (38°C) are common, and days sometimes reach around 107°F (42°C). Frequent, short rains cool things off a bit, but the summer humidity makes things uncomfortable for people from cooler climates. The rest of the year, it's cooler, with temperatures generally around 77°F (25°C), sometimes rising to 88°F (31°C).

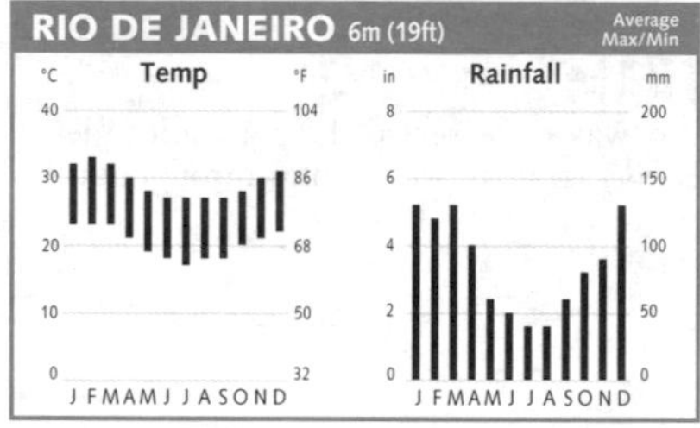

COURSES

Rio makes a fine setting for soaking up an exhilarating dose of the tropics, but if action is what you're after, there's a wealth of opportunities for visitors, from diving to surfing to honing one's volleyball game on the sands. See the Sports & Activities chapter (p180) for more information on surfing, hang gliding, volleyball, dance classes and more.

Cooking

There are many cooking classes available in Rio de Janeiro. Those wanting to learn how to make a decadent pot of *feijoada* (black beans and pork stew) or *moqueca* (seafood stew cooked in coconut milk) should book a private class with Cook Rio (☎ 8606 7497; www.cookrio.com). Classes last around two hours, cost R$108 per person, and at the end of the preparation, you get to enjoy the fruits (and meats) of your labor.

Language

Most language institutes charge high prices for group courses. You can often find a private tutor for less. Hostels are a good place to troll for instructors, with ads on bulletin boards posted by native-speaking language teachers available for hire. **Instituto Brasil-Estados Unidos** (IBEU; Map pp76–7; ☎ 2548 8430; www.ibeu.org.br; 5th fl, Av Nossa Senhora (NS) de Copacabana 690, Copacabana) is one of the oldest, more respected language institutions in the city. It has four different levels of classes from beginner through to advanced. Classes typically meet two hours a day, three days a week. The cost for a four-week course is about R$1000. For information, stop by or visit the website. IBEU also has a decent English library.

CUSTOMS REGULATIONS

Travelers entering Brazil can bring in 2L of alcohol, 400 cigarettes, one personal computer, video and still camera. Newly purchased goods worth up to US$500 are permitted duty-free. Meat and cheese products are not allowed.

At Galeão international airport, customs use the random-check system. After collecting your luggage, you pass a post with two buttons; you push the appropriate button depending on whether you have anything to declare. A green light allows you to proceed straight through; a red light means you've been selected for a baggage search. They are usually fairly lenient with foreigners.

DISCOUNT CARDS

Tourist offices in Rio, such as Riotur (p228), currently give out a free pass, which nets you a small discount (5%) at a few bars, shops and restaurants. See www.riopass.com for more info.

ELECTRICITY

The current is almost exclusively 110V or 120V, 60 Hz, AC. Some hotels also have 220-volt current. The most common power points have two sockets, and most will take both round and flat prongs. If you're packing a laptop – or any electronic device – be sure to use a surge protector.

Electrical current is not standardized in Brazil, so if you're traveling around the country it's a good idea to carry an adapter. For more information on electricity, plugs and other curious tidbits, visit www.kropla.com.

EMBASSIES

Many foreign countries have consulates or embassies in Rio. If they're not listed here, you'll find consulates listed in the back of Riotur's bimonthly *Rio Guide.*

Argentina (Map p84; ☎ 01122-2553 1646; consar.rio@openlink.com.br; sobreloja/1st fl 201, Praia de Botafogo 228, Botafogo)

Australia (Map pp90–1; ☎ 01122-3824 4624; honconau@terra.com.br; 23rd fl, Av Presidente Wilson 231, Centro)

Canada (Map pp76–7; ☎ 01122-2543 3004; rio@international.gc.ca; 5th fl, Av Atlântica 1130, Copacabana)

France (Map pp90–1; ☎ 01122-3974 6699; www.ambafrance.org.br; 6th fl, Av Presidente Antônio Carlos 58, Centro)

UK (Map p84; ☎ 01122-2555 9600; www.reinounido.org.br; 2nd fl, Praia do Flamengo 284, Flamengo)

USA (Map pp90–1; ☎ 01122-3823 2000; www.embaixadaamericana.org.br; Av Presidente Wilson 147, Centro)

EMERGENCY

If you have the misfortune of being robbed, you should report it to the **Tourist Police** (Map p66; ☎ 3399 7170; Rua Afrânio de Melo Franco 159, Leblon; 24hr). No major investigation is going to occur, but you will get a police form to give to your insurance company.

To call emergency telephone numbers in Rio you don't need a phonecard. Useful numbers include the following:

Ambulance ☎ 192

Fire ☎ 193

Police ☎ 190

GAY & LESBIAN TRAVELERS

Rio is the gay capital of Latin America. There is no law against homosexuality in Brazil. During Carnaval, thousands of expatriate Brazilian and gringo gays fly in for the festivities. Transvestites steal the show at all Carnaval balls, especially the gay ones. Outside Carnaval, the gay scene is active, but less visible than in cities like San Francisco and Sydney.

You may hear or read the abbreviation GLS, particularly in the entertainment section of newspapers and magazines. It stands for Gays, Lesbians and Sympathizers, and when used in connection with venues or events basically indicates that anyone with an open mind is welcome. In general, the scene is much more integrated than elsewhere; and the majority of parties involve a pretty mixed crowd.

The Rio gay guide (www.riogayguide.com) is an excellent website full of information for gay and lesbian tourists in Rio, including sections entitled 'Bars & Cafés,' 'Carnival in Rio' and 'Rio for Beginners.' It's available in German, English and Portuguese versions.

For more details on gay life in Rio de Janeiro see p170.

HOLIDAYS

On public holidays banks, offices, post offices and most stores close. Public holidays include the following:

New Year's Day January 1

Epiphany January 6

Dia de São Sebastião January 20 (St Sebastian Day; p20)

Carnaval February or March (to plan your dates for Carnaval, see p51)

Easter March or April

Tiradentes Day April 21

Dia de São Jorge April 23 (St George Day; p21)

Labor Day May 1

Corpus Christi May or June

Dia de Independência do Brasil September 7 (Independence Day; p22)

Our Lady of Aparecida Day October 12

All Souls' Day November 2

Proclamation Day November 15

Black Consciousness Day November 20

Christmas Day December 25

School break coincides with Rio's summer, running from mid-December to mid-February. It's when the city gets overrun with both Brazilian vacationers and travelers from abroad. Another break occurs in July, when Brazilian vacationers come to Rio.

INTERNET ACCESS

Most top-end hotels and a few midrange ones have the technology to allow you to plug in your laptop and get high-speed internet access from your room. Wi-fi is slowly catching on.

Internet cafés are prevalent throughout Rio, with Copacabana having the highest concentration of them. Most places charge between R$4 and R$8 an hour.

Central Fone Centro (Map pp90–1; basement level, Av Rio Branco 156; 9am-9pm Mon-Fri, 10am-4pm Sat); Ipanema (Map p64; Rua Teixeira de Melo 47; 9.30am-8pm)

Cyber Café (Map pp90–1; Av Rio Branco 43, Centro; 9am-7pm Mon-Fri)

Fone Rio (Map pp76–7; Rua Constante Ramos 22, Copacabana; 8am-midnight)

Letras e Expressões Ipanema (Map p64; Rua Visconde de Pirajá 276; 8am-midnight); Leblon (Map p66; Av Ataúlfo de Paiva 1292; 24hr)

Locutório (Map pp76–7; Av NS Copacabana 1171, Copacabana; 8am-2am)

Telerede (Map pp76–7; Av NS de Copacabana 209A, Copacabana; 8am-2am)

LEGAL MATTERS

In Brazil, 18 is the legal drinking age; it's also the legal age of consent and the minimum driving age.

You are required by law to carry some form of identification. For travelers, this generally means a passport, but a certified copy of the relevant ID page will usually be acceptable.

The police in Rio are very poorly paid, with the honest ones needing two or three other jobs to make ends meet. Corruption and bribery are not uncommon.

Marijuana and cocaine are plentiful in Rio, and both are very illegal. An allegation of drug trafficking or possession provides the police with the perfect excuse to extract a not-insignificant amount of money from you – and Brazilian prisons are brutal places. If you are arrested, know that you have the right to remain silent, and that you are innocent until proven guilty. You also have a right to visitation by your lawyer or a family member.

MAPS

The company Quatro Rodas produces the best maps of Rio and of Brazil. Its guide *Ruas Rio de Janeiro* has detailed maps of city streets published in book format. It's updated annually and is available at newsstands and bookstores (priced around R$30).

Riotur (p228) also provides a useful (and free) map of Rio de Janeiro, which has a detailed street layout. It's available from their information booths.

MEDICAL SERVICES

Some private medical facilities in Rio de Janeiro are on a par with US hospitals. The UK and US consulates (p221) have lists of English-speaking physicians.

Brazilian blood banks don't always screen carefully. If you need an injection, ask to have the syringe unwrapped in front of you, or use your own.

Hospitals

Hospital Ipanema (Map p64; ☎ 3111 2300; Rua Antônio Parreiras 67, Ipanema)

Miguel Couto Hospital (Map pp70–1; ☎ 3111 3781; Av Bartolomeu Mitre 1108, Gávea)

Pharmacies

Pharmacies stock all kinds of drugs and sell them much more cheaply than in the West. However, when buying drugs anywhere in South America, be sure to check the expiration dates and specific storage conditions. Some drugs that are available in Brazil may no longer be recommended, or may even be banned, in other countries. Common names of prescription medicines in South America are likely to be different from the ones you're used to, so ask a pharmacist before taking anything you're not sure about.

There are scores of pharmacies in town, a number of which stay open 24 hours. In Copacabana try **Drogaria Pacheco** (Map pp76–7; Av NS de Copacabana 115 & 534; 24hr). In Ipanema, visit **Drogaria Pacheco** (Map p64; ☎ 2239 5397; Av Visconde de Pirajá 592).

MONEY

Since 1994 the monetary unit of Brazil has been the *real* (R$, pronounced hay *ow*); the plural is *reais* (pronounced hay-*ice*). The *real* is made up of 100 *centavos*. Most prices in this guide are quoted in *reais*, though some hoteliers prefer to list their rates in less-stable currencies like US dollars and euros.

Coins come in the usual denominations, and there is both a one-*real* coin and a one *real* note.

Brazilian bank notes are printed in different colors with different animals on each, so there's no mistaking one denomination for another. In addition to the green one-*real* note (hummingbird), there's a blue two (hawksbill turtle), a violet five (egret), a scarlet 10 (macaw), a yellow 20 (lion-faced monkey), a golden-brown 50 (jaguar) and a blue 100 (the not terribly romantic grouper fish).

Over the last five years the real has proven to be a strong, stable currency.

ATMs

ATMs are the handiest way to access money in Rio. Unfortunately, there has been an alarming rise in card cloning, with travelers returning home to find unauthorized withdrawals on their cards. Always cover your hands when inputting your pin number and don't leave ATM receipts inside the bank.

Banco do Brasil, Bradesco, Citibank and HSBC are the best banks to try when using a debit or credit card. Look for the sticker of your card's network (Visa, MasterCard, Cirrus or Plus) on the ATM, and you may have to try a few machines before finding one that accepts your card. Even though many ATMs advertise 24-hour service, these 24 hours usually fall between 6am and 10pm. This is really for the best, since it's unwise to withdraw money after dark. On holidays, ATM access ends at 3pm.

You can find ATMs in the following locations:

Banco 24 Horas (Map pp90–1; outside Carioca metro stop, near Av Rio Branco, Centro)

Banco do Brasil Centro (Map pp90–1; Rua Senador Dantas 105); Copacabana (Map pp76–7; Av NS de Copacabana 1292); Galeão airport (3rd fl, Terminal 1)

Citibank Centro (Map pp90–1; Rua da Assembléia 100); Ipanema (Map p64; Rua Visconde de Pirajá 459A); Leblon (Map p66; Av Ataúlfo de Paiva 1260)

HSBC (Map pp90–1; Av Rio Branco 108, Centro)

Changing Money

Good places to exchange money include the following:

Banco do Brasil Centro (Map pp90–1; 2nd fl, Rua Senador Dantas 105); Copacabana (Map pp76–7; Av NS de Copacabana 594); Galeão airport (3rd fl, Terminal 1)

Citibank Centro (Map pp90–1; Rua da Assembléia 100); Ipanema (Map p64; Rua Visconde de Pirajá 459A)

Easier than dealing with banks is going to *casas de câmbio* (money exchanges, usually shortened to *câmbios*). Recommended *câmbios* include **Casa Aliança** (Map pp90–1; Rua Miguel Couto 35C, Centro; 9am-5.30pm) and **Casa Universal** (Map pp76–7; Av NS de Copacabana 371, Copacabana).

Credit Cards

Visa is the most widely accepted credit card in Rio; MasterCard, American Express and Diners Club are also accepted by many hotels, restaurants and shops.

Credit-card fraud is rife in Rio, so be very careful. When making purchases keep your credit card in sight at all times.

To report lost or stolen credit cards, ring the following emergency numbers:

American Express ☎ 04134-3233 6266

Diners Club ☎ 0800 784 480

MasterCard ☎ 0800 891 3294

Visa ☎ 0800 891 3680

Tipping

Most service workers get tipped 10%, and as the people in these services make the minimum wage – which is not nearly enough to live on – you can be sure they need the money. In restaurants the service charge is usually included in the bill and is mandatory; when it is not included in the bill, it's customary to leave a 10% tip. If a waiter is friendly and helpful, you can give more.

There are many other places where tipping is not customary but is a welcome gesture. The workers at local juice stands, bars and coffee corners, and street and beach vendors, are all tipped on occasion. Parking assistants receive no wages and are dependent on tips, usually the equivalent of R$2. Gas-station attendants, shoe shiners and barbers are also frequently tipped. Taxi drivers are not usually tipped, but it is common to round up the fare.

NEWSPAPERS & MAGAZINES

Ownership of Brazil's media industry is concentrated in the hands of a few organizations. O Globo, based in Rio, controls one of the nation's leading newspapers and TV networks.

Foreign-Language Press

In Rio you will find three daily newspapers in English: the *Miami Herald*, *USA Today* and the *International Herald Tribune*. They are usually on the newsstands by noon.

Imported newspapers and magazines are available, but are quite expensive. Several bookstores in Ipanema and Leblon offer foreign-language publications. See Shopping (p112) for details.

Portuguese-Language Press

The *Jornal do Brasil* and *O Globo* are Rio's main daily papers. Both have entertainment listings. *O Povo* is a popular daily with lots of gory photographs.

The country's best-selling weekly magazine is *Veja*. In Rio, it comes with the *Veja Rio* insert, which details the weekly entertainment options (the insert comes out on Sunday). It's a colorful, well-produced magazine, and it's not difficult reading if you're learning Portuguese. *Isto É* has the best political and economic analysis, and reproduces international articles from the British *Economist*, but it's not light reading. It also provides good coverage of current events.

For something a little more low-brow, check out *O Dia*, which keeps Cariocas up-to-date with all the latest scandals. Environmental issues (both national and international) are covered in the glossy monthly magazine *Terra*.

ORGANIZED TOURS

There are many ways to experience Rio, whether by boat, helicopter, jeep or good old-fashioned walking. Joining an organized tour is also a good way to meet other travelers. For hiking and climbing tours, see p180.

Bay Cruises

With its magnificent coastline, Rio makes a fine backdrop for a cruise. Tours depart from the Marina de Glória (Map p87), and you can purchase tickets in advance from 8am to 4pm Monday to Friday. Bay cruises include the following:

Macuco Rio (Map p87; ☎ 2205 0390; www.macucorio.com.br in Portuguese; Marina de Glória, Glória; boat tours R$50-100) Offers daily tours in a high-velocity speed boat, which can carry 28 people. The first trip heads south to the pristine Cagarras Archipelago all the way to Redondo Island, where you can spot migratory birds and perhaps dolphins, turtles and even whales at certain times of the year. The other route heads to the north passing beside the Museu do Arte Contemporânea (MAC) and historic sites along the bay. Both tours last just under two hours, with a choice of morning or afternoon cruises.

Marlin Yacht Tours (Map p87; ☎ 2225 7434; www.marlinyacht.com.br; Marina de Glória, Glória; cruise R$40-70) Offers several daily tours aboard its large 30-person schooners to Cagarras Island, stopping for a beach swim along the way. It also offers sunset cruises, sailing and diving trips, and is known for its fishing tours.

Saveiros tours (Map p87; ☎ 2225 6064; www.saveiros.com.br; Marina de Glória, Glória; cruise R$40-70) Saveiros leads daily two-hour cruises out over Baía de Guanabara in large schooners. The route follows the coastline of Rio and Niterói with excellent views of Pão de Açúcar (Sugarloaf),

SHOULD I STAY OR SHOULD I GO?

Favela tours are now among the most popular day tours you can book in the city, but many visitors wonder if it's little more than voyeurism taking a trip into the Rocinha 'slums.' In fact, there can be some positive things that come out of the experience. Local residents, who feel marginalized by their own government, are often flattered that foreigners take such an interest in them. Projects focused on the arts are growing in the favelas; and one of the best ways to support the community directly is to purchase locally made paintings and handicrafts.

Choosing a guide is also essential. Try to get the lowdown before you sign up. Does he or she give time or money to the community? If so, how much and where does it go? Does the guide live in the favela? While the majority of agencies operating in Rocinha are simply opportunists, there are a few who are bringing more than just tourists to the neighborhood. Ask around, as for those who are interested in seeing Rocinha from the inside – as a volunteer – there are numerous ways to get involved.

the MAC, Ilha Fiscal and the old fort of Urca. You'll sail under the Niterói bridge.

Velho Marineiro (☎ 7845 6033; www.traineira.com.br; per person R$80) Rio's newest aquatic venture is a small party boat that heads out for a four-hour cruise around Rio. The tour entails music, a barbecue, free drinks, and stops for swimming along the way. Tours run only when there's enough demand (10 persons or more), which is fairly often in the summer. The tour operator will pick you up on the day of the tour.

City Tours

There are a number of private guides who can lead customized tours around the city, taking in the major daytime sights, leading nightlife tours and organizing just about anything Rio has to offer. Recommended guides include the following:

Aurélio Curtim (☎ 9223 9945; www.aurelioriоguide.com) Offers low-key tours around the city; also rents apartments.

Brazil Expedition (☎ 9988 2907; www.brazilexpedition.com; tours R$70) The friendly English-speaking guides from Brazil Expedition run a variety of traditional tours around Rio, including trips to Cristo Redentor, nightlife tours in Lapa, game-day outings at Maracanã and favela tours.

Lisa Rio Tours (☎ 2237 4615; www.lisariotours.com) This new outfit leads a variety of unique tours around the city, including a trip around colonial Santa Teresa, stopping at Parque das Ruínas; exploring the historic district of Centro; tours around Niterói, and most fascinating of all, an Afro-Brazilian history tour, with visits to a cemetery, a museum and other spots.

Madson Araújo (☎ 9395 3537; www.tourguiderio.com) English-speaking guide offering custom-made day- or night tours around Rio.

Marcelo Esteves (☎ 9984 7654; marafes@terra.com.br) A multilingual Rio expert offering private tours around the city.

Favela Tours

The pioneer of favela tourism, **Marcelo Armstrong** (☎ 3322 2727, 9989 0074; www.favelatour.com.br; per person R$60), takes small groups on half-day tours to the favelas of Rocinha and Vila Canoas near São Conrado. The itinerary includes an explanation of the architecture and social infrastructure of the favela – particularly in relation to greater Rio de Janeiro. The trip also includes a walk through the streets, and a stop at both a community center and a handicraft center where visitors can purchase colorful artwork made by locals. A portion of Marcelo's profits goes toward social causes in the favela. To avoid paying a commission, call him direct (don't book through hotels or other middle men).

Alternatively, you could try **Be A Local** (☎ 9643 0366; www.bealocal.com.br; per person R$60-120), a popular outfit that offers daily trips into Rocinha (you'll ride up by motor-taxi, and walk back down), with stops along the way. Be a Local also organizes a night out at a *baile* funk party in Castelo das Pedras on Sunday night, and organizes trips to Maracanã on game days.

Helicopter Tours

In business since 1991, **Helisight** (☎ 2511 2141; www.helisight.com.br; per person R$150-875) offers eight different tours, lasting from six minutes to 60 minutes. From one of its four helipads, helicopters travel around Cristo Redentor, from where you can get a bird's-eye view of Rio's most famous monument. Helisight also has flights over the Parque Nacional da Tijuca and above the mountains and beaches. Helipad locations are in Parque Nacional da Tijuca facing Corcovado; on Morro da Urca, the first cable-car stop up Pão de Açúcar; on the edge of Lagoa; and Pier Mauá downtown at the docks.

Jeep Tours

Excursions led by Jeep Tour (☎ 2108 5800; www.jeeptour.com.br) travel to the lush Parque Nacional da Tijuca in a large, convertible jeep. Four-hour tours, which cost around R$80 per person, consist of a stop at the Vista Chinesa, then on to the forest for an easy hike, and a stop for a swim beneath a waterfall, before making the return journey. On the way back, you'll stop at Praia do Pepino, the landing strip for hang gliders from nearby Pedra Bonita. Other excursions offered by Jeep Tour include trips to Angra dos Reis (where forest meets sea) and a coffee *fazenda* (plantation). The price of all tours includes pick up and drop off at your hotel.

Or if you are looking for a unique four-wheel-drive adventure, Hoca Tour (☎ 3472 7576; www.hocatour.com.br; per person R$200-300) is unmatched. This outfit runs small group excursions west of town along rutted roads, launching over dunes and splashing through rivers. Trips last between four and 12 hours, and include stops for beachside swims, a dip in a waterfall, plus lunch (not included) at a restaurant in the countryside.

Tram Tours

Run by the Museu do Bonde (Tram Museum), Bonde Historico (☎ 2240 5709, 2524 2508; per person R$6; 10am Sat) offers guided tours of the Santa Teresa neighborhood to illuminate historic points along the journey from downtown to Silvestre and back, with a stop at the Museu do Bonde. Trams depart every Saturday at 10am, from the tram station (*bonde* to Santa Teresa) on Rua Lélio Gama in Centro.

Walking Tours

Run by art historian Professor Carlos Roquette, who speaks English and French as well as Portuguese, Cultural Rio (☎ 9911 3829; www.culturalrio.com.br; tours from R$100) offers visitors an in-depth look at social and historical aspects of Rio de Janeiro. Roquette has a wealth of Carioca knowledge (and a quirky sense of humor) and he feels as comfortable discussing Jobim and the bossa nova scene as he does the sexual indiscretions of the early Portuguese rulers. Itineraries include a night at the Theatro Municipal, colonial Rio, baroque Rio, imperial Rio and a walking tour of Centro. He's been in business for over 20 years, and has led thousands of private walking tours.

POST

Postal services are decent in Brazil, and most mail seems to get through. Airmail letters to the USA and Europe usually arrive in a week or two. For Australia and Asia, allow three weeks.

There are yellow mailboxes on the street, but it's safer to go to a *corréió* (post office). Most *corréiós* are open 8am to 6pm Monday to Friday, and until noon on Saturday.

Other branches include Botafogo (Map pp78–9; Praia do Botafogo 324), Ipanema (Map p64; Rua Prudente de Morais 147) and Copacabana (Map pp76–7; Av NS de Copacabana 540).

Any mail addressed to Poste Restante, Rio de Janeiro, Brazil, ends up at the post office in Centro (Map pp90–1; Rua Primeiro de Março 64). The post office will hold mail for 30 days and is reasonably efficient. A reliable alternative for American Express customers is to have mail sent to the American Express office (Map pp76–7; ☎ 2548 7056; Level 1, Av Atlântica 1702, Copacabana).

SAFETY

Rio gets a lot of bad international press about violence, and unfortunately it's not all hype. The crime rate is high, and tourists are sometimes targeted. To minimize your risk of becoming a victim, you should take some basic precautions. First off: dress down and leave expensive (or even expensive-*looking*) jewelry, watches and sunglasses at home.

Copacabana and Ipanema beaches have a police presence, but robberies still occur on the sands, even in broad daylight. Don't ever take anything of value with you to the beach. Late at night, don't walk on any of the beaches.

Buses are well-known targets for thieves. Avoid taking them after dark, and keep an eye out while you're on them. Take taxis at night to avoid walking along empty streets and beaches. That holds especially true for Centro, which becomes deserted in the evening and on weekends, and is better explored during the week.

Get in the habit of carrying only the money you'll need for the day, so you don't have to flash a wad of *reais* when you pay for things. Cameras and backpacks attract a lot of attention. Consider using disposable cameras while you're in town; plastic shopping bags also nicely disguise whatever you're carrying. Maracanã football stadium is worth a visit, but take only your spending money for the day and avoid the crowded sections. Don't wander into the favelas at any time, unless you go with a knowledgeable guide.

If you have the misfortune of being robbed, slowly hand over the goods. Thieves in the city are only too willing to use their weapons if given provocation.

TELEPHONE

Rio is not known for its efficient telephone service, which hasn't improved much after privatization. Lines cross and fail frequently. The only solution is to keep trying.

Public phones are nicknamed *orelhôes* (floppy ears). They take a *cartão telefônico* (phonecard), which are available from newsstands and street vendors. The cheapest cards start at R$5 for 20 units. All calls in Brazil, including local ones, are timed. Generally, one unit is enough for a brief local call (but calls to cell phones will quickly burn through your phonecard). The phone will display how many units your card has left. Unless you're very lucky, you will have to try at least two or three phones before you find one that works.

Wait for a dial tone and then insert your phonecard and dial your number. For information, call ☎ 102. The Portuguese-speaking operator can usually transfer you to an English-speaking operator.

To phone Rio from outside Brazil, dial your international access code, then 55 (Brazil's country code), 21 (Rio's area code) and the number.

Cell Phones

The cell phone is ubiquitous in Rio and goes by the name *celular* (this is also the nickname given to hip flasks of liquor).

Cell phones have eight-digit numbers, which usually begin with '9' or '8'. If you have an unlocked GSM phone (using the 900MHz and 1800MHz wavelengths, the same as used in Europe), you can simply buy a SIM card (called a *chip*) for around R$10 to R$16. To buy the card, you'll need your passport or at least a copy of it. Among the major carriers of Tim, Vivo, Oi and Claro, most Cariocas rate Tim as having the best, most hassle-free service. You can then add minutes by purchasing *cartões pre-pago* (pre-paid cards) from any newspaper stand. Cards come in denominations of R$20, R$40, R$60, which you'll burn through at the rate of around R$1.80 per minute for a local call.

If you'd rather rent a phone, ConnectCom (☎ 2215 0002; www.connectcomrj.com.br) has the goods, and will even deliver to your door. With advance notice, they'll also give you a number before you arrive. Phone rental is R$10 a day plus call charges.

Long-Distance & International Calls

International calls aren't cheap in Brazil. If you haven't heard of Skype (www.skype.com) and plan to make long-distance calls from Brazil, we highly recommend you acquaint yourself with this service. Skype will allow you to make free or very inexpensive international calls from many internet cafés, hostels and guesthouses.

If you'd rather call from a landline, your best bet is buying an Embratel phonecard from a newsstand (sold in denominations of R$20 and R$80). These have a bar on the back that you scratch off to reveal a code to enter along with the number you are calling (instructions are printed on the cards in English and Portuguese). You can make calls through some pay phones. Rates run about R$2 a minute for calls to the US, R$3 a minute to Europe and about twice that to Asia and Australia.

Many internet cafés in Copacabana also have private phone booths for making calls. Rates, which fluctuate quite a bit, generally run at about R$1 to R$2 per minute for calls to the US and Europe, and much more to Australia and Asia. In Copacabana, try Telenet (Map pp76–7; Rua Domingos Ferreira 59, Copacabana; 9am-10pm Mon-Sat, 11am-9pm Sun), Telerede (Map pp76–7; Av NS de Copacabana 209A, Copacabana; 8am-2am) or Locutório (Map pp76–7; Av NS Copacabana 1171, Copacabana; 8am-2am). In the center of town there is Central Fone (Map pp90–1; basement level, Av Rio Branco 156, Centro; 9am-9pm Mon-Fri, 10am-4pm Sat). In Ipanema, Central Fone (Map p64; Level B, Rua Vinícius de Moraes 129, Ipanema; 9.30am-8pm Mon-Fri, 11am-6pm Sat & Sun) also offers international phone calls.

To make a call to other parts of Brazil, you need to select the telephone company you want to use. To do this, you must insert a two-digit number between the 0 and the area code of the place you're calling. For example, to call Búzios from Rio, you need to dial ☎ 0 + xx + 22 (0 + phone company code + Búzios city code) + the seven- or eight-digit number. Embratel (code 21), Intelig (code 23) and TIM (code 41) are several big carriers.

Unfortunately, you cannot make collect calls from telephone offices. Public phones and those in hotels are your best bet. For calling collect within Rio dial ☎ 9090 + phone number; to call collect within Brazil, dial ☎ 90 + phone company code + area code + phone number. A recorded message (in Portuguese) will ask you to say your name and where you're calling from after the beep. For international collect calls, try dialing ☎ 0800-703-2111.

TIME

Brazil has four official time zones. Rio, in the southeastern region, is three hours behind Greenwich Mean Time (GMT) and four hours behind during the northern hemisphere summer. Rio also observes daylight savings time, pushing the clocks one hour forward from late November to late February.

TOURIST INFORMATION

Riotur is the generally useful Rio city tourism agency. It operates a tourist information hot line called Alô Rio (☎ 0800 285 0555, 2542 8080; 9am-6pm). The receptionists speak English and are very helpful. Riotur's useful multilingual website, at www.riodejaneiro-turismo.com.br, is also a good source of information.

All of the Riotur offices distribute maps and the bimonthly *Rio Guide*, which is packed with information and major seasonal events. You'll find information kiosks at the following locations:

Centro (Map pp90–1; ☎ 2271 7000; 9th fl, Praça Pio X; 9am-6pm Mon-Fri)

Copacabana (Map pp76–7; ☎ 2541 7522; Av Princesa Isabel 183; 9am-6pm Mon-Fri)

Galeão airport Terminal 1 (Domestic Arrival Hall; ☎ 3398 3034; 7am-11pm); Terminal 2 (International Arrival Hall; ☎ 3398 2245; 6am-11pm)

Novo Rio bus station (Map pp60–1; ☎ 2263 4857; Av Francisco Bicalho 1, São Cristóvão; 8am-7pm)

TRAVELERS WITH DISABILITIES

Rio is probably the most accessible city in Brazil for disabled travelers to get around, but that doesn't mean it's always easy. It's convenient to hire cars with driver-guides, but for only one person the expense is quite high compared to the cost of the average bus tour. If there are several people to share the cost, it's definitely worth it.

The metro system has electronic wheelchair lifts, but it's difficult to know whether they're actually functional. Major sites are only partially accessible – there are about 10 steps to the gondola base of Pão de Açúcar for instance; and although there is access to the base of Cristo Redentor, there are about two dozen steps to reach the statue itself.

The streets and sidewalks along the main beaches have curb cuts and are wheelchair accessible, but most other areas do not have cuts. Many restaurants have entrance steps, and most of the newer hotels have accessible rooms.

The Centro de Vida Independente (Map pp70–1; ☎ 2512 1088; www.cvi-rio.org.br in Portuguese; Rua Marquês de São Vicente 225, Gávea) can provide advice for travelers with disabilities visiting Brazil.

Those in the USA might like to contact the Society for Accessible Travel & Hospitality (SATH; ☎ 212-447 7284; www.sath.org). SATH's website is a good resource for disabled travelers. Another excellent website to check is www.access-able.com.

VISAS

Brazil has a reciprocal visa system, so if your home country requires Brazilian nationals to secure a visa, then you will need one to enter Brazil. US, Canadian, Australian and New Zealand citizens need visas, but UK and French citizens do not. You can check your status with the Brazilian embassy or consulate in your home country.

Tourist visas are issued by Brazilian diplomatic offices. They are valid upon arrival in Brazil for a 90-day stay. They are renewable in Brazil for an additional 90 days. In most Brazilian embassies and consulates, visas can be processed within 24 hours. You will need to present one passport photograph, a round-trip or onward ticket (or a photocopy of it), and a valid passport. If you decide to return to Brazil, your visa is valid for five years.

The fee for visas is also reciprocal. It's usually between US$20 and US$50, though for US citizens visas cost US$100.

Applicants under 18 years of age wanting to travel to Brazil must also submit a notarized letter of authorization from a parent or legal guardian.

Business travelers may need a business visa. These are also valid for 90 days and have the same requirements as a tourist visa. You'll need a letter on your company letterhead addressed to the Brazilian embassy or consulate, stating your business in Brazil, your arrival and departure dates and your contacts. The letter from your employer must also assume full financial and moral(!) responsibility for you during your stay.

For up-to-the-minute advice on visa requirements for Brazil, check the Lonely Planet website at www.lonelyplanet.com.

Entry/Exit Card

On entering Brazil, all tourists must fill out a *cartão de entrada/saida* (entry/exit card); immigration officials will keep half, you keep the other. They will also stamp your passport and, if for some reason they are not granting you the usual 90-day stay in Brazil, the number of days will be written beneath the word *Prazo* (Period) on the stamp in your passport.

When you leave Brazil, the second half of the entry/exit card will be taken by immigration officials. *Tip: Don't lose your card while in Brazil! If you do lose it, you could miss your flight dealing with immigration hassles.* Typically, if you lose the card you'll be required to pay a fine (upwards of R$150) at the Banco do Brasil before you're allowed to leave.

WOMEN TRAVELERS

In Rio, foreign women traveling alone will scarcely be given a sideways glance. Although machismo is an undeniable element in the Brazilian social structure, it is less overt here than in many other parts of Latin America. Flirtation (often exaggerated) is a prominent element in Brazilian male-female relations. It goes both ways and is nearly always regarded as amusingly innocent banter. You should be able to stop unwelcome attention by merely expressing displeasure.

WORK

Brazil has high unemployment, and visitors who enter the country as tourists are not legally allowed to take jobs. It's not unusual for foreigners to find work teaching English in language schools. The pay isn't great (if you hustle you can make around R$1500 a month), but you can still live on it. For this kind of work it's always helpful to speak some Portuguese, although some schools insist that only English be spoken in class. Private language tutoring may pay a little more, but you'll have to do some legwork to find students.

To get this type of work, log on to a Brazilian web server like terra (www.terra.com.br in Portuguese) or uol (www.uol.com.br in Portuguese) and search for English academies. You should also ask around at the English-language schools.

Volunteering

Río Voluntário (☎ 2262 1110; www.riovoluntario.org.br in Portuguese), headquartered in Rio de Janeiro, supports several hundred volunteer organizations, from those involved in social work and the environment to health care. It's an excel lent resource for finding volunteer work.

One notable volunteer organization is Rio-based Iko Poran (☎ 04121-2205 1365; www.ikoporan.org), which links the diverse talents of volunteers with needy organizations. Previous volunteers have worked as dance, music, art and language instructors among other things. Iko Poran also provides housing for volunteers.

Several other local organizations that currently accept volunteers and donations: Família Santa Clara (www.familiasantaclara.org.br), an orphan age that helps at-risk children, and Projeto Uerê (www.projetouere.org.br), which helps youth in poor communities in Rio.

The UK-based Task Brasil (www.taskbrasil.org.uk) is another laudable organization that places volunteers in Rio. Here, you'll have to make arrangements in advance and pay a fee that will go toward Task Brasil projects and your expenses as a volunteer.

See Action Without Borders (www.idealist.org) for the best volunteer opportunities.

LANGUAGE

Portuguese is one of the top 10 or so most commonly spoken languages in the world, with around 200 million speakers globally. The majority of them – 186 million at last count – hail from Brazil, the only Portuguese-speaking country in South America. Brazilian Portuguese differs from European Portuguese, owing in part to New World influences: Portuguese colonists first arrived in the 16th century, and as they came into contact with the Tupi tribes living along the Atlantic coast, they adopted the Tupi language to such an extent that Tupi, along with Portuguese, became the lingua franca of the colony. The Jesuits had a great deal to do with this, since they translated prayers and songs into Tupi, and in so doing recorded and promoted the language. The situation lasted only as long as the priests. Tupi was banned when the crown expelled the Jesuits in 1759, and Portuguese remained the country's official language.

Tupi wasn't the only language to have an influence on the development of Brazilian Portuguese. In the 19th century, the Bantu and Yoruba languages arrived in Brazil, brought by African slaves. At the same time, European Portuguese went through linguistic changes as it came in contact with French (Napoleon Bonaparte, who invaded Portugal, played his part in the semantic evolution), while Brazilian Portuguese retained some of its earlier features. Today the differences between the two variations are about as pronounced as those between American English and British English.

Although Portuguese shares many lexical similarities with its romance-language cousin Spanish, the two are quite different. Spanish speakers will be able to read many things in Portuguese, but will have great difficulty understanding Brazilians. English is still not commonly taught in Brazil, except in the more exclusive private schools. Fortunately Brazilians are quite patient, and they appreciate any effort to speak their language. If you want to learn more of the lingo than we've included here, pick up a copy of Lonely Planet's comprehensive but user-friendly *Brazilian Portuguese Phrasebook*.

PRONUNCIATION

A characteristic of Brazilian Portuguese is the use of nasal vowels. Nasalization is represented by n or m after a vowel, or by a tilde over it (eg ã). The nasal i exists only approximately in English, with the 'ing' in 'sing', for example. Nasal vowels are pronounced as if you're trying to force the sound out your nose rather than your mouth, creating a similar sound to when you hold your nose.

SOCIAL

Meeting People

Hello.
Olá.
Hi.
Oi.
Goodbye.
Tchau.
Please.
Por favor.
Thank you (very much).
(Muito) obrigado/obrigada.
Yes/No.
Sim/Não.
Excuse me.
Com licença.
Sorry.
Desculpa.
Do you speak (English)?
Você fala (inglês)?
Do you understand?
Você entende?
I (don't) understand.
Eu (não) entendo.

Could you please ...?
Você poderia por favor ...?

repeat that	repetir istos
speak more slowly	falar mais devagar
write it down	escrever num papel

Going Out

What's on ...?
O que está acontecendo ...?

locally	aqui perto
this weekend	neste final de semana
today/tonight	hoje/á noite

OI, CARA! (HEY, GUY/GAL)

A few phrases and gestures can go a long way in Brazil, and making an effort with the language – or getting your point across – is something Brazilians will greatly appreciate. *Diria* (slang) is a big part of the Carioca dialect spoken by the residents of Rio. Here are a few words and phrases to help you along.

babaca (ba·*ba*·ka) – jerk
bunda (*boon*·da) – bottom/arse
Eu gosto de você. (*e*·oo *gosh*·too zhi vo·*se*) – I like you.
Falou! (fa·*low*) – Absolutely!/You said it!.
Fique à vontade. (feek a van·*tazh*) – Make yourself at home.
fio dental (*fee*·oo den·*tow*) – dental floss, aka bikini
gata/gato (*ga*·ta/*ga*·too) – good-looking woman/man
Nossa! (*no*·sa; lit, 'Our Lady') – Gosh!/You don't say!
sunga (*soong*·ga) – tiny Speedo-type swim shorts favored by Carioca men
Ta ótimo/Ta legal! (ta *a*·che·moo/ta lee·*gow*) – Great/Cool/OK!
Tudo bem? (*too*·doo beng) – Everything OK?
Tudo bem. (*too*·doo beng) – Everything's OK.
Valeu. (va·*le*·o) – Thanks.
Vamu nessa! (va·moo·*ne*·sa) – Let's go!

Where can I find ...?
Onde posso encontrar ...?

clubs	um lugar para dançar
gay venues	lugares gays
places to eat	lugares para comer
pubs	um bar

Is there a local entertainment guide?
Existe algum guia de entretenimento dessa área?

PRACTICAL

Question Words

Who?	Quem?
What?	(o) que?
When?	Quando?
Where?	Onde?
How?	Como é que?
Why?	Por que?
Which?	Qual/Quais? (sg/pl)

Numbers & Amounts

0	zero
1	um
2	dois
3	três
4	quatro
5	cinco
6	seis
7	sete
8	oito
9	nove
10	dez
11	onze
12	doze
13	treze
14	quatorze
15	quinze
16	dezesseis
17	dezesete
18	dezoito
19	dezenove
20	vinte
21	vinte e um
22	vinte e dois
30	trinta
40	quarenta
50	cinquenta
60	sessenta
70	setenta
80	oitenta
90	noventa
100	cem
200	duzentos
1000	mil

Days

Monday	segunda-feira
Tuesday	terça-feira
Wednesday	quarta-feira
Thursday	quinta-feira
Friday	sexta-feira
Saturday	sábado
Sunday	domingo

Banking

Where's ...?
Onde tem ...?

an automated teller machine	um caixa automático
a foreign exchange office	uma loja de câmbio

Where can I ...?
Onde posso ...?
I'd like to ...
Gostaria de ...

cash a check	descontar um cheque
change money	trocar dinheiro
change travelers checks	trocar traveller cheques

Post

Where is the post office?
Onde fica o correio?

I want to send a ...
Quero enviar ...

fax	um fax
letter	uma carta
parcel	uma encomenda
postcard	um cartão-postal

I want to buy ...
Quero comprar ...

an aerogram	um aerograma
an envelope	um envelope
stamps	selos

Phones & Cell/Mobiles

I want to make ...
Quero ...

a call (to ...)	telefonar (para ...)
a reverse-charge/ collect call	fazer uma chamada a cobrar

I'd like a/an ...
Eu gostaria de ...

adaptor plug	comprar um adaptador
battery for my phone	comprar uma bateria para o meu telephone
cell/mobile phone for hire	alugar um cellular
phone card	comprar um cartão telefônico
prepaid cell/ mobile phone	comprar um cellular pré-pago
SIM card for your network	comprar um cartão SIM para sua rede

Internet

Where's the local Internet café?
Onde tem um internet café na redondeza?

I'd like to ...
Gostaria de ...

check my email	checar meu e-mail
get online	ter acesso à internet

Transport

When's the ... (bus)?
Quando sai o ... (ônibus)?

first	primeiro
last	último
next	próximo

What time does it leave?
Que horas sai?
What time does it get to (Parati)?
Que horas chega em (Parati)?

Which ... goes to (Niterói)?
Qual o ... que vai para (Niterói)?

boat	barco
bus	ônibus
plane	avião
train	trem

Is this taxi free?
Este táxi está livre?
Please put the meter on.
Por favor ligue o taxímetro.
How much is it to ...?
Quanto custa até ...?
Please take me to (this address).
Me leve para (este endereço) por favor.

FOOD

breakfast	café da manhã
lunch	almoço
dinner	jantar
snack	lanche

Can you recommend a ...?
Você pode recomendar um ...?

bar/pub	bar
café	café
restaurant	restaurante

Is service/cover charge included in the bill?
O serviço está incluído na conta?

See p128 for more information on food and dining out.

EMERGENCIES

Help!
Socorro!
It's an emergency.
É uma emergência.
Could you please help?
Você pode ajudar, por favor?
Call a doctor/an ambulance!
Chame um médico/uma ambulância!
Call the police!
Chame a polícia!
Where's the police station?
Onde é a delegacia de polícia?

BRAZILIAN DISHES

Acarajé A specialty of Bahia made from peeled brown beans mashed with salt and onions, and then fried in *dendê* (palm oil). Inside these delicious croquettes is *vatapá* (dried shrimp, pepper and tomato sauce).
Angú A kind of savory cake made with very fine corn flour called *fubá,* mixed with water and salt.
Bobó de camarão Manioc paste cooked and flavored with dried shrimp, coconut milk and cashew nuts.
Camarão á paulista Unshelled fresh prawns (shrimp) fried in olive oil with lots of garlic and salt.
Canja A hearty soup made with chicken broth; often a meal in itself.
Carangueijada Crab cooked whole in seasoned water.
Carne de sol A tasty salt-cured meat, grilled and served with beans, rice and vegetables.
Caruru A popular Brazilian dish of African origin, *caruru* is made with boiled okra or other vegetables mixed with grated onion, salt, shrimp, chili peppers and *dendê*. Traditionally, a saltwater fish such as *garoupa* (grouper) is added.
Casquinha de carangueijo or siri Stuffed crab, prepared with manioc flour.
Cozido Any kind of stew, usually with vegetables (such as potatoes, sweet potatoes, carrots and manioc).
Dendê Palm oil; decidedly strong stuff. Many non-Brazilian stomachs can't handle it.
Dourado A scrumptious freshwater fish found throughout Brazil.
Farofa Otherwise known as cassava or manioc flour, it is a legacy of the Indians, for whom it has traditionally been an essential dietary ingredient; it remains a Brazilian staple.
Feijoada The Carioca answer to cassoulet. See p132
Frango ao molho pardo Chicken pieces stewed with vegetables and covered with a seasoned sauce made from the blood of the bird.
Moqueca A kind of sauce or stew, as well as a style of cooking from Bahia, which is properly prepared in a covered clay pot. Fish, shrimp, oyster, crab or a combination of those are served with a *moqueca* sauce, which is defined by its heavy use of *dendê* and coconut milk, and often contains peppers and onions.
Moqueca capixaba A *moqueca* from Espírito Santo that uses lighter *urucum* (from the seeds of the berrylike fruit of the annatto tree) oil from the Indians instead of *dendê*.
Pato no tucupi Roast duck flavored with garlic and cooked in *tucupi* sauce, which is made from the juice of the manioc plant and *jambu,* a local vegetable. A very popular dish in Pará.
Peixada Fish cooked in broth with vegetables and eggs.
Peixe a delicia Broiled fish usually served in a sauce made with bananas and coconut milk.
Petiscos Appetizers.
Picanha Thin cut of rump steak.
Prato de verão Literally, a 'summer plate,' which is served at many juice stands in Rio. It's basically a fruit salad.
Prato feito Literally a 'made plate,' usually a serving of rice, beans and salad, with chicken, fish or beef. Sometimes abbreviated to 'PF'.
Pirarucu ao forno *Pirarucu,* the most famous fish from the rivers of Amazônia, baked with lemon and other seasonings.
Tacacá An Indian dish of dried shrimp cooked with pepper, *jambu,* manioc and much more.
Tutu á mineira A bean paste with toasted bacon and manioc flour, often served with cooked cabbage.
Vatapá A seafood dish with a thick sauce made from manioc paste, coconut and *dendê*. Perhaps the most famous Brazilian dish of African origin.
Xinxim de galinha Pieces of chicken flavored with garlic, salt and lemon. Shrimp and *dendê* are often added.

HEALTH

Where's the nearest ...?
Onde fica ... mais perto?

(night) chemist	a farmácia (noturna)
dentist	o dentista
doctor	o médico
hospital	o hospital
medical centre	a clínica médica

I'm ill.
Estou doente.

I need a doctor (who speaks English).
Eu preciso de um médico (que fale inglês).

I have (a) ...
Tenho ...

diarrhoea	diarréia
fever	febre
nausea	náusea
pain	dor
sore throat	dor de garganta

GLOSSARY

See p55 for more Carnaval terms.

açaí – juice made from an Amazonian berry
agouti – small rodent; looks like a large guinea pig
a quilo – per kilo

baía – bay
baile – dance party in the favelas
baile funk – dance, ball
bairro – neighborhood
baixo – popular area with lots of restaurants and bars
banda – street party
barraca – food stall
batida – mixes of *cachaça*, sugar and assorted fruit juices
berimbau – stringed instrument used to accompany *capoeira*
bloco – see *banda*
bonde – tram
bondinho – little tram
boteco – small neighborhood bar
botequim – bar with table service

cachaça – potent cane spirit
caipirinha – *cachaça* cocktail
câmbios – money exchange
Candomblé – religion of African origin
capoeira – Afro-Brazilian martial art
capela – chapel
cara – guy, dude (slang term used for male or female)
Carioca – resident of Rio
carro – car
cartão telefônico – phone card
celular – cellular (mobile) phone
cerveja – beer
cervejaria – pub
chocante – cool, excellent
chope – draft beer
chorinho or choro – romantic, intimate samba
churrascaria – traditional barbecue restaurant
cidade maravilhosa – nickname for Rio de Janeiro (literally 'marvelous city')
convento – convent
corréio – post office

escola de samba – samba school
estação do metro – metro (subway) station
estrada – road

farmácia – pharmacy (chemist)
favela – shanty town
fazenda – ranch, plantation, large farm
feijoada – black beans and pork stew
feira – open-air market
festa – party
forró – traditional fast-paced music from the northeast of Brazil
frescão – air-conditioned bus
frescobol – game played on the beach with two wooden racquets and a rubber ball
futebol – football (soccer)

gafieira – dance club/dance hall
gente – people

igreja – church
ilha – island

jardim – garden

lagoa – lake
largo – plaza
legal – cool, excellent
livraria – bookshop

malandros – con men
mar – sea
Mata Atlântica – Atlantic rainforest
mirante – lookout
morro – mountain
mulatto – person of mixed black and white ancestry
museu – museum

novela – TV soap opera

onibus – bus
orelhôes – public telephones
orixá – spirit or deity of the Candomblé religion

pagode – relaxed and rhythmic form of samba; first popularized in Rio in the 1970s
parque – park
ponte – bridge
posto – lifeguard station
pousada – guest house
praça – square
praia – beach

reais – plural of *real*
real – Brazil's unit of currency
refrigerante – soft drink
rio – river
rodoviária – bus terminal
rua – street

salgados – bar snacks
sobreloja – above the store; first floor up
suco – juice bar
supermercado – supermarket

trem – train

Zona Norte – Northern Zone
Zona Sul – Southern Zone

BEHIND THE SCENES

THIS BOOK

This 6th edition of Rio de Janeiro was written by Regis St Louis, with contributions from Dan Littauer (Gay Rio, p170), Carmen Michael (Rio's Malandros, p32; The Dance Halls of Old, p36; Samba da Mesa p166), Tom Phillips (Brazil's Favorite Politico, p38; Baile Funks, p168) and Marcos Silviano do Prado (Carnaval Party Planner, p51). Regis also wrote the 4th and 5th editions, while editions one to three were written by Andrew Draffen, with contributions from Heather Schlegel on the 3rd edition. This guidebook was commissioned in Lonely Planet's Oakland office and produced by:

Commissioning Editors Jennye Garibaldi, Kathleen Munnelly

Coordinating Editor Dianne Schallmeiner

Coordinating Cartographer Anthony Phelan

Coordinating Layout Designer David Kemp

Managing Editor Geoff Howard

Managing Cartographer Alison Lyall

Managing Layout Designers Adam McCrow, Celia Wood

Assisting Editors Anna Metcalfe, Helen Yeates

Assisting Cartographers Jolyon Philcox, Andrew Smith

Assisting Layout Designers Katherine Marsh, Cara Smith

Cover Designer Pepi Bluck

Project Manager Eoin Dunlevy

Language Content Coordinator Quentin Frayne

Thanks to Lisa Knights, Wayne Murphy, Michael Ruff, Sarah Sloane, Adam Stanford

Cover photographs Carnaval dancer using public telephone at Copacabana Beach, Tom Morrison/Getty Images (top); Window and door of house in Jardim Botânico district, John Pennock/Lonely Planet Images (bottom).

Internal photographs by Lonely Planet Images, and by John Maier Jr p4 (#2 & 3), p5 (#4, 6 & 7), p6 (#2), p7 (#4 & 6), p8 (#2), p9 (#4 & 5), p10 (#4), p11 (#1), p12 (#3), p13 (#5, 6 & 7), p14 (#2 & 3), p15 (#5 & 6), p16 (#2 & 4); Ricardo Gomes p3, p4 (#1), p5 (#5), p7 (#5), p8 (#3), p9 (#6 & 7), p10 (#2), p11 (#2 & 4), p12 (#2), p13 (#4), p14 (#1), p15 (#4 & 7), p16 (#1 & 3); John Pennock p2, p6 (#1), p10 (#3), p11 (#3), p12 (#1); Judy Bellah p6 (#3), p8 (#1); Lee Foster p10 (#1).

THANKS

REGIS ST LOUIS

In Rio many people helped along the way, and I'm grateful to all who provided advice and friendship. I'd like to thank Marta Miller for her hospitality, Cristiano Nogueira and friends for great nights out in Rio, Marcelo Castro for some superb adventures, Aurélio Curtim for Rocinha fun and Cândida Botafogo for her kindness (and obvious cooking talents). I'd also like to thank all the readers who wrote in with suggestions. At Lonely Planet, I'd like to thank Kathleen Munnelly and all the behind-the-scenes talents for superb work on this edition. Lastly, *beijos* to the women of my life, Casssandra and Magdalena.

THE LONELY PLANET STORY

Fresh from an epic journey across Europe, Asia and Australia in 1972, Tony and Maureen Wheeler sat at their kitchen table stapling together notes. The first Lonely Planet guidebook, *Across Asia on the Cheap*, was born.

Travelers snapped up the guides. Inspired by their success, the Wheelers began publishing books to Southeast Asia, India and beyond. Demand was prodigious, and the Wheelers expanded the business rapidly to keep up. Over the years, Lonely Planet extended its coverage to every country and into the virtual world via lonelyplanet.com and the Thorn Tree message board.

As Lonely Planet became a globally loved brand, Tony and Maureen received several offers for the company. But it wasn't until 2007 that they found a partner whom they trusted to remain true to the company's principles of traveling widely, treading lightly and giving sustainably. In October of that year, BBC Worldwide acquired a 75% share in the company, pledging to uphold Lonely Planet's commitment to independent travel, trustworthy advice and editorial independence.

Today, Lonely Planet has offices in Melbourne, London and Oakland, with over 500 staff members and 300 authors. Tony and Maureen are still actively involved with Lonely Planet. They're traveling more often than ever, and they're devoting their spare time to charitable projects. And the company is still driven by the philosophy of *Across Asia on the Cheap*: 'All you've got to do is decide to go and the hardest part is over. So go!'

OUR READERS

Many thanks to the travelers who used the last edition and wrote to us with helpful hints, useful advice and interesting anecdotes:

Alex Angeloudes, Pascal Bardouil, Benedetta Bini, Annabelle Binns, Geoff Brandt, Jennan Carnell, Vicki Chan, Melonie Chapman, Dorothy Chatwin, Piotr Chrusciel, Thalita Coelho, Vasco Almeida E Costa, Paulo Dias, Tim Farnsworth, John Guy, Barb Harvey, Steve Hazel, Dick Hazelwood, Nicole Hoff, Dubeaux Ingrid, Cameron James, Philipp Lamprecht, Kimberly Lasalandra, Davina Maiolo, William Millard, Susan Monteiro, Andreea Nicoara, Emilia Nieminen, Leo Otte, Sara Pavanello, Scott Pearson, Fabrice Perrier, Korey Pulas, Kathryn Radford, Marcelo Rodel, Harvey Schwartz, Charlieu Stephen, Yvonne Tan, Paul Toombs, Danielle Uzeda, Susanne Wolfgarten, Jeane Yarrow, Nenad Zivanovic

SEND US YOUR FEEDBACK

We love to hear from travelers – your comments keep us on our toes and help make our books better. Our well-traveled team reads every word on what you loved or loathed about this book. Although we cannot reply individually to postal submissions, we always guarantee that your feedback goes straight to the appropriate authors, in time for the next edition. Each person who sends us information is thanked in the next edition – and the most useful submissions are rewarded with a free book.

To send us your updates – and find out about Lonely Planet events, newsletters and travel news – visit our award-winning website: www.lonelyplanet.com/contact.

Note: We may edit, reproduce and incorporate your comments in Lonely Planet products such as guidebooks, websites and digital products, so let us know if you don't want your comments reproduced or your name acknowledged. For a copy of our privacy policy visit www.lonelyplanet.com/privacy.

Notes

Notes

INDEX

See also separate indexes for:

000 map pages
000 photographs

ARTS

CINEMA

PERFORMING ARTS

DRINKING

EATING

AMAZONIAN

BAHIAN

BISTRO

BRAZILIAN

BUFFET

CAFE

CHURRASCARIA

CONTEMPORARY

CREPERIE

DELI

ECLECTIC

FEIJOADA

FRENCH

FRENCH THAI

FRUIT MARKET

GERMAN

ICE CREAM

ITALIAN

JAPANESE

JUICE BAR

LEBANESE

MIDDLE EASTERN

PATISSERIE

PERUVIAN

PIZZA

PORTUGUESE

SALAD BAR

SANDWICHES

000 map pages
000 photographs

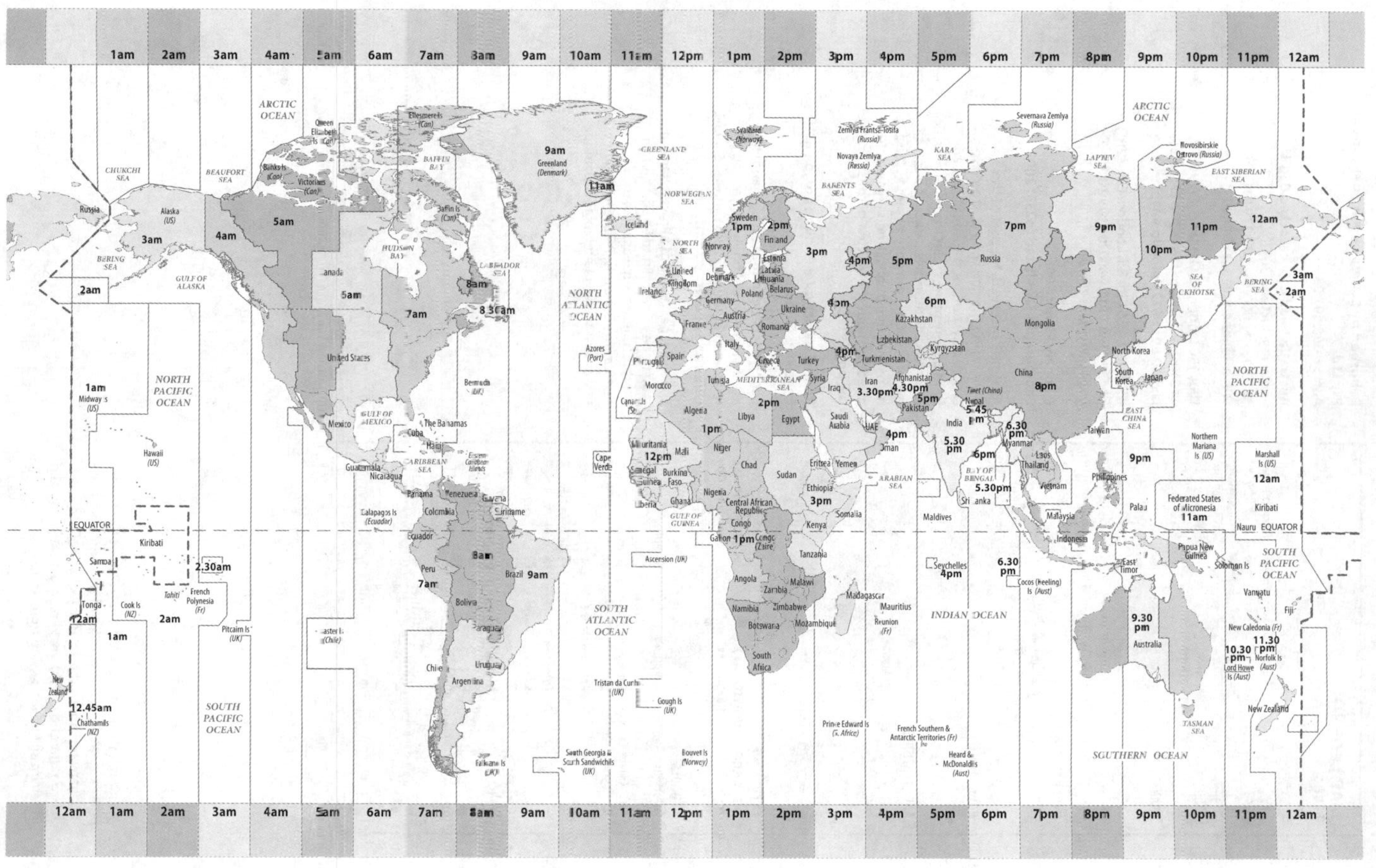

1am
2am
3am
4am
5am
6am
7am
8am
9am
10am
11am
12pm
1pm
2pm
3pm
4pm
5pm
6pm
7pm
8pm
9pm
10pm
11pm
12am
ARCTIC OCEAN
CHUKCHI SEA
BERING SEA
BEAUFORT SEA
GULF OF ALASKA
NORTH PACIFIC OCEAN
SOUTH PACIFIC OCEAN
EQUATOR
Russia
Alaska (US)
Hawaii (US)
Midway Is (US)
Kiribati
Samoa
Tonga
Cook Is (NZ)
Tahiti
French Polynesia (Fr)
Pitcairn Is (UK)
Chathams (NZ)
New Zealand
12.45am
2.30am
Banks Is (Can)
Victoria Is (Can)
Queen Elizabeth Is (Can)
Ellesmere Is (Can)
Baffin Is (Can)
BAFFIN BAY
HUDSON BAY
LABRADOR SEA
Canada
United States
Mexico
GULF OF MEXICO
Cuba
The Bahamas
Haiti
CARIBBEAN SEA
Guatemala
Nicaragua
Panama
Galapagos Is (Ecuador)
Easter Is (Chile)
Colombia
Venezuela
Guyana
Suriname
Ecuador
Peru
Bolivia
Brazil
Paraguay
Uruguay
Argentina
Chile
Falkland Is (UK)
Bermuda (UK)
8.30am
Greenland (Denmark)
NORTH ATLANTIC OCEAN
SOUTH ATLANTIC OCEAN
Azores (Port)
Cape Verde
Canary Is (Sp)
South Georgia & South Sandwich Is (UK)
Tristan da Cunha (UK)
Gough Is (UK)
Ascension (UK)
Bouvet Is (Norway)
GREENLAND SEA
NORWEGIAN SEA
NORTH SEA
Iceland
Ireland
United Kingdom
Portugal
Spain
France
Morocco
Algeria
Mauritania
Senegal
Mali
Burkina Faso
Guinea
Liberia
Ghana
Nigeria
Niger
GULF OF GUINEA
Gabon
Congo
Congo (Zaire)
Central African Republic
Chad
Libya
Tunisia
Angola
Namibia
Botswana
South Africa
Zambia
Zimbabwe
Malawi
Mozambique
Tanzania
Kenya
Ethiopia
Somalia
Eritrea
Sudan
Egypt
Svalbard (Norway)
Norway
Sweden
Finland
Denmark
Germany
Poland
Austria
Italy
Estonia
Latvia
Lithuania
Belarus
Ukraine
Romania
Greece
Turkey
MEDITERRANEAN SEA
Syria
Iraq
Saudi Arabia
Yemen
UAE
Oman
Iran
Afghanistan
Pakistan
Turkmenistan
Uzbekistan
Kazakhstan
Kyrgyzstan
3.30pm
4.30pm
BARENTS SEA
KARA SEA
Novaya Zemlya (Russia)
Zemlya Frantsa-Iosifa (Russia)
Severnaya Zemlya (Russia)
ARABIAN SEA
Madagascar
Mauritius
Reunion (Fr)
Seychelles
Maldives
Prince Edward Is (S. Africa)
French Southern & Antarctic Territories (Fr)
Heard & McDonalds (Aust)
INDIAN OCEAN
India
5.30pm
Nepal
5.45pm
Tibet (China)
Sri Lanka
BAY OF BENGAL
Myanmar
6.30pm
Cocos (Keeling) Is (Aust)
China
Mongolia
Laos
Thailand
Vietnam
Malaysia
Indonesia
Philippines
Taiwan
EAST CHINA SEA
North Korea
South Korea
Japan
East Timor
Palau
Australia
9.30pm
SOUTHERN OCEAN
LAPTEV SEA
EAST SIBERIAN SEA
Novosibirskie Ostrovo (Russia)
SEA OF OKHOTSK
Northern Mariana Is (US)
Federated States of Micronesia
Papua New Guinea
Solomon Is
Marshall Is (US)
Nauru
Vanuatu
New Caledonia (Fr)
Fiji
Lord Howe Is (Aust)
10.30pm
Norfolk Is (Aust)
11.30pm
TASMAN SEA

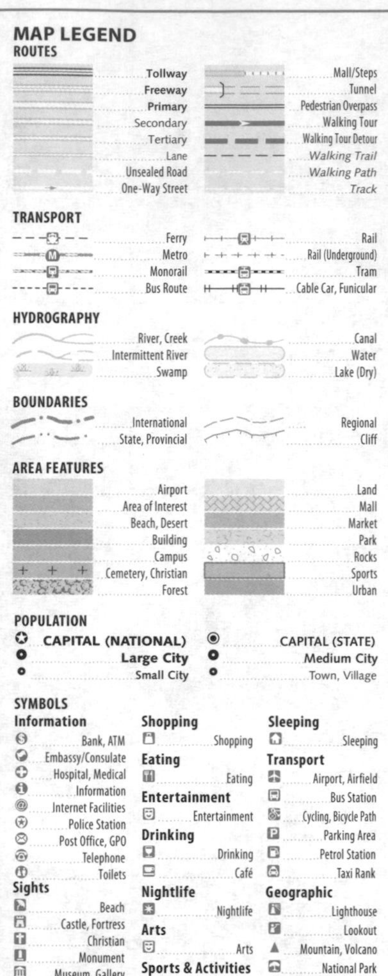

Published by Lonely Planet Publications Pty Ltd
ABN 36 005 607 983

Australia Head Office, Locked Bag 1, Footscray, Victoria 3011,
☎03 8379 8000, fax 03 8379 8111,
talk2us@lonelyplanet.com.au

USA 150 Linden St, Oakland, CA 94607,
☎510 250 6400, toll free 800 275 8555,
fax 510 893 8572, info@lonelyplanet.com

UK 2nd fl, 186 City Rd, London, EC1V 2NT,
☎020 7106 2100, fax 020 7106 2101,
go@lonelyplanet.co.uk

Printed by Hang Tai Printing Company. Printed in China.